Samuel B
'More P

Bloomsbury Studies in Historicizing Modernism
Series Editors: *Matthew Feldman*, Senior Lecturer in Twentieth Century History, University of Northampton, UK; and *Erik Tonning*, Senior Researcher, University of Bergen, Norway

Associate Editor: *Paul Jackson*, Lecturer in History, Open University, UK

Editorial Board: *Professor Chris Ackerley*, Department of English, University of Otago, New Zealand; *Professor Ron Bush*, St. John's College, University of Oxford, UK; *Dr Finn Fordham*, Reader in 20th Century Literature, Royal Holloway, UK; *Professor Steven Matthews*, Department of English, Oxford Brookes University, UK; *Dr Mark Nixon*, Director, Beckett International Foundation, University of Reading, UK; *Professor Shane Weller*, Department of Comparative Literature, University of Kent, UK; *Professor Janet Wilson*, Deptartment of English, University of Northanpton, UK

Bloomsbury Studies in Historicizing Modernism challenges traditional literary interpretations by taking an empirical approach to modernist writing: a direct response to new documentary sources made available over the last decade. Informed by archival approaches to literature, and working beyond the usual European/American avant-garde 1900–1945 parameters, this series reassesses established views of modernist writers by developing fresh views of intellectual backgrounds, working methods and manuscript research.

Katherine Mansfield and Literary Modernism, edited by Janet Wilson, Gerri Kimber and Susan Reid

Reframing Yeats: Genre and History in the Poems, Prose and Plays, Charles Ivan Armstrong

Samuel Beckett's 'German Diaries 1936–37', Mark Nixon

Samuel Beckett's 'More Pricks Than Kicks', John Pilling

Samuel Beckett's 'More Pricks Than Kicks'
In a Strait of Two Wills

John Pilling

BLOOMSBURY
LONDON • NEW DELHI • NEW YORK • SYDNEY

Bloomsbury Academic
An imprint of Bloomsbury Publishing Plc

50 Bedford Square
London
WC1B 3DP
UK

1385 Broadway
New York
NY 10018
USA

www.bloomsbury.com

Bloomsbury is a registered trade mark of Bloomsbury Publishing Plc

First published 2011
Paperback edition first published 2013

© John Pilling 2011

John Pilling has asserted his right under the Copyright, Designs and Patents Act, 1988, to be identified as Author of this work.

All rights reserved. No part of this publication may be reproduced or transmitted in any form or by any means, electronic or mechanical, including photocopying, recording, or any information storage or retrieval system, without prior permission in writing from the publishers.

No responsibility for loss caused to any individual or organization acting on or refraining from action as a result of the material in this publication can be accepted by Bloomsbury or the author.

British Library Cataloguing-in-Publication Data
A catalogue record for this book is available from the British Library.

ISBN: HB: 978-1-4411-5947-2
       PB: 978-1-4725-2572-7
       ePDF: 978-1-4411-0588-2
       ePUB: 978-1-4411-6358-5

Library of Congress Cataloging-in-Publication Data
A catalog record for this book is available from the Library of Congress.

Typeset by Newgen Imaging Systems Pvt Ltd, Chennai, India
Printed and bound by CPI Group (UK) Ltd, Croydon, CR0 4YY

For Jenny Halstead

The powers of evocation of this Italianate Irishman were simply immense, and if his Dream of Fair to Middling Women, *held up in the* limae labor *stage for the past ten or fifteen years, ever reaches the public, and Walter says it is bound to, we ought all be sure to get it and have a look at it anyway. ('What a Misfortune')*

Contents

Series Editors' Preface		ix
Preface		x
Acknowledgements		xii
Abbreviations		xiv
Chapter 1:	*The Disruptive Intelligence*	1
Chapter 2:	*My Sometime Friend Belacqua*	26
	Seul et à deux: 'Walking Out', 'Love and Lethe', 'Fingal'	26
	Rare Movements of Compassion: 'Dante and the Lobster', 'Ding-Dong', 'Yellow'	47
	Ensemble Pieces: 'A Wet Night', 'What A Misfortune', 'Draff'	70
	Three Stories More: 'The Smeraldina's Billet Doux', 'Echo's Bones', 'A Case In A Thousand'	92
Chapter 3:	*How it Went in the World*	118
	The Early Reviews	118
	The Belated Afterlife	120
	The Longer Perspectives	122
Chapter 4:	*The Statement of a Compromise*	126
Chapter 5:	*Notesnatchings: Allusions, Borrowings and Self-Plagiarisms in* More Pricks Than Kicks	141
	'Dante and the Lobster'	144
	'Fingal'	149
	'Ding-Dong'	154
	'A Wet Night'	157
	'Love and Lethe'	176
	'Walking Out'	183
	'What A Misfortune'	190
	'The Smeraldina's Billet Doux'	208
	'Yellow'	210
	'Draff'	220

Chapter 6:	*Addenda*	233
	How (or How *Not*) to 'Get Over' Joyce	233
	A Note on Swift	237
	An Unknown Letter	239
	A Note on Editions	240
Bibliography		242
Index		250

Series Editors' Preface

This book series is devoted to the analysis of late nineteenth- to twentieth-century literary Modernism within its historical context. *Historicizing Modernism* thus stresses empirical accuracy and the value of primary sources (such as letters, diaries, notes, drafts, marginalia or other archival deposits) in developing monographs, scholarly editions and edited collections on Modernist authors and their texts. This may take a number of forms, such as manuscript study and annotated volumes; archival editions and genetic criticism; as well as mappings of interrelated historical milieus or ideas. To date, no book series has laid claim to this interdisciplinary, source-based territory for modern literature. Correspondingly, one burgeoning subdiscipline of Modernism, Beckett Studies, features heavily here as a metonymy for the opportunities presented by manuscript research more widely. While an additional range of 'canonical' authors will be covered here, this series also highlights the centrality of supposedly 'minor' or occluded figures, not least in helping to establish broader intellectual genealogies of Modernist writing. Furthermore, while the series will be weighted towards the English-speaking world, studies of non-Anglophone Modernists whose writings are ripe for archivally based exploration shall also be included here.

A key aim of such historicizing is to reach beyond the familiar rhetoric of intellectual and artistic 'autonomy' employed by many Modernists and their critical commentators. Such rhetorical moves can and should themselves be historically situated and reintegrated into the complex continuum of individual literary practices. This emphasis upon the contested self-definitions of Modernist writers, thinkers and critics may, in turn, prompt various reconsiderations of the boundaries delimiting the concept of 'Modernism' itself. Similarly, the very notion of 'historicizing' Modernism remains debatable, and this series by no means discourages more theoretically informed approaches. On the contrary, the editors believe that the historical specificity encouraged by *Historicizing Modernism* may inspire a range of fundamental critiques along the way.

Matthew Feldman

Erik Tonning

Preface

... in a strait of two wills ...
(Dream of Fair to Middling Women, 'A Wet Night')

This is the first full-length study of Beckett's first work of published fiction, *More Pricks Than Kicks* (1934). I analyse the book as the product of competing tensions in Beckett, some personal and some generic, as figured in the character and *alter ego* Belacqua, Belacqua Shuah as he appears in 'What A Misfortune' and in 'Draff'. Of the 'young thought' of Belacqua we learn in *Dream of Fair to Middling Women* (35, hereafter *Dream*) that it was 'stocked ... and confused in a way that was opposed to its real interests'. The confusion did not diminish when, *Dream* having failed to make any impact, Beckett felt compelled to continue. But the terms in which it could be thought through underwent some decisive changes.

More Pricks Than Kicks has never been granted the close attention from which it benefits, and from which it can also suffer. For a number of reasons, as I try to show, Beckett's own attitude to the book – his first appearance before the general public as a creative writer – was extremely dismissive, even by his own typically severe standards. This study seeks to retrieve what most matters in *More Pricks* and also deals with a number of related issues arising out of its conception, execution and reception.

Chapter 1 discusses how the collection came into being, and explores the tensions out of which it grew. Chapter 2 groups together nine of the ten stories in three groups of three, with a fourth grouping of three more 'odds', one of them ('The Smeraldina's Billet Doux') published in *More Pricks*, one ('Echo's Bones') omitted from it and one ('A Case In A Thousand') showing how Beckett tried to move on beyond it. Chapter 3 shows how *More Pricks* was received on its publication in 1934, how it came to be reprinted in 1970 and how academic criticism has struggled to cope with it, initially in the non-ideal conditions of there being no reprint, and subsequently with the challenge of competing with more obviously compelling and more fully achieved work, the work which gained Beckett fame and an international reputation. Chapter 4 offers a conspectus view of Beckett as storyteller, and Chapter 5 supplies notes on details easily lost to view in the act of reading. In Chapter 6, four 'Addenda' deal with ancillary issues arising from discussions conducted in the body of the book. The bibliography is a selective one, orientated towards *More Pricks* rather than to the very wide field of Beckett Studies as a whole. There is an index of names and texts referred to in the first four chapters and the 'Addenda', and of substantive points of reference in Chapter 5.

I have written this book, subtitled *In A Strait of Two Wills*, in the hope of stimulating further exploration of one of Beckett's most neglected works, and in the belief that *More Pricks Than Kicks* is a much more substantial achievement than anyone, Beckett himself included, has been willing to acknowledge.

Acknowledgements

My thanks, as always, go to Edward Beckett and the Estate of Samuel Beckett as administered by Rosica Colin Ltd., especially for permissions to quote unpublished material, and to Cambridge University Press for permission to cite *The Letters of Samuel Beckett 1929–1940* (CUP, 2009). For permission to quote from *More Pricks Than Kicks*, I thank Paul Keegan and Faber and Faber Ltd.

I am also very grateful for the permissions granted by the Beckett International Foundation at the University of Reading, the Department of Manuscripts at Trinity College Dublin, and the Harry Ransom Humanities Research Center at the University of Texas at Austin.

An inspiration over almost 40 years has been James Knowlson, Emeritus Professor of French Studies at the University of Reading, Beckett's authorized biographer, and a close friend never too busy to offer advice, information and moral support, for which relief much thanks as ever. Seán Lawlor, with whom I have been editing Beckett's *Collected Poems and Translations* for Faber and Faber (due to appear in 2011), was the unwitting instigator of this book. He has been an almost daily sounding board throughout its writing, and he has saved me from much error and confusion, for which I thank him most warmly.

Matthew Feldman and Erik Tonning have been the most patient and encouraging editors I could have wished for, and have tolerated my idiosyncrasies with more forbearance than I doubtless deserve. It was a pleasure to receive so much help and support from Colleen Coalter acting on behalf of the manuscript sent for approval to the Board of Continuum appointed for this series; my thanks go to them all. In America Molly Morrison and my copy editor Heather Hambleton have laboured long and sensitively with my manuscript, and I thank them both most warmly, hoping our paths may someday cross in real terms, rather than in the ether we have inhabited together. Specific debts are given, hopefully with my gratitude plain to see (if inevitably sometimes left unexpressed), at the appropriate points in the body of the text and more particularly in the 'Addenda' and 'Notesnatchings' sections, but for her help with the difficult subject of Beckett and Dante I pay special tribute to Daniela Caselli, and for his expertise with Chatto and Windus archives to Andrew Nash. David Tucker very kindly shared with me information which enabled me to better understand why the projected reprinting of *More Pricks Than Kicks* in 1964 fell through.

My son Sam has been a supporter in ways he knows nothing of, not to mention those he knows only too well, and my dedicatee has been important to me beyond measure.

Abbreviations

Disjecta – *Disjecta: Miscellaneous Writings and a Dramatic Fragment* [Human Wishes], edited by Ruby Cohn (London: John Calder, 1983)
DN – Beckett's *'Dream' Notebook*, edited, annotated and with an introductory essay by John Pilling (Reading: Beckett International Foundation, 1999)
Dream – *Dream of Fair to Middling Women*, edited by Eoin O'Brien and Edith Fournier (Dublin: The Black Cat Press, 1992)
HRHRC – Harry Ransom Humanities Research Center, University of Texas at Austin
JOBS – *Journal of Beckett Studies*, old series (o.s.) and new series (n.s.)
LSB – *The Letters of Samuel Beckett 1929–1940*, edited by Martha Dow Fehsenfeld and Lois More Overbeck (Cambridge: Cambridge University Press, 2009)
PTD – *Proust* and *Three Dialogues with Georges Duthuit* (London: John Calder, 1965)
SBT/A – *Samuel Beckett Today/Aujourd'hui*
TCD – Trinity College Dublin
UoR – Beckett International Foundation, University of Reading

The abbreviations used in Chapter 5 are listed in its headnote.

Editions Used

As indicated in the Bibliography, I have wherever possible used the Faber and Faber reprints of Beckett's works throughout.

Chapter 1

The Disruptive Intelligence

The influences of nature are great, but they do not enable the disruptive intelligence, exacting the tumult from unity, to invert its function.
('The Essential and the Incidental'; *Disjecta*)

Beckett's *More Pricks Than Kicks* became what it is more by accident than by design, more by default than by its own will-to-form. It grew alongside and – for a long time – very much in the shadow of Beckett's first attempt at a novel, *Dream of Fair to Middling Women*, which was not (*pace* Cassandra Nelson's claim, based on the late Richard Seaver's introduction to the New York Arcade edition of *Dream* [1993, vi]), written 'in a matter of weeks' (Faber and Faber, 2010, viii), but in fact between May 1931 and July 1932. *More Pricks* was to endure a still longer gestation, and – well before he was in a position to put a whole volume of short stories together – Beckett seems to have thought it had 'never been properly born', much like the later novel *Watt* (1941–5: 'Addenda') and the little girl of the play *All That Fall* (1956). In the wake of the wreck of *Dream*, Beckett found *More Pricks* something of a spar to cling to, but as such very much a mixed blessing, a product of finding himself 'in a strait of two wills', like the St Augustine in whom he had found the phrase (*Beckett's 'Dream' Notebook* [hereafter *DN*], item 155 [hereafter referred to by item number alone]). Beckett was 'in a strait of two wills' in the sense that he was constricted in his movement and obliged to exercise strategic control over his material, while remaining the prey of competing impulses. *More Pricks* was not the novel he had set his heart on. But it was the next best (or, as it must often have seemed, the next worst) thing: a congeries of stories which could be left looking as if it might once have been a novel in its own right (but see my assessment of this issue in Chapter 3), when in fact it was something quite different and quite itself, even if it had only come into being *faute de mieux*, in the space left by a novel which had not come off.

Generically speaking, it suited Beckett's multiple purposes to think of *More Pricks* as 'Short Stories', as his (failed) application for a teaching post at the University of Cape Town titles it, perhaps understandably (*LSB*, 524). This was not to be a contribution to 'ars longa' (*Dream*, 168), and so not 'a large elephant and big' ('Echo's Bones', 8). Beckett had been forced to jettison *Dream*, which in parts at least had offered to be a Beckettian attempt to emulate the Joyce of *Work In Progress* (subsequently *Finnegans Wake*). Beckett had seen *Work In Progress* as 'that something itself' ('Dante . . . Bruno.Vico..Joyce' [1929]; *Disjecta*, 27) and had made *Dream* uniquely 'itself' by a devil-may-care approach to composition which made nonsense of the traditional distinctions between form and content. These old bugbears could not be dissolved in *More Pricks Than Kicks*, with the shorter form of fiction forms keeping content to the fore. But just as he was 'in a strait' generically, so was he emotionally. Beckett realized that the book, however constituted, could not help but fall between two stools: that of self-expression ('self-extension'; *Disjecta*, 19) and that of space-filling, creativity and the construction of a commodity. And it is surely symptomatic that later, in the spring of 1938, after reading the philosopher Kant seriously for the first time, Beckett summed up his feelings in the terse phrase 'short stories antinomial' (as jotted down in the so-called *'Whoroscope' Notebook*; UoR MS 3000; cf. a less specific grounding for the same idea in Farrow, 100).

The *Oxford English Dictionary's* third definition for *antinomy* reads: 'A contradiction between conclusions which seem equally logical, reasonable or necessary; a paradox; intellectual contradictoriness (after Kant)'. There was probably nothing so definitional operating in 1933; at that point it was simply a battle between dramatization and 'draff', a word meaning 'the lees left after brewing', which Beckett had found in both Chaucer and Thomas à Kempis (*DN*, 590, 1167). *Draff*, Beckett's working title for the whole enterprise (although probably only once he had realized that it might become such a thing), it was *not* to be, under the wise eye of Chatto's commissioning editor Charles Prentice. The implications, however, of 'waste', 'afterthought' and 'fit only to be thrown away', conveyed by the word 'draff', were never separable from Beckett's attitude in later life to *More Pricks*.

With a copy text finally established some 2 months after Beckett thought he had finished the book – there had been a kerfuffle over a possible eleventh story, 'Echo's Bones' (see Chapter 2: 4) – Beckett could write at the end of it all: 'So it goes in the world' (*More Pricks*, 181; all page references are to the 2010 Faber paperback reprint of *More Pricks Than Kicks*). How much he cared about how *More Pricks* went in the world can be inferred from an unpublished letter of 7 May 1934 (HRHRC) to his friend A. J. Leventhal.

This letter – in which Beckett is trying (if not trying very hard) to cloak some murky transactions in Rupert Street, Soho, with a veneer of decency and a modicum of business-like impersonality – contains the phrase 'So it comes in the world'. As *More Pricks* was coming into the world – it was to be published just over a fortnight later, on 24 May 1934 – the book obviously remained mired, in Beckett's mind, in the dualities and contradictions which had ultimately enabled it to come into being, but which had continuously hampered its progress. By this late stage, there was obviously '[n]othing to be done' (*Waiting for Godot*, Act 1, 5). No doubt Beckett was, like Belacqua in 'Dante and the Lobster', 'hop[ing] for the best' and 'expect[ing] the worst' (10). But he was also 'bogged' in a kind of limbo, 'so bogged that he could move neither backward nor forward' (3). 'Will [Belacqua's] next appearance' – Prentice had asked Beckett about 'Echo's Bones' before the story had even been begun – 'be a kick or a prick?' (letter of 4 October 1934; UoR). Neither man had long to wait for an answer. But once 'Echo's Bones' had been jettisoned as surplus to requirements, Belacqua's 'next appearance' was as Prentice had first received it, in a (suitably tidied up) *More Pricks Than Kicks*. 'I hastened to assure him', notes the narrator of the story 'Ding-Dong' regarding his earlier dealings with his 'sometime friend Belacqua', 'that he had a perfect right to suit himself in what, after all, was a manoeuvre of his own contriving' (35). This was very much the spirit in which Beckett had written or 'contriv[ed]' *More Pricks*, and it had worked as well, or as badly, as could have been expected. But Beckett could obviously not expect to condition the response of 'the world', the world having for the most part not the slightest idea who Samuel Beckett was. In any event, the world paid him and his book the time-honoured compliment of indifference in the face of anything new, odd or unfamiliar. *More Pricks* was a resounding failure, something of a publisher's nightmare in fact, as the following figures register in no uncertain terms. Chatto and Windus had printed 1,500 sets of sheets, but only 500 were ever bound up. Of these, more than 90 were sent *hors commerce* or for review. Seventy-seven were sent to the English-speaking colonies. By September 1934, 4 months after publication, 358 copies had been sold. By March 1935, 10 months in, one more free copy had been given away and 19 more copies sold, leaving 26 bound copies. Of these, 22 were sold between 1935 and 1946, at the average rate of 2 per year. By then everyone connected with *More Pricks* was entitled either to feel profoundly dispirited by its fate or to think that it was better forgotten. No doubt Beckett never could have been induced to feel even lukewarm about it, given the way it had grown in lieu of *Dream*, even if the novel had failed for quite different reasons.

On publication Beckett had given a copy of *More Pricks* to his grieving mother in the family home at Cooldrinagh in the southern Dublin suburb of Foxrock, where it had been not so much coolly received as almost totally disregarded (letter of 31 December 1935 to Thomas MacGreevy). Even with Beckett more or less established in the public eye some 20 years after the *succès de scandale* of *Waiting for Godot*, his first published book of fiction made little headway. In the interim, copies of the book had become so rare that, for all practical purposes, *More Pricks* was invisible. If it had 'never been properly born', Beckett was determined to keep it that way, at least until the pressure to reprint it proved irresistible (see Chapter 3).

The sales figures help to explain why there are fewer than 35 copies of the 1934 edition in public and/or university library collections around the world and why so very few are ever offered for sale at auction – copies in the original dust jacket are rare beyond the dreams of avarice, and beyond the experience of almost all antiquarians, whether buyers or sellers. Even Beckett, on the few occasions when he felt he would like to give copies of *More Pricks* as presents to friends, had to rely on someone else being fortunate enough to find one for him, or simply admit (as in a letter to Aidan Higgins of 3 December 1951; HRHRC) that he did not possess one. The copy that he eventually inscribed for Higgins, which is now in the Beckett collections at Washington University in St Louis was acquired by the good offices of Mary Hutchinson, as indicated by letters to her of 13 June and 31 July 1957 (HRHRC). On discovering that he did not own one, she found Beckett a copy of *More Pricks* which had once belonged to the poet David Gascoyne. Beckett wrote to her: 'Though I have not the courage to read it I am very glad to have it'. But Beckett did not keep it for long: the Higgins inscription dates from November 1957.

The failure with *Dream* could, with time, be forgotten. But with *More Pricks*, which had flickered briefly in the public domain, the embarrassment and self-loathing lingered. It is perhaps not wholly surprising that something of the sad 'fiasco' of *More Pricks* survived to reappear in *Krapp's Last Tape* more than 20 years later: 'Seventeen copies sold, of which eleven at trade price to free circulating libraries beyond the seas. Getting known' (*Krapp's Last Tape*, etc., 10). In practice, readers almost never get to know Beckett first by way of *More Pricks*. Their first encounter is typically through *Godot* or *Endgame*, or (not much more helpfully, but at least by way of prose fiction) with *Murphy* or *Molloy*. It is usually through one or other of these that a received idea of Beckett begins to form. *Murphy* is obviously a much more substantial achievement than *More Pricks*. And the very quality of these later works militates against a warm, or even very sensitive, appreciation of the earlier. But the apparent failure of the stories to 'live up to' the received idea of Beckett – as derived almost exclusively from later work – is really not surprising. And of course it may indeed be that *More Pricks* is best forgotten as a clever, but essentially negligible, apprentice work by a young man of 28 who had still to find his own voice, and who would have to wait some time – more than 10 years – to do so.

In spite of much good work on *More Pricks Than Kicks*, some of it unfortunately confined to doctoral theses, assessments of it have left us with an unclear picture and a mixed outcome. This book has been written to re-assess what gives *More Pricks* its particular and idiosyncratic value. Although it will inevitably raise many more questions than it can hope to answer, it will at least reach conclusions as to *how* 'it' goes in *More Pricks*. It is not my intention to turn the picture round so far that the book becomes something other than the disaster it was in the 1930s or (as is hardly likely to be achieved) becomes capable of commanding an interest comparable to that of *Godot* and its progeny. This would be as counterproductive as the view which currently prevails, namely that *More Pricks* is hardly worth the bother of rediscovery and redefinition. My purpose is the much more modest one of re-examining the evidence, giving *More Pricks* more room to breathe than it typically enjoys and trying to see as clearly as possible *why* it is as it is, flaws and all. And, of course, I discuss how it might be better enjoyed for *what* it is, rather than neglected, or discounted, in favour of what it is not.

* * *

No manuscript or typescript of *More Pricks* seems to have survived, and unless and until any do emerge we shall never know the exact details of how and when the stories came to be written and how they were revised for publication. If the work was more assured of attention, this might not much matter, but as things stand there can obviously be no appeal back from the outcome to the circumstances of conception. Beckett remembered (in a letter of 6 July 1971 from Santa Margherita to Ruby Cohn; UoR) the first story in the collection ('Dante and the Lobster') as the first written and thought that it was much earlier than the others, although he did not specify how much earlier:

> Re More Pricks Than Kicks I forget. I suppose more or less the order in which published. 'Dante and the Lobster' certainly the first and by a long way – when there was no thought of that unhappy work.

The published placement of the story, combined with this letter, suggests that 'Dante and the Lobster' must indeed have been the first. But Beckett's notion that the other stories followed in much the same order as that in which they appear is probably best seen as an inability on his part to summon up sufficient interest to pursue the matter further, together with a quite understandable sense that it had all happened too long ago to make very much difference. If, as was almost certainly the case, Beckett worked on all ten of the stories as a group, introducing echoes between and across them that were not necessarily part of their original inspiration, he could certainly be forgiven for taking the line of least resistance and simply shrugging his shoulders. This said, an extremely provisional order of composition, one which might well have to be revised in the unlikely event of any relevant documents coming to hand, is the following:

'Dante and the Lobster': ?1930
'Walking Out': (?first) version before 15 August 1931
'The Smeraldina's Billet Doux': before, probably well before,
    5 July 1932
'A Wet Night': after January 1932, and before 5 July 1932
'Ding-Dong': ?late 1932, and before 23 March 1933
'Fingal': after 5 January 1933, and by Easter (23 April) 1933
'Yellow': after 3 May 1933, and probably before 13 May 1933
'What A Misfortune': after April 1933, and before July–August 1933
'Love and Lethe': before July–August 1933
'Draff': before 7 September 1933

(The dates here are derived from published and unpublished letters to Thomas MacGreevy and Charles Prentice. An earlier provisional dateline of mine is discussed by Lawlor (2009, 65, n. 1), pointing out that *A Samuel Beckett Chronology* is slightly different again. The difficulties intrinsic to this exercise have not lessened over time!)

If we can assign 'Dante and the Lobster' more or less securely to about 1930 (in any event, *after* the 1929 story 'Assumption', published in *transition*, no. 27), eight of the other nine stories were very probably composed over roughly 2 years, between about mid-1931 and mid-1933, with 'Draff', the tenth and last (the eleventh was jettisoned, an issue I shall deal with separately) written after the death of Beckett's father on 26 June 1933. Two stories – 'A Wet Night' and 'The Smeraldina's Billet Doux', the latter not in fact a 'story' as the word is usually understood, although it tells several – must have been written by mid-1932, when Beckett sent his *Dream* novel to

Charles Prentice at Chatto (letter of 5 July 1932; UoR), since they are taken over almost verbatim from the novel. Beckett told MacGreevy in a letter of 13 May 1933 (*LSB*, 157) that he wanted a sufficient number of stories, ideally a dozen, to put before a publisher to have some hope of their being accepted. This perfectly legitimate strategy did some favours for *More Pricks* in terms of its achieving a positive response although it was still not quite long enough to satisfy Prentice (hence the addition of 'Echo's Bones'). But Beckett's recourse to *Dream* material has done the whole collection few favours in the eyes of posterity, since the two stories can easily be dismissed as mere space-fillers, and the collection as a whole looks less original than it really is. It remains only a slight contribution in terms of originality. I think the issue is more complex and complicated than that, but I do not want to make claims for either 'A Wet Night' or 'The Smeraldina's Billet Doux' which they are unable to sustain, and the facts of the case, insofar as we can understand them, will presumably always tell against both of them in the long run.

The troubled history of the ultimately jettisoned story 'Echo's Bones' can be reconstructed in greater detail. Charles Prentice wrote asking for one extra story on 29 September 1933, a request Beckett could only satisfy about a month later, in late October/early November. Prentice promptly and ruefully returned it, as Beckett told MacGreevy on 5/6 November 1933 (*LSB*, 171). Only then was a long labour at an end, with the last act a labour lost. Pre-publication, by contrast, ran smoothly. With some help from MacGreevy, Beckett dealt very professionally with the proofs sent by Prentice. Prentice told Beckett (4 December 1933; UoR) that he already had a 'good lot' of proofs; he acknowledged receipt of Beckett's corrections on 7 December 1933, having sent him the balance of the proofs (for the last two stories, 'Yellow' and 'Draff') a day earlier. Last minute alterations were made to 'Draff' in light of the failure of 'Echo's Bones', and Prentice praised 'the new little bit at the end' in a letter of 11 December. Prentice wrote again on 18 December to say that MacGreevy had gone over all the proofs again, and on 20 December he thanked Beckett for sending back the full set of corrected proofs. The whole process took less than a month, a tribute to the postal service of the day as well as to everyone involved. But perhaps the most telling aspect of all this, in light of the later disfavour into which *More Pricks Than Kicks* fell in Beckett's eyes, is how doggedly determined he was, over 'the last ditch' (25), to see things through to a conclusion.

* * *

The 2-year, or 2-year-plus, gestation of *More Pricks* was a long run for Beckett, who had written *Dream* in just over a year and would later go on to write *Murphy* over 11 months (August 1935–July 1936). *Watt*, written in 'dribs and drabs' was to take the best part of 4 years and more (February 1941–May 1945), *Molloy* about 6 months (May–November 1947), *Malone Dies* (*Malone meurt*) also about 6 months and *Comment c'est* (*How It Is*) more than 2 years (December 1958–August 1961). Of these, only the time taken over the latter is of much help as a comparison, since *Watt* was for the most part written, and at the same time *not* written, under the very difficult circumstances of eluding capture by the Gestapo. But *More Pricks* was, unlike any of these, a book of short stories, and as such (even with a common 'hero') the stories were separate entities, emerging when – and only when – Beckett felt in the mood to write them. In a 1934 book review of a novella-length prose work by the poet Eduard Mörike (*Mozart on the Way to Prague*), Beckett writes that Mörike's talent was 'sporadic, eager in attack and rapidly exhausted' (*Disjecta*, 61). This was probably not the way Mörike himself thought of his 'talent' – it sounds more appropriate to a percussive, naturally 'decaying' instrument like a pianoforte – but it is uttered by Beckett with such confidence that he must have been familiar with similar impulses, perhaps never more so than when writing short stories. In *Dream*, Beckett recorded how demanding he was finding 'ars longa' (168), and he may have turned to stories in part for relief from that, only to find that *ars brevis* required a similar commitment, albeit differently distributed.

How much familiarity Beckett had with the short story form is a matter of guesswork, like so many of one's dealings with *More Pricks*. In Ireland, or in Anglo-Irish literature, there were short stories aplenty, from a rich folklore to the work of such writers as Seán O'Faoláin and Frank O' Connor (to name only them), with Joyce's great *Dubliners* collection (published 1914) probably the only one that really mattered to Beckett, although he seems to have done what he could to fly by that net. In England there was Saki (the pseudonym of H. H. Munro; cf. a letter to MacGreevy of 7 September 1933, comparing the relative difficulty of reading Saki and 'Dante and the Lobster') and Ronald Firbank, both of whom were to leave their mark on *More Pricks*. Between England and Ireland, as it were, there was Oscar Wilde, two of whose stories Beckett mentioned, together with his 'Poems in Prose', in his first letter to Thomas MacGreevy (*LSB*, 12). In France there were a number of figures, with Maupassant (cf. my later discussion of 'What A Misfortune' in Chapter 2) perhaps at the head of them. *Dream* (37) even pays a backhanded compliment of a kind by describing an alcoholic concoction (a liqueur or cocktail) that 'went to your head and settled your stomach' as 'like a short story by [François] Mauriac', which may well be gesturing in the direction of Mauriac's (long) short story/novella *Thérèse Desqueyroux* (1927; cf. *Dream*, 80). In Russia there was Chekhov, or the 14 volumes of Constance Garnett's translations of his stories into English, which there seems to be no evidence of Beckett having read. (The reference to 'the cliché machine', Ippolit Ippolititch, a teacher of history and geography and a minor character in Chekhov's ['Tchekov's] story 'The Teacher of Literature', noted in Beckett's *'Whoroscope' Notebook* [fol. 75], must be later than *More Pricks* and is found amid material which seems to date from his 6 months in Germany in 1936–7; perhaps Beckett actually read the story in German. Much later, in August 1965, he told Barbara Bray that he had read and liked Chekhov's 'A Boring Story'.) Beyond these, if indeed as far as these, Beckett probably did not feel much disposed to go, or did not feel any need to go. There were plenty of models for him, had he wished to pursue the matter, but none, seemingly, that appealed to Beckett as a mentor or absolute master (except, inevitably but also inimitably, Joyce), and he did not want it to appear that he had 'gone Joyce' in *More Pricks*, as many thought he had with 'Sedendo et Quiescendo' on the rocky road to *Dream*. In an undated (probably 12 July 1931) letter to Prentice (UoR) MacGreevy told him: 'He went Joyce in it ['Sedendo et Quiescendo'], though he denies it is Joyce' (cf. Beckett to Prentice, 15 August 1931; *LSB*, 81).

The young Beckett was too unruly a writer to have accepted anyone else's method anyway, and he clearly did not think of the short story as a mode in which much distinction (with certain very honourable exceptions) could be achieved, or one in which a writer could expect, or should seek, to achieve much distinction. In Beckett's hierarchy of forms in the early 1930s, the poem was uppermost, the novel a necessity and the play an optional extra. There was no need, and no room, for the short story to enter the lists. This attitude may help to explain why it took Beckett a relatively long time, about 2 years, to write ten stories (only eight if 'A Wet Night' and 'The Smeraldina's Billet Doux' are put back in their original context), and several weeks to find inspiration for the jettisoned eleventh story, 'Echo's Bones'. Chekhov and Maupassant, to name just two of the more widely admired short story writers, would surely have written much more quickly and would certainly have written many more stories during a period of composition lasting longer than 18 months. Julian Barnes has pointed out that 'in 1884 [Maupassant] published more than a story a week; in 1886 three every two weeks' ('On we sail', *London Review of Books*, 5 November 2009, 25). And, if only for comparison's sake, it may be worth noting that Elizabeth Bowen wrote more than 80 short stories, and William Trevor has written over 100.

But Beckett's difficulties with the short story form became manifest just when the whole *More Pricks* enterprise began to assume a kind of reality in his mind. 'This writing is a bloody awful grind', he told MacGreevy on 13 May 1933:

> I did two more 'short stories', bottled climates, comme ça, sans conviction, because one has to do something or perish with ennui. Now I have five. But I don't think I could possibly invite a publisher to wipe his arse with less than a dozen.

Beckett went on to tell MacGreevy that he was really finding it increasingly difficult to go on, and that he felt that his writing was inevitably suffering as a result, although he still had 'hopes of its all coming in a gush like a bloody flux' (*LSB*, 159).

The 'gush' had to give way to hard labour, inspiration to perspiration. In the wake of the first of his father's two heart attacks, Beckett told MacGreevy (letter of 22 June 1933) that before it he had accomplished about 'half or two-thirds enough', but had been obliged to leave it as it stood in the hope of inspiration returning. The death of his father 4 days later meant that this did not happen, but Beckett must have tried to assuage his grief by putting some pieces of an emerging 'jigsaw' together, and perhaps even adding some pieces ('Love and Lethe'? 'What A Misfortune'? 'Yellow'? 'Draff', certainly.) to the 'five' he had counted on 13 May. There must also have been some revision of the whole collection: Beckett told MacGreevy in a letter of late 1933 that he had worked on them assiduously before even sending them to Charles Prentice (*LSB*, 172). Most, if not all, of this revision was probably undertaken in the intervening period between 26 June 1933, the day Beckett's father died, and the despatch of ten 'contes' (as Beckett called them, in the letter to MacGreevy of 7 September 1933, presumably because they could hardly be considered *nouvelles*) to Charles Prentice at Chatto.

There was a ready market for short stories in England and Ireland (and also in the USA), at least in magazines, which often paid contributors. No doubt the conditions for a successful collection of stories in book form could have been better, but they were not markedly worse than they might have been at any other time. Charles Prentice told Beckett: 'Short stories are chancey [*sic*] things, on which the library and the bookseller turn a poached-egg eye' (letter of 25 September 1933; UoR). He was, however, glad to be able to accept something by Beckett for publication after he had turned down both *Dream* and a collection of poems (letters of 19 and 27 July 1932; UoR) on the basis that neither could possibly succeed. Prentice must have hoped that, with Chatto accepting Beckett for the first time as a creative writer rather than as an essayist and literary critic (as in *Proust*, published by Chatto in 1931), the prospect would please.

But Beckett had already turned his own poached-egg eye on the short story form: he had noted down Chaucer's tongue-in-cheek assessment of 'The draf of stories' in the B-text of his *Legend of Good Women* (*DN*, 1167). With eyes on Parnassus, or on his own version of it, Beckett could easily try to forget the commodity aspects of publishing, which were of course just as applicable to the appearance of a novel or a collection of poems as to anything else. No doubt the mere whiff of entering a competitive market had something to do with Beckett's antipathy to the short story form, given that he had already expressed in *Proust* (*PTD*, 76) his hostility to the whole business of the 'penny-a-line vulgarity of a literature of notations'. It was not Beckett's nature (as can be seen in *Dream*, 173) to want to add to a literature of 'vulgarity'. A stray remark in an undated (1934) letter to Morris Sinclair (*LSB*, 215) suggests that Beckett was defensively unable to imagine himself being taken seriously in any activity whatsoever, especially one with either practical or utilitarian consequences. This letter shows Beckett assuming the combined roles of actor, impersonator, comedian and clown, and in some ways better defines his prevailing attitude in the early 1930s, certainly during the gestation of *More Pricks*. Here Beckett could not hope to avoid 'vulgarity' altogether, and he found himself obliged to make some common cause with 'plausibility' and with some fairly conventional 'concatenation[s]' (*PTD*, 82). There was always active in Beckett a rather high-minded disinclination to compromise, as later reflected (in the dialogues with Duthuit) in the notion of the artist as, at least ideally, 'too proud for the farce of giving and receiving' ('André Masson'; *PTD*, 112). But the writer of *More Pricks* is more vulnerable than proud, intent on a performance and on playing a role, primed to receive whatever may come his way, and skilled enough to give it back with interest. Without actively setting out to please an audience, Beckett's hope that there might actually be one somewhere kept him flexible in his repertoire of effects and exceptionally alert in the employment of rhetorical devices, if not necessarily very good at judging what would work and what would not. Somehow or other the show had to go on, and the showman had to ensure that it went on, not least because *Dream* had been hobbled by the narrator's willingness to 'call the whole performance off' (112).

Dream, although very different from *More Pricks*, is obviously very helpful to us in showing why the latter is as it is. There are even moments in *Dream* when Belacqua's excursions into literary theory anticipate what Beckett will only really act on in the collection of stories which grew, awkwardly and painfully, out of *Dream*. One such is the passage in which he envisages a more subtle way of opening up a 'tinned Kultur' (161) by not succumbing to 'the desire to bind for ever in imperishable relation the object to its representation' (160). *Dream* for the most part accomplishes this ambition by riding roughshod over all conventional developmental constraints, but Beckett seems to be so busy expressing himself that he cannot imagine how his novel ever could find its ideal reader. *Dream* is written (in a way befitting its failure to impress publishers) without any real conviction on Beckett's part that the public might ever be in a position to read it and understand his intentions. But, as if recognizing that in *Dream* he could only fail to please publishers, the public and (by definition) himself, in *More Pricks* Beckett seems prepared either to abandon, or at least temporize with, the 'dream' of working with 'not a trace ... of the premises in the conclusion' (161). In postulating such a dream Beckett was obliged to concede that it 'presents certain difficulties in the manner of manipulation' (161), and in his *Proust* essay he wrote: 'No amount of voluntary manipulation can reconstitute in its integrity ... the will [that] has – so to speak – buckled into incoherence' (*PTD*, 72). But even in *Dream*, in committing himself to 'whatever premises you fancy', Beckett had realized that 'You will have to live on them, you cannot get rid of them'. 'The public', he adds, 'never spots the deception ... the public is too busy admiring the seamless tights of the performer and listening to the patter of the parable' (161). The writing of *More Pricks* gave Beckett the opportunity to pursue a much closer relationship between 'the performer', 'the patter', 'the parable' and 'the public', if only by way of a much more controlled 'manipulation'. In his Paris Diary for 20 June 1934 (HRHRC), George Reavey registered *More Pricks Than Kicks* as a 'faithful portraiture of [Beckett's] curious psychological reactions', but Reavey had not read *Dream*. It would perhaps be more apt to think of *More Pricks* as *un*faithful 'portraiture', and necessarily so, given Beckett's strenuous attempt to reduce his own presence in the narrative proceedings and keep what was really troubling him pretty securely under wraps.

One of the difficulties which threaten to bedevil discussions of the *More Pricks* stories – as we have seen, seeking to establish the order in which they were composed is itself irksome – is the negative evidence of how few of them were sent out to editors of magazines, and the lack of interactivity in this area in the MacGreevy letters. One story ('Walking Out') had been turned down by J. B. Pinker in August 1931, and another (it is not clear exactly which one, but it may have been 'Ding-Dong') failed to impress Seumas O'Sullivan at the *Dublin Magazine*, where Beckett had succeeded in placing his poem 'Alba' in the autumn of 1931. When this story was returned, Beckett told MacGreevy that he had considered trying the *Adelphi* magazine but was uncertain as to whether this would be worth the effort (letter of 23 April 1933; *LSB*, 154). His discouragement is palpable, even though he went on to tell MacGreevy that he had written another story (probably 'Fingal'). But one reason why he felt so discouraged was the failure of the much more ambitious *Dream of Fair to Middling Women* to find favour anywhere. This failure made it impossible to see a short story collection as anything more than a climb-down, a failure made worse by *Dream* being sent back by publishers with monotonous regularity. It speaks volumes for Beckett's diminishing confidence that he gave some stories (he does not even tell MacGreevy which ones) to a representative from the firm of Methuen, Colin Summerford (letter of 13 May 1933; *LSB*, 157). In any event, nothing came of what looks like little more than a half-hearted gesture, probably not much helped by Beckett having too few stories to show anyone. Yet it was MacGreevy whom Beckett considered one of the few of his friends who might like one story or another. In a letter headed '21st' [21 March 1933; *LSB*, 153, n. 1] Beckett describes the story sent to O'Sullivan as one which he believed MacGreevy at least might appreciate, having the day before told him, in French, that he was concentrating really hard on it (*LSB*, 153). Whether the reference is to 'Ding-Dong' or to 'Fingal' – there is an echo of the last sentence of the latter in the letter to MacGreevy – is perhaps of less importance than the fact that Beckett knew, deep down, that his way of writing short stories was unlikely to appeal to a wide audience. Six months later, however, in the letter to MacGreevy of 7 September 1933, with *More Pricks* under consideration at Chatto, Beckett summoned sufficient bravado to claim that, if people could read Saki, then they could read anything, even 'Dante and the Lobster'.

Beckett had kept MacGreevy fully briefed as to his trials and tribulations in trying to place *Dream* with publishers, although he had apparently not seen fit to communicate any final decision to give up on it. It comes as something of a surprise therefore to discover that Beckett seems to have told MacGreevy nothing about sending a collection of stories to Chatto, and only felt able to announce their acceptance – and the brief glimmer of satisfaction which this had brought him – about a month after receiving the go-ahead from Prentice. Beckett's insouciance in keeping MacGreevy *au courant* with these developments can be seen in the letter (9 October 1933; *LSB*, 166) in which Beckett was obliged to reveal (for the first time?) what the book was to be called, an issue which had been under consideration between Beckett and Prentice since early September. MacGreevy had presumably never seen *More Pricks* as Beckett had sent it to Chatto and must have been somewhat surprised that the acknowledged deficiency of having only five stories in mid-May (*LSB*, 157), plus the hiatus following Bill Beckett's first heart attack in June (letter of 22 June 1933), had nonetheless resulted in a typescript sufficient to secure Prentice's support for the venture. But MacGreevy seems to have taken all this in his stride, since he was more than happy to help in any way he could when the proofs of the book were sent from the printers and continued to assist Prentice with them right up until the point when the book went into production. Beckett may or may not have been embarrassed by the way he had kept MacGreevy largely in the dark as to what was going on. But over the whole long gestation of *More Pricks*, any comments on the stories, even with Beckett having so close a confidant as MacGreevy, were sufficiently rare that one might suppose that any hopes which Beckett may once have had for them had been given up long before they were collected in book form. He had, however, made it clear (notably in the 21 March 1933 letter) that he could be 'caught up' by them, even when his struggles with the short story format had reminded him that it was not, as indeed it never would be, his preferred medium of self-expression.

* * *

The short story suffered, in Beckett's eyes, from its inevitably cramped dimensions, and from its relative intolerance of the experimentation beloved by *avant-garde* writers who were in principle (if not, of course, in practice) indifferent to their reception by the general public, or anyone narrowly confined (as 'Walking Out' puts it) by 'the pot-hooks and hangers of civility' (98). Beckett had conceived no specific plan for *More Pricks Than Kicks*, and he had no models which he was prepared to follow. Symptomatically, when the book was on the point of appearing, he took umbrage at the very suggestion that he was following anyone else's successful formula, and he was adamant in telling Nuala Costello, in a letter dated 10 May 1934, that he had never read either James Stephens or T. S. Eliot (!), that he had not been influenced by Joyce (!!), and that behind his book she should look for the influence of Grock, Dante, Chaucer, Bernard de Mandeville and Uccello (!!!) (*LSB*, 208). (I discuss this claim in Chapter 4.)

This was in response to a no doubt well-intentioned 'puff' for *More Pricks* which had appeared as from 'Anon' on page 6 of *The Observer* of 6 May 1934 and which Beckett considered 'sufficiently imbecile' (*LSB*, 208). The 'puff' had mentioned Eliot, Joyce and *The Crock of Gold*, but had also said that 'The Dubliner in hospital' [i.e. 'Yellow'] is a triumph' and that 'elsewhere, minor brilliancies abound'. In writing to Nuala Costello, a very intelligent woman and a friend of Lucia Joyce's (it was at the Joyces and in Paris that Beckett had met Nuala, although a letter to MacGreevy of 7 September 1933 suggests she is a new friend), Beckett was silent about the praise he had received and concentrated only on what had displeased him in the pre-publication hype. He obviously expected Nuala Costello to be as clever and as complicated as he was. This was a kind of compliment in its way, but not one which was guaranteed to bring Nuala as close as he might have liked, as events later proved. It seems reasonable to suppose that among the 'thousand tender fancies' in the letter to her, Beckett was nourishing a number of less tender fancies about Nuala herself. Nuala may just possibly have missed this point, but she would have had to be a lot less intelligent than she was to have missed the main point of Beckett's remarks: none of the so-called major influences are short story writers. Nuala may not have heard of all these figures (notably Mandeville who, unlike Grock, Dante, Chaucer and Uccello, is not explicitly invoked in *More Pricks*), and she must have realized that Beckett had his tongue at least partly in his cheek. The remarks were Beckett's way of suggesting that there were really no 'major influences', or at least no positive ones, since the writers mentioned by 'Anon' in the *Observer* could only be considered negative, or not in any way formative.

Beckett may have learned from Nuala's reaction to this outburst not to respond to the reviews when the book had appeared, and Nuala could certainly be forgiven if Beckett's somewhat toxic cocktail of emotions did not win her or her affections, although she continued to meet Beckett occasionally over the next 18 months (see *LSB*, 273–5). Beckett's letter to her of 10 May 1934 shows, though, how very isolated he felt, as a person and a writer, and how little he wanted to be inscribed in the prevailing literal or cultural mainstream of the day. The combination of extreme individualism and overweening arrogance, partly fuelled by the pretence that he had no interest in fame or celebrity anyway, may not look very appealing to us even today. But the implication that only he himself could really hope to understand or appreciate what he had achieved, or failed to achieve, in *More Pricks* is worth taking seriously, given how little commentators have made of it in more than seven decades since.

Beckett's strategy in *More Pricks* was to appear to obey, within limits, the conventions of the short story, right down to the (unsurprising?) 'surprise' or 'O Henry' ending – 'Yellow' is perhaps the best example – while all the time eroding expectations from within. The difficulty here was that no rules could be applied to what was an essentially guerrilla activity, without a controlling metaphor or theme (see Lawlor 2009, 50). The activity had to be – or seem to be – random, casual or ancillary to some other purpose, as if it could be considered 'antinomial' and not really a serious claim on anyone's attention. To this end there had to be some constants against which other, more aberrant, practices could figure, and this required some lip service to be paid to the 'ordinary' conventions of storytelling, the better to score points off them. At the same time, one of the fundamental aspects of novel-writing could also be hinted at: a 'hero' and a place (or places) where such a hero might fictionally be imagined operating in interaction with others. There are two constants in *More Pricks*: the character of Belacqua, and the city and environs of Dublin (Dublin is even in the Smeraldina's mind as she writes from Germany). Differently modelled, *More Pricks Than Kicks* could easily have become a novel, although hardly an experimental one of the kind that *Dream* had offered to be. Instead, *More Pricks* became that most unusual of things: an experimental book of short stories, a point quietly but visibly made, amid much that is kept hidden by the adoption of an unusual – and frankly eccentric – way of punctuating any spoken word (no comma after its initial manifestation, a device Beckett was careful to insist on in his correspondence with Prentice. The revised 1934 version of 'Dante and the Lobster' removes as many of the commas from the much more conventional 1932 *This Quarter* version as possible). Beckett seems never to have been tempted to adopt the Joycean speech-dash for spoken dialogue, a choice which even in its small way is, of course, entirely consistent with his not wanting to stand in Joyce's shadow any longer than circumstances obliged him to. For anyone feeling a little short-changed in this respect, in the last knockings of 'Draff' Beckett makes a point of writing, ' "No gardener has died, comma, within rosaceous memory" '(181), as if he has just remembered that he 'ought' to have supplied hundreds and hundreds more commas, which (had he done so) would never even have been noticed!

The two constants of *More Pricks* are separable from one another, but obviously not unrelated. Belacqua has no greater love for the city of Dublin than his creator had, although he likes the countryside north and south of it. But he suffers too much from self-love, or at least self-regard, to feel either a great love or a great loathing for anything but himself. He feels comfortable, no more, in his chosen stamping-ground around Trinity College, or not far from it (as in 'Ding-Dong'). This is an area he knows like the back of his hand, and he can negotiate it without falling foul of poets and intellectuals more often than he can tolerate ('The aesthetes and the impotent' of 'Ding-Dong', 35). This is something of an achievement given exactly where he is, and to accomplish it he needs to know the rat runs which can be exploited in an emergency (or simply out of the front door of the Grosvenor Hotel in Westland Row ['A Wet Night', 47], for example). It is difficult, however, to think of Belacqua as really belonging where he is, familiar though it all is to him. He would probably be much the same wherever he was, as his excursions north and south of the city tend to confirm. In 'Ding-Dong' the narrator actually tells us that 'as for sites, one was as good as another' (31), and, a little later, 'for the moment there were no grounds for his favouring one direction rather than another' (33).

Why he is *as* he is is not something that much occupies Belacqua (cf. Beckett on 'motive' in 'Echo's Bones', 16), and he accepts himself, or Beckett presents him, as a kind of given. He is not much disposed to change his behaviour, nor is he apparently much changed by what happens to him. Death, we are told in 'Draff' (172), has 'already cured him' of the 'naïveté' of supposing that it can make up for life's losses, but life cannot teach him very much because (as with his toast in 'Dante and the Lobster', 6) he seeks to 'vanquish it utterly', if only in a succession of trivial triumphs. Given what he is given to, he has no real plan as to how to achieve this, which is perhaps one reason why circumstance conspires from time to time to outwit him and a medical error can cause his demise.

Beckett had used Belacqua as the 'principal boy' of his jettisoned novel *Dream* (19, 38, 40, etc.), and he must presumably have asked himself whether there was enough life left in Belacqua for a collection of short stories. (*More Pricks* tends to reduce Belacqua's presence from roughly halfway through.) The difficulty was that Beckett did not have sufficient interest in anyone else, which effectively obliged him to stick with Belacqua as long as he could. Collections of short stories do not of course typically require a single hero or the same one in all of them, nor are they expected to. But Beckett knew Saki, and Saki had done this more than once, in *Reginald* (1904) and *The Chronicles of Clovis* (1911). Saki had also shown, through Reginald (who reappears in the first story of *Reginald in Russia* [1910]) and the much more successful Clovis, that the use of the same figure in multiple, unconnected situations need not restrict an author's range. Hemingway later did so, with *in our time* in 1925.

Of course any choice of this kind precludes other choices, so the issue of range really becomes a question of how adequate the single figure is for the particular purposes of a particular story. Given Beckett's purposes in *More Pricks*, Belacqua serves him well for the most part, even if the stories cannot be considered uniformly successful. *Dream*, whatever it had failed to achieve, had at least left Beckett fairly clear as to what could be expected of Belacqua and what could not. The Belacqua of *Dream*, Beckett had discovered, could 'scarcely fail to keep on [letting us down]' (113). Could he be equally relied upon to do so in the more 'exploded' medium of the short story, but to the benefit of the collection as a whole? From every point of view Belacqua was very nearly ideal as someone who could antagonize others, even if his most accomplished antagonist is himself. And by the very adoption of the short story form, continuity could be abandoned in favour of 'disfaction', 'a breaking-down and multiplication of tissue', a *'cupio dissolvi'* (*Dream*, 138). It would have to be an effort differently distributed, but it was in no way under duress to compose itself into a unity. The idea of unity is never quite abandoned in *Dream*, even if it can temporarily be seen as 'involuntary' in any novel (*Dream*, 132). But it could easily enough be willed away in this new, if inevitably inferior, medium, at least until the process of revision had to be undertaken.

Dublin mattered less to Beckett than Belacqua, and here the question of range becomes a much more vexed one, partly because *Dubliners* (as its very title leads us to expect) paints a larger canvas covering a much wider spectrum of human experience. But Beckett was not attempting to write another *Dubliners*. His social range is as narrow as his geographical sweep, if there is such a thing as the latter in *More Pricks*. There are almost no poor people in *More Pricks*, except in 'Ding-Dong', although the old man in 'Fingal', the pedlar in 'Ding-Dong' and the tinker in 'Walking Out' seem in somewhat straitened circumstances. Poverty and its associated social ills, disease and prostitution (both rife in Dublin), leave almost no mark on the stories, although there is a girl 'debauched in appearance' in 'Ding-Dong' (35). There is correspondingly little interest taken, except once again in 'Ding-Dong', in the life of the streets, even with all the street names of a given neighbourhood on display. An even more visible presence in the Dublin of Beckett's childhood, youth and early manhood – the Catholic Church – is not much in evidence either, the only real exception being the Jesuit who cunningly leaves the Polar Bear to pay his fare ('A Wet Night'). Really, the only details that suggest these stories must be set in Dublin are horse-riding, alcohol (the only foodstuffs that Belacqua consumes are toast in 'Dante and the Lobster' and scallions in 'What A Misfortune'), death and an overarching anxiety about sexuality – stereotypes that Beckett enjoys because he can play with and against them. However, none of these details, small or large, is unique to Dublin, even if the setting can, as it chooses, make them seem as if they might be.

Joyce's achievement of making Dublin the type and measure of humanity at large, wherever it might find itself, is completely alien to Beckett's intentions, with the very quality of *Dubliners* militating against the possibility that similar intentions could in any way have prospered. But to say, as David Pattie has written in a recent essay (Gontarski [ed.], 182–95) that 'where Joyce finds more and more levels of meaning (to the extent that, in *Finnegans Wake*, the city contains everything), Beckett drains the Dublin landscape of most of its culture and history' (183) is to miss the use to which Beckett puts this 'culture and history' in *More Pricks*, a book to which Pattie, like so many other critics, pays only passing attention. The role of the city and its environs in the collection as a whole is, as we shall see, a more complex matter, although it is evident that Belacqua in *More Pricks* is only ever *of* Dublin, even when he is actually *in* it and walking through many of the streets in it (as notably in 'Ding-Dong', from the Phoenix Park west of the city centre to Lombard Street to the east of the centre), perhaps especially when much of the action in several of the other stories is occupied with describing his movements *away* from it.

Beckett's Dublin is certainly not Joyce's, and this difference is reinforced by the arrangement of the stories in *More Pricks*, which works against the *Dubliners* structural 'model' of childhood, youth, middle age, public life and so on. The only concession in *More Pricks* to the arc of 'birth to death', or beginning to ending, is that the collection starts (as many a story might) with 'It was morning' – a phrase added to the 1932 version of 'Dante and the Lobster' – and ends in the darkness of the cemetery. From the outset, Belacqua is 'stuck', indeed 'so bogged that he could move neither backward nor forward' (3). But there would be no stories at all if the collection did not appear to progress forwards, periodically look backwards, and in the end stay pretty much where it was. By engineering a 'moon rise' in 'Dante and the Lobster', and by having 'the moon on the job' in 'Draff' at the end, Beckett manages to suggest that not much movement has taken place between whiles. The opening of 'Ding-Dong' suggests that movement does matter, given that Belacqua has 'enlivened the last phase of his solipsism . . . with the belief that the best thing he had to do was to move constantly from place to place' (31). But the story as a whole privileges a movement without purpose, the occupation of an 'interval', nothing more. Connections and disconnections inevitably occur, as insisted upon by the footnotes which from time to time point out echoes from one story to another, and by other echoes and pre-echoes throughout, and they occur so frequently that they almost amount to a surrogate conservation of outlook, even as other conventions are disregarded. They are among the 'little things that are so important' introduced suspiciously late in the day in 'What A Misfortune' (132). They are, as it were, relics of the 'little encounters and contretemps' (127) of which *More Pricks* is made. But they refuse to coalesce into a 'unity'.

Beckett's interest in these 'little things' was probably part of his scepticism as to what a short story could be expected to achieve. It may also have been a way of dramatizing, and at the same time tacitly disparaging, what he took to be the small-mindedness of Dublin. Even so, as Edwin Muir was one of the few early critics (*The Listener*, 4 July 1934) to realize, there is also a kind of devotion to the 'little things' of which much can be made, a dimension apparent in the very first story ('Dante and the Lobster'), where the preparation of a toasted sandwich for lunch is given unusual prominence. Beckett's way of paying realism back for its perceived deficiencies, or its 'vulgarity' (*PTD*, 76), is to insist on mundane details for all, or for all the little, they are worth. If they make less impact in *More Pricks* than they would in, say, Chekhov, this is because of the way they are modelled (though I shall say more about them in a later section of this chapter). They seem almost to possess a life of their own, rather than the power to illuminate the life of which they are supposedly a part.

* * *

The 'little things' are, of their very nature, less visible than what Ruby Cohn (in her discussion of 'Dante and the Lobster', *Canon* 45) has aptly called 'disjunctions'. These latter occur partly as a consequence of the pressure on space in the short story form. This pressure has certain consequences for the content a short story can, or can ever hope to, contain. There is no room for a theory of history (à la *War and Peace*), or for interpolated tales (as in picaresque literature, or as in many eighteenth-century novels, or as in Dickens), or for anything essayistic (*Moby-Dick*) or resembling a feuilleton (Dostoevsky, Robert Musil). The form simply has to discharge its business fairly swiftly, without appearing thereby to suffer in terms of depth, context or continuity. Beckett could hardly have written many stories without accepting these restrictions on his natural tendency (as evidenced in *Dream*) to spread his wings and go 'up the rigging' (138). But Beckett was not comfortable making a virtue of necessity without exposing the vice, as he saw it, at the heart of it, and one type of exposure he was keen to exploit in *More Pricks* was the making manifest of the very restrictions he would have liked to do away with, or not have had to endure in the first place. To this end he devised disjunctions in several shapes and sizes:

1. Blatant narratorial intrusions;
2. Surprising transitions within a sentence, or from one paragraph to another, or from one focalized topic to another;
3. Dialogues either not obviously promoting the narrative, or presenting one or other of the participants as pursuing their own thoughts without necessarily making any useful contribution to the narrative;
4. Shifting lexical registers to create juxtapositions which seem either unnecessary in, or inappropriate to, a given situation;
5. Laboriously constructing, or constituting, a character whose 'life' as such, or whose physical characteristics, may not have much, or any, bearing on the role that the story expects or requires them to play;
6. Highlighting apparently insignificant details while downplaying the conventionally more important ones, thereby occupying much of the (inevitably limited) narrative space with occasions on which nothing much seems to be happening;
7. Openly flaunting the gaps in continuity which no reader, however competent, can hope to fill, so that differential blocks of narrative can be juxtaposed with one another;
8. Refusal of the 'rule' that the narrator or implied author knows all that is required for the provision of the story;
9. Surprising or recondite analogies and/or allusions;
10. Burying some connections so deeply into the narrative fabric that even an exceptionally alert reader is likely to miss them or, in the unlikely event of having registered them, be left wondering what to do with them;
11. Inventing absurd names, or names that flaunt their foreignness;
12. Elision of pronouns;
13. Allusions which only the writer himself could possibly know anything about, which adds 'insult' to the 'injury' of the refusal under category 8 above.

Other categories, or subsets of categories, could obviously be proposed, and the 13 categories here are by no means watertight. But they can be turned into serviceable tools for dealing with some of the strategies in a collection not primarily known for its subtlety. They can be briefly illustrated to provide a background for the stories individually, as I shall subsequently treat them.

1. The blatant intrusions are not especially subtle: 'Let us call it winter' ('Dante and the Lobster', 13); 'friend of the family (what family?)' ('Draff', 173).
2. Surprising transitions: ' . . . For the tiller of the field the thing [what thing?] was simple' ('Dante and the Lobster', 5); 'Though he [Mr Tough] might be only able to afford a safety-bicycle he was nevertheless a man of few words' ('Love and Lethe', 85).
3. Dialogues: applicable to almost anything 'spoken'. Dialogues, or double monologues, are at their most numerous and conspicuous in 'A Wet Night'. Any exchange between men who rightly or wrongly think themselves witty (e.g. in 'What A Misfortune') seems to promote very little. Any exchange between a man and a woman skirting around some issue ('Fingal', 'Love and Lethe', the end of 'What A Misfortune') seems just to peter out.
4. Registers: 'The itch of this mean quodlibet' ('Dante and the Lobster', 3); 'It [Pearse Street] was a most pleasant street, despite its name' ('Ding-Dong', 34); the nationalist hero and martyr looking a little less heroic as his name is implicitly broken down into 'pee' and 'arse'; 'a slush, a teary coenaesthesis' ('Draff'; 167).
5. Laborious construction: Of the Smeraldina, in a long paragraph close to the start of 'Draff', after we have been told that 'bodies don't matter' (167), a detailed description which goes much further than could ever be 'justified' narratively.
6. Apparently insignificant details: 'He knew a man who came from Gorgonzola . . . ' (12; added to the 1932 version of 'Dante and the Lobster').
7. Gaps: visual gaps in 'Dante and the Lobster' and 'A Wet Night' (the latter inheriting them from *Dream*, 199 ff.), when a story which might benefit from them ('What A Misfortune') has none; verbal gaps (two, at least) in 'Fingal' – Winnie as the 'last girl' (17) when we have not yet met the first, and Winnie finding the surrounding scenery 'dull', which is only recorded by Belacqua quoting the word back to her (17).
8. Disavowal of 'necessary' knowledge: 'tending whatever flowers die at that time of year' ('Dante and the Lobster', 13); 'Wisps of snipe and whatever it is of grouse' ('Love and Lethe', 86; the missing term is a 'covey' or 'coveys'); 'looking up (why up?)' ('Draff', 170).
9. Recondite allusions: to Shakespeare's *Hamlet* in 'Dante and the Lobster' – 'It [the prospect of eating toast] would be like smiting the sledded Polacks on the ice' (6) – or to Stendhal, for example, in 'A Wet Night' (47; the Comte de Thaler is a minor character, only mentioned twice, in *Le Rouge et le Noir*).

10. Buried connections: the 'infernal' basement in 'Dante and the Lobster' and the fire as a kind of inferno in 'Draff', both re-applying Dante; Schubert in 'Ding-Dong'; Proust in 'Yellow' (see my later treatment of these stories).
11. Names: Belacqua (with the surname 'Shuah' added first in 'What A Misfortune', but only given any prominence, very late in the day, in 'Draff'), an 'impossible' Italo-Hebraic combination derived from Dante's *Purgatorio* and commentaries thereon, and from the Biblical book of Genesis (cf. *DN*, 311, 313–15, 425), which Beckett concocted in a reversal of his own initials in order to emphasize, and at the same time to obscure, that he is indolent and a masturbator. (Compare the 'S.B.B.' autograph on the Hotel Léopold menu for the 'Déjeuner "Ulysse"' in June 1929, and the signature 'S. B. Beckett' on early letters to correspondents whom he did not know very well.) Other fantastical combinations include: Hermione Näutzsche ('What A Misfortune'; a 'nautch-girl' as in the poem 'Sanies I', but with Nietzsche and Shakespeare's *The Winter's Tale* in tow); Jimmy the Duck Skyrm (also in 'What A Misfortune'); the 'bboggs' family in 'What A Misfortune' (cf. a letter to MacGreevy of 22 June 1933); 'Tiny' Quin, a huge man, who is also nicknamed 'Hairy' and 'Capper'; Zaborovna Privet and Haemo Gall in 'Echo's Bones' (with 'Mick Doyle' a deliberate come-down). There are many names quite as strange as these in the works of Ronald Firbank.
12. Elision: To whom do 'his' in 'his mother' and 'him' in 'good enough for him' ('Dante and the Lobster', 5) refer? Cain – the tiller of the field – and Belacqua are all connected by the confusion (cf. the essay by Kay Gilliland Stevenson).
13. Material impossible to grasp: Ruby knowing an unpublished revision of a Beckett poem ('Love and Lethe', 90), of which only Beckett himself, or a very close friend, could possibly have knowledge; Hairy quoting from a passage in Ovid's *Metamorphoses* which Beckett had translated (128; *DN*, 1118).

* * *

All these 'disjunctions' are, in their different ways, disturbing reminders of how flagrantly, and sometimes deviously, *constructed* these stories are, much like the poems by Beckett which had given him the feeling that they were '*construits*' (letter to MacGreevy of 18 October 1932; *LSB*, 134). The dislocations are 'little things' in themselves, but they loom large, like 'Tiny' Quin, a man with more than one nickname (unlike most of us). In the writing of *More Pricks* Beckett was hyperaware of tensions in himself; for the most part, the stories disguise these, though there are two distinct occasions when the traces are foregrounded and apparently raised as debatable issues. It is precisely at a (self-imposed) lull in the development of 'What A Misfortune' that the narrator elects to tell us that 'these are the little things that are so important' (132) and obliges us to see the sentence by giving it a paragraph to itself. But it is not very clear, and neither is it meant to be, whether the 'importan[ce]' here depends upon the 'little things' which might naturally occur in life or on these particular 'little things' as presented in this story, or at this point in the story. The gratuitousness of the narrative gesture here acts as a reminder of the contingencies on which literature necessarily depends if it is to exist at all, and on which life may also hang. But it is only in literature that such a remark can point in more than one direction. In life it could almost certainly only be applied, or judged as necessary, after a sequence of events believed to be over, from which a simple moral of a kind could then be deduced.

Equally striking is the narratorial intervention in 'Walking Out', which raises the question: 'Is all this merely ridiculous?' (99, after a description that epitomizes Lucy's physical characteristics). The question is left unanswered, although it is not obviously a rhetorical question. The difficulty is to know whether 'all this' refers to the collection as a whole, or only to the matters presented in the paragraph in 'Walking Out' which this question brings to an end. Of course it may not matter, since the question asked, at least in this way at this time (quite possibly in an addition to the story while preparing the whole collection for publication), is unanswerable. It is no more measurable than the statement about the importance of 'little things' in 'What A Misfortune'; it is only true or false as a reader chooses, or does not choose, to endorse it. Neither the statement nor the question illustrates anything. Rather, they are illustrations, at these two distinct moments, of the author's own scepticism as to what he is about. Neither of them is, by any criterion of relevance, actually needed, and the positions which they occupy cannot be considered 'justified'. The reader is being led to consider what may be genuine issues, which turn out to be undecidable on the basis of what else is being given. Now while it is obviously the case that the reader always comes to a piece of writing as second best – since he or she did not originate the writing – at the same time, only the reader can decide what is genuinely important and what is 'merely ridiculous'. It is only through reading, in fact, that these stories, or indeed any fiction, 'live' at all.

* * *

There is not much point in wishing the *More Pricks* stories to be other than they are, although there may be some point in seeing how they work and what they are primed to work with and against. Most readers, finding that there is one character who appears in all of them, will read *More Pricks* in the order in which the stories are presented on the contents page. But this threatens to turn *More Pricks* back into the novel it was never intended to be, and for critical purposes it is, I think, more profitable and more interesting to divide the ten stories (or nine stories and a letter) into three groups of three, within which features distinctive to each group can be discerned. 'Walking Out' treats of Belacqua's first marriage (insofar as it treats of marriage at all), 'Fingal' of 'the last girl' he went with and 'Love and Lethe' makes its limited impact in a placement between the two. These three are (if the phrase has any meaning in this context) 'love stories'. The second group ('Dante and the Lobster', 'Ding-Dong' and 'Yellow') deals with wider issues of the mind and the world on which that mind seeks to have some effect. Wider still are the ensemble pieces of the third group ('A Wet Night', 'What A Misfortune' and 'Draff'), the last of which Belacqua has necessarily been removed from as a living principle, even if he continues to occupy the thoughts of others and remains a kind of spectral 'presence' or ghost in the machine even after he has been put in his coffin and buried. And the one 'story' left, 'The Smeraldina's Billet Doux', falls in a category of its own, whatever purposes it may have served in *Dream*, where at least it had Lucien's letter to Belacqua (19–22) and Jem Higgins's love letter to the Alba (152–4) for company. It does no real harm to 'The Smeraldina's Billet Doux' to treat it separately, and here I situate it in Subsection 4 of Chapter 2, alongside, if in no way interactive with, two other stories which are more or less 'odds', one of them ('Echo's Bones') intended for *More Pricks* – an attempt to address Charles Prentice's qualms over the size of the book – and the other ('A Case in a Thousand') written after its publication and after Beckett knew that *More Pricks* had failed to make its mark. But for now it is perhaps best to leave all these backgrounds and foregrounds to *More Pricks Than Kicks* and look more closely at what 'has to be taken or left' (*Dream*, 13), by turning first to Belacqua's (last?) attempt at 'gallantry' (17).

Chapter 2

My Sometime Friend Belacqua

1. *Seul et à Deux:* 'Walking Out', 'Love and Lethe', 'Fingal'

From now on till the end there is something very secco and Punch and Judy about their proceedings.

(*'Love and Lethe'*)

Each of these stories – 'Walking Out', 'Love and Lethe' and 'Fingal' – builds on the structures already de-stabilized in *Dream* by way of 'the Smeraldina-Rima' in section 2 of the novel and 'the Alba' in section 3, even though the contrast between the two real-life originals behind those characters (Peggy Sinclair and Ethna MacCarthy) has in *More Pricks* been abandoned as too 'binary' (*Dream*, 28) to be of much use in a short story collection. *More Pricks* is more imaginative than *Dream* in two senses: more of the events imagined are specific to a Belacqua who has been obliged to experience the aftermath of taking 'the dull coast road home' (*Dream*, 143) to Dublin and its environs, and narrative material less personal to Beckett's own experience is brought under control for more specific purposes, with a closer attention to detail. The female figures in *Dream* seem, much as in a dream, to float into and out of the narrative consciousness or to be summoned up for no particular reason at any given point in the novel, as if they were little more than reflex projections and phantasms being obsessively pursued, or (as in the case of the Smeraldina, when circumstances permit) pursuing Belacqua. In *More Pricks* the female figures, though much more numerous, are not allowed so much freedom and are less dominant; they are effectively taken up and dropped as each particular story sees fit to do so. In *Dream* the threat of 'a love passage' (189) can be more or less continuously ironized, but there is much more space for development, and for an often bewildering range of emotions. In *More Pricks* the movement away from 'ars longa' (*Dream*, 168) entails more situational intrigue and a generally more 'secco' approach ('Love and Lethe', 87) to what had been too rich and ripe a brew in the novel. This was no doubt one reason, among many, why Beckett had decided to call his book *Draff* by the time he sent the stories to Chatto, alluding to the lees left after the process of creating a more heady and inebriating concoction.

'Walking Out'

The existence (by August 1931) of a version of 'Walking Out' – which was briefly under consideration by the agent J. B. Pinker (*LSB*, 82), who sent it back to Beckett – suggests that it was probably the second of the *More Pricks* stories to be written, more than a year before 'Dante and the Lobster' appeared in *This Quarter*. A 1933 letter to Beckett from Charles Prentice further suggests that Beckett had offered to change the title (which Prentice liked) for one now lost. The extant title is in many ways very apt, although one of the meanings of the title that was finally adopted has itself now almost been lost. In the days when the words *courting* and *courtship* still had some meaning, one 'walked out' with one's beloved (compare Gretta Conroy describing her relationship with Michael Furey to her husband Gabriel in Joyce's 'The Dead', *Dubliners*, 220, 316, n. 88), either on the way to becoming 'betrothed' or engaged – as Belacqua and Lucy are here – or on the way to being married, as eventually happens here – or is said to have happened, since the only wedding we actually see taking place in *More Pricks* is in 'What A Misfortune'. But at the beginning of the story Belacqua is 'walking out' in the countryside (on his own) and – at least as Lucy sees it, or thinks she sees it – is also in danger of 'walking out' on her, or on her potential sexual claims upon him, in favour of 'unacceptable' voyeuristic practices. Belacqua dignifies these with a phrase 'sursum corda' (lift up your hearts) adapted from the Latin Mass of the Roman Catholic Church. The heart of Charles Prentice, at least, seems to have been uplifted by the double meaning of Beckett's original title, almost an illustration of what 'Ding-Dong' calls a 'double response, like two holes to a burrow' (36). The idea that walking out *with* someone might better be achieved by walking out *on* them was obviously attractive to Beckett.

Much of 'Walking Out' describes Belacqua doing just that – walking out – and later running and stumbling out of Tom Wood chased by the outraged Tanzherr. But obviously a title cannot, of its very nature, contain everything that a given story seeks to encompass. This, it turns out, is a story which also depicts Lucy *riding* out and an unnamed Lord (one is bound to think of

Lord Gall of the jettisoned 'Echo's Bones') *driving* out. Overarching them is the otherwise unremarkable activity of *looking* out, simply seeing things, or hoping to see them, from a distance, without any actual participation in them. When looking out is prompted by more or less 'natural' desires (more so in the case of Lucy, less so in the case of Belacqua), it seems as if this is likely to lead to a disastrous outcome, although again more so in the case of Lucy, less so in the case of Belacqua. At the same time, if one does not look out (in the sense of being alert to danger), especially at dusk and then as night falls, that too can lead to an unwanted and unforeseen event: disablement on Lucy's part, embarrassment on Belacqua's. Beckett is sufficiently disinterested, or cunning enough to seem so, to simply present the events as they occur, although Belacqua is clearly granted his wish (a sexless marriage) and Lucy has to forego hers, unless a marriage of any kind was all she had in mind. The narrator leaves matters to what he calls, tongue in cheek, an 'adverse fate' (101) that, much like God, 'sees' everything. The narrator does so, however, after having introduced the figure who (with Belacqua's 'bitch' dog a close second) is probably the least prey to desire of all the human and animal characters in the story. This is the vagabond left, after encountering Belacqua and his dog early in the story, 'peering out through his sector' as yet one more voyeur, although all he sees is 'the grey of the road with its green hem' (101). The vagabond is not given a name, and is in any case about to disappear into the 'dark' of non-narration, superfluous to the business of the dénouement (a marriage), but more 'real' in standing alone. Jeri Kroll very shrewdly assesses the vagabond, and also the groundsman in 'Draff' later, as a kind of *figura* of Beckett himself, a notion which assumes extra importance over Beckett's sense of his 'Peter-Panitis' (Knowlson, 1996, 178; cf. the alleged 'infantilism' of Proust [*PTD*, 57]), and the 'gerontophilia' of the letter to MacGreevy of 8 September 1935 (*LSB*, 274). Also illustrative in this connection are two entries in Beckett's German diaries: 'shall I never learn to cease thinking of myself as young' (18 December 1936); and 'I wish I were an old man/Or an old woman' (2 March 1937; compare the 'two further women [. . .] the one of a certain age, the other not', in 'Yellow' [163]).

Belacqua's first name (we only learn that it is his first by being told of his second on the wedding invitation in 'What A Misfortune' and in the obituary in 'Draff'; his full name, Belacqua Shuah, has been well described by Leslie Hill as an 'inverted S. B.' and a 'reversed monogram'; 7, 112) is as absurd and literary as he himself is. His very name is 'dark' (once its meaning has been decoded), and he favours the dark, or the near-dark ('definitely dusk', 102), for his nefarious activities. By contrast, Lucy's first name (the only one she is given) is synonymous with light, although it is she who goes out in search of enlightenment as to her lover's doings. The story effectively pays her back for going *out*, outside her 'fixed' role, or rather outside the role fixed for her by her given name. Lucy, we may suppose, lacks the 'inner light' which might have been derived from her own mind, as in the inscription on the redeemed wedding ring in 'What A Misfortune'. Disabled by her accident, Lucy never achieves the light, but her 'hopes of a place in the sun' (105), a phrase which effectively endorses Belacqua's preference for the dark, are forever disappointed. Yet, as his own experience demonstrates, the world of the dark has its own dangers, which one may not always escape with impunity.

'Walking Out' plays the *More Pricks* trick of surrounding what would be the focal point in a more conventional story – the accident – with lots of much more trivial business. It is the latter, not the former, that interests Beckett. The typical hinge of the plot is thereby disfigured, much as '[p]oor little Lucy' is to be. In the same way, the true 'hero' of the story proves to be not Belacqua but the vagabond, 'this real man at last' (98). This assessment of someone apparently of no importance threatens to turn the characters who occupy the bulk of the action into mere bit-part players, of little significance, not 'real' men or 'real' women. Given this, how much can it matter if one of them is 'dreadfully marred' (103) and the other rendered, at least for a time, 'half insensible' (105)? Like the details of Lucy's physiognomy, these things may be 'merely ridiculous' (99) or in danger of becoming so.

While 'Walking Out' necessarily concerns itself with Lucy and Belacqua (and specifically with Belacqua's motives for walking out), Beckett's principal interest seems to be in describing physical movement, or (in the case of the dog going over the wall) the difficulty of achieving it. The bitch, a Kerry Blue like the dog Beckett himself owned, apparently makes it home unaided after Belacqua's fight with the Tanzherr although we are not told how, probably because Belacqua himself is '[u]nable to understand how he reached home' (105). In the absence of detail, the story's angle of vision implicitly conveys Belacqua's sense of his own superiority over the bitch and, by extension, over Lucy. However – though the narrator presents Belacqua thinking 'what a splendid thing it is when all is said and done to be young and vigorous' (97) – when all actually has been said and done, and when his opponent has soundly beaten a Belacqua who has been 'fighting like a woman', the narrator drily observes: 'So much for his youth and vigour' (105). Forward movement has been stalled, or wished away, in a trajectory which is all 'out' and no 'back'. This is to some extent also true of Belacqua in 'Ding-Dong', in spite of that story's invocation of the 'boomerang' effect.

Beckett cunningly anticipates an outcome which (from a number of points of view) is really no outcome at all by beginning his story of movement and moving by way of its opposite: a pause or halt. A kind of hiatus is occurring precisely when, ordinarily, events ought to be getting under way. But Belacqua has 'paused, not so much in order to rest as to have the scene soak through him' (95). It is fundamental to Belacqua's personality (as Beckett conceives of it) that, although he actually *does* very little here (or in any of the later stories), he is never really at 'rest', except perhaps inevitably in 'Draff', and even there he is given what would normally be considered signs of life, 'grinning' away in his coffin (175). Here Beckett emphasizes the *scene* at the outset in order to establish how important things *seen* will be in the development of the story. But looking and seeing are matters hedged round with multiple ironies. To look with desire is not to see the whole picture. To *fore*see is impossible, and nature is happily blind to what humanity makes of it, given that 'fate' sees all. The wood is said to be 'the root of all the mischief' (102), but Lucy 'saw nothing' of it, and of course she does not see the 'most quarried lovers' (as they are described in the 1932 poem 'Serena I') who are ensconced there. The story pays Lucy back, behind her back – St Lucy is the patron saint of seeing and eye complaints (cf. *DN*, 774) – by obliging her to run the gauntlet of suffering from her own ocular deficiencies. How far this reflects Beckett's wish to punish Lucia Joyce – in some sense a model for Lucy, as I suggest in the relevant notes in chapter 5 – remains unclear, But it remains a possibility, especially when 'The Smeraldina's Billet Doux' (see Section 4 of this chapter) treats Peggy Sinclair in terms that are far from flattering, and when 'Fingal' becomes a kind of 'walking out' on the Winnie Coates figure later associated with 'decency' (167). In 'Walking Out', which is a story effectively beginning the series of reversals which will ultimately add up to *More Pricks Than Kicks*, the usual pieties and traditional wisdoms come under pressure from the 'real' events as they are presented. In this connection, or in this exploitation of disconnection, we can hardly help but register that the corncrake here – there are corncrakes lurking in *Molloy*, part 1 (13) later; they 'used to be common in Ireland' (Boland, 238) – is only ominous in its 'death-rattle' (103) because tradition and Belacqua would have it so. In the dénouement no one actually dies, whatever and whomever Beckett may be trying to 'kill off', wish away (cf. 'Be off, puttanina' behind the back of the Lucia Joyce figure in *Dream* [51], the 'Syra-Cusa') or simply put behind him.

The single potentially active omen-like element in this situation is present only in its absence: the cuckoo (95, 103). Keen as he is to be cuckolded by a 'cicisbeo' (96) – an Italian word which contrives (twice) to contain two letters from the name 'Lu*ci*a' – Belacqua naturally laments this, as if nature ought to reflect his desires. But in due course, a surrogate sexual partner will not be needed: 'the question of cicisbei does not arise' (105). Beckett is probably making wry play here with Frederick Delius's popular 'On Hearing the First Cuckoo in Spring'. He certainly intends to exploit loopholes in the long tradition of pastoral literature and the idea that 'in the spring a young man's fancy lightly turns to thoughts of love' (compare *Dream*, 188, on the shortcomings of 'the Springtime' as opposed to winter). One literary source known to Beckett in the early 1930s – beyond Shakespeare, some of whose 'pastoral' plays he had studied at TCD – was John Fletcher's play *The Faithful Shepherdess* (1608; cf. *SBT/A*, 16, 214–5, items 46 and 47). Beckett was interested not in the faithfulness of the Shepherdess but rather in the lustfulness of the Sullen Shepherd, the villain of the piece, who is characterized in the *'Whoroscope' Notebook* as 'winning, loathing and flying' on the basis of his self-proclaimed 'blessed destiny' in a speech in Act 2, scene 3 (cf. Ackerley 1998, 52–3). Fletcher presents this figure in Act I, scene 2 of *The Faithful Shepherdess* as 'one that lusts after every several beauty,/ But never yet was known to love or like', and the Sullen Shepherd figure sufficiently impressed Beckett to reappear in Neary's memory (*Murphy*, chapter 4, thinking back to chapter 1) as the model, or rather anti-model, for 'conducting . . . amours' (33). But Beckett's Belacqua in 'Walking Out' (which almost certainly pre-dates any of the 'For Interpolation' material in the *'Whoroscope' Notebook*) is, or is presented as, more of a sad case than a villain. As early as the second paragraph of 'Walking Out', Belacqua is obliged to confront the 'vivid thought' that he 'must be past [his] best' (95), even as he looks forward to the unspecified (as yet) pleasures of the wood, pleasures which in the event turn out to be more bucolic and burlesque than pastoral. The Sullen Shepherd entry in the *'Whoroscope' Notebook* is, however, a useful reminder of how, even as early as 'Walking Out', Beckett had already taken elements from a genre to which he did not wish to subscribe and combined them according to his own subversive creative purposes. Indeed, it seems clear that Beckett rather liked the way storytelling modes like pastoral could contain elements not just saccharine but also 'sullen'. (He had studied Milton's *Comus* during Michaelmas Term at TCD in the autumn and early winter of 1924 [cf. Smith, 168]; he could remember Guarini's *Il Pastor Fido* and Tasso's *Aminta* 10 years after he had left university [cf. *LSB*, 361; Pilling 2009, 7]; and he later entered quotations from Pope's *Pastorals* in his *'Whoroscope' Notebook*.) Whether he thought of the genre of Pastoral in the radically unconventional way soon to be analysed by William Empson in *Some Versions of Pastoral* (London: Chatto and Windus, 1935) seems unlikely, but Beckett must at least have been familiar with Empson's name (and perhaps some of his early poems) by way of the Cambridge University journal *Experiment*, of which Empson (later supported by Jacob Bronowski and George Reavey) was a founding editor. In a letter to MacGreevy of 6 January 1931 Beckett told his friend that Reavey was intending to publish one of his poems in *Experiment*, claimed that he did not care one way or the other and then decided that he would prefer them not to publish it. (The seventh and last issue of *Experiment* came out in Spring 1931, which meant that the question of whether to accept or decline very swiftly ceased to have any relevance.) But 'Walking Out' effectively demonstrates that Beckett did not require instruction from Empson, or from any of the other young Cambridge luminaries, on how easily the constituent forms and the ancillary contexts of a given literary convention could be separated for utterly different purposes. 'Walking Out' is explicitly set, and deliberately set up as taking place, on 'one of those Spring evenings when it is a matter of some difficulty to keep God out of one's meditations' (95), but the story actually develops without experiencing any real difficulty of this kind, and indeed with relatively few 'meditations' of any kind. The 'spilt religion' aspect of Pastoral, its shepherds mere by-blows of the Good Shepherd, is left looking empty, and it seems that 'God' has no control over these 'fateful' events (95) anyway.

'We did not meet many animals', says Camier (who can remember a goat) to Mercier (who remembers a parrot; *Mercier and Camier*, 99). 'Walking Out', however, is unusually rich in animals. There are, to be sure, 'no horses' (though there will be a 'jennet') and 'no cats', but there are 'legions of sheep and lambs' (95), larks (twice mentioned), a bitch and a corncrake. At one point Lucy even thinks of Belacqua as a 'lizard' (99) and a 'creepy-crawly' (101). Towards the end the 'Fräulein and friend' in the wood – figures bringing Smeraldina material into this Lucy story, just as 'Lucy will intrude on the Thelma material in 'What A Misfortune' – seem to be rutting away like animals, although all that can be seen is a 'flutter and a gleam of white in a hollow' (104), which almost transforms them into birds. (Cf. the Alba in *Dream*: ' "Are we birds?" ', 195.) Of these animals the most memorable are the jennet (a small pony of Spanish origin) who 'hoped, before it died, to bite a man' (a hope it will not be able to satisfy, 96) and the old Kerry Blue bitch who has few hopes left. The latter either tries to remain seated – later she is 'sitting in the ditch' (100), and later still tethered (104) – or 'ma[kes] herself at home' (97) by urinating on the down-and-out's trousers, a detail remembered later, in

1933, and worked into the echoic maelstrom of 'Echo's Bones' (20). Both these creatures, for all the 'emblems of the spring' and 'pastoral clamour' (98) surrounding them, are in their different ways doomed. The jennet is spared from a life of 'servitude' by a 'superb silent limousine' (103). The bitch, after briefly contributing to the 'whole group' as pictured in a 'sector' (101) of the tinker's 'old high-wheeled cart', is conspicuously omitted from the final tableau of Lucy and Belacqua married. Neither the jennet nor the bitch prove to be of much use as a 'partner in life's journey' (as Lucy thinks Belacqua might be, 99), since the journey of the former leads to its death, and the journey of the latter only gives much 'pleasure' to its master when he can give her 'a vigorous heave on the grey hunkers' (97). It is subsequently revealed, in the opening paragraph of 'What A Misfortune' (109), that Lucy has been only a 'partner in life's journey' for 2 years. She has been, as Malone will later be, 'given [. . .] birth to into death' (114).

The pattern 'birth to [. . .] death' is a 'given' of 'Walking Out', the 'newborn lamb' (97) figuring against a small Spanish pony which 'expire[s]' (in French; 103) under the wheels of a large luxury German car, and all for love. Unlike the *l'Amour* and *la Mort* of 'Love and Lethe' (91), this is a 'private joke' (*Dream*, 67) hidden in plain view, privileging privacy over disclosure, as epitomized by the privacy of the tinker, his 'private life . . . not acquired . . . but antecedent', beyond all 'civility' (98). In a way, the story also respects – as public taste might expect it to do – the privacy of the lovers in the hollow. These are not 'things seen' or at least not seen very clearly, however much 'Walking Out' may emphasize looking (Belacqua), looking out (Lucy) and 'peering out' (the vagabond, 101). The real drift of the story, indeed, is towards moments when there is nothing very specific to be seen. It is symptomatic that Belacqua, while waiting for Lucy to turn up at their rendezvous, replicates the 'eagerness' which is fated to get her into difficulties, but, wisely perhaps, '[g]radually . . . he cease[s] to look for her and look[s] at the scene instead' (103). As it is a gradually 'darkling' landscape anyway (103, as with Keats's listening in 'Ode to a Nightingale'), the scene offers as little to the eye as the 'performance' (104) to follow, and it is part of the story's technique of reversal that on encountering the lovers Belacqua surprises himself by 'not looking at all but staring vacantly into the shadows' (104). This is effectively the final 'proof', which has been hinted at throughout, that all the looking in 'Walking Out' has to be measured against the more intimate pleasure of listening: if not to the cuckoo, then to the 'crex-crex' of the corncrake, and to Schubert's '*An die Musik*' at the end. Lucy, who has been 'spared' from *seeing* the prolepsis of this final tableau in the 'high plume of smoke waxing and waning, like a Lied' (102) – when she could hardly be expected to see a pre-echo – has obviously also failed to *listen* for the limousine which will kill her jennet and mar her beauty. 'Poor little Lucy!' (102) seems very apt in the circumstances; for as 'Belacqua saw all these things' (as of course the narrator does) she 'saw nothing' (102), and as it happens an 'adverse fate' has conspired to make the limousine ('a Daimler no doubt' [103], when presumably what marque it may or may not be is wholly irrelevant to the outcome) a 'silent' one. The irony is redoubled when the jennet expires, '*sans jeter un cri*' (103). Even listening, perhaps, may be an activity fraught with danger, although in 'Walking Out' it seems the best policy is not to speak (for fear one might find, like Belacqua talking to Lucy, that one has 'gone too far'; 100), but rather to listen (even if only to what is silent), and if one really must look, it is best to see nothing (that 'rare postnatal treat' as chapter 11 of *Murphy* registers it). What we do hear, in this Irish landscape, precisely because dialogue has ended and because spoken speech of any kind has dwindled almost to nothing (in musical terms, a *diminuendo al niente*), is, of all things, two words in German ('wie heimlich!' [102]; '*wie heimatlich!*' in 1934 [153; my emphasis]), the one gesturing towards an idea of domesticity, and the other towards a (foreign!) homeland. In Joyce's *Dubliners* this detail would, or could, form part of an 'epiphany' and as such would highlight the focal 'point' of the story, like the gold coin in Corley's palm at the end of 'Two Gallants'. But here there is no epiphany, no focus, and indeed nothing visual in what is more and more a 'night-piece' (cf. Schubert's Lied '*Nachtstück*'). Here there is no light, because 'Walking Out' has effectively 'walked out' on itself, by shifting – without in any way emphasizing the shift – from the outer scene to the inner, and from a parody of pastoral conventions to an adaptation of stanzas five and six of Keats's 'Ode to a Nightingale'. (In stanza four of the poem, line 38, Keats insists: 'But here there is no light').

The fifth stanza of Keats's poem begins: 'I cannot see what flowers are at my feet'. The sixth stanza pivots on the prayer 'Take into the air my quiet breath' (cf. 'Dante and the Lobster' and the poem 'Serena I') and on the idea that it would be 'rich to die' (a feeling also to be found in Schubert's '*Nachtstück*', if not in '*An die Musik*'). It must have given Beckett a great deal of pleasure to imply that Keats's Ode, which is at no point *visible* here (with the only obvious external referent being a Schubert song), ties the conclusion of 'Walking Out' to the only other story in which, at this point in time – August 1931 at the latest – Belacqua has figured: 'Dante and the Lobster'. (Compare Beckett's *Proust* on 'the plagiarism of oneself' [*PTD*, 33]). Keats is very cunningly left *invisible*, as his nightingale is, because his poem cannot be *heard*. The strategy underpins what the story – much more obligingly though not much more openly – is telling us explicitly by way of what can be seen and heard in it. In 'Walking Out', Belacqua cannot see, and ultimately chooses not to see, what he has walked out to look at, which might as well have been flowers in the end. As Vandervlist emphasizes (1991, 75), 'both the initial target (romance conventions) and the alternative (unromantic and 'perverse' solitary pleasures) are undermined'. Belacqua's breath, it seems, must be quiet enough, as 'quiet' as Keats is striving to be, for him not to be heard. But the ever-active 'adverse fate' ensures that he falls foul of a rotten bough which snaps off with a 'loud report' (104), much as the revolver in 'Love and Lethe' will. Beyond telling us what we are (and seem to be meant to be) looking at, 'Walking Out' invites us to see, if not exactly by looking, that nature has its own order and fate its own agenda, whereas human life is a prey to disorder. There may be a kind of harmony in a Keats ode, but here the only real remedy is beyond words. It is part of the marital harmony between Lucy and Belacqua that, even though they 'sit up to all hours', 'they never *allude* to the old days' (105; my emphasis). They are (or at least he is) 'happily married' (105), and this, it is implied, is 'how to be happy though married' – the title of the book by 'Hardy' [Edward John, not Thomas!] remembered by Maddy Rooney in *All That Fall* more than 25 years later (*All That Fall*, etc., 31). With Keats operating as a kind of 'ideal real' (*PTD*, 75), Schubert's song – itself a hybrid of words and music (though we are not given any music here, as we will be, courtesy of Beethoven, in 'What A Misfortune') – is what allows the story to end in 'a queer old lesson in quiet' (172). Best of all, '*An die Musik*' is being used here 'in order to rest' when 'to rest', as the very first sentence of 'Walking Out' suggests (95), might have been the better policy to begin with. (Cf. the 'Ruheort', the place of rest, in line 12 of the Johann Mayrhofer poem '*Nachtstück*' as set by Schubert, D. 672, op. 36, no. 2.) At this point all narrative activity simply has to end, if only by appearing to comply with the 'happy ever after' requirement. This seems to be gesturing towards the kind of possible future bliss which no story ever finds it profitable to pursue, and it is perhaps the only narrative convention which this story has not yet seen fit to undermine. But the wry final words are designed to subvert that convention too, a reminder that all 'hopes of a place in the sun' (105) have here to be foregone.

* * *

'Love and Lethe'

If there were a 'natural' order at work in *More Pricks*, 'Walking Out' would have come earlier in the collection, certainly before 'Love and Lethe', which immediately precedes it. In a novel either one of the stories would have had to be sacrificed, or the first would have 'foreshadowed' and the latter 'reflected' the second. The published arrangement here subordinates the former (in its first version, at least, one of the earliest of the stories) to protect the latter (probably one of the last to be written) from any accusations of déjà vu. The two stories may well have been written, or originally conceived, some 2 years apart, 2 years in which *Dream* made no headway and had to be jettisoned. During this time Beckett's understanding of what a short story could and could not do took on clearer definition, but did not necessarily guarantee him much pleasure in the form. (To see him relishing the form one needs to turn to other very late stories like 'What A Misfortune', 'Draff' and 'Echo's Bones'.) By the time of 'Love and Lethe', Beckett must have been close to having a sufficiently (as he hoped) large collection of stories, although no doubt equally close (as he must have feared) to losing patience with the whole enterprise. How much he cared by then, with the devastating death of his father either about to happen or having just occurred we can only guess. But a few years later, having settled finally in Paris, Beckett cared enough about 'Love and Lethe', perhaps because of its relative straightforwardness, to attempt a French translation of it. In a letter to George Reavey written after 24 October 1938 (*LSB*, 644–5) Beckett told him that he was translating a revised 'Love and Lethe', possibly (he thought) as unsuccessful as the original story had been, although no such translation into French – there is also the barest trace of such a possibility in a letter to the same correspondent written 4 years earlier (*LSB*, 212) – seems to have survived.

If we think of 'Love and Lethe' as one of the latest stories for the collection, we might perhaps expect it to show less signs of strain than are visible elsewhere, and it is notably brisk and businesslike, with none of the baroque encrustations of, say, 'What A Misfortune'. In showing few signs of strain, however, 'Love and Lethe' also largely dispenses with the finer subtleties of some of the earlier stories. It is not without them, but Beckett is intent on advertising its brightness and brittleness. To this end he prefers short paragraphs to longer ones, restricts himself to brief and/or terse dialogic exchanges, highlights Mr Tough's suitably tough vocabulary, twice intervenes with glosses for the reader and even avails himself of the visual aid of the licence plate/notice with its absurd message ('TEMPORARILY

SANE', 89). Although the narrator decides at one point that 'we need not allow [Ruby's] outside to detain us' (81), not much visible effort is put into giving the character any inner depth. The narrator detains himself during a 'lull' in 'this incredible adventure' – a lull, needless to say, of his own making – with some background allegedly designed to make it less 'unintelligible' (80). But the reader, whom the narrator fears may be inclined to 'pooh-pooh' this material, finds that the narrator has been ahead of him or her in the 'pooh-pooh' stakes, since the portrait of Ruby that emerges is little more than the 'series of staircase jests' (82), her personal estimate of her own life. A kind of devil-may-care mood prevails, with Belacqua little more than an 'adult desperado' (83), especially when driving, and Ruby ('one of those ladies who have no use for a petticoat', 88) more than ready to shed her skirt in order to 'storm the summit' of the mountain. 'We state the facts', says the narrator, 'We do not presume to determine their significance'; Belacqua's real motives are said to be 'subliminal to the point of defying expression' (82) and are left unexpressed.

Long before we reach this 'non-determination', however, the significance of these particular facts has ceased to matter much. We could, for example, have been told which text Ruby is quoting from just before she pours herself a third double whiskey, even if her quotation is immediately deemed an 'irrelevance'. (No one in 1934, and very few readers today, could possibly know that she is actually quoting from Beckett's own revision to part of the conclusion to his 1930 poem 'Whoroscope'!) There is a similar irresponsibility in the narrator's refusal to disclose what Belacqua is really hoping to 'pull . . . off' (88), although we are told in the penultimate paragraph that 'at least on this occasion, if never before nor since, he achieved what he set out to do' (91). We are not given Ruby's evaluation of the 'occasion', but we can at least suppose she is satisfied, given that she only tolerates Belacqua 'in the hope that sooner or later . . . he would so far forget himself as to take her in his arms' (82).

Far from forgetting himself, Belacqua has decided that in their suicide pact Ruby is to be the one to go first, just as she has preceded him up the mountain (he has 'enjoyed a glimpse of her legs', 86). But as things turn out, the 'problem of precedence' (90) is no problem at all. The only potential problem which might affect their 'inevitable nuptial' (91) occurs in a bizarre transposition of material derived from Pierre Garnier's *Onanisme, seul et à deux* (cf. *DN*, 426): the revolver goes off by allusion to Onan bringing himself off (Genesis 38.9). One is left free to suppose that, without the transposition, or under the duress of a more 'adverse fate' ('Walking Out', 101), Belacqua might have been disabled from any immediate satisfaction of intimacy. The 'detonation' so shocks Ruby that 'for fully a minute she thought she was shot' (91). We later learn that the parson in 'Yellow' actually was shot and 'was transfixed'. But here – so as not to offend 'decency' (167) – the outcome is only the *petit mort* of orgasm. This is 'suitably' dignified by the narrator's appeal to the authority of 'one competent to sing of the matter' (91): the poet Ronsard, the 'lecherous laypriest' of the 1929 poem 'Return to the Vestry' who also offers 'Deliverance from Love' in *Dream* (175). As *Dream*, however, reveals, Beckett also has a very different, much better known, poet in mind: T. S. Eliot. The last lines of Eliot's *The Hollow Men* (1925) read: 'This is the way the world ends/ Not with a bang but a whimper'. The endorsement of Ronsard in 'Love and Lethe' reinforces an explicit critique of Eliot in *Dream*: 'The bang is better than the whimper. It is easier to do' (177). Too easy, perhaps, for the good of the story; the music here, promoting a nuptial by way of a loud bang, looks like a way of backing out so as to have done with these hollow people.

Ruby is seen by her mother as 'very strange' (85), although 'the most astounding thing' in the story is actually said to be a 'high mesh wire fence, flung like a shingles round the mountain' (86), the point of which Belacqua cannot grasp, on first seeing it (86). But no one can seem strange for long compared to Belacqua, and the backstory of Ruby's amours and gallants makes it seem quite understandable that she should be keen 'to end with a fairly beautiful bang' (83), especially given her (unspecified) 'incurable disorder' (82). There is perhaps too much 'verisimilitude' (82) in this backstory for it to live long in the mind, and Ruby is not expected (by the doctors, or by the readers of 'Love and Lethe') to live long, hence the brief obituary 'Ruby duly' in 'Draff' (161). The narrative voice adds to this sense of an existence hardly worth maintaining by imagining, at the very end, what life will be like for Belacqua 'when Ruby is dead' (91), which happens much later on (by narrative report, rather than by way of the 'bang' or report of a gun). This 'flash forward' technique is one of the few technical accoutrements used here that is not also tried in 'Walking Out', the death of Lucy held over until the beginning of 'What A Misfortune'. ('Yellow', almost certainly written close in time to 'Love and Lethe', also depends in part on imagining what will have happened when the whole *More Pricks* experience is over and done with, '[y]ears later' [160].)

It is against this (apparently) unimaginable, or not to be narrated, future that the narrator wishes Belacqua and Ruby, in a 'rare movement of compassion' (cf. Dante in 'Dante and the Lobster', 11), a 'night . . . full of music' (91), a periphrasis used by Beckett in his early writing to mean sexual intercourse (as, for example, in chapter 5 of *Murphy*). This 'music' motif is itself a throwback, and something of a throwaway line across the page, to Schubert's *'An die Musik'* at the end of 'Walking Out', and further back – in terms of the way the stories are arranged – to Belacqua at the end of 'Ding-Dong', listening to the music of the spheres, and of 'supply and demand', just before setting off for Railway Street, the site of many notorious brothels in the 'Monto' district of Dublin. Beckett must have known the lines in Keats's 'Ode on a Grecian Urn' (stanza 2) which claim that 'Heard melodies are sweet, but those unheard/ Are sweeter', and he seems often to have worked on this basis on his own behalf in a number of the *More Pricks* stories. There may also, as I have suggested above, be an 'unheard' melody (by way of T. S. Eliot) here, but the emphasis at the end of this story falls on the heard melody (*'l'Amour'* and *'la Mort'*), and although the revolver has gone off, the story does not quite come off. In 'Love and Lethe' Belacqua's 'apparent gratuity of conduct' (82) is matched by this manifestly gratuitous intervention by the narrator, never at his most subtle in 'Love and Lethe'. The unattributed Ronsard quotation which equates death and sex (cf. Belacqua 'like a bridegroom' in 'Yellow', 164) seems to reduce the potential interest (and the 'strange'-ness) of a suicide pact to a rather trivial joke. The joke is nowhere near as well told, or so well integrated into the fabric, as the 'sottish jest' in 'Yellow' (163), one of only two stories in the collection (with 'Dante and the Lobster') which seem to close off, rather than open out into, a life or lives that might continue. But in 'Yellow' the reason for such a closure is contained within the events that have gone before, whereas in 'Love and Lethe' the strategy seems of a piece with the 'deed *ex nihilo*' (82–3) for which the narrator has earlier hoped to be forgiven. In spite of the wit deployed here it is difficult not to feel that comparing 'Love and Lethe' with almost all the other *More Pricks* stories leaves it looking more of a makeweight, and more of an afterthought, than a through-composed entity in its own right. This may be an inevitable consequence of reading back from its 'natural' comparator 'Walking Out', but it helps to explain why the story was placed where it is.

* * *

'Fingal'

Of the three stories which deal directly with Belacqua's idiosyncratic treatment of girlfriends on the way (or not) to becoming his wife, 'Fingal' has the lightest touch, so light that it threatens to defeat the reader intent on significant action and development as readily as Belacqua 'hands over' Winnie Coates to Dr Sholto. There is nothing inherently dramatic or shocking here – no voyeurism, no suicide pact – other than perhaps the discourtesy shown towards Winnie (who 'wins' nothing, except perhaps Sholto). She has 'walked out' with Belacqua, only to be walked out on, but with the consolation of a 'master of the situation' (27) and his car waiting in the wings. Winnie, we are told, can be 'sulky' and can indulge in 'beastly punctilio' (22) when she chooses. But she suffers none of the indignities visited on Lucy (whose beauty is terribly marred) or Ruby (whose skirt, in a life she sees as doomed to 'staircase jests', just has to come off). Winnie is said to be 'pretty, hot and witty, in that order' (17), but these are qualities in her which have largely to be taken on trust, since none of them is given any play in the story. Belacqua is twice described as a 'sad animal' (17, 21), as in the *omne animal post coitum triste* tradition ascribed to Aristotle (as Winnie in *Happy Days* remembers). But even when this Winnie is described as 'all anyway on the grass' (19), coitus seems to be about the last thing on either of their minds.

As for being 'witty', Winnie at least keeps her wits about her, resisting Belacqua's flannel about a 'magic land' and a 'land of sanctuary' – this in an Ireland oddly spiced with memories of a 'short stay abroad' (18) – even if she keeps her thoughts largely to herself. If Belacqua really is 'as wax in her hands' (19, as a later footnote in 'Walking Out' insists that we remember he was), he can hardly be said to be in her grip, and he is plainly not in the grip of one specific passion or another, as in 'Walking Out' and 'Love and Lethe'. The relationship between the two is so mild and slight that it scarcely seems to be one at all (and, for once, marriage does not follow, whereas even in 'Love and Lethe' a kind of 'nuptial' does occur). Winnie, indeed, describes Belacqua in her conversation with the 'stout block of an old man' as 'just a friend' (25), and Dr Sholto has already been mentioned as a 'friend' they can visit together (20). Belacqua, for once unable to indulge in secrecy ('Walking Out') or in low cunning ('Love and Lethe'), is somewhat hamstrung in the case of Winnie, obliged to fill their brief time together with random glimpses of his past and with mostly trivial chit-chat. Certain aspects of their conversation which reveal their temperamental incompatibility can be, and have been, seen as anticipating the exchanges between Belacqua and Thelma in 'What A Misfortune' (Kroll 1974, 285). But the mood here is less feverish, and aptly so, given that Belacqua and Winnie are not engaged to be married, and never will be man and wife. The much more important companion for Belacqua here is a bicycle, the labourer's bicycle which he happens to have come across earlier, and it speaks volumes for the power relations between him and Winnie that Belacqua should be permitted to find it again just when he is looking for an opportunity to abandon a relationship which is obviously (unlike the bicycle!) going nowhere. At this point, Winnie – unknown to herself – is more like 'wax in [*his*] hands' than the other way around. But although she now finds herself 'beg[inning] to feel that she had made a mess of it' (26) and is said to be 'furious for several reasons' (26), she does not seem unduly concerned that she has been left in the lurch. It is Sholto who worries on her behalf that she may have to 'hang around here all night' (26), but the 'lovers' went out in the morning and – although Winnie has 'kept her eye on the time' (24–5) – there is nothing to suggest that it is very late yet.

Almost the only suggestion of romance in this supposedly 'magic land' is supplied by the old man with his hazy tale of Swift and Stella, which Winnie, perhaps not so 'witty' as she may once have seemed, takes time to digest: ' "You mean", she said, "that he lived there [in the 'square bawnless tower'] with a woman?" ' (26). This may be intended to suggest that the tale has moved her to think a thought totally uncharacteristic of her (given what 'Draff' identifies later as her 'decency', 167), and it does seem to be precisely this which prompts her to think she has 'made a mess of it' (26). But the indicator is so slight that Winnie comes across as more interested in acquiring knowledge than emulating Stella, a Stella who comes to seem more like a fairytale princess in a tower than a real person. Winnie can perhaps hardly be expected to see stars – or, more particularly, a long dead *Stella* – in 'star[ing] out across the grey field', as it is not yet (despite Sholto's mention of it) night (26). Unlike Ruby Tough in 'Love and Lethe', Winnie is not given the slightest opportunity to feel 'starry' (91). What appears to matter most to her is the meaning of a word ('motte') given in an old man's Dublin vernacular. The concentration on this detail has prompted C. J. Ackerley (2008, 66, n. 10) to criticize Frederik N. Smith for invoking Madame de la Motte in this connection, but the poem 'Sanies II' and the *'Dream' Notebook* both mention this historical figure, a prisoner under the duress of Marie Antoinette – just as Stella was metaphorically a prisoner of Swift (or so the old man thinks, insisting three times that 'He kep her there', 26) – which makes the parallel at least as valid as Ackerley's suggestion that Beckett has Swift's publisher, Benjamin Motte, uppermost in his mind. Winnie, intellectually superior to Ruby Tough and more resourceful than Lucy, is presented as thoughtful and in contemplation of what secrets the tower may still hold, and just possibly harbouring murderous intentions, given the way women (Stella, Madame de la Motte, and Winnie herself) seem to become victims, if only by staying put. Belacqua, by contrast, who finds the crenels on a wall 'as moving . . . and moving in the same way, as the colour of the brick in the old mill at Feltrim' (22), cannot be stayed by a mere word which he is not there to hear. He (in some ways very aptly) gets on the move, takes decisive action and proves swifter on the stolen bicycle (if only because he has a head start) than his pursuers can match in the car. The odd effect of this is to make Winnie look the more thoughtful of the two, but also the more stuck, having been 'laid aside' (Ackerley 2008, 64), with Sholto's car her only way out ('run her down'; 26). (Beckett re-jigs these motifs in 'Sanies I' by way of his 'proud Swift bicycle', a fond memory as late as a letter to Barbara Bray of 2 November 1971 [TCD], and in the phrases 'dismounted to love' and 'cadge a lift'.) Belacqua, for his part, looks little better than an opportunist, preferring 'a memorable fit of laughter' to anything that might be construed as 'gallantry' (17).

Much later in his life, Beckett told Barbara Bray that he had been reading, while on holiday, the Abbé de Brantôme's lively but scurrilous *Lives of Gallant Ladies*. But at this point in time Beckett must, one supposes, have associated the word *gallant*, and indeed the very idea of 'gallantry' (cf. 'Yellow', 155), more with the 'Two Gallants' of Joyce's *Dubliners* than with anything more *outré*. In Joyce's story the gallants of the title seem more concerned to score off a woman than to score with her, and the tarnished (in moral terms), shining (in physical terms) gold coin, a guinea piece, is the 'prize' for their efforts. Here, with Belacqua having 'dropped' Winnie (who has 'won' Sholto as a consequence) and having made off courtesy of a speedy bicycle, the prize is making it to the pub, and probably to the 'snug' bar, where in Ireland at the time women were never very welcome and were effectively discouraged from entering. The only fly in this ointment, a small price to pay apparently, is the publican, given the name of Taylor (the name of a real publican in a real public house in Swords in the 1920s as *Thom's Directory* indicates, and as *The Beckett Country* shows in a photograph [239]), who finds Belacqua's behaviour – he knows nothing of Belacqua's behaviour thus far – not much to his liking. There is a nice play even here: the publican's initials ('M. R.') being transformed into the common-or-garden 'Mr' (27). Oddly, the name of the 'young man on a bicycle' who has seen Belacqua on a bicycle is given four times as 'Tom' (cf. 'Tom Wood' in 'Walking Out'), but any suggestion of Belacqua as a 'peeping Tom' is here – not unnaturally, given the way he skedaddles – cleverly soft-pedalled by the old man assuring Sholto that 'he would keep his eyes open' (26), although doing so has effectively been rendered pointless by Belacqua's swift move.

It seems probable that the principal *raison d'être* for the writing of 'Fingal' was a desire on Beckett's part to record his own encounter in the country with the idiot savant old man who actually told him the 'tale' of the tower and of Swift and Stella. Beckett informed Thomas MacGreevy about this in a letter dated 5 January 1933 (*LSB*, 150). This is a splendid example of what, if you are lucky, you can find on your travels, much closer to home than any 'magic land' abroad. At the same time, the old man's vignette seems almost to belong more to the story as an abstract entity than to any of the participants in it. The most memorable moment in 'Fingal' occurs in a story told outside the frame of the principal story: 'Little fat Presto [the name 'given to Swift by the Italian-born Duchess of Shrewsbury, who could not remember the English word *swift*', Ackerley 2008, 64], who 'would set out early in the morning, fresh and fasting, and walk like camomile' (26). This surprising interpolation works well, in part because of Belacqua's memory of himself (in a phrase borrowed from section 1 of *Dream*) as 'a little fat overfed boy' (22), but also because up to this point, and before coming across the bicycle, Belacqua has obviously been obliged to walk, as Swift was long ago. But perhaps the real 'point' of this cluster of associations is to demonstrate that Swift and Stella's still enigmatic relationship (as posterity has tried to see it) can be re-activated in a kind of literary 'steal' which will figure alongside the theft of the bike. Swift is out of kilter with this 'magic land' with its real names and real places, imagined as coming 'down from Dublin' at almost the same point in the story that Dr Sholto reveals he '[has] to go up to Dublin' (26); thus, Swift and Stella are safe beyond retrieval by the scholars. Belacqua is, in any event, 'safe' in Swords (27), having made a swift and dramatic move, if not really a move to or from anywhere. Like Joyce's two gallants, he gets what he wants in the end, but without the story suggesting that this is a meaningful achievement. Even though Belacqua does not end up in this story back south of Dublin in Foxrock (where Beckett was born), he completes at least part of his favourite 'boomerang' procedure of 'out and back' ('Ding-Dong', 31). Beckett associated this throughout his life with a phrase he had come across in Thomas à Kempis's *The Imitation of Christ*, which he had copied into his *'Dream' Notebook* (*DN*, 576). In 'Ding-Dong', the phrase or the idea is 'translated' as a 'glad going out and sad coming in' (36), from which Belacqua is explicitly dissociated in his characteristic reversal of the terms. The figure said (twice) to be a 'sad animal' is in the end saved and 'safe', and has achieved what Dr Sholto would call a 'pleasantly appointed sanctum' (24). The outcome is given an extra fillip by the narrator stepping in, in a manner that at once closes and opens up the story, to tell us that Belacqua is the real 'master of the situation', having made himself invulnerable in Taylor's public house in Swords 'before they [Winnie and Dr Sholto] were well on their way' (27).

* * *

Charles Prentice, in writing to Beckett (4 October 1933; UoR) to encourage him on the addition of an eleventh story to *More Pricks* – the '10,000 yelps' of 'Echo's Bones' (letter of 2 November 1933; UoR) – asked whether Belacqua's next (and last) adventure was more likely to be a 'prick' or a 'kick'. (Jeri L. Kroll usefully points out that one of the meanings of the word *yerk* as used later in 'Yellow' [164] is 'kick' [1974, 268].) The letter suggests that for Prentice, who had perhaps been encouraged by Beckett to think in these terms, the eye-catching title of the collection, a replacement for *Draff*, was best understood as indicative of a conflict between active and reactive forces, with the experience of pain and suffering in one corner and the limited ability to cope with it in the other. The otherwise merely incidental TCD 'squib' of *The Possessed* partly confirms this in its conceit of an intellectual debate conducted as if it were a boxing match (*Disjecta*, 99); in 'Echo's Bones', the idea is kept alive in the 'battle' which 'rage[s]' when Belacqua meets Lord Gall. But Prentice by this time knew that Beckett was not offering him a book of love stories – he had read *Dream*, a novel of 'unparalleled obscenity' in some eyes (letter to MacGreevy of 27 August 1932) – even if only two stories ('Dante and the Lobster' and 'Ding-Dong') dispensed altogether with love as a trigger for the events in them. And Beckett knew that he had begun the long slog towards *More Pricks* (with 'Dante and the Lobster') without much consideration of whether love stories might provide 'staffage' (*Molloy*, 63) if the going were to get tough, and with no idea that it might do so. Beckett was never in fact very much concerned with 'love' as ordinarily understood, preferring (as in the applied Spinoza, such as it is, of chapter 6 of *Murphy*) what he was to call 'amor intellectualis', intellectual love, with any sexual elements left in it rarefied or at least modified by the more compelling exercise of 'mind'. But there had to be some human interest if the enterprise was to stand a chance of success, and the subject of love and his own failures in that area were certainly much on Beckett's own mind.

In these three stories we can see Beckett partially complying with the felt need to appeal to his potential audience by way of an ever-popular subject, but at the same time undermining the genre and shifting the time-honoured structures of comedy into the bargain. In 'Walking Out', 'Love and Lethe' and 'Fingal', *More Pricks* observes the 'rule' that a love comedy – whether as play, poem or novel – must move towards a focal point of final consummation (a point suitably obscured in the forest of error in 'Walking Out'), while leaving the 'decency' (167) of privacy so the reader's imagination can fill in the vacancy or supply the 'happy ever after'. But by complying with this 'rule', Beckett underscores his critique of a convention rather more difficult to negotiate. In these three stories, and indeed in *More Pricks* as a whole, the emphasis falls not, as it typically does elsewhere, on the more or less legitimate ways in which men and women conduct themselves in the business of moving towards marriage. Beckett's interest, by contrast, is in the ways in which his Belacqua can best avoid what marriage would usually mean, since Belacqua seems not to possess very many of the impulses which might easily induce a young man to think of marrying. Far from Beckett (in the guise of Belacqua) confirming Dr Johnson's famous claim that 'marriage may have some pains, but celibacy few pleasures', he reverses the idea as if determined to demonstrate that it really is a matter of more pricks than kicks (in the sense in which Prentice chose to understand the tag), and much more than a matter of (as Lucy in 'Walking Out' sees it) finding a 'partner in life's journey' (101). In so doing he gives notice, as it were, that elsewhere, even with 'amor intellectualis' as a substitute, he will not concern himself overmuch with the subject, but rather with a different kind of journey, a journey either into the mind or out into the world. In 'Love and Lethe', Ruby Tough is said to have discovered how '[t]he grapes of love, set aside as abject in the days of hot blood, turned sour as soon as she discovered a zest for them' (81). But Belacqua does not share her 'zest' and is seeking to keep cool. 'Fingal' is similar in the way its 'magic land' seems little more than bombast, with Swift and Stella, secure from the prying eyes of posterity, mere hearsay, much more mysterious than posterity would have them be. 'Fingal' establishes fairly early on that its scenery specifics are not much more than a 'pretext', as if Beckett were afraid that they might give something away that would be better hidden. But the pretext which has most obviously been dispensed with in each of these three stories is that which dictates that a comedy must end in a marriage to which both parties have become gradually more committed. There is, to be sure, a marriage of a kind at the end of 'Walking Out', and a 'nuptial' of a rather different kind at the end of 'Love and Lethe'. But 'Fingal' breaks the mould, and in its 'looseness & ease' (letter to MacGreevy of 3 February 1931, congratulating him on his study of T. S. Eliot; *LSB*, 64) is one of the more quietly experimental stories in *More Pricks*. None of these three stories moves in a conventional way to its resolution, whether as deferred (as in 'Fingal') or kept short and sweet (as in 'Walking Out' and 'Love and Lethe'). But 'Fingal', even though it contains less risqué material than the other two, is in many ways the most daring of the three from a technical point of view, notably in its 'refusal' of the classic comic trope of marriage or '[coming] together' (91) as a dénouement.

Belacqua nevertheless manages three marriages in *More Pricks Than Kicks:* to Lucy in 'Walking Out', to Thelma in 'What A Misfortune' and to the Smeraldina at some point between her 'billet doux' and her appearance as a widow in 'Draff' – although the third and last of these marriages ends 'after less than a year' (167). Just how far these marriages reflect some need on Beckett's part to dramatize aspects of his own personal life by way of the 'secret occasions' of narrative (178) – Peggy Sinclair had died only a few months before Beckett wrote 'Draff' – it is obviously very difficult to say. The fact that we never see Belacqua participating in the married state (even after the wedding in 'What A Misfortune') enables Beckett, for whatever private reasons, to focus on Lucy's beauty being 'dreadfully marred' ('Walking Out'), on the old joke that *l'amour* and *la mort* are not far apart ('Love and Lethe'), on the need to be quick-witted when an opportunity to escape entanglement offers itself ('Fingal'), and later, in 'Draff', on the aftermath of a marriage that is over. Jeri L. Kroll sees Belacqua's aversion to sex lessening as the collection progresses (1974, 326). And this certainly seems to square with the Belacqua who is most happily married as the 'bridegroom' in 'Yellow' with the death for which he has, unwittingly, kept a day free (cf. *PTD*, 17).

It was almost certainly a combination of personal tensions, experiments with form and conventional comic strategies, and some awareness of commercial considerations that made these three stories what they are. But Beckett needed to widen the canvas which had been so love-bound in *Dream* if he was ever to move on from it at all. Even with love and its discontents not quite abandoned in the rest of this collection, there was still a need to colonize new territories, and Beckett cleared a space in which to do so. Having discharged his 'responsibilities' both to tradition and to his idiosyncratic 'individual talent', Beckett was left with the freedom to pursue a different quarry, the troubled inner world of the mind, and in due course to chart the behavioural oddities of the world outside and beyond it, which are the areas to which I turn in Sections 2 and 3 of this chapter.

2. Rare Movements of Compassion: 'Dante and the Lobster', 'Ding-Dong', 'Yellow'

In a less tight corner he might have been content to barricade his mind against the idea. But this was at best a slipshod method, since the idea, how blatant an enemy soever and despite the strictest guard, was almost certain to sidle in sooner or later under the skirts of a friend, and then the game was up.

('*Yellow*')

Grouping these three stories together serves to separate them from the three focused on Belacqua's love life ('Walking Out', 'Fingal', 'Love and Lethe') and the three that place him in the company of other figures who are on the face of it at least as important as he is – for the duration of a story, at any rate ('A Wet Night', 'What A Misfortune', 'Draff'). The love stories, if one can call them that, contribute to a kind of *éducation sentimentale*, if nothing like so penetrating or thoroughgoing as that of Frédéric Moreau in either of the two versions Flaubert wrote with this title. Beckett uses a citation from part II, chapter 6 of Flaubert's second *Education sentimentale* as the epigraph to 'Les Deux Besoins' (*Disjecta*, 55), with the key phrase in the passage chosen being 'Sénécal put his hand in front of the man's mouth' (*A Sentimental Education*, 288). But 'Dante and the Lobster', 'Ding-Dong' and 'Yellow' are also, in their way, educational, and in each of them it is women who are engaged in 'education by provocation' (*Disjecta*, 79). Each of them in their different ways, as I shall show, activates a version of a spiritual principle that Belacqua is unable, or unwilling, to develop on his own behalf, with each of the figures viewed as intermediaries akin to Beatrice in Dante's *Divine Comedy*, Miranda in Shakespeare's *The Tempest*, and the so-called Shekinah of Jewish mythology (cf. Kroll 1978, 21–2). In all three stories Belacqua has something to learn, and the narrator (who has been compelled to '[give] him up . . . because he was not *serious*'; 'Ding-Dong', 32) has something to impart, from the preparation of toast ('Dante and the Lobster') to the proper conduct of a surgical operation ('Yellow'). The narrator, by definition, knows everything there is to be known. But in all three stories, at least one woman knows more, or thinks she knows more, than Belacqua, and she gives him something to think about, very appropriately it would seem, since all three of these stories focus on what is going on in Belacqua's mind.

'Dante and the Lobster'

'Dante and the Lobster' is easily the best known of all the *More Pricks* stories, and almost the only one of them to have lived any kind of life independent of the collection as a whole. (One is not as a consequence obliged to consider it the best simply because of its wider circulation, although almost all commentators seem to do so, in spite of when it was written, at a time when Beckett had almost no experience in writing short stories conventional or otherwise; only 'Assumption' is earlier.) As we have already seen at the beginning of Chapter 1, Beckett remembered 'Dante and the Lobster' (in a letter of 4 January 1982 to Ruby Cohn; UoR) as the first Belacqua story to have been written, and he was of the opinion that it must have been written much earlier than the others. But this may have been for no better reason than that 'Dante and the Lobster' works with materials deriving from Beckett's real life as a TCD student in 1925–6, nearly 6 years before the original version of 'Dante and the Lobster' appeared in the *émigré* magazine *This Quarter*, and 8 years before a revised version of it was placed in *More Pricks Than Kicks*. In her *Canon,*, Ruby Cohn very reasonably says, 'It is unlikely that Beckett's attention was called to McCabe by an old newspaper' (47). Presumably, there are no grounds for supposing that Beckett's sense of 'Dante and the Lobster' as separate from the others requires us to backdate its composition that far. It must, I take it, postdate 'Assumption' (1929). There is at least some internal evidence in the story that points towards 1930 (it contains some details also to be found in the essay *Proust*, written in the late summer of 1930), and at the time of composition the very idea of a book of short stories – assuming the idea had even suggested itself – was so obviously secondary to Beckett's commitment to *Dream* that it can scarcely have been even an afterthought. This said, there is a 1931 letter to Charles Prentice which envisages 'seven spectral petals' (15 August; *LSB*, 82), apparently planned to accompany the story 'Walking Out', presumably the second Belacqua story to be written and the first to suggest to Beckett that 'Dante and the Lobster' might be more than an isolated phenomenon.

With *Dream* still a live issue in Beckett's eyes, and a character still called Belacqua at the heart of the novel, neither 'Dante and the Lobster' nor 'Walking Out' could contain much of an inkling of how 'doomed' ('Love and Lethe', 79) he was to be in 2 or 3 years. But time is established in 'Dante and the Lobster' as fundamental to life and death, and as the earliest of the *More Pricks* stories it possesses something of an 'early' feel – very much so in its separateness in *This Quarter* – such that it can now seem a world away from us in a number of its specifics. The Dublin we are introduced to here, as we meet it 80 years later, looks somewhat old-fashioned, with even a little old-world charm. The bedsitter life of a student has not changed a great deal over the decades, although Belacqua's residence looks much less glamorous than Beckett's rooms at 39 New Court in TCD must have been in reality. (The student accommodation was serviced by a staff of servants, as in some of the older collegiate universities today.) In a similar way, the idea of a private lesson in Italian given (in real life by Bianca Esposito) outside the college boundaries would today probably only resonate with students attending Oxford, Cambridge, Durham, Edinburgh and the like, and the notion of a grocer's shop just round the corner and a fish shop not much further afield looks rather a throwback in our age of supermarkets. The life of these Dublin streets has also long gone. There is a quasi-medieval lamplighter doing his rounds on a bicycle ('*jousting* [my emphasis] a little [gas] light into the evening') and a horse gone down, with 'a man sat on its head': 'I know', Belacqua thinks, 'that that is considered the right thing to do. But why?' (13). This is as much of an enigma to him as the 'impenetrable passage' in Dante's *Paradiso*, which he has been studying, and very comparable with Beckett's bafflement in his notes on Dante (specifically raised at a number of passages in the *Paradiso*) at TCD (see *SBT/A*, 16). It is pretty much a measure of how different life is nowadays that we would be very surprised even so much as to see a horse in the street, let alone know what ought to be done with one apparently in some distress, like the 'old hack foundered in the street' in the first of the much later *Texts for Nothing* (1950–2).

Presumably none of these 'old-world' details would have been found very unusual by Dubliners in the late 1920s and early 1930s, however remote from contemporary Londoners they may have seemed. (And, of course, times change: no Londoner in the 1930s would have been surprised by the sheep in Kensington Gardens in chapter 5 of *Murphy*.) But it is the way that Beckett handles these details that link them both to the time of writing and to the longer perspectives of literary history. For Beckett it is important that none of this 'local colour' is given the potential to generate the kind of 'epiphany' which can excite Joyce's Stephen Dedalus to aesthetic flights in *Stephen Hero* and *A Portrait of the Artist*. (For Joyce's own 'Epiphanies', see *Poems and Shorter Writings*, ed. Richard Ellmann, A. Walton Litz and John Whittier-Ferguson [London: Faber and Faber, 1991], 155–200; for a critique of commentators who find Joycean 'epiphanies' in 'Dante and the Lobster' and elsewhere, see the first of my Addenda.) Although Beckett is far too concerned with pursuing his own quarry to be bothered to emphasize the divergence, in this first *More Pricks* story he is already 'walking out' on Joyce and Joyce's early writings, much like his own Belacqua is 'walking out' on his fiancée Lucy. There is a tacit refusal to suggest that the ordinary constituent elements of life need to be invested with a special power designed to lift them to a higher plane.

The world of 'Dante and the Lobster' seems sufficiently old for a poet writing in medieval Italian to look a living part of it, even with his complex system of rings and circles, rewards and punishments, predicated on a pre-Copernican, Ptolemaic concept of space which is obviously one still believed in by the pedlar of 'Ding-Dong'. But in 'Dante and the Lobster' there is the overarching view that nothing much ever changes. It is always a matter of 'where we were, as we were', whether in the mouth of the Ottolenghi or shortly after (13), linking the end of the second section of the story to the beginning of the third section, the tripartite structure being a nod in Dante's direction. But even so, Dante is obviously something of an optional extra up against the demands of lunch and dinner, which are never likely to go out of date. The less recondite pleasures of unbuttered toast, 'rotten' Gorgonzola and a '[l]epping fresh' lobster make a less enigmatic mark than Blissful Beatrice's 'proof', which offers Dante the pilgrim and Belacqua the pursuer of knowledge something of a headache. Belacqua is determined to 'not concede himself conquered' (3) by these mysteries of *The Divine Comedy*, although it seemingly has very little to teach him compared to what his aunt's dinner will reveal. At least Dante can be 'slammed . . . shut' (3), as if his poem were the two 'toasted rounds' which 'clave the one to the other on the viscid salve of Savora [a sweet and spicy mustard nowadays mostly to be found, if at all, in delicatessens]' in Belacqua's sandwich (6).

Not for the last time in *More Pricks* – the last time is as far away as the last paragraph of 'Draff' (173) – is literature shown up as being an empire of signs with little application to the realities of life, however memorable or enigmatic either life or literature may be. Dante's 'superb pun' (16) generates thoughts in Belacqua's mind, but neither he nor the native Italian Ottolenghi can resolve the paradox it contains. Similarly, 'Take into the air my quiet breath' (14) – from the section of 'Ode to a Nightingale' in which Keats hopes to 'die upon the midnight with no pain' – is not of much help to the lobster on its way to the 'cruel pot', even if (for a moment or two) it looks as though this might be the lobster's very own contribution, rather than a stray caption from Belacqua. (Beckett had already quoted Keats's phrase in a 1930 letter to MacGreevy [*LSB*, 21] and in *Dream* [107], and he would use it again in the poem 'Serena I' and the novels *Murphy* and *Watt*; see *Faber Companion*, 297.) Not even Keats, apparently, can supply much more than the 'rapid shorthand of the real facts' (3), Belacqua's understanding (such as it is) of Blissful Beatrice's 'proof' in the *Paradiso*.

Belacqua's interest in food is consistent with his memory of himself as 'a little fat overfed boy' ('Fingal', 22), a phrase borrowed from the first page of the jettisoned novel *Dream*. But 'Dante and the Lobster' is just about the only story in the collection in which Belacqua eats anything at all, his preferred habit being the consumption of alcohol. (In 'Yellow', alcohol is obviously out of the question, but then so is eating; in 'Echo's Bones', voracious eating is for the most part left to the groundsman Mick Doyle.) Even so, 'Dante and the Lobster' acknowledges the Dublin 'fact' that alcohol – in this case two pints of draught and a bottle of stout for the outlay of half-a-crown – is at least as necessary to life as the bread secured, without losing much ground, by the poor girl 'debauched in appearance and swathed in a black blanket' standing in the cinema queue in 'Ding-Dong' (35). This said, despite the local details establishing Dublin as the backdrop for 'Dante and the Lobster', in this particular story (unlike 'Ding-Dong') Dublin seems to be simply the place where these events happen, because they have to happen somewhere. There is none of Joyce's affection for 'dear old dirty Dub' as manifested in *Dubliners*, *Portrait*, *Ulysses* and *Finnegans Wake*. In 'Dante and the Lobster' we are as much 'IN THE HEART OF THE HIBERNIAN METROPOLIS' as Leopold Bloom in the newspaper office of 'Aeolus' (*Ulysses*, 147), but Dublin seems almost to have shrunk to the size of a village, with the 'metropolitan' dimension reserved for the more or less recondite literary allusions. In its mood, if not in its actual setting, 'Dante and the Lobster' begins the process in *More Pricks* whereby Belacqua moves, erratically but symptomatically, away from the city centre and out, either north towards Swords ('Fingal'), south towards Foxrock ('Walking Out'), west towards Galway ('What A Misfortune') or ultimately to the Redford cemetery at Greystones ('Draff').

In 'Dante and the Lobster', Belacqua is unwilling to 'concede himself conquered' (9) by the difficulties of Dante, and Beckett was certainly unwilling to concede himself conquered by any pre-existent literary presentations of Dublin, of which Joyce's was obviously (for him) the most compelling and the one he most needed to circumvent. Yet, oddly, there are perhaps more Irishisms here than elsewhere in *More Pricks*, except in stories of much greater length:

- He turned it over on its back to see was the other side any better [for 'to see if it was'] (7).
- Incontinent bosthoons (9).
- Bating, of course, the lobster [for 'except', as in the 1932 version, 230] (10).
- 'Lepping' he [the fishmonger] said cheerfully [for 'living' or 'lively' or 'brand spanking new' in its freshness] (10).
- 'Well', she [Belacqua's aunt] said, 'It is to be hoped so indeed' (19). [This is not exclusively Irish, but it has a distinctive Irish flavour. Belacqua has used 'well' rather differently earlier (7), and differently again at the very end].
- It is not (14). [In itself this is just a simple and devastating way of being declarative. But it has more than a trace of the Irish way, apparently deriving from Gaelic, of saying 'No', as in 'It is' for 'Yes'. Hairy Quin points out what he sees as the inadequacies of Gaelic in 'Draff' (177).]

'Local colour' of this kind occurs throughout the collection. But here it serves to establish Belacqua's estrangement from his surroundings and sets up some nice ironies of a loosely 'international' nature which will also be exploited later. Belacqua no more knows what 'lepping' means than he knows 'the French for lobster' (he says 'fish', but a lobster [Fr. *homard*] is, strictly speaking, a crustacean). His native Dublin demotic is, we infer, as strange to him as the enigma in Dante's *Paradiso*. Why this should be is obviously a constituent element in Belacqua's essential homelessness and what we might also call his perversity. Why, we might well ask, is he so ignorant of 'lepping' and lobsters when he is learning difficult medieval Italian, and obviously also knows some French (if not *homard*)? This continues to look odd when his Professoressa (and also her colleague, the French teacher Mlle Glain) can speak English without a trace of foreignness and move equally comfortably into an exchange couched in French. Yet we might hardly notice these details if the story did not also contain a 'superb pun' in Italian, not to mention a snatch of Neapolitan song on the subject of Napoleon (with the two elements – Neapolitan and Napoleonic – almost forming an anagram), the former allegedly 'untranslatable', the latter left untranslated. There would have to be more than this to make an Italianized Dublin to match the 'Italianate Irishman' Walter Draffin from later in *More Pricks* (128), even with the mention – an addition to the 1932 version of 'Dante and the Lobster' – of an Angelo, born in Nice but an inhabitant of the North Italian town of Gorgonzola (7). But this addition is not just one of the 'random recollections' as Stevenson, in an otherwise exceptionally acute essay (44), sees it; each of these little details in sum makes Dublin feel less rooted in its own time and place than it might otherwise be. Perhaps Belacqua, for it is he who makes it seem so, is in a way justified in seeing Dublin as no place in particular.

Issues of language and register occur all across *More Pricks*, but perhaps nowhere more concentratedly than in 'Dante and the Lobster'. It is not so very surprising that Beckett, a formidable linguist, should privilege such issues in a story which contains an actual language lesson – quite similar in its way to the language lesson handed out by the pedlar in 'Ding-Dong' – and a culinary lesson on how to cook lobsters. What really concerns Beckett, however, is the way in which language, and even the highly considered and sophisticated language of literature, leaves behind enigmas more puzzling than the real life situations from which it effectively distracts us. Stevenson points out (38) very helpfully that the popular notion that the moon is made of green cheese has more to do with how the story moves than Dante's *Paradiso* or Shakespeare's *A Midsummer Night's Dream*, and the snatch of popular Neapolitan song certainly seems to stimulate Belacqua to independent thought (ill-considered, immature or superficial as it may be) more than Dante's *Paradiso* does, the *Paradiso* being rather too orthodox to satisfy him for long. Stevenson also usefully observes (37) that Dante enters the sphere of the moon at noon (*Paradiso* I, 43–5), which is just when Belacqua goes out, and one of the many differences between the one pilgrim and the other is that, for the latter 'it was morning . . . '. Stevenson further suggests (39–40) that literature, by way of re-contextualization, entails 'readjustments of vision', but it is not really a match for life in any meaningful sense, running either parallel to it, or actually at odds with it.

This is a judgement further reinforced by Wai Chee Dimock, who emphasizes that the story 'invokes the tripartite structure of *The Divine Comedy* only to short-change it drastically' (Gontarski and Uhlmann [eds.], 200). Sam Slote effectively squares the circle by emphasizing (26) that the story's way of reading the *Commedia* is 'an allegory of the horror of the realisation of the complete and utter absence of allegory in the world below', and adds that 'such a realisation was already indicated in the *Commedia* since the machine of the world is too complex for allegory'. Beckett's view of this had been expressed in the summer of 1930, while writing (perhaps side by side with 'Dante and the Lobster') his *Proust* essay under the influence of his first reading of the philosopher Arthur Schopenhauer: 'Here [i.e. with 'Dante's allegorical figures'] allegory fails as it must always fail in the hands of a poet' (*PTD*, 79; cf. *The World as Will and Representation*, volume 1, Third Book, subsection 50, which contains Schopenhauer's view that allegories are nothing but hieroglyphics). Later, in 1936, in an appreciation of Jack Yeats's *The Amaranthers*, Beckett took a more severe line: 'There is no allegory, that glorious double-entry, with every credit in the said account a debit in the meant' (*Disjecta*, 90). The whole complex issue of how Beckett read Dante is compellingly analysed by Daniela Caselli (2005), but the simplest thing to say about how Belacqua reads him is to emphasize that what the narrator intends to show here, even if he does not openly say so, is an aesthete and an intellectual, adrift in the higher reaches of a difficult and alien theology, quite unfit for any pilgrimage more demanding than the acquisition of Gorgonzola cheese and a lobster.

One can read a long way into 'Dante and the Lobster', judging what is said and what is meant, without taking much account of the one Dublin 'fact' in it that ties the story to the public sources of life there in 1926: 'the rather handsome face of McCabe the assassin' (4). Jeri L. Kroll was the first scholar to investigate the events that lie behind this (see JOBS [o.s.] 2, 1977), and there is little that can usefully be added to her account. (Beckett is almost certainly remembering the circumstances surrounding the murder, and very accurately, about 4 years on from the time it was committed.) But it is, of course, on this peg that Beckett hangs Belacqua's interest in the timeless issues of pity and piety and the exact relationship between them. Part of Beckett's point here must be that there is more to be learned from a face in the newspaper (and, later, from the 'face' of the bread for Belacqua's toast) than can be gleaned from 'running' your brain against an 'impenetrable passage' in Dante (3). Dante the pilgrim as 'misinformed poet' (later, in 'Draff' [the footnote on 177], though not named, he becomes 'competent', as if he might be the similarly unnamed Ronsard from the end of 'Love and Lethe', which of course he isn't!) is at a considerable disadvantage compared with the ordinary people of Dublin, readers of the *Evening Herald* newspaper. Stevenson shrewdly points out (44), in relation to the *Herald*, that 'no messenger is to appear in this story', and it is true that none of the readers of the newspaper can alter the outcome at Mountjoy Prison the next day. We are told that 'the food [Belacqua's lunch] had been further spiced [it already has Savora mustard on it] by the intelligence ... that the Malahide murderer's petition for mercy, signed by half the land, having been rejected, the man must swing at dawn in Mountjoy and nothing could save him' (10). This information, this 'intelligence', prompts Belacqua to prodigies of thinking. But just as nothing can save McCabe, so nothing can be done to save the lobster which is to be cooked for Belacqua's dinner. The story connects Dante, McCabe and the lobster, although all it explicitly insists on is 'lunch, lobster, lesson', in that order (10). Belacqua can only connect Dante and McCabe, and leaves the lobster out (from ignorance of cooking practice). Of the Ottolenghi we learn that Belacqua 'did not believe it possible for a woman to be more *intelligent* or better *informed*' (9, my italics). Even the Ottolenghi, however, is helpless in the face of a pun, and she is naturally of less help than Belacqua's aunt when it comes to the lobster, whose ultimate fate has merely been deferred by the prompt actions of Mlle Glain. We can draw our own conclusions: one can be 'intelligent' and 'informed' (or even a 'bluestocking' like Mlle Glain), but of no real use in the face, and the fate, of a murderer (McCabe) and of a creature to be murdered (the lobster).

'Dante and the Lobster' has been much praised, partly because it is so much better known than most of the other *More Pricks* stories. But Beckett obviously thought it could be improved (cf. 'Oliver the improver', 10) from its 1932 version. As Kay Gilliland Stevenson has very ably shown, Beckett made several small changes to tighten up its effects, and also to 'increase the tension, the balance, or ambiguity, of Belacqua's presentation [and] the tension between judgment and charity' (37). Stevenson even goes so far as to see 'what might be called an improvement in [Belacqua's] character' (41) and demonstrates how, for all the continuing 'ambiguity', the 1934 version is more coherent than the 1932 version. She emphasizes the equations of Belacqua and Dante (39), Belacqua and Cain (40), Belacqua and Beatrice (41), Belacqua and the lobster (40–1), and even Belacqua and the executioner, at the same time admitting (42) that not all of these details are absent from the 1932 version. The 1934 version contains a little (but only a little) more material than the 1932, but the later version really improves upon the earlier by being much more to the point, even as it multiplies ambiguities. A reader of the story in 1932 could only have known that he or she had had (or had not had) an experience, and in the nature of the case it could only be an experience on its own, an experience without consequences, as it were. Revised, and placed at the head of a collection like *More Pricks*, 'Dante and the Lobster' is obviously better situated to prepare for, and figure against, what follows. Yet the 'reasonably alert reader' imagined by Stevenson (43), who could have registered the story's essentially clear, tripartite structure even in 1932, needs the other stories to see that this one remains separate from them in the relative clarity of its concerns.

'Dante and the Lobster' must have given Beckett an idea of what could be achieved even in the 'minor' genre of the short story. But to exploit the possibilities there obviously had to be more stories on hand, and (an even more important matter) enough stories with which to interest a publisher. By August 1931 Beckett had what he called a 'whore's get' version of 'Walking Out' (letter to Prentice, *LSB*, 82), which was turned down and returned to him by the celebrated literary agent J. B. Pinker, and later revised for *More Pricks*. But it was not until more than a year later that 'Dante and the Lobster' appeared in Edward Titus's magazine *This Quarter*, which thereafter immediately ceased publication. If Beckett read the runes, the omens were not good. Yet it must have been Titus's 'courtesy' (*LSB*, 128) that gave Beckett some incentive to write more stories and kept alive in him an intermittent flicker of interest in the form, as *Dream* met nothing but incomprehension and rebuff. By the time of 'Ding-Dong', probably the third of the stories to be written, Belacqua has already become the narrator's 'sometime friend' (31), but there was still some time to fill before Beckett realized that his sometime friend was in any case, like the lobster, 'doomed' ('Love and Lethe', 79).

* * *

'Ding-Dong'

We know from a letter of April 1933 to Thomas MacGreevy (headed '23rd', *LSB*, 153–5) that the editor of the *Dublin Magazine*, Seumas O'Sullivan, had returned a short story to Beckett, probably one that had been sent about a month earlier, finding it unsuitable but conceding that he was no doubt 'behind the times'. O'Sullivan could not have had much time to absorb what Beckett's 'Dante and the Lobster' story in *This Quarter* might be telling him – only 3 or 4 months had passed – and he may not even have seen it. If the story he rejected was (as seems quite likely) 'Ding-Dong', O'Sullivan's reaction, unimaginative as it obviously seemed to Beckett, was in many ways understandable. There is no obvious connection between the story and its title, and no consensus even now as to how the title ought ideally to be read. James Acheson has proposed a source in Joyce's *Ulysses*; Ruby Cohn (in her *Canon*, perhaps following Robert Cochran) has suggested the Spirits' response to Ariel's dirge 'full fathom five' in Act I, scene 2 of Shakespeare's *Tempest*, which Beckett had studied at TCD in the Hilary (Spring) Term in early 1925. The latter, even with allowances made for the passage of time, is perhaps the more likely, since there are spirits of various kinds being consumed or imagined in 'Ding-Dong', and Ferdinand finding 'nothing of earth' in the sounds he is hearing, which remind him of his drowned father, sets up the idea of Heaven at the end of 'Ding-Dong'. (Robert Cochran, in his 1991 study, even goes so far as to suggest that Belacqua in 'Ding-Dong' is like a 'charmed Ferdinand' [10].) But there are at least two meanings of 'ding-dong' in ordinary speech, the language of 'the woman of the people' in this story, which may also lie behind the title: a family or social gathering or get-together, either at home or in the pub, typically with songs and the like, a sort of 'knees-up'; and a vigorous debate or quarrel, 'a right old ding-dong'.

It may not, however, have been the title that gave O'Sullivan problems, if indeed 'Ding-Dong' was the story in question. For in 'Ding-Dong' Beckett was attempting to do something with the short story for which he had no obvious model in his three previous attempts at the form ('Assumption', 'Dante and the Lobster' and 'Walking Out'): introducing into the fabric as a significant figure in his own right the narrator, here an actual, living 'I' figure at some time in touch with, and in conversation with, the lead character Belacqua, even if the two of them have subsequently gone their separate ways. O'Sullivan could have seen (if indeed he *had* seen) that in 'Dante and the Lobster' everything is presented from outside the frame, as it were, with even the surprising last words uttered as if the narrator had no personality of his own and was not even a person in any meaningful sense. (Harry Vandervlist in his 1991 thesis aptly points out that the 'It is not' conclusion in 'Dante and the Lobster' 'seems to belong neither to Belacqua nor to the narrator' [82, n. 6], and no doubt much the same could be said of 'Take into the air my quiet breath' just above it.) But in 'Ding-Dong' the narrator openly 'trespasses' on, or wanders onto, his own stage for the space of seven lengthy paragraphs and even returns some two or three pages later for another full paragraph. In his more conventional role of recessed tale-teller, he says of Pearse Street that it was 'full as it always was with shabby substance and honest-to-God coming and going' (38). At least one of the comings and goings in this story is his own, which may be more a matter of 'shabby substance' than of 'honest-to-God' dealing, even if his familiarity with Belacqua has been offered as a kind of earnest of authenticity and accuracy. If this was in fact what turned O'Sullivan against 'Ding-Dong', he would no doubt have applauded a curious reprint of the story (in *A Dublin Anthology* [Dublin: Gill and Macmillan, 1994], 3–8), which quite simply omits the opening seven paragraphs and hacks off Beckett's title into the bargain!

It seems to matter little to Beckett whether the short story form will tolerate this kind of narratorial intervention; instead, he applies the tactic for all it is worth, at least until the more ordinary business of the story – and there is much business being done, in a very ordinary locale – has to take over. This was not something Beckett ever tried again (although Sam and Watt are sometime friends), and the adoption of a first-person perspective in the much later *Nouvelles* meant that he did not have to. It was not an experiment that could have been expected to work more than once or twice at best, and Beckett no doubt left this as the one example of its kind in *More Pricks* in order to further destabilize an already very diverse, if not actually 'ramshackle' (*Dream*, 139), book of stories. 'Ding-Dong' could thereby, henceforth and for ever (the meaning of the Latin motto Belacqua sees as 'implicit behind the whole length of [TCD's] southern frontage'), remain incommensurable with any of the other stories, at least 'it was to be hoped so, indeed' (34). But time in the usual sense of the word, as distinct from *sub specie aeternitatis*, seems much less of an issue here than in 'Dante and the Lobster' or in 'Yellow', where Belacqua has 7 hours to while away before his operation.

In 'Ding-Dong', issues of place – the Dublin streets, the pub, the seats in heaven – occupy Belacqua's attention, just as they did Beckett's in a letter written on 27 February 1934 to Nuala Costello from London (*LSB*, 184 ff.), also concentrating on specific locations and with only a few weeks to wait before *More Pricks* would be published. As if anticipating the 'junction' of Cremorne Road and other streets (though this takes place almost 18 months later, at the start of *Murphy*), Beckett describes to Nuala Costello the junction of d'Olier, College, Pearse and Townsend Streets (the latter is where the 'woman of the people' in 'Ding-Dong' lives), 'if I have not forgotten my Dublin' (*LSB*, 184). Writing 'Ding-Dong' either in late 1932 or early 1933, Beckett could hardly have forgotten 'his' Dublin, since that was where he then was. Place, for once in this collection, seems, and to some extent proves, a matter of real concern to Beckett, which is why, after the narrator's long introduction, we are simply set down 'on the particular evening in question' (33; cf. 'on this particular occasion', 36), its particularity dependent more on what happens and where it happens than on exactly when it happens, although that also matters. Dusk has invaded the last section of 'Dante and the Lobster', and all of 'A Wet Night' takes place in darkness, but only here in 'Ding-Dong' does the night-time setting seem to be an essential component of the story and the scene, rather than a merely incidental gesture designed to maintain continuity. Only night-time could give much point to the 'blind paralytic' who becomes 'a star the horizon adorning if you like' (34), or to the splendid picture in the pub, a 'spectacle' which Belacqua 'gradually ceased to see' (compare his similar reaction to the 'performance' in 'Walking Out'; 104). (The picture is more of an aural than a visual one, in anticipation of the 'music' at the very end of the story.) Similarly, the countenance of the female pedlar can only meaningfully have 'lighted her to her room in Townsend Street' (39) in a story that is overwhelmingly a 'night-piece' (Beckett's description of an unfinished play, probably 'Fragment de théâtre II', and certainly with thoughts of Schubert's song *'Nachtstück'*, – one of the silent intertexts in 'Walking Out' [see above] – in a letter to Barbara Bray of 10 September 1958).

The long introduction to 'Ding-Dong' threatens the integrity of the story (which it otherwise seems to want to promote) by approaching it crabwise, which could be part of a tendency to privilege disaggregation and disunity throughout the collection. The first-person mode was the way forward, though it took Beckett more than a decade (and the creation of Arsene in *Watt*) to realize it. But the way detail connects with detail in 'Ding-Dong' also adds a dimension of integration evident to anyone alert enough to pick it up. The narrator's interventionist activity (cf. *Disjecta*, 65, on the 'conflict between intervention and quietism') is on display at the start, but only the better to disguise his subterranean, or subtextual, activity later on. One example of the latter, perhaps the best, is the 'great major symphony of supply and demand . . . fulcrate on the middle C of the counter' in the pub (36). This is obviously in accord with the concern in 'Ding-Dong' for commerce of different kinds. But Beckett is almost certainly thinking here of Schumann's famous description of Schubert's Ninth Symphony (the so-called great C major) as characterized by its 'heavenly length'; in 'Ding-Dong' Schubert becomes an 'ideal real' (*PTD*, 75), just as he was earlier in 'Walking Out'. This becomes more than a merely local effect when the 'woman of the people' who is selling seats in heaven, describes heaven as a place which goes 'rowan an' rowan an' rowan', 'dropping the d's and getting more of a spin into the slogan' (39). The obvious reference-point for this 'spin' within the story is 'the big Bovril sign' (43), a Dublin landmark which will reappear in 'A Wet Night', presumably written (as part of *Dream*, ready for submission to publishers by July 1932) before 'Ding-Dong'. But the 'spin' which Beckett gets into this moment has very little to do with a sign that can be seen; this is much more like what 'Walking Out' calls a 'waxing and waning [. . .] fume of signs', and at precisely the point in that story where Lucy 'saw nothing' (102). For the seat-seller's dropped 'd's are, in musical terms, just as 'fulcrate on the middle C' as the supply and demand over the counter, and aptly so, given that 'commerce' of a kind is operative in both cases. In what offers to be, or is received as, the territorial paradise of the lowly pub, there lurks the root of all evil – money – although only here and in 'What A Misfortune' is money of much concern to Belacqua, the 'dirty low-down Low Church Protestant high-brow' ('Yellow'[163]; a phrase expanded from *Dream* [100] and 'A Wet Night' [66]) with a house and garden in fashionable and prosperous Foxrock to go back to, should he ever choose to do so.

A subtle connection like this – it becomes even more subtle with 'Walking Out' *behind* 'Ding-Dong' in terms of the date of composition, and *yet to occur* for the reader reading *More Pricks Than Kicks* sequentially – is the product of what *Dream* calls 'flagrant concealment' (148); but the connection is so subtle that it takes even longer to emerge than the narrator's account of his relationship with his 'sometime friend'. It implies a background much more recessed than the one we are offered as in some way explicative or corrective of the ideas of Belacqua. In both its introduction and its development, 'Ding-Dong' is as front on in its perspective as most of the other *More Pricks* stories, which leaves Beckett all kinds of room to be, as it were, hidden in plain view for anyone with eyes to see, or simply to play games that even a 'competent' reader (to match the 'competent' singer [Ronsard] of 'Love and Lethe' [91] or the 'competent poet' of 'Draff' [177], Dante!) might find it difficult to follow. Whether these games were worth playing was probably not uppermost in Beckett's mind, though they must have pleased him in what he saw as a laborious task: the production of enough short stories to attract a publisher. He was predictably less pleased when Seumas O'Sullivan found he was too much 'behind the times' to pick up on what was going on in 'Ding-Dong'.

* * *

'Yellow'

There was no money to be made from the *Dublin Magazine*, or from anywhere else, with 'Ding-Dong': Beckett thought of sending the same story on to the *Adelphi* (*LSB*, 154), which also rejected it. By the time – several months later – that Beckett came to write 'Yellow', he seems to have given up much hope of placing his stories in the magazines of the day, although he was beginning to have enough stories to make up some kind of collection. A mixture of hope and realism marks 'Yellow', Belacqua having been admitted to hospital for two minor ailments, the treatment for which ought to have gone much more swimmingly than it does. 'Yellow' is an attempt to make light of this, relying on the reapplication of a 'sottish jest' (163) to settle Belacqua's hash. But behind 'Yellow', as is obliquely indicated by placing the story *after* 'The Smeraldina's Billet Doux', lies a death that Beckett would have found difficult to articulate other than by making light of it. On the day Beckett was cured (as Belacqua is not to be) of his own minor ailments, Peggy Sinclair, his 'sometime' *innamorata*, died of tuberculosis. Her failure to survive reminded Beckett that he had. Seven weeks later, on 26 June 1933, his beloved father died, a much more devastating blow, since he seemed to be recovering from a first heart attack only to succumb to a massive second one. (Beckett had twice been taken into the nursing home, for two different operations, which have been run together for Belacqua purposes.) Even though we cannot know exactly when 'Yellow' was written, it seems more than likely that this second death lies behind the way the story refers, no less than seven times, to Belacqua's 'late family', of whom we have heard nothing previously in *More Pricks*, although at least some of them had been given a few brief roles to play in *Dream of Fair to Middling Women*. Belacqua, who is trying on for size the theatrical (and for him philosophical) masks of tragedy and comedy before being taken down to the operating theatre, is preparing a face to meet other faces and is himself a mask for Beckett's real feelings, which were still causing him pain as late as 'Draff' and beyond it, while writing 'Echo's Bones', 'A Case In A Thousand' and 'Lightning Calculation' (see Section 4 of this chapter). The death that, as it were, 'cure[s]' Belacqua of his 'naïveté' ('Draff', 172) was in part the price he had to pay for Beckett's inability to deal directly with the death of his father.

'Yellow' adopts the 'coming and going' motif of 'Ding-Dong' and turns it into a kind of structural principle, with nurses and cleaners bustling about. But Beckett is really more interested in what happens when a Belacqua typically seen as 'mov[ing] constantly from place to place' ('Ding-Dong'; 31) can be brought to a halt, and granted the 'stasis' for which he so longs, however difficult it may be to maintain. Belacqua's confinement to bed sets him free in his mind, and he will in due course be set free from the physical world altogether by an inept hospital staff. Beckett must have known Montaigne's great essay 'To philosophize is to learn how to die'; in 'Yellow', Belacqua is learning – as he did in 'Dante and the Lobster' and 'Ding-Dong' – a lesson, but with no tutor other than himself and those around him. Belacqua's long morning in the nursing home may be 'dull' and 'irksome', but his mind is lively. He is perhaps at his liveliest (and not just in his mind, with so many females around) just when his life is about to end. In terms of the overall title of the collection, these thoughts are 'kicks' against the 'pricks' – here literally the pricks of pre-med – even if the latter outlast the former in (on this occasion) an unanswerable and irreversible way. As Jeri L. Kroll aptly says, 'The slow seepage of light throughout the story indicates that Belacqua's time is running out, though he is unconscious of it', she adds, 'Earlier, in "Love and Lethe", the narrator calls him "the doomed Belacqua" . . . though not because the hero's suicide attempt is destined to succeed' (1974, 343).

Belacqua's choice (it is actually Beckett's 'choice'; for Belacqua it is a discovery) of a Donne paradox – which I will explore in due course – nicely masks Beckett's play with a motif from Shakespeare's *Romeo and Juliet* (a play that he had studied at TCD in the Trinity [Summer] term of 1925): 'The bawdy hand of the dial is now upon the prick of noon'. This (as indicated in the 'Notesnatchings' section) is from a speech made to the Nurse (!) by Mercutio. Noon, a key point of reference for Dante also (cf. 'Dante and the Lobster'), is when Belacqua is *down* to go *down* to the operating theatre (and Dante also moves, or thinks he is moving, downwards), although of course noon is the time on the dial of a clock when its two hands point directly *upwards*. The pedlar in 'Ding-Dong' seems to conceive of her version of heaven as up above, and Belacqua, who here believes God to be 'good if we only know how to take Him' (152), is kicking from the start against the prick of being taken 'down' (151, '*Down*' on 162). He is as much at war with things outside him as he had been in 'Dante and the Lobster', but also at war in his mind. Belacqua is presented as in quest for 'a suitable engine of destruction' (154), although it will be made crystal clear that the world always has one of these to hand, whether it be in the shape of a negligent surgeon or unexpected accidents such as have already occurred in 'Walking Out' and 'Ding-Dong'. Belacqua's chosen 'engine of destruction' is his mind. But, as Beckett was to tell readers of the Christmas number of *The Bookman* in a review of Sean O'Casey's *Windfalls*, published some 7 months after *More Pricks*: 'A man's mind is not a claw-hammer' (*Disjecta*, 83). If this is so, then the mind is not, or not necessarily, an efficient tool to be applied to a recalcitrant (metaphorical) nail or two, and as such, even with sufficient force and leverage applied, not a very effective 'engine of destruction' (154). Belacqua's only cure, although he knows it to be 'of no avail', is a phrase he has read 'somewhere' (either in the Hone and Rossi biography of Swift[*LSB*, 150], or in the Bible): 'I am what I am' (152). We are told by the narrator that Belacqua 'liked it and made it his own'; however, it is obviously no more his own than the Donne paradox, his initial valuation of which he forgets (Kroll 1974, 267). Even Belacqua's death is not his own, since it has been anticipated by that of the parson who had qualms about saying 'By God' in an amateur *theatrical* production that he (mistakenly, if understandably) thinks is merely a 'secular occasion' (162).

'I am what I am' proves to be of no more practical value, whether as 'engine of destruction' or as 'cure', than any of the other literary texts with which Belacqua's mind is so well stocked from the outset. If it is a 'save' of a kind it is one only in the sense that it temporarily keeps a problem at bay, and has proved a fortunate find – in its way a fortunate fall – for a creative adaptation from a book (or books) Beckett had recently been reading. But it is no match for medical negligence operating against a background of hyperefficient nurses and the like, all of whom discharge their duties with exemplary attention to detail and despatch, their speed anticipating the outcome and contrasting nicely with the long, slow hours Belacqua must while away. Belacqua is constantly worrying, pointlessly, about the questions 'Am I what I am, or seem to be?' and, bigger still, 'Who, or what, am I?' This is one reason, although of course not the only one (with 'I am what I am' [twice] behind it), for the capitalization of the parson's 'BY CHRIST! I *AM* SHOT!' (162, italics in the text, but partly to emphasize the connection between one text and another). What one *is*, or might *be*, is left looking like a mere mind exercise over an intractable fact: that one is 'doomed' ('Love and Lethe') one way or another way, and quite as likely to die by accident as by design, even if (as in 'Love and Lethe') you seek to forestall the event by the ruse of a suicide pact.

'Yellow' was touted as a success (though not by name) in a publishers' blurb for *More Pricks* in the *Observer* of 6 May 1934, just over a fortnight before publication, and it was accepted as such (once again, with no title given) in the review of the collection in *The Times Literary Supplement* some 3 months afterwards (24 July 1934; see section III:1). 'Yellow' does indeed prosper compared to a number of the other stories because, with Belacqua unable to *do* very much and confined to his mind, Beckett can keep his own *mind* on the job at hand, shaping and crafting a story which is not just a success in the collection as a whole but is able to stand on its own. Everything in 'Yellow' is engineered with unusual precision and with almost no distractions, even if Belacqua's 7-hour wait necessarily consists of nothing but distractions. Like the phrase from Hardy's *Tess of the D'Urbervilles* with which Belacqua wakes up (he has been sleeping with a book and its heroine rather than with a woman!), 'Yellow' is from start to finish 'manipulated' (151), with the final tableau turning the hospital into a 'charnel-house' (156), and Belacqua's sense that there are 'limits' to the relevance of the 'laughing philosopher' Democritus turned on its head by a 'jest' that has missed one mark and hit another. There has been high-quality entertainment in what Belacqua thinks of as 'a dreadful situation' (145), and it is kept alive long enough to deliver when the truly 'dreadful' outcome occurs.

'Yellow' is one of the few stories in *More Pricks* to put its literary baggage on display in an apparently open illustration of how Belacqua has 'lived in his mind' (153), with the mind here a 'last ditch' (cf. Winnie in 'Fingal'; 25) in more senses than one, and with more authors than one. In 'Yellow' we find Donne in the company of Swift, Thomas Hardy, and Daniel Defoe. (It is as if Beckett, like Robinson Crusoe, has got all his [literary, in Beckett's case] 'gear ashore, the snugger to be' [153].) One may not 'be' for very long, but one can certainly lengthen a long wait with these temporary helps. But there is in fact even more literature at work, or in play (cf. 'Draff'; 175), in 'Yellow' than meets the eye, although it is the narrator's eye rather than Belacqua's which points us towards it, in an attempt by Beckett to get even more 'spin' ('Ding-Dong', 39) into the story's otherwise apparently unhelpful title. When 'two further women' ask Belacqua to 'stand on the mat', they search ('in vain' we are told; cf. chapter 11 of *Murphy*) for 'signs of discomposure' in his 'yellow face', which has become a 'mask' (163). Later, on being anaesthetized, Belacqua has 'terrible yellow yerks in his skull' (164). But both of these instances have been prepared for by a peculiar moment earlier, when Belacqua looks at a 'grand old yaller wall' (159) and fails to see his 'light dying' (*Endgame*, 11). Belacqua does not and cannot know that, as in the *Mene mene tekel upharsin* of the book of Daniel in the Bible, he has been weighed in the balance and found wanting. But the Bible was almost certainly not the literary text that Beckett had most in mind here, or so it would seem, given the reappearance a moment or so earlier of the 'asthmatic in the room overhead' (153). This is a kind of homage in the direction of the goat (or constellation Capricorn, visible from December to January, the time of Beckett's first operation at the nursing home) who 'coughs at night in the field overhead' in T. S. Eliot's 'Gerontion' (*Poems*, 1920; compare the uses to which Beckett has put T. S. Eliot's 'The Hollow Men' in 'Love and Lethe'). But when Beckett decides to emphasize that, as things are now, 'the coughing aloft had greatly abated since he first heard it' (159), this is almost certainly because he has yet another literary quarry up his sleeve to 'justify' the title of his story.

The spelling 'yaller', which sounds American, is cunningly calibrated to throw us off the track, reinforcing what looks like a subtext on our hero's cowardice in the face of minor surgery. The undisclosed referent is the character Bergotte in Proust's *La Prisonnière* (*Remembrance of Things Past*, vol. 9 [*The Captive*, I], 243ff.). Bergotte, who has been ordered to rest after a 'by no means serious' attack of uraemia, decides to abandon the policy he has adopted of staying at home and 'ceas[ing] to go out of doors' (*Captive*, 243). So he goes out, to look at a Vermeer canvas (*Street in Delft*), lent by the Mauritshuis in The Hague. A Parisian art critic has identified in the picture 'a little patch of yellow wall' so beautifully painted that it is 'sufficient in itself' (*Captive*, 249). *B*ergotte, a writer (like *Be*lacqua and *Be*ckett), looks at this detail and laments the fact that his own books are so inferior by comparison:

> 'That is how I ought to have written', he said. 'My last books are too dry, I should have gone over them with several coats of paint, made my language exquisite in itself, like this little patch of yellow wall'.

Bergotte dies a few moments later, and Proust's narrator discusses for the best part of a paragraph whether this writer is 'permanently dead' or 'not wholly so' (*Captive*, 250, 251). Beckett does not choose to follow Proust in these speculations, perhaps because although Belacqua is his alter ego (as Bergotte is Proust's), he is uninterested, or striving to be uninterested, in the whole question of literary fame or living forever. His Belacqua is soon to be dead, unlike Bergotte who is (in Proust) 'not wholly and permanently dead' (251). The patch of yellow wall was not wholly and permanently dead for Beckett, as it happens, since it figures as one of the crucial determinants in how 'something changed' one summer's day for Arsene in *Watt*, and is used by Arsene in his 'short statement' as part of a semi-systematic programme, a lesson to be learned, and in effect a warning of the change(s) awaiting Watt in the time he will spend at Mr Knott's house, which will entail the 'death' of a former self. Ironically enough, it seems to be a warning from which Watt learns very little, just as Belacqua in 'Yellow' does not see what the significance of his 'yaller wall' really amounts to.

The apparently insignificant detail of the 'grand old yaller wall' is discussed by Zurbrugg (1988, 221–3), is referred to by Ackerley in his annotated *Murphy*, 'Demented Particulars', and is very shrewdly assessed by Lawlor (2009, 52) as a 'coded intimation of mortality'. But the issues here are perhaps themselves more complex than immediately meet the eye, just as the unnamed authors have (almost) failed to do. Indeed, this detail is full of significance only if we at once look at it, look away from it and look beyond it. And for the detail to do its work we have to know where to look and how to look. We have to 'draw the blind, both blinds' (159) on the window and the actual wall, and open our minds to what the wall is telling us, not as Belacqua sees it, but behind his back, as it were. Already a marked man – marked by the ticking of the clock, the interruptions and injections of the nursing staff, the inability to put his carefully considered plan into 'execution' (156) – the 'old yaller wall' does indeed, as Lawlor suggests, 'identify' (2009, 52) him as already effectively a dead one. But if, as seems likely, the old asthmatic in the nursing home is 'really' Marcel Proust, he too is ('really') already dead and at the same time 'not wholly' so, since he can be re-imagined coughing in Dublin for the purposes of 'Yellow', 'making things easier for me' (153) – 'me' being both Belacqua and Beckett. Or Beckett at least: Belacqua, in spite of having died in 'Yellow', will still be called upon to act as a kind of live presence in 'Draff' and – however unwillingly Beckett may have complied with Prentice's request for yet more *More Pricks* – will have to be recalled to life, or to a kind of life, in the story 'Echo's Bones'. (Beckett puts the strategy to even better use in chapter 12 of *Murphy*, where the dead protagonist might almost as well be alive, given the amount of attention he is receiving; and it is no doubt highly symptomatic that Beckett [in a letter to MacGreevy of 7 July 1936; *LSB*, 350] tried to console himself for what he considered the shortcomings of the mortuary scene – which he had always thought of as 'the necessary end' – with 'Perhaps it is saved from anticlimax by [the] presence of M. all through'.) 'Yellow', for which Beckett had some materials deriving from his brief stay in the Elgin Nursing Home in Lower Mount Street shortly after Christmas 1932, was probably not finalized, and may not even have been begun, until after a second sojourn there in May 1933. It was, as indicated above, after he had been discharged from this second stay that Beckett learned of the death of Peggy Sinclair in Germany, on the same day that he had been operated on. It is possible that 'Yellow' received further attention after the death of Beckett's father on 26 June 1933, although it will presumably never be possible to link the story to a death much more devastating for Beckett than the news of Peggy Sinclair's had been. But the placing of 'Yellow' *after* 'The Smeraldina's Billet Doux' and *before* 'Draff' suggests that at least the first of these deaths, and possibly also the second, was used by Beckett as a kind of mask, if not for the actual death of one (or two) loved one(s), then for the effective death of his alter ego Belacqua, as if Beckett had increasingly come to realize that he simply had to get beyond him somehow. Much as the figure of Bergotte had been used by Proust to keep at least some of his own fear of death under a modicum of literary control, so Beckett very cunningly appropriates the strategy for his own similar purposes in this story. It joins with other examples of what Lawlor aptly calls 'covert resurrectionism' (2009, 66, n. 23), but it does so within a felt need to be much more 'covert' than *Dream* could ever have been (an issue, or complex of issues, which I deal with as relevant in Chapter 5), in the hope that *More Pricks* at least might have some kind of a future.

Exactly how closely Beckett associated his *More Pricks* collection with the sudden death of his father, in his mind if not necessarily in any direct use of material in the actual stories, it is impossible to say, even though 'Yellow' was (with 'Dante and the Lobster') one of the only two *More Pricks* stories which Beckett claimed to remember in later life (see the letters to Higgins, Boyle and Bray referred to in the second part of Chapter 3, 'How it went in the world'). But as my discussion of 'Draff' will subsequently show, it was this death that most preyed upon Beckett's mind as he prepared the book for publication, and one reason for his unusually hostile attitude to it in later life, since his father had not lived to see the fruits of a labour that Beckett had undertaken in large part (due to the failure of *Dream*) to 'justify' in the eyes of his family his having given up the prestigious job of lecturer in French at TCD. It must have been particularly distressing that, when copies of *More Pricks* arrived at 'Cooldrinagh', the book was met with a stony silence, a response Beckett self-tormentingly noted in a letter to his friend MacGreevy (see Chapter 1). There was even less interest in it at home than there was to be for *Echo's Bones and Other Precipitates*, although there was inevitably something of a public response (see Chapter 3), if only because *More Pricks* was not – or was not intended to be – a limited edition. As we now know, it effectively became one, selling only 20 or so more copies than *Echo's Bones* could ever have sold.

* * *

No fully involved reader of *More Pricks Than Kicks* would be tempted to confuse these three stories one with another. They do, however, have more in common than meets the eye, precisely because the eye has to, as it were, look away from them, towards literature and music, for real interconnectivities to be registered. Literature, it would seem from 'Yellow', can do things life cannot really be expected to do, even if life (or death or – in 'Draff' – 'the world') usually wins in the end. But the lessons which these three stories – 'Dante and the Lobster', 'Ding-Dong' and 'Yellow' – teach are not simple and straightforward, and there is no textbook to which to refer when the going gets tough (as the Ottolenghi promises she will do when she gets home). (Literature, to which Beckett may have turned in the hope of clarifying things, only makes real life more complicated.) What links the three stories – over and above the ideological aspects of each – are the females whom Belacqua has (for once) had to take seriously. These are the key figures with whom Belacqua is in contact (though not in love with) in each story, and it is largely in these women, rather than in

Belacqua, that the 'rare movements of compassion' (11) originate, even if Belacqua is prompted by them to make half-hearted gestures of a similar kind. There are men in these stories, from the grocer and fishmonger of 'Dante and the Lobster', to the 'dockers, railwaymen and joxers [cab-drivers]' of 'Ding-Dong' (39), to the doctor of 'Yellow'. But Belacqua considers himself ineffably superior to all of them: he can give the grocer a lecture on how to keep Gorgonzola, the *hoi-polloi* in the pub pose no threat to his fantasies and he never even considers the doctor who will so significantly contribute to his demise. In this last case this is because he is surrounded by no less than six rather domineering females: 'Was it the same woman? . . . What a number of women there seemed to be in this place!'

In all three of these stories it is the so-called weaker sex that is in a position to teach Belacqua a lesson. Each of the many women, in their different ways, manoeuvres Belacqua to where she wants him. But at least three of these women win from Belacqua a more than grudging admiration, even as he finds them something of a mystery (like Blissful Beatrice). The Ottolenghi is a 'sweet creature' ('Dante and the Lobster'); the 'woman of the people' is 'of very remarkable presence indeed' and 'a triumphant figure' ('Ding-Dong'); and the day-nurse in the hospital, given the name Miranda (as in Shakespeare's *Tempest*), is a 'divine creature', even if she 'just misse[s] being beautiful'. Beckett nowhere (except perhaps in an allusion in 'What A Misfortune', 124) comes close to saying so out loud, but the Ottolenghi, the pedlar woman and Miranda are all versions of the Shekinah, the divine female intermediary and intercessor of orthodox Jewish mythology (a motif Beckett had found in Carlyle's *Of Heroes and Hero-Worship*; *DN*, 298), and all of them are avatars of the Blissful Beatrice who plays this role in Dante's *Divine Comedy*. Beatrice in 'Dante and the Lobster', the woman with her Ptolemaic heaven in 'Ding-Dong' and the 'divine creature' Miranda in 'Yellow' are all part of the same connective tissue, even if they are to be found in three different stories.

Each of these fragments of the Shekinah contribute something to the reader's (if not always to Belacqua's) understanding of the difference between 'pity' and 'piety', judgement and mercy, which ought ideally, Belacqua thinks, to be one and indivisible, but which in practice turn out to be too often at loggerheads. In 'Dante and the Lobster', Belacqua asks himself:

> Why not piety and pity both, even down below? Why not mercy and Godliness together? A little mercy in the stress of sacrifice, a little mercy to rejoice against judgment. He thought of Jonah and the gourd and the pity of a jealous God on Nineveh. (13)

'Ding-Dong' is a little less abstract, and a little more prepared to compromise:

> ... he would say that the only place he could come to anchor and be happy was a low public-house. ... But as they closed at ten, and as residence and good faith were viewed as incompatible, and as in any case he had not the means to consecrate his life to stasis, even in the meanest bar, he supposed he must be content to indulge this whim from time to time, and return thanks for such *sporadic mercy*. (36, my italics)

Later in the same story the narrator intervenes to foreclose upon all this:

> The implications of this triumphant figure [the 'woman of the people' but also the literary figure of 'a dimmer on a headlight'], *the just and the unjust*, are better foregone' (38, my italics)

'Yellow' steps back from these issues or at least appears to do so, as if they might indeed be 'better foregone'. But even in 'Yellow' we have 'For himself, to do him justice ... ' and 'This was a godsend and no error. Not the phrase [from Donne] as a judgment, but its terms, the extremes of wisdom that it rendered' (155). Donne's phrase (from one of his *Paradoxes and Problemes*) moves the emphasis away from mercy and judgement towards laughter and weeping and by extension towards Heraclitus and Democritus; 'Yellow' manages very successfully to keep these 'extremes' on speaking terms with one another, as if they at least cannot be usefully separated. (This was certainly Beckett's later 'take' on them in a letter of 27 February 1934 to Nuala Costello, in which he seems to wish to be situated apart from, though mindful of, Democritus and Heraclitus, alone in his own space, 'a place where sighing is out of melancholy and not out of torment' [*LSB*, 185]. Beckett had presumably read Freud's 1920 essay on 'Mourning and Melancholia' from *Beyond The Pleasure Principle* in the meantime.) Donne's paradox runs:

> Now among our wise men, I doubt not but many would be found, who would laugh at Heraclitus weeping, none which would weep at Democritus laughing. (154–5)

Dante's 'superb pun' may or may not be translatable, but this Donne paradox – dealing with pre-Socratic philosophers on whom Beckett had either already taken notes, or was about to do so (TCD 'Philosophy Notes') – at least proves adaptable (for Beckett's purposes, if not Belacqua's) to what happens later. The irony, as Kroll very shrewdly recognizes (1974, 267), is that 'Belacqua ignores his initial evaluation of the Donne paradox, to be caught by it in the end'. But it is the narrator, not Belacqua – since it is only the former who can be numbered 'among our wise men' – who has learned from what literature has to teach us: 'Laugh! How he did laugh, to be sure. Till he cried' (163).

There are a number of ways in which these three stories reflect upon each other, of which only the most important are explored here. The first and the last of the three were, perhaps significantly, two (of only three *More Pricks* stories, 'The Smeraldina's Billet Doux' being the third) that were returned temporarily to the public domain in magazines before the inevitable reprint of the collection as a whole, although even 'Ding-Dong' can stand on its own, as I have tried to show. Together, separated as they are, they are more than a match for the three stories in which Belacqua pursues – by walking out on – his lovers and wives-to-be, despite the self-love from which (even here) he can never be entirely schooled, whatever these powerful Shekinahs may think. The obverse of this self-love, felt by Beckett if not by his alter ego Belacqua, was self-loathing and an inability to take pleasure in anything so much associated in his mind, if only once all the stories had been gathered together for public consumption, with the sudden and devastating death of a beloved father. There was never to be any relief from this for Beckett, but he did at least try before abandoning *More Pricks* to its own fate to find relief of a different kind, modelling a different balance of the relationship between 'figure' and 'ground', in the three stories to which I now turn. Each of these stories situates Belacqua still somewhat removed from his own sensibility, but now in a much more peopled landscape, a context necessarily wider in its focus than the ones which, in establishing him as the key figure overall, also emphasize his pitifully limited scope.

3. Ensemble Pieces: 'A Wet Night', 'What A Misfortune', 'Draff'

There was something so bright and meaty about the assembly, something so whorled in its disposition with the procession coiled in the midst waiting to move off, that Walter was slowly but surely put in mind of a Benozzo fresco and said so . . . it was obvious that until the procession uncoiled itself there could be no relief for the congestion.

('What A Misfortune')

Just as there are three *More Pricks* stories which are principally concerned with Belacqua's love life, and three largely focused on the life of his mind, so there are three – 'A Wet Night', 'What A Misfortune' and 'Draff' – in which he plays his part, wittingly or unwittingly, in settings for the most part given over to others, or at least involving a number of figures otherwise ancillary to him in the rest of the collection. At first these stories almost look as if they might have strayed in from another collection which just happens also to have a character called Belacqua in its cast list. It may or may not be significant that the second and third of these stories were – or so I suppose – composed late in the day, when Beckett's patience with Belacqua was beginning to wane, even if the ultimately jettisoned 'Echo's Bones' required him to be 'reborn'. Perhaps, if nine stories could have delivered a book of sufficient length to Chatto, Beckett would have stopped there. But, as so often with Beckett, 'the danger is in the neatness of identifications' (*Disjecta*, 19). And by including 'A Wet Night', probably written (when it was intended to form part of section 3 of *Dream*) at least a year or more earlier than the other two stories, any neat definition there might have been was already in jeopardy.

Beckett's situation in late June 1933 was unenviable on at least two major counts: he was grieving over the death of his father and realizing that his first attempt at a novel, *Dream of Fair to Middling Women*, had failed to find favour with some six or seven publishers, after more than a year of doing the rounds. At some point Beckett must have decided to cut his losses and salvage what he could from *Dream* in an attempt to save what might yet amount to a suitably substantial book of stories. Minor – very minor – revision was undertaken of the relevant pages from *Dream* that would make 'A Wet Night' a candidate for inclusion. This very act was a virtual admission that *Dream* possessed almost no 'unity', 'involuntary' (*Dream*, 132) or otherwise. How much Beckett may have wished that there might be other sections of *Dream* which could be so readily recycled we shall never know. It was at least sensible of him to reject as a possible selection the part of the novel he thought of (as indicated in a letter of 15 August 1931 to Charles Prentice) as 'They go out for the evening' (*LSB*, 81), arguably *Dream* (87–109) at its most colourless and lifeless. This section, although a distinct episode, does not in fact separate very readily from *Dream*, although in presenting quite a large number of characters other than Belacqua it might have served some of Beckett's other purposes. 'The Smeraldina's Billet Doux' he obviously did think could be taken out, which meant that (with 'A Wet Night') he had two bodies of material to bulk out what was otherwise several pages too few for comfort. But he had only two, and Beckett's only other recourse was to pillage *Dream* for odd phrases which could be liberally sprinkled across *More Pricks*, the only really substantial exception to this tactic being a paragraph (or most of one) that could be used early in the last story (as Beckett first thought of it), 'Draff'.

'A Wet Night'

For anyone with *Dream* to hand, or in mind, it is almost impossible to separate 'A Wet Night' from its original context, easy as Beckett seems to have found it. But the very few readers of *More Pricks* in 1934 suffered from no such difficulty and were faced only by the challenge of what they were to make of what was before them. With 'A Wet Night', however, some of the challenges were at least tempered by the socially specific scene presented in it, and by time-specifics (it is Christmas Eve in Dublin) which could be keyed in to a familiar masterpiece, already by general consent considered one of the greatest of all short stories, Joyce's 'The Dead'. It was at once a brave and foolhardy decision on Beckett's part to even hint at a comparison with Joyce, whose *Dubliners* he really did not want to compete with (and could hardly hope to emulate). It was no less a rash move for Beckett to virtually invite the comparison by way of a fairly feeble and lacklustre, perhaps because half-hearted in spirit, pastiche of the last paragraph of 'The Dead' (which, in *Dream*, Beckett had warmed up for earlier; 145). But whatever Beckett lost by this move he gained by suggesting to any potential reader that here was something that could be viewed in roughly the same plane, if not necessarily of the same depth and penetration. And in setting himself this test, Beckett created for himself a space in which he could explore (more patiently than in the 'Sedendo et Quiescendo' section of *Dream*) the extent to which, and the manner in which, he differed from Joyce. Beckett must have been gratified, if perhaps also slightly surprised, when Charles Prentice wrote to him (after receiving section 3 of *Dream*) to say that he was 'at [his] best' and 'on [his] own' there, and 'right away from Joyce' (letter of 5 July 1932; UoR). It was probably this response which contributed to the selection of 'A Wet Night' for inclusion in *More Pricks*, whenever Beckett finally decided that he was in need of 'staffage' (*Molloy*, 63). Prentice's positive reaction may have been relief that Beckett had not decided to choose other night scenes from *Dream*, since this 'wet' night in Dublin from section 3 of the novel shows many more signs of life than its lacklustre equivalent in Kassel at the Barberina at the end of section 2.

Joyce's 'classical temper' and impersonal stance, the artist as a god paring his fingernails, come under immediate pressure in 'A Wet Night', with four challenging opening paragraphs of self-evidently and self-consciously mannered prose announcing a narrator determined to say things his own way, however oblique or obscure that way may be at first sight. Beckett's differential 'take' on narrative procedure is signalled by the terse 'Not so Belacqua' in paragraph two (43), following hard upon 'Mistinguett would do away with chalets of necessity [street urinals, public toilets]. She does not think them necessary'. The joke here is not such a sparkling one that it cannot be missed, blurred as it is by just how much else is going on. It is as if the sheer bustle of 'the season of festivity and goodwill' has galvanized the prose such that it can hardly pause on anything without bringing a host of others in its train. It seems somehow symptomatic in this connection that, in the description of the blind paralytic under his arcade, we are told that 'he was there one minute and gone the next' (43). Almost all the details gathered here are in much the same state of flux and ephemerality. If the 'seven phases' of the Bovril sign look almost orderly by comparison, that is only because they are mechanically controlled. This Christmas Eve, to be sure, Belacqua's own moves may not be so very different from his customary ones, but his thoughts seem to have an unusual and compelling freedom to them, a freedom perhaps in part due to them having first figured in the wild world of *Dream*, rather than in the more constrained world of *Draff/ More Pricks*. Belacqua walking (as distinct from driving a hired car ['Love and Lethe'] or the car on loan for the wedding ['What A Misfortune']) is Belacqua in his element: grounded, dilatory, almost a 'happy body' (43), as if flaneuring around were a version of the expulsion of waste matter. He is braced for encounters but not disabled by them, 'well adrift' but not much bothered by being so, and – with Chas at least – sufficiently resourceful to be 'casting off with clean hands' (45). Later encounters expose how chancy his methods actually are, but even at the end of 'A Wet Night' he is, in his own way, 'happy'; he has been the beneficiary of good fortune and is not too discontented. Relatively few of the 'pangs' of 'Walking Out' or the shafts of feeling '[p]ast the worst of his best' in the same story (95–6) encumber Belacqua in 'A Wet Night', and nothing commits him to any apparently irreversible decision, like getting married or getting ready for a surgical operation. Even when night falls, and there is no Bovril sign to see by, it is a case of 'darkness visible'; he discovers his hands 'face upward' and the pain in his stomach has become 'so much better' (75).

But there is much to happen, and not all of it to Belacqua, before then. And it may be that the very diversity of material, the fact that things are happening to other people, gives the impression that Belacqua has been offered some much needed relief, some shelter from the spotlight he is haplessly prone to stumbling or 'waddl[ing]' into (47). Perhaps with Grock (and, who knows, God) in his heaven, all's right with the world, or at any rate with this world, on this night, even with the saviour Christ, as it were, still waiting to be born. The news from the Venerilla that the Alba's party dress buttons up behind even prompts Belacqua at this point to utter, 'Praise be to God . . . and his blissful Mother' (49), for this third piece of good fortune follows the brushing off of Chas and being 'rude on the sly' (47) on encountering the Poet.

Five portraits or snapshots follow – of the Alba, the Polar Bear, Chas among the students, the Poet with his 'strong composition' and finally the Frica. In each, the focal character assumes some self-importance, but falls short of any actual triumph. The Alba will be 'belle of the ball', but she is 'sullen' (49); the Polar Bear matches the Jesuit in his absurdity, though not in cunning, and the burden of his bus fare has to be borne; Chas makes waves, but leaves the students puzzled as to what he means by his 'divulgation' of 'sense' (52–3); the Poet is thinking of how best to 'conquer the salon' but is 'under stress' (54), and not just poetic 'stress'; the Frica thinks she has won her battle of one-upmanship with the Countess of Parabimbi, but the latter's '*frescosa*' (56) is very much a backhanded compliment. These minor reverses notwithstanding, the feeling that nothing much can go wrong at the Christmas party grows as the guests begin to assemble, even if Belacqua may be as unreliable (and perhaps as sozzled) as Freddy Malins 'on rather shaky legs' in 'The Dead' (*Dubliners*, 185). The high spirits are such, even without the provision of liquor (only soft drinks are to be served), that everyone obviously believes they are having a good time. Of course it is all a performance, and indeed something of a pre-performance (an 'Ante-Purgatory' in Dantean terms), since the Frica knows that she will have to 'round them up for the party proper to begin' (63), just as Beckett has had to 'round them up' in the first place (in *Dream*, and subsequently from *Dream*) for there to be any party or any story. Since the narrator has been obliged to 'round them up' without Belacqua coming into contact with them – Belacqua arrives late at the party, brought back by the narrative equivalent of a 'rescue' (68) – any idea that Belacqua might be the 'hero' of the story suffers further qualification. There is nothing, however, in 'A Wet Night' that corresponds with the 'crucial loss of interest in himself' (139) which Belacqua suffers in 'What A Misfortune', or the 'He did not pause to consider himself' (153) moment in 'Yellow'. What we are really being asked to admire, since Belacqua's conduct with the Civic Guard can only diminish him in our eyes, is the narrator's skill in organizing disparate blocks of material to bring the actual party (the 'party proper', 63) closer, while delaying the moment when everything and everyone can come together, and the later moment when Belacqua and the Alba cannot. The two sudden irruptions of guests into the swing of things ('the gaggle of nondescripts', 56; the 'arriv[al] . . . in a body', 59) figure against the ground of a deferral deliberately undertaken to seem in retrospect something of a performance on the part of the narrator, much more of a *deus ex machina* here than he had even been in 'Ding-Dong', but much less visible.

The actual performances at the party proper – a recitation in French ('old vulgar French' in *Dream*, 224), a Scarlatti Capriccio, a song in Gaelic and a 'recent composition' by the Poet bringing up the rear (his poem effectively buried, since it does not need to be repeated again, by 'an outburst of applause', 72) – are ignored by the guests, who are only really interested in how they themselves are performing, the situation somewhat resembling the situation of the court and the 'rude mechanicals' at the end of Shakespeare's *A Midsummer Night's Dream*. (In 'The Dead', most of the entertainment has little effect on Gabriel Conroy because he is too bound up in his own private thoughts, whereas Beckett is interested in exposing the public aspect of the Frica's party as an absurd charade.) The best, or the most successful, performance is in a one-to-one exchange between Belacqua and the Alba (72). Belacqua's 'borrowed quodlibet' (borrowed from St Augustine, *DN*, 182; also borrowed from *Dream*, 235) prompts the Alba to cap it with the magic words 'See me home' (72). (In *Dream* she says: 'Will you see me home? . . . Will you?' [236]. Beckett is almost certainly thinking back privately here to taking Ethna MacCarthy, the real-life inspiration for the Alba, home in a car that crashed, injuring her quite seriously, after a Christmas Eve party in 1931, an event that left him feeling guilty for decades.) There is a lovely irony in Belacqua, briefly a St Augustine, not being obliged (apparently 'A Wet Night' is silent in this respect) to perform anything else, or in any of the more obvious ways, on reaching 'Casa Alba' (a designation unique to 'A Wet Night'). *Dream* is more explicit here, if not wholly so: 'You didn't suppose, it is to be hoped, that we were going to let him spend the night there' (240). In *Dream* this comes immediately after a cod-Joyce portmanteau word allegedly uttered by 'a Leipzig prostitute', who for the purposes of 'A Wet Night' – in accordance with what has *not* happened – becomes 'a divine creature' (73). Anything so potentially committing as the Alba and Belacqua spending the night together would of course damage what has certainly been a 'wet' night (too much rain, too much to drink), but was never likely to become a hot one, as anticipated in a previous encounter between them in *Dream* ('He has not lain with her. Nor she with him', 177).

'A Wet Night' treats the Alba – the dominant female figure in *Dream*, section 3, and described there as 'royal' (177) – with a degree of affection and a kind of awe which elevates her above any of the other women who appear in *More Pricks*. The very suggestion (as made in 'What A Misfortune', 120) that she might once have been 'an old flame of the groom' looks about as preposterous an idea as any sexual shenanigans between herself and Belacqua. The exploration of this 'old flame' aspect is more fully and acutely explored in *Dream* in a series of encounters between the two, meetings which are conducted with a delicacy, even an elegance, not otherwise much evident there. (In real life, Ethna MacCarthy was only an 'old flame' in the sense that Beckett's hopes of her becoming a 'flame' at all had been disappointed, although *Dream* shows through the various meetings between Belacqua and the Alba how the latter became, and remained, so much more than a mere 'flame'.) Even in 'A Wet Night', in which the centrality of the Alba has to compete with the gathering of the clans and the absurdity of society's behaviour, it is possible to feel the poignancy of Belaqua seeing her home, as if there might really be something more to him than the shuffling and awkward scapegrace we have seen, if certainly nothing that would induce her to become emotionally involved with him. The long account of the Alba in her 'sunken kitchen' (49; with some material from *Dream*, 54 and 176, imported into it – Belacqua's aunt also has her kitchen in the basement) getting ready for the Frica's party is almost the only extended treatment in *More Pricks* of a woman thinking, planning and acting for an achievable purpose, orientated towards a 'reality of preference' (50) rather than the life of fantasy for which most of the work's other female figures (Lucy, Ruby, Winnie and the Smeraldina) have to serve as unwitting models. The Alba is too much 'a woman of the world' (50) to be a Beatrice, and (as we have seen) the Shekinah figures can only exercise a temporary ascendancy over Belacqua, at the periphery of his consciousness. The Alba is 'a woman of the world' because she is *in* the world but not *of* it, because she can deal with the world without becoming mired in it; on both counts she achieves a level of 'distinction' (49) which is not granted to any of the others. Significantly, surely, Beckett added a phrase to the equivalent description of her in *Dream* (208) to underline the Alba's ability to make light of the petty achievements which seem to matter so much to the Dubliners on show here. They are seen as little more than 'masks' in *Dream* (207), but here the Alba is indifferent to 'a palm that she had merely to open her eyes and assume' (49). The story effectively awards her the palm for sailing through the party with her dignity intact. One reason why Belacqua so much admires the Alba is her complete disregard for the social norms by which even he is ensnared. The Alba possesses the remarkable ability to walk out of the spotlight – both here and again in 'What A Misfortune' – in a way that, quite unlike Belacqua's own fluctuating capacity to do so, offends no one. It is part of the strict, if somewhat perverse, logic of *More Pricks* that in 'What A Misfortune' she should have become 'Alba Perdue' or 'Miss Perdue' (120, 129), as unobtainable as Marcel's 'Albertine Perdue' in Proust's *Recherche*; she is later said to have died 'in the natural course of being seen home' ('Draff', 167) by someone other than Belacqua. But 'dead' as she may be in relation to Belacqua's amatory hopes, in Beckett's memory she cannot so easily be killed off; she even reappears twice in the story 'Echo's Bones' (19, 27–8) as a natural leader, commanding 'a submarine of souls' with exemplary aplomb!

The beneficial effects of the Alba seem to survive her return to the security of 'Casa Alba' (74), and something of her benign presence appears to have mollified even the 'uneasy' Belacqua. At the end of 'A Wet Night' it is Christmas morning, though for Belacqua it is inevitably more a matter of the morning after the night before, or at least part of the night before. But the pain in his feet abates after he has thrown away his boots (Beckett wore footwear in imitation of Joyce's, but had bigger feet), and he can then offer the compliments of the season (in what is an usually civil gesture, for him, one not found in *Dream* [240]) to 'some early bird' (74). There may be a faint trace here (as later with the phrase 'more in sorrow than in anger' at the very end of the story) of Shakespeare's *Hamlet* – a much more frequent reference point throughout *More Pricks* than it ever is in *Dream* – with Beckett thinking of the pleasing fiction of harmony between the soldier Marcellus out on the battlements in Act I, scene 1, and the 'Bird of Dawning' that is said to sing all night long on Christmas Eve. The phrase 'more in sorrow than in anger', which is in *Dream* (241), occurs in Act I, scene 2 of *Hamlet*.

This faint trace of Shakespeare is given extra 'spin' by the equally faint trace of Dante (author of *The New Life* or *Vita Nuova*) by way of Belacqua adopting the quasi-foetal, knee-and-elbow position of his namesake in the *Purgatorio*. But to say that Belacqua is reborn on Christmas morn is to say more than Beckett is prepared to say, even if in real terms he has actually been reborn from *Dream*. There is simply the requirement made of him to 'move on', which Belacqua is 'only too happy' to comply with (75), having started out a 'happy body' (43). There are no stars to be seen, and no suggestion of any dawn that might follow. But for Belacqua this is 'a consummation devoutly to be wished', better even than any consummation that might be offered him by the Alba. In 'A Wet Night', a 'quite black night' (compare the end of the first section of *Watt* many years later) reigns over the open-ended closure of the story. But it is not 'submarine and oppressive' like the darkness in the wood in 'Walking Out' (104). Belacqua's hands are 'opened . . . in unison' (74), an almost perfect illustration of how Beckett likes, if he can (and here he can do so without a reader necessarily noticing it), to end a *More Pricks* story by invoking music or musical terminology (cf. 'Walking Out' and 'Ding-Dong'). It would surely have ruined the prevailing party mood of this story had it been otherwise.

'A Wet Night' ends as Beckett's *Dream* ended, and with almost the same words: Belacqua moving unhurriedly, if a little uncertainly, and without the wherewithal to go back into the centre of the city. (*Dream* is, for once, clearer in its implications: the phrase 'by the time he reached Ballsbridge' [241], south of his current location, is omitted from 'A Wet Night'.) But *Dream* ends in this way, with 'END' underlining the fact, having earlier (114, 149) toyed with the idea of a quite different 'last scene' or 'terminal scena'; this non-termination keeps things 'middling' and moving, which is how they began. This way of ending seems appropriate enough in its context and better than any other 'terminal scena' might have been, perhaps because it also gestures vaguely towards the 'commodius vicus of recirculation' which operates in *Finnegans Wake* (3), a dream work and a work in progress. But the end of 'A Wet Night' works differently, even with much the same material deployed. Although the repetition of 'happy' (43, 75) suggests a measure of 'recirculation', 'A Wet Night' – like 'Fingal' and 'Ding-Dong' before it – privileges inconsequential continuity. 'Ding-Dong' offered the image of a 'boomerang' – out and back – as a kind of model, but failed to exemplify it in what transpires, and in fact several of the stories ('What A Misfortune' is perhaps the best illustration) avoid resolution at the point of termination. In *More Pricks* it is even more obvious than in *Dream*, which still seems to hold out some hope, that there can be no *nostos* or return as in the *Odyssey* or Joyce's *Ulysses*. In the particular case of 'A Wet Night' there is no need to even think of such a thing and no organic way of achieving it. The bustle of its beginning makes it apt that the story should remain 'on the move' (cf. 'Serena III'), and the conclusion leaves little doubt that there is really no obvious place to go. 'Love and Lethe', the next story in the non-sequential sequence, complicates the idea by homing in on the Toughs in Irishtown, to the east ('nearer the sea', 74) of the Leeson Street/Ballsbridge neighbourhood. But by relying on a suspense motive which is not in the end going to deliver its promise, the idea of 'moving on' remains alive even there. 'There is an end', wrote Kafka in one of his *Zürau Aphorisms*, 'but no way: what we call a way is only hesitation'. 'A Wet Night', with or without the benefit of Kafka, makes the best of a bad job in relying on recycling rather than radical revision.

* * *

'What A Misfortune'

The 'quodlibet' Belacqua borrows and adapts, from *Dream* (235) and from St. Augustine, the Father of the Christian Church, divides the 'mind' and the 'memory', the former indifferent to the indifference it contains, the latter 'not sad', even though it has 'sorrow' in it (72). The sorrows and sadnesses, or 'pricks', that frequently afflict Belacqua in *More Pricks* have no real equivalents in 'A Wet Night', and they are also in fairly short supply in 'What A Misfortune' and (for good reason, no doubt!) 'Draff'. 'What A Misfortune' is easily the longer of these two late stories, and indeed only matched in length by 'A Wet Night'. It is *More Pricks* at its most sustained and also at its most demanding; only the jettisoned story 'Echo's Bones' really approaches it in terms of complexity. The difficulties (as in 'Echo's Bones') are largely local, but they are so numerous that the structure of 'What A Misfortune' threatens to get lost, whereas 'Echo's Bones' follows a basically simple triadic pattern, and the ideas behind it remain essentially clear. There is enough richness in 'What A Misfortune' for this not to matter much, although it may be that Beckett has here tried to do more than even a long short story could be expected to do. This probably reflects Beckett's view that the short story, as a form, could only ever be 'antinomial' and ancillary, or a rather trivial footnote to the much more substantial achievement of a full-length novel. However, in 'What A Misfortune', Beckett pulls out just about all the stops to try to persuade himself that it might be otherwise.

One of the prompts towards 'What A Misfortune' – there were many, although none sufficiently direct to be called influences – may have been the 'scorching phrase' from Maupassant: *'phylloxera of the spirit'* (131). The Rachel Burrows lecture notes (TCD) show Beckett taking a sideswipe at Maupassant as a writer of much less interest than Proust, Stendhal, Flaubert or Gide. But he must have found time to read the little-known story 'Divorce', which first appeared in the magazine *Gil Blas* (21 February 1888), and which was later collected in *Le Rosier de Mme Husson*. (It was not one of the *Six Contes*, edited by Harold P. Sloman [Cambridge University Press, 1914, etc.] set for student study at TCD in Beckett's time there, as indicated in the *Dublin University Calendar*.) In the Maupassant story, the phrase reads 'phylloxéra des âmes' (Pleïade, vol. 2, 1017–18), and the very title of the story obviously does not bode well for the wedding of Belacqua and Thelma bboggs. As we only learn three stories later, in 'Draff', they are divorced by death, Thelma having 'perished of sunset and honeymoon that time in Connemara'. She has, and indeed they have, obviously 'gone west' (140) in a more than literal way, with Beckett no doubt remembering Michael Furey and Gretta Conroy in Joyce's 'The Dead'. But here at least they are together, and the only death recorded is the one to come in the case of Thelma's father who (like Beckett's father) 'died in the end of a clot' (130). This suggests that 'What A Misfortune' must have been finished after 26 June 1933, or at least altered during the revision of all the stories for their presentation to Charles Prentice, although it may well have been begun before that date. But in *More Pricks* deaths occur randomly, from the lobster of 'Dante and the Lobster' to the accidental death of Belacqua in 'Yellow', so this could be no more than a bizarre coincidence, a 'misfortune' quite unanticipated.

The difficulties of 'What A Misfortune' begin with its title, and then permeate the story to its end, the point where the characters 'went further' (140), but the story does not. We are never told *what*, or what *kind* of *misfortune* is at issue, and it does not seem to help matters very much (even with Kroll [1978, 32] making a very interesting case for it) when an origin for the phrase can be found in Voltaire's *Candide*: '*Che sciagura d'essere senza coglioni*' ('What a misfortune it is to be without your testicles'; 53). Beckett had used the first two words of this Italian phrase in his 1929 squib on the vexed question of the import of contraceptives into the Irish Free State ('Che Sciagura'), and there is a faint echo of it later, in Malone's paragraph beginning 'What a misfortune', after he has dropped his *pencil* (49). In 'What A Misfortune', however, neither contraception nor testicles make very much sense (even if writing is occasionally mentioned) as inspirations for the title, which suggests that the misfortune in question must be the wedding to which Belacqua has, no doubt unwisely, committed himself. A letter of 22 September 1935 (*LSB*, 276 ff.) to MacGreevy slightly complicates this picture, with Beckett imagining himself a month or so later, having agreed to act as best man at his friend Geoffrey Thompson's wedding down at Lulworth Cove, 'booked for the misfortunes of Hairy' (*LSB*, 277), who is Belacqua's best man in this story. (The role of '*stand*ing best man', as the 'local doc' has done for some unspecified friend, has catastrophic consequences for Belacqua in 'Yellow', and there is an implied question mark over whether Dr Nye in 'A Case In A Thousand' is, metaphorically speaking, the 'best man' in the circumstances. See Section 4 of this chapter.)

Belacqua's love for Thelma, we are told, is a 'divine frenzy' and 'none of your lewd passions' (110). Indeed, the 'intense appeal' of Thelma 'from the strictly sexual *stand*point' (111) is precisely that she has no sexual appeal at all; there would be no point in *stand*ing with her, at the altar or anywhere less public. (With his best man Hairy, by contrast, 'Belacqua stood' [128], the better to see himself in the pier glass.) Beckett borrows and adapts a phrase from Diderot (from his 'Ceci n'est pas un conte'; *DN*, 583) to say: 'She brought neither the old men running nor the young men to a standstill'. He follows this with a phrase designed to show what – physically – Thelma is: 'To be quite plain . . . ' (111). The marriage, then, is what the world would call a marriage of convenience, in which connection one can hardly help thinking of the 'toilet requisites' (111) which were once touted by Thelma's father and which have helped to form the basis for his prosperity. The 'convenience' of the marriage for Belacqua is that Thelma is, or will soon be, 'a girl of substance', a good prospect in financial terms for a Belacqua with an 'inconsiderable' fortune, albeit one of some 'distinction', being 'unearned' (110). Belacqua's frenzy seems, then, not so much 'divine' as mired in the chicanery of commodity exchange; in fact, money matters (which also figure prominently in Maupassant's 'Divorce') are much to the fore in the early part of 'What A Misfortune'. Money has not brought much happiness to the bboggses, but it has conferred on them, or on Otto Olaf at least, some prestige and social status. Otto Olaf inflates this by his grandiose style. He is ever ready to promote himself even in such an ordinary activity as singing, a performance prompting Belacqua to admire, or to seem to admire, his 'real three dimensional organ' (113), even if someone else's organ has proved vital in the conception of Thelma.

Whatever love there may once have been in the bboggses' marriage has been compromised by Otto's complaisance and Bridie's adulteries, one of which has given her Thelma as a by-blow. This means that the bride that her father is 'giv[ing] away' (132) is not, strictly speaking, his to give, and the man to whom he is giving her (for whom Otto has 'contempt', 112) does not want to be a bridegroom in the primary sense of the word. There is a tension here, or an equation, between private vices and public virtues, advertised in the words *public* and *private* at the end of the second paragraph of 'What A Misfortune'; however, the notions they engender are effectively present throughout, and explicitly so in the case of Walter Draffin's drinking habits (114). Beckett told Nuala Costello (10 May 1934; *LSB*, 208), with whom (for a time) he fancied himself in love, that one of the authors he had in mind during the writing of the *More Pricks* stories was Bernard de Mandeville, the seventeenth–eighteenth century poet-philosopher of *The Fable of the Bees*, which swiftly became notorious for its suggestion that private vices must inevitably lead to public virtues.

The wedding, as dramatically proclaimed by the insertion of a 'visual aid' (the invitation to it, 111; cf. the sign in 'Love and Lethe' [88] and the 'insertion' in the press in 'Draff' [163]), is a necessarily public event, and the married couple are not even left on their own as they go off on honeymoon. They have the ghost of Lucy, from 'Walking Out', with them 'the best part of the way down to Galway', and Lucy has been referred to on no fewer than six occasions earlier. What Belacqua privately thinks and feels is for the most part either kept to himself, conveyed in snippets to his best man or given to us by the narrator in curlicues of cryptic information. His private vices (sufficiently well known by now, after 'Walking Out' and 'Fingal', for Beckett not to have to enumerate them) certainly do not seem to stand in the way of his public benefits. Beckett is also, of course, remembering the lines in *Hamlet* which speak of how 'the funeral bake-meats did furnish forth the marriage tables' (as found in 'Fingal', 21) in another second marriage, although he is obliged to soft-pedal this if Otto and Bridie are not to become Old Hamlet and Gertrude, with Walter Draffin as Claudius!

If it seems doubtful in this situation that the public benefits of a marriage, any marriage, could possibly last, there is always Otto Olaf's business success to suggest otherwise, since sexual success (despite his 'real three dimensional organ') looks very much a secondary matter. Even Walter Draffin does not care much about sexual conquest, since his principal concern is with his 'book' (116, 125; 'given away' to him by Beckett!). Belacqua as a writer of, say, poetry ('Calvary by Night', for example, a Beckett poem 'given away' to 'the Poet' in 'A Wet Night'), is hereby absolved from having to furnish us with any examples of his work, which leaves Otto Olaf's businesslike sense of him in that role looking like just one more judgement of surface over depth. Sex has, in 'What A Misfortune', been reduced, by neglect almost, to the level of just another commodity to be bought and sold, and Belacqua for the most part seems blissfully unaware of it. Only at the very end does the narrator imagine a beaver (alleged to cut off its testicles at the appearance of danger) astride a mule (a hybrid unable to propagate its species) and have Belacqua lose his 'favour of veronica' (as it is called in 'Draff', 175), which has 'wormed its stem out of the slit [!]' in his buttonhole (140). On page 128, this is 'a purple tassel of veronica, fixed in the wrong lapel', and obviously, given Thelma's supposed parentage, this is not the first tassel to have been fixed in the wrong lapel in a wider sense. Perhaps we are indeed intended to infer that testicles and misfortune go together.

But it seems equally likely that the 'misfortune' is not so much to be without, or without the will to use, your testicles, but to be without the means (supposedly available to the beaver) to continue in spite of them. This is part of the double bind in which public benefits depend on the social niceties being observed, even if private vices lurk behind them. The wild comedy of 'What A Misfortune' works with these contrasts and this bind, exploiting the gaps and the connections between them, with an arch and omniscient narrator – similar to, although nothing like so proficient as, Fielding (especially in *Tom Jones*) – controlling the events at whim. Even here, however, the narrator cannot show complete disregard for the social niceties operative on storytelling as a successful commodity exercise in its own right. The 'jigsaw' puzzle has to fit together, however recalcitrant the pieces may look as distinct items alongside one another.

Beckett relishes these juxtapositions – the more heterogeneous the better – more fully, or at least for longer, in 'What A Misfortune' than anywhere else in *More Pricks*, almost as if he were determined, in some final fling of effort, to exhaust the possibilities of the form he has forced himself to choose. The exceptional complexity in (and of) 'What A Misfortune' is due to the conscious and manifest exercise of a will elsewhere more honoured in the breach than the observance. This may be one reason why 'A Wet Night' has no less than seven breaks in its transmission, breath pauses which may or may not reflect actual breaks in the compositional process, whereas 'What A Misfortune' has none. 'What A Misfortune' becomes a more difficult read than any of the other stories because it never lets up. The 'comic relief', as Beckett later told George Reavey in connection with *Murphy* (letter of 13 November 1936; *LSB*, 380–1; *Disjecta*, 103) also has to work hard, given that there can be no real relief in writing, and more particularly in writing in this form.

At one point in 'What A Misfortune', Otto Olaf (or the narrator on his behalf) sees the wedding circus to come as, more accurately, a 'circus wedding' (116). The term 'vaudeville' (PTD, 92) seems equally applicable. Anthony Farrow (152) sees this aspect as dependent on 'doubles', perhaps prompted to do so by the numerous *doubles entendres* in the story, which he understandably chooses not to examine too closely. But it may be more profitable to see it as dependent on a more idiosyncratic and distinctively Beckettian 'law' of substitution and transformation. Thelma, for example, is not only a substitute for the dead but not forgotten Lucy, but also for the otherwise forgotten Ruby. Walter is a substitute for Otto Olaf in the marital bed first, but later for Belacqua as Walter takes the Alba home. The long discussion of who are to be the bridesmaids at the wedding – a kind of parody of the College of Cardinals in Rome choosing a new Pope – involves a whole gallery of possible substitutes, endlessly substituting for one another. The length of the discussion implies that the possible substitutions could go on for ever before in the event a group of six, one of them the Alba, are found acceptable and fit for purpose, but obviously as people much of a muchness. Similarly, Capper Quin, in some ways a mere henchman for his 'principal' (122), feels the need to have an assistant in 'one Sproule', and so on. Beckett's strategy here can be seen as an illustration and realization of what he means when, in the *Proust* essay, he speaks of an 'endless series of renovations' and of 'the comedy of substitution' (*PTD*, 28–9).

Words and phrases from other *More Pricks* stories (and often from *Dream*) also take on new life here as substitutes for genuinely new material. The 'sullen' Alba's 'See me home', Belacqua excusing himself, and 'Happy dawg' (now given to Sproule) are all imported and/or re-adapted from 'A Wet Night'. The number plate (127) recalls to mind the one actually given a number in 'Love and Lethe' (89). The 'cruel stroke of midday' (127) which fails to wake Belacqua up is taken from the time of his operation in 'Yellow' (151) and the time he went to his kitchen in 'Dante and the Lobster' (3). The plan, if plan it can be called, is not so much 'Never one without two' (as in *Dream*; 'seldom' in 'A Wet Night'), but, better still, 'Never two without three', which is Belacqua's estimate of the tots of whiskey left in the bottle he is sharing, or trying to share, with Ruby in 'Love and Lethe' (89). It is in the same spirit that Beckett cannot resist combining quotations from very diverse sources, as he had already done throughout *Dream*, sources which might have been ill-adapted to one another, if not actually incompatible. There are so many of these that 'What A Misfortune', like 'Echo's Bones' after it, really needs annotation for the sheer adroitness of Beckett to be appreciated (see Chapter 5).

Part of the success of 'What A Misfortune' is attributable to Beckett avoiding any prolonged verbal sparring (like, for example, that engaged in by Belacqua and Winnie in 'Fingal', or by Belacqua and Lucy in 'Love and Lethe') between Belacqua and Thelma. They have just one brief exchange quite early on about the 'period clock' purchased as a 'present' – with Beckett having some fun with the intrinsic contrast between 'period' and 'present' (122) – and an equally brief one at the end of the story after stopping in the car on the way out west to Galway. Much of the space in the interim is occupied by rapid-fire dialogues between Hairy and Sproule, Hairy and Draffin, and Hairy and Belacqua, with the focus widened later on to give voices even to the wedding guests. This tactic enables Beckett to imply that Belacqua and Thelma will never amount to much, but is also part of a strategy very shrewdly recognized by Farrow (147), who writes of how the lead figure 'is a less interesting Belacqua ... [in] that he has ceased to be himself as we have come to know him. From this point on it will be a less distinct or a more ghostly Belacqua who will figure in these stories'. Just before 'What A Misfortune' ends, indeed, it actually presents a Belacqua who 'stood like a stock at gaze', and the narrator adds: 'It was from this moment that he used to date in after years his crucial loss of interest in himself, as in a grape beyond his grasp' (139). What this does not, of course, tell us, is why this 'loss of interest' might occur, now or later. Belacqua, by this point in the composition of *More Pricks*, had almost certainly come to seem to Beckett more a liability than a benefit. Given the circumstances, however, Beckett had to try to 'save the appearances' – as in a note on the technical definition and function of the strategy of 'hypothesis', jotted down early in the *'Whoroscope' Notebook* – by situating Belacqua against a gaggle of others, *primus inter pares* for once, and by situating this particular story at a point where it might best promote a gradual decline in Belacqua's importance, rather than first in the collection as a whole. The next (so-called) story is a letter from the Smeraldina, after which Belacqua is bed-bound, not in much of a position (try as he might) to engage in 'gallantry' in 'Yellow', and fit only to be buried, sexual issues having to be left to others (in 'Draff').

The strengths of 'What A Misfortune' proved of little assistance in the general 'misfortune' which was to befall *More Pricks*, but its intransigence could never have made it a popular success on its own, as might have occurred (and in a way did occur) in the case of 'Dante and the Lobster' or 'Yellow'. Like Walter Draffin's speech at the wedding, 'What A Misfortune' is 'too densely packed to gain the general suffrage' (135), as was recognized early on by the reviewer of the collection in the *TLS* [see Chapter 3]. Beckett has here applied, but twisted, the time-honoured conventions of comedy and burlesque in a way which public taste, even today, might still find unacceptable. This 'circus wedding' is an even more preposterous performance than those engaged in by the guests in 'A Wet Night'. But the truths told, in spite of the hubbub on the surface and the concentration on surfaces (notably, what the women are wearing), are in their way quite as devastating as anything in Mandeville's *Fable of the Bees*.

* * *

'Draff'

'Draff' is concerned with '[the way] it goes in the world', as its last sentence tells us. (The phrase is actually taken, as a much later undated letter of January 1955 [UoR] to Pamela Mitchell almost reveals, from the Brothers

Grimm story 'How the Cat and the Mouse Set up House'.) The 'world' is present at the beginning in the form, almost literally the form, of a *newspaper* obituary (sent in by *telephone*, which generates the metaphor of a *telegram*), and the reality quotient is maintained thereafter by the undertaker, the parson, the gardener, the groundsman and the specifics which the supposedly grieving widow, or more often her maid, has to consider. 'Draff' was Beckett's provisional title (perhaps found quite late in the day) for the whole collection, which he was prepared to change on the advice of his editor Charles Prentice. It is a technical term meaning the lees left after brewing, and there is a slightly 'after the Lord Mayor's show' feel to this story, even with Belacqua still (as a body) *on* earth for half of it, and only *in* the earth at the end. (The situation of the autopsy over Murphy is anticipated here, by keeping the dead body of Belacqua on permanent display.) Even so, there is considerable daring on Beckett's part in 'killing off' a Belacqua whose presence has, in any case, been diminishing in various ways since 'Walking Out'. In 'Draff' he obviously cannot walk out, but has to be carried out; other things have to be carried out on his behalf. 'There is', the narrator of *Murphy* will later tell us, 'no return game between a man and his stars' (chapter 5; 55), even if a published 'Echo's Bones' story could have proved him wrong.

The 'world' in 'Draff' is seen not just in the human terms of 'sympathy' or self-interest, self-love or social concern, public or private (Mandeville's ideas are again, though muted, mobilized). Overarching the human dimension are the fundamental categories on which human existence seems to depend: time and space. Of Hairy Quin we learn that 'he was greatly improved, commerce [a word last heard in 'Ding-Dong', but a subject dealt with in 'What A Misfortune'] with the things of time had greatly improved him' (171). The dead Belacqua, by contrast, has a 'timeless mock' on his face (173). This clear-cut distinction between them underpins the idea that 'Belacqua dead and buried, Hairy seemed to have taken on a new lease of life' (177). The Smeraldina, perhaps ominously for Hairy's hopes, has herself 'died in part' (177; her real-life equivalent, Peggy Sinclair, had in fact died several months earlier), and is seen as living in a kind of predicateless present, satisfying her immediate needs with eggs lightly boiled, and at a loose end, vague about any possible future. Hairy has future assignations with the Smeraldina very much in mind. By contrast, the stout-drinking groundsman (later, in 'Echo's Bones', given the name Mick Doyle) is given the whole spectrum of past, present and future, and also what looks like the most intelligent assessment of it: 'He strained his ear for the future, his future, and what did he hear? All the ancient punctured themes recurring . . . Very well. Let the essence of his being stay where it was' (174). The groundsman re-animates the 'listening' which has a part to play in 'Walking Out' and other earlier stories, and the scene is '[d]arkling' in much the same way as it had been for the Keats of 'Ode to a Nightingale'.

Spatial considerations are, appropriately enough, more precisely mapped. There is a long and penetrating account of the Smeraldina's body (much of it purloined from *Dream*), which is oddly prepared for by a curt dismissal at the start and whisked way by another one at the end. She is equally closely scrutinized in the manner of 'prepar[ing] her weeds' and leaving the floor 'strewn with . . . bright cuttings' (169). Space actually invades the story with a curious interpolation (itself an 'insertion', with a 'minus' of its own):

One insertion in the Press
Makes minus how many to make a black dress? (169)

But Beckett seems to have rather tired of this kind of interventionist trick by this point, having used up most of his complement of breaks in the visual continuity of the narrative texture in 'A Wet Night' (four times) and 'What A Misfortune' (nine indented interpolations). The insertions that really matter in 'Draff' are of Belacqua's body in his coffin, for which he has to be measured, and of both body and coffin in a grave, which has to be dug and 'upholstered' by someone inserting himself in it (cf. a letter to MacGreevy of 25 July 1933). The grave has necessarily to be a matter of 'down, down, down' (173), as even the Belacqua of 'Yellow' would have been forced to acknowledge. But Beckett amuses himself hugely by harping on the word 'up' throughout: the word occurs, either on its own or in combinations, some 25 times! (cf. 'Echo's Bones', 5, Belacqua to Zaborovna: ' "When you say 'put me up' . . . what do you mean exactly?" '.) Of all these examples perhaps the most telling is the one which has Belacqua 'grinning *up* at the lid' (my emphasis; 175; cf. *Dream*, 146) of his coffin, a favourite notion of Beckett's and a perfect epitome of the 'timeless mock' (173) – it is as if he has not actually died – noted earlier. But so full of life is this little, apparently negligible, word 'up' that we find it even in the '*up*holstered' grave and the '*up*turned box' on which the gardener sits grieving for a while, even if '[l]ike most of us, he is grieving for himself' (Kroll 1977, 56). These, Beckett seems to be saying (although he only does so 'out loud', and only then *en passant*, in 'What A Misfortune') are 'the little things that are so important' (132). Considerations of space in 'Draff' certainly matter as much, if not more than, considerations of time, even with more 'human' considerations emerging as 'all too human' in both the breach and the observance. But of course everything that goes 'up' (including Mr Malacoda, 163, and the parson 'churning up the avenue', 170) must come down, or go 'down, down, down', like Hairy into the grave pit (173).

The spatial dimension is reinforced in 'Draff' by the most memorable descriptions of landscape to be found in *More Pricks*, though 'Fingal', 'Love and Lethe' and 'Walking Out' also have their moments in this respect. In 'Fingal' we learn that 'landscapes were of interest to Belacqua only in so far as they furnished him with a pretext for a long face' (23), and the landscapes in 'Walking Out' are largely exercises in applied pastoral ('Croker's Gallops') or modifications of elements from fairytales (Tom Wood). (A paragraph in 'What A Misfortune' links 'pastoral' and 'fairy tale' [110].) But in 'Draff', landscapes interest Beckett for more complex reasons and work towards more various ends. There is no 'long face' here, but rather a kind of tranquillity, perhaps because the landscape that matters is the cemetery, with the mountains behind. This is Redford cemetery at Greystones (cf. O'Brien, 98 ff.), where Beckett's father had been buried in late July 1933 (cf. the 'uterine/pre-uterine' aspect of 'the rocks at Greystones', *Watt* typescript, HRHRC, 149). A letter to Nuala Costello of 10 May 1934, a fortnight before the publication of *More Pricks*, describes Beckett's visit to 'The Country Boneyard' (*LSB*, 209) at Stoke Poges in Buckinghamshire, the site of Thomas Gray's *Elegy*. But Beckett may well have had in mind Gray's famous line 'And leaves the world to darkness and to me' several months earlier while writing 'Draff', as well as Donne's 'A Nocturnall (i.e., Nocturnall) upon *St Lucies* Day' – even though the implied literary reference seems to be to Paul Valéry's poem 'Le cimetière marin'. At the end of 'Draff', the groundsman who has dug the grave is left, as if he too is dead or might as well be, with 'the company of headstones' and 'the hills observing their Attic vigil in the background' (180). The groundsman decides it is 'A classico-romantic scene', which is a judgement both temporal and spatial in its way, given that ' [s]o it goes in the world' (181), and also out of it.

Beckett seems to be trying for an exceptionally complex narrative effect here in the tension between what 'goes in the world' and what the parson, thinking of the dead Belacqua, piously describes as 'there where there is no time' (170). *More Pricks*, and indeed Beckett himself, has had to move on (as recommended by the Civic Guard at the end of 'A Wet Night'), and the collection has complied with the 'rule' that narrative must always do this, however often a retardation can be introduced, whether for suspense purposes, or to fill in a background, or even simply to forestall forward movement. But Beckett wants in 'Draff' – intended as the last story – to suggest that things have not moved very far since he began the first story 'Dante and the Lobster' (one reason why there are several motifs in 'Draff' that look back to the beginning). A renewed 'commerce with the things of time' (171) underpins a number of time indicators in 'Draff', and chronology obviously rules the roost – 'As a writer he is not altogether at liberty to detach effect from cause' (*PTD*, 11) – given that Belacqua has to be dead before he can be buried. But the drama of the story is in the moment rather than in the sequence of events, as if sequence in itself might ultimately be of limited significance when the essence of living, so utterly different from being dead, is to be found in the passing moment, the moment which is always the same in the sense that it must always be passing. There is no invocation here of the pre-Socratic philosophers mentioned in 'Yellow', but the essentially philosophical notions of recurrence and non-recurrence, of 'the one and the many', are almost certainly part of the substructure of 'Draff'.

Dream emphasizes the importance of 'stases' (35) which it cannot find room for, whereas *More Pricks* is in large part dependent on 'pauses' – in spite of all the fairly feverish movement – on which each of the stories finds it necessary to focus. 'Draff' typifies this general tendency by ending with what is at once a kind of stasis *and* a kind of movement forward into a future beyond any narrating. The splendid final sentence is very cunningly devised to keep us 'where we were, as we were' (13) at the same time that it points (like the thinking of the groundsman earlier, 173) towards an (inconceivable) future. Sequence is inevitably obliged, whether it be operative in a novel or a book of short stories, to come to some kind of halt; narrative has the power (as in the open-ended non-resolutions of 'Ding-Dong', 'A Wet Night' and 'What A Misfortune', for example) to go 'further' into a kind of void which simply cannot fall within the frame of articulation. So – in the many and varied senses of the word *so* – it goes in the world.

There are more '[l]ittle remains' (179) in 'Draff' than immediately meet the eye, and Charles Prentice was well within his rights in thinking it made a better end for the collection than 'Echo's Bones', especially with the revised ending supplied by 'Echo's Bones'. But humankind, 'modulating from porridge to marmalade' (167) and concerned mainly for its own state of health (as the gardener and even the groundsman also are), cannot bear very much reality and does not come well out of it all. For the Smeraldina, 'a husband . . . was oakum in the end the same as everything else, prophylactic', little better than a space-filler even if there is 'some sentimental factor in play (or at work) complicating the position' (175). For Hairy, there is 'the inevitable something more' (173; an 'inevitable nuptial' [91] he seems to hope, though presumably *not* marriage), the 'little something extra' (174) which the narrator cannot bring himself to name. But all that this story can supply Hairy with is the prospect of a *vita nuova* to be enjoyed with Belacqua gone, and with his widow to make up to; yet, the drive out with the Smeraldina into 'the heart of the purple mountains' exhausts Hairy's 'petrol supply' (179–80). The other characters are similarly baulked. For the parson, there is no time to turn (or 'cock up', 178; cf. the late 1933 poem 'Serena III') the other cheek and, indeed, little inclination to exercise Christian forgiveness of the couple who have turfed him out of the car on 'the drive back from the grave' (178). For the gardener there are the difficulties he has to suffer on not finding his vital resources, rose on his watering-can and the line to 'put down' his broccoli, the one stolen, and the other appropriated. For the undertaker Mr Malacoda (cf. the poem 'Malacoda', begun in 1933, but later revised) there is only his 'impatience to cover' (174), no time for more than 'a quick flirt' with Mary Ann (174), and only a job like any other to be done. The Smeraldina, thinking 'That was what he was there for, that was what he was paid for' (175), is unwittingly reprising the Cain figure of the first story 'Dante and the Lobster', although in reference to *Dream* (7) and the 1933 poem 'Spring Song', rather than a straightforward echo. And for the groundsman there is only the consolation of thinking of a quotation from Diderot that Beckett had jotted down in his *'Dream' Notebook* (cf. *Dream*, 175), even if it is manifestly a fantasy.

Only the groundsman, a grounded man, a man with his feet on the ground (though his mind is on a Diderot pleasantry), emerges from all this with very much credit. As Jeri L. Kroll says of him, '[He] is, in fact, one of the most attractive figures in *More Pricks Than Kicks* . . . he is neither a caricature, nor is he ridiculed' (1974, 351), and may even be a surrogate 'persona for the author' (ibid., 350). This perhaps privileges the groundsman over the 'real man at last' – the tinker whom we met briefly in 'Walking Out' – and also over the 'gentlewoman of the people' in 'Ding-Dong'. But in what was certainly (initially) intended to be the last *More Pricks* story, we seem to be once again in the presence of a real man secure in a real scene, a figure who (unlike Belacqua) can 'continue to exist in the same modest way, among the defunct' (Kroll, 354). Yet in their total effect, both the scene and the mood at the end of 'Draff' are such a mixture of grief, relief, acceptance and irony that even the groundsman's simple consolations look rather paltry: 'He sang a little song, he drank his bottle of stout, he dashed away a tear, he made himself comfortable' (181). No doubt Belacqua is 'grinning up at the lid' through all of this, because it is not much of a 'world' to leave, or to leave behind, peopled mostly by the lees of humanity, the 'draff' of swine which Beckett had found in Thomas à Kempis (*DN*, 590; cf. *Dream*, 46). It was also an ideal way of bringing to an end what (by way of Chaucer; *DN*, 1167) he had come to think of as the 'draf of stories', the relics left over from a more heady brew. It was no substitute for being 'made steadfast for ever' (*DN*, 579; from Kempis), but Beckett had stuck to the task, and he could now make himself as 'comfortable' as his circumstances permitted.

'The end, the beginning, is among the hills', Beckett wrote some 3 years later in an assessment of Jack B. Yeats's 'imaginative adventure' *The Amaranthers* (*Disjecta*, 90), which he thought a 'lovely book' (*LSB*, 334). But the end of *More Pricks*, with the hills away in the distance, is much more a matter of what can be seen, felt and heard in the dark. Jack Yeats's 'birds of paradise' (*LSB*, 334) are a far cry from Beckett's 'earth that is Purgatory' (*Disjecta*, 33), and the graveyard effectively becomes the narrow 'world' to which we will all ultimately be confined. The mood here very much resembles that of the first stanza of Donne's 'A Nocturnall (i.e., Nocturnall) upon *St Lucies* Day, being the shortest day' – a text which would surely have moved Beckett even without the St Lucy/Lucia Joyce connection so prominent in *Dream* and so well hidden in *More Pricks* – where we read of how:

> The world's whole sap is sunk:
> The general balm th'hydroptic earth has drunk,
> Whither, as to the bed's feet, life is shrunk,
> Dead and interred; yet all these seem to laugh,
> Compared with me, who am their epitaph.

The groundsman has 'dashed away a tear' (181) and threatens to become, unknown to himself, something of a tutelary spirit in the genius of the place. But it falls to the impersonal narrator to write the 'inscription' which Hairy Quin seems to be unable or unwilling to remember, and to supply the appropriate 'epitaph': 'So it goes in the world'. This sober ending – resembling 'It is not' (14) in that it seems to belong to nobody (cf. the issues raised in the headnote to Chapter 5) – is much better adapted to 'Draff' than it is to 'Echo's Bones', just as at least one joke in the former is 'much more effective' (Lawlor, 2009, 68, n. 75) than it is in the latter, some of the material from which was obviously carried over, or back, in a late revision of 'Draff' (letter of 11 December 1933 from Charles Prentice; UoR). A story beginning with a wry reminder of the writer behind *More Pricks* ('**Shuah, Belacqua**', my emphasis) ends in the anonymous presence of the 'world', with the one waving a kind of 'farewell' (cf. *Dream*, 12) to the other. But in the aftermath of death – as distinct from the moment of death as staged in 'Yellow' – Beckett's propensity to joke has met with something that is obviously no laughing matter, however much resignation he has been able to muster.

In the next section of this study I turn to the 'billet doux' which I deal with as apart from, though it is also of course a part of, *More Pricks*. I go beyond the collection to two stories (with the trace of a third) which came after 'Draff', before turning to how it/they went 'in the world', and then offer a conspectus view of Beckett as storyteller in Chapter 4.

4. Three Stories More: 'The Smeraldina's Billet Doux', 'Echo's Bones', 'A Case In A Thousand'

The two most important of the 'fair to middling' women in *Dream* (the Smeraldina and the Alba) reappear in *More Pricks*. A third – the Syra-Cusa, based on Lucia Joyce – has apparently accepted banishment from the proceedings: 'Be off, puttanina' (*Dream*, 51). *More Pricks* is sufficiently impersonal in its manner, in spite of a few cracks here and there, for the figure of Lucy, a recurrent reference point in the collection, to seem quite unrelated to the Syra-Cusa of *Dream*, even if at least some aspects of Lucia Joyce may have been incorporated into the characterization. Lucy for the most part plays a wholly new role in *More Pricks*, and a much more important one than any the poor Syra-Cusa could possibly have sustained. And neither of the Syra-Cusa's 'rivals' in *Dream* – both of them much more dominant there – are given a comparable prominence in *More Pricks*, although both figure briefly in new contexts: the Alba as a bridesmaid at the wedding in 'What A Misfortune' and the Smeraldina as a widow in 'Draff', where she is shown facing, and apparently tolerating, the amatory attentions of Hairy Quin. We also catch a glimpse of the Smeraldina, or someone very like her (she speaks German when roused!), in the Tom Wood scene in 'Walking Out', although there she becomes almost indistinguishable from her surroundings and from her partner the Tanzherr (cf. *Dream*, 92–3). She does, however, receive the kind of backhanded compliment that none of Belacqua's other women – fair, middling or otherwise – receive in *More Pricks*, Beckett having at some point decided to recycle *Dream* (55 ff.), thereby generating the only first-person speaking voice in a collection which (unlike *Dream*) tries – for the most part successfully – either to keep personal issues under wraps, or to adopt a quasi-impersonal narrative mask to put them under manipulative pressure.

The inclusion of 'The Smeraldina's Billet Doux' means that hers is the only personal voice we hear in *More Pricks*, beyond the dialogues cunningly engineered by the thoroughgoing impersonal narrator, who occasionally even volunteers his own personal voice, though very rarely (and only at length at the beginning of 'Ding-Dong'). Presumably Beckett would not have entertained this strategy for more than a moment if it had not further enabled him to 'exact . . . tumult from unity' (*Disjecta*, 83). But there were other 'sentimental factor[s] in play (or at work) complicating the position' ('Draff', 175). For between Beckett sending *Dream* out to publishers and sitting down to plan something which might add up to a book of stories, the real-life equivalent of the Smeraldina – Peggy Sinclair – had died on 3 May 1933 of tuberculosis (*LSB*, 158).

Beckett had met Peggy, his cousin, in Dublin in the summer of 1928, on a visit from Germany with her family. Subsequently Beckett visited her in Kassel-Wilhelmshöhe on at least five occasions, and Lucia Joyce claimed later that Peggy had visited Beckett during his 2 years in Paris (1928–30). During necessarily prolonged periods apart, Beckett and Peggy Sinclair naturally exchanged letters (cf. *Dream*, 31), none of which have survived. After their relationship failed ('he knew and so did she, [i]t was all over bar the explanations' [*Dream*, 109]), Beckett, back in Dublin at TCD, went to the lengths of asking his friend Thomas MacGreevy to remove the traces of Peggy he had left behind in his rooms at the Ecole Normale Supérieure (letter of 5 October 1930). MacGreevy must have obliged, and no doubt Beckett hoped thereby to expunge a painful episode from his memory. The survival of the Smeraldina into *More Pricks*, however, suggests that the medicine did not quite work. The 'bump[ing] off' ('Echo's Bones', 24) of Belacqua in 'Yellow' is obviously a separate matter, though the net effect, oddly enough, was not dissimilar. It was obviously difficult for Beckett to believe that the dead actually were dead, when stories could make them 'redivivus' (*LSB*, 167; compare the quotation from *Mercier and Camier* in the headnote to Chapter 5).

It is as an 'odd' that I deal here with the 'billet doux', with two other 'odds' ('Echo's Bones' and 'A Case In A Thousand') to follow, only the last of which helped Beckett to put the whole *More Pricks* catastrophe into some kind of perspective.

'The Smeraldina's Billet Doux'

The Smeraldina-Rima is not demonstrable. She has to be taken or left. Belacqua did a little of both. She obliged him to.

(*Dream of Fair to Middling Women*)

Beckett is having so much fun in 'The Smeraldina's Billet Doux' that it would seem a shame to spoil it with a critical assessment of what is for the most part an exercise in ventriloquism. With 'Text' (as published in *The New Review*, also extracted from *Dream* [83]), it was Beckett's first assumption of the female voice – which he would not use again until writing *Happy Days* 25 years later – and it was probably prompted by an unpleasantly vindictive desire to score points off his sometime lover Peggy Sinclair. This billet doux was almost certainly written – if we discount the idea that it was an actual letter that Beckett once received from Peggy – with more than half an eye on the Molly Bloom monologue ('Penelope') which concludes Joyce's *Ulysses*. Molly's monologue famously ends with a ringing 'Yes' in a verbal imitation of orgasm, and it presents Molly between sleep and waking, perhaps on the point of waking up from a wet dream. Beckett's Smeraldina is, by contrast, wide awake, really concentrating hard, if not quite hard enough (to judge from her linguistic problems). Another difference between the two is that Molly's freely associating psyche seems to remove moral considerations (Joyce considered the episode 'amoral', not inviting judgement from any moral standpoint), whereas the Smeraldina threatens to fall within moral strictures, betrayed as she is by her linguistic shortcomings into a veritable barrage of double entendres, euphemisms and tonal slips typically foregrounding sexual matters. Try as she might – and she may not be trying very hard – to be suitably demure and 'correct' in these areas, she comes across as so deeply intrigued by them as to have an unhealthy interest. But the film which she has been to see has, she claims quite justifiably, 'nothing to do with Love (as everyone understands the word)' (143), and the reader is left free to apply the phrase to her billet doux also. Indeed, the whole performance is in so many ways so innocent that it would be absurd to bring any moral censure upon it. In a second burst from the Smeraldina in *Dream* ('Text', from *Dream* [83], as published in *The New Review*), she seems to be the epitome of a much more sophisticated sensuality, buttressed by a much greater acquaintance with English literature and the plays of the Jacobean dramatist John Ford in particular (see Pilling 1999b). But 'Text' is not offered as a billet doux, and in *Dream* it is left 'suitably' obscure that it is as if Beckett were the Smeraldina that is writing it, whereas here his 'presence' is pretty much unavoidable, given the letter writer's insistence on 'Bel, Bel' (143).

The Smeraldina's erratic proficiency in English – in *Dream*, Belacqua wonders how she can speak her 'native tongue' quite so badly (84) – is contrasted with her more natural facility in German from what seems to have been a long residence in Germany. This leads to her saying, in practice and in *writing*, both more and less than she intends. Her intense, sometimes almost sublime, emotions are left looking absurd, although from time to time, as if by accident, she hits a Beckettian nail on the head (notably with 'death is the onely thing'; 143). As already indicated, we do not know, and will now never know, how closely this billet doux resembles Peggy Sinclair's actual letters to Beckett. But 'The Smeraldina's Billet Doux' almost defies credulity in itself: how, we might ask (which is not quite the same question as Belacqua's in *Dream*), could anyone get so much English right while continuing to get so much wrong, or just plain wide of the mark? Some of the Smeraldina's idiomatic phrases would have taken a non-native speaker several years to learn – Peggy had of course been born of Dublin parents – and at the same time some of her mistakes would have been eradicated in an attentive student in just a few weeks. The Smeraldina has apparently not been paying sufficient attention to her studies: her 'blue letter' (144) is some kind of reminder or warning as to her future conduct and commitment. But this letter, 'blue' or otherwise, is largely an exercise in setting words free to see what might become of them.

Beckett clearly realized that even intimate letters (such as this one is supposed to be) rely to a large extent on being constructed from pre-existent material, and perhaps even on previous love letters written to someone else. It was a theme he was to return to in 1936 in the poem 'Cascando'. 'The Smeraldina's Billet Doux' conveys this idea very well, but at the same time manages to demonstrate how letter-writing, even with some inevitably recycled materials, catches the passing moment as nothing else can, which is both its strength and its limitation as a literary device outside of the epistolary novel. Just as the Smeraldina is sitting pen in hand and, it would seem, about to draw her remarks to some kind of conclusion, a letter from Belacqua arrives (145). We are not told what this letter contains, although the tenor (and some of its content) can be inferred from *Dream* (62). This is a reminder, even if Beckett did not intend it as such, that we would not normally violate the unwritten 'rule' that you do not read intimate letters which are not addressed to you. But 'The Smeraldina's Billet Doux' is of course itself a violation of the rule, and it contains a good deal of detail that no doubt a real Smeraldina and a real Belacqua would not really have wished to see bandied about in the public domain.

There is no dateline for 'The Smeraldina's Billet Doux', although on internal evidence – 'Two more weeks of agony pain and sadness' until the '23th' (144) – it would have to be something like '9 December', with a Christmas visit by Belacqua to Kassel in the offing. The year may not much matter, but it cannot be earlier than 1929 – the film *Der Lebende Leichnam* was made in 1928 but only premiered in Berlin in February 1929 – which leaves plenty of time for George Gershwin's hit 'The Man I Love' ('I never longed so much for the man I love', 144) to have crossed the Atlantic from America (unlike the lover of the Smeraldina's new friend, or many of his letters: 'the man she loves, at present he is in Amerika'; 144) and become all the rage in Germany. Gershwin's song was written for, and later dropped from, the musical *Lady, Be Good*. Beckett no doubt wanted to imply that the Smeraldina, with someone to watch over her, is trying to be, and will always try to be, good, even if she may not always be successful; another very popular Gershwin song, 'Someone to Watch over Me', featured in the 1926 musical *Oh, Kay!*

Musicals, films and even classical music (Beckett has Beethoven's 'ferne Geliebte' [*DN*, 1109] in mind, 143) are seen in 'The Smeraldina's Billet Doux' as little more than pleasant pastimes, even if they each, in their different ways, achieve a certain artistic quality. There is also a 'little white statue' (147), quite possibly art deco in style – almost certainly a sensual one. But the Smeraldina clearly takes a particular interest – an interest Belacqua obviously shares – in literature. She quotes Goethe's *Faust*, and quotes it to some effect. She also quotes accurately from another play, although she seems to have forgotten the source – it is Grillparzer's play on the Hero und Leander story *Des Meeres und der Liebe Wellen* – and has obviously completely forgotten the context in which the line quoted occurs. Far from being a prevision of a lovers' tryst, which is what the Smeraldina wants to make it, *'Der Tag will kommen und die stille Nacht'* is, in Grillparzer's play, an expression of relief at the prospect of certain death.

In 'The Smeraldina's Billet Doux', this Grillparzer reference operates – as do many of the literary triggers in *More Pricks* (Dante, Donne, Keats, Joyce, etc.) – as a questionable 'pointer', easily quoted, but less easily negotiated. This strategy is effectively begun on the very first page of section 2 of *Dream*, in only the third paragraph of the actual text, by giving the Peggy Sinclair character the full name of 'the Smeraldina-Rima' (3, and throughout section 2). This eye-catching compound –occasionally shortened to 'Smerry', which is how the Smeraldina refers to herself (*Dream*, 60; *More Pricks*, 140) – is Beckett's way of associating her with two quite unrelated literary heroines: La Esmeralda in Victor Hugo's *Notre-Dame de Paris* (1831) and Rima in W. H. Hudson's *Green Mansions: A Romance of the Tropical Forest* (1904). How well Beckett actually knew either of these novels remains open to question. In a letter to Mania Péron of September 1951, Beckett told her he had been trying to read *Notre-Dame de Paris*, but was finding it 'impossible', so his closest encounter with it most probably came in the form of the film *The Hunchback of Notre Dame* (1923). Perhaps Hudson had been similarly upstaged by the controversial nude Epstein statue (1922) of Rima in Kensington Gardens (mentioned in chapter 5 of *Murphy*). If, however, we choose to go behind Beckett's back, as it were – as with the Grillparzer quotation he has certainly gone behind the Smeraldina's – it seems slightly ominous that, in both these novels, the heroines die tragically. Both are apparently free spirits, a gypsy girl in the Hugo and a 'bird-girl' (cf. *Dream*, 15) in the Hudson. But La Esmeralda is left hanging on a gibbet (book 11, chapter 2), and Rima is burned to death in a fire in the forest. (As indicated in the section on 'Draff' in 'Notesnatchings', some use of Dante's *Inferno* also seems to be present in the mix.)

Beckett must have swiftly registered that, given her tuberculosis, Peggy Sinclair might not live long. But calling her 'the Smeraldina-Rima' in *Dream* – which the other members of the Sinclair family had not read – could hardly be remedied by reducing the 'Rima' element simply to the 'bird-face' of 'Draff' (168), or at least not as long as the 'billet doux' remained a candidate for inclusion in *More Pricks*. Beckett was '[g]lad to hear' from Peggy's brother Morris (*LSB*, 214, 215) that their father bore him no ill will, but it seems that Beckett's rather tasteless resuscitation of the Smeraldina did not go down at all well in Kassel. Did Beckett, one wonders, subsequently regret his inclusion of the 'billet doux' – which seems later to have been the point at which he abandoned his struggle with the proofs of the proposed 1964 edition of *More Pricks*, as documented in Chapter 3 – not just because it upset the Sinclairs, and not just because it came to seem a rather desperate remedy for the shortfall of material imperilling the acceptance of *More Pricks Than Kicks*? It seems almost absurd to say so, but there are enough significant deaths hidden in the fabric of *More Pricks* for Beckett to have started to think that, in anticipating one death (by way of La Esmeralda and Rima), he had unwittingly predicted, and in some sense 'caused', another. The billet doux's 'death is the onely thing' would have looked rather different to Beckett after the events of May and June 1933, however good a jest it was a year or more earlier.

'Smerry' seems happily oblivious of any of the dark implications lurking in her favourite literature. But in her own limited attempts at describing the beauties of the natural world, which are a heady mixture of literature and virtual illiteracy, the dark reasserts itself and offers its own satisfactions. Probably her best effort in this connection occurs early on:

Comeing home there was a new moon, it looked so grand ofer the black trees that it maid me cry. I opened my arms wide and tried to imagine that you were lieing against my breasts and looking up at me like you did those moonlit nights when we walked together under the big chestnut trees with the stars shining through the branches. (143)

Her subsequent excursions into literary landscape sound a bit more strained and mechanical, even if her memory of 'last summer' (in real life either 1929 or 1930) is suitably rosy and sets up an effective contrast with the present much more wintry scene:

Now the snow is all melted and the wood is as black as ever and the sky is allways grey except in the early morning and even then one can onely see spots of red between the black clouds. (146)

The snow that has 'melted' here is intended to figure against what the Smeraldina's mother ('Mammy', as often in *Dream*) is hoping for over the impending Christmas period:

She says the time is flying, it will be no time till Xmas and she says she hopes Frau Holle makes her bed ofen. (146)

Presumably this distinctively German idiom appealed to Beckett in its combination of 'bed' and a name that could almost be read as 'Hölle' (Hell), but what 'Mammy' is hoping for here are the frequent falls of snow that are more than likely to occur in Kassel at Christmas time.

* * *

How much more we as readers now (as distinct from our relatively few predecessors in 1934) are able to make of 'The Smeraldina's Billet Doux' may depend on what is known of Beckett's attitude to Germany and German things, which is arguably a more promising area of inquiry than any lingering resentment Beckett may have felt about how Peggy Sinclair had treated him, or (perhaps more painfully) embarrassment at remembering how he had behaved towards her. 'Beckett and Germany' obviously becomes an even more compelling issue in relation to his German Diaries of 1936–7. But there are earlier indicators, for example, in a letter to Thomas MacGreevy of 21 November 1932:

I'm reading German and learning a little that way. Always when it's coming up to Xmas I get the German fever . . . But I won't see any of it this year [unlike in 1929, 1930–1 and 1931–2], no Homer dusks or red steeples [cf. lines 1–2 of the poem 'Dortmunder']. And soon I will be tired of the Brothers Grimm machinery.

Beckett's most recent visit to Kassel before this letter, during which he wrote the poem 'Dortmunder', had been in January 1932, before he finished *Dream* (begun close to May 1931), but after he and Peggy Sinclair had separated, apparently amicably, as a couple potentially, if never actually, *promessi* ('A Wet Night'). Although in the letter to MacGreevy Beckett seems to have come close to questioning his own need for romantic nostalgia, it is equally evident that more than a few relics of it survived in his memory. His own nostalgia is a much more complicated matter than the nostalgia of the Smeraldina for a time ('last summer') that may not come again – in strict terms, of course, it simply cannot – or her hopes for a future for herself and Belacqua which, even though they have been married by the time of 'Draff', neither of them can long enjoy. (In *More Pricks* we never see them together. 'Draff' tells us that they have been married 'less than a year', and the Smeraldina does not visit Belacqua in hospital in 'Yellow', where he is almost inundated by the number of women who are looking after his needs.)

Beckett's nostalgia is bound up with literature, but literature he is trying to distance himself from. An earlier letter to MacGreevy (29 May 1931; *LSB*, 78–9) shows Beckett put off by what he finds 'flabby' in Goethe and in his *Werther*, understandably a first port of call for Beckett in a literature and a language which he had never been formally taught. So perhaps it was unwise of the Smeraldina to invoke *Faust*, even if Beckett was later to go on to take copious notes from it (see Dirk van Hulle's essay in *SBT/A*, 16). Beckett probably knew the words the billet doux was quoting not directly from *Faust*, but rather from Schubert's famous song 'Gretchen am Spinnrade'. The words convey a sense of incurable pain which can easily be matched in Beckett's private correspondence, and a nagging, anguished awareness of the horizon of death which seems never to have left him. This is why the Smeraldina starts out by saying that 'death is the onely thing' and why Beckett gives her the line from Grillparzer at the end of her billet doux, at the same time hoping that the alert reader will not forget the tragic context from which the line is taken. (It is no accident that Grillparzer's play also flickers faintly into view in *Malone Dies*.) No doubt Beckett's feelings in these areas needed nothing specifically German to stimulate them, or to keep them at the forefront of his mind. But he may well have been a little disappointed at finding them so fully and articulately developed in a culture with which he was only indirectly familiar, with that very familiarity dependent on a love affair now definitively over. 'The Smeraldina's Billet Doux' may simply have been extracted from *Dream* to add a few (but really only a very few) pages to *More Pricks Than Kicks*, although it is certainly possible that Beckett did so in an attempt to expel feelings difficult to express, which the Smeraldina, even with all her linguistic errors to blur them, so memorably conveys.

'The Smeraldina's Billet Doux' had something of an afterlife, although ironically when it did so (and when Beckett had reached precisely this point in reading the Grove Press proofs for their proposed reprint of *More Pricks Than Kicks* – this would have been the first American edition), it was borne in upon Beckett that the project was a 'ghastly mistake' (letter to Barney Rosset of 20 October 1964), that he would much rather repay the advance he had received than go any further with it, and that he would advise his English publisher likewise. Perhaps this self-censorship was belated reparation of a kind. But with all the parties to the situation long dead, 'The Smeraldina's Billet Doux' can of course be enjoyed, or by the same token endured, without worrying too much over its darker implications. It can be seen either as a well sustained, if rather perverse, performance or, alternatively, as one that outstays its welcome and becomes a rather pointless exercise, simply a useful variant on the 'de-stabilization' principle operative throughout *More Pricks Than Kicks*. In the terms offered by *Dream* (13), it has to be 'taken or left'. However we choose to react to it, 'The Smeraldina's Billet Doux' can stand or fall on its own, as was true of its appearance in *Dream*, and still true on its reincorporation into *More Pricks*, a collection to which it hardly seems to belong in any meaningful sense, and from which it could very easily have been extracted, had not Charles Prentice found 'Smerry's letters . . . as superb as ever' (letter of 5 July 1932; UoR), amidst much else that obviously gave him something of a headache ('It would be stupid to query things I admit I can't quite get hold of'). Prentice's letter seems to raise the intriguing possibility that *Dream* may once have contained more than one billet doux, but no doubt both Prentice and Beckett were happy, or happy enough, to settle for just one in the very different world of *More Pricks Than Kicks*.

'Echo's Bones'

Say what you will, you can't keep a dead mind down.

('What a Misfortune')

The twenty-eight-and-a-half typed pages of 'Echo's Bones' (housed in the Lawrence E. Harvey collection at Dartmouth College, New Hampshire) were written in late 1933 in an attempt to comply with Charles Prentice's sense that the *More Pricks* collection would benefit from the addition of another story. Beckett obviously experienced some difficulty in adding material to a book he was ready to forget and leave to others, especially after working hard on revising it as a whole. After some 5 weeks he sent Prentice what the two men seem to have come to think of as '10,000 yelps' (letter from Prentice to Beckett, 2 November 1933; UoR), only for Prentice to realize that the new story, far from adding to the potential success of *More Pricks*, would actually leave it much more vulnerable to criticism. Obviously very embarrassed at having to recommend its omission, Prentice was compelled to ask whether Beckett would accept, with the book's best interests at heart, that Chatto proceed with it in its original format; Beckett had really no option but to agree. If 'Echo's Bones' had been added to *More Pricks*, it would have been, with 'A Wet Night' and 'What A Misfortune', one of the three longest stories. But, the story effectively became (by accident rather than design) an epitome of the principle of 'draff'. *Draff* had been, or had become, Beckett's provisional working title, which had itself become a casualty of the editorial negotiations that Prentice and Beckett had been conducting for some months in a cordially collaborative manner.

Beckett told MacGreevy (*LSB*, 170–3) that he had put a lot of effort into writing 'Echo's Bones', and evidence of this is everywhere on the surface of the story, which is often as difficult to follow as 'What A Misfortune'. Generically speaking, it is a brilliant but very conflicted mishmash, ultimately not one thing but many. As such, it was a kind of confirmation of what Beckett had been up to in *More Pricks* proper. But it is in no sense a culmination of the collection, the tensions within which could never have been resolved in some final 'statement' akin to that of Joyce in 'The Dead' at the end of *Dubliners*. 'Echo's Bones' begins in Beckett's version of the Gothic or ghost story mode, in Irish writing perhaps best epitomized by Sheridan LeFanu, whose *In A Glass Darkly* of 1872 contains a story ('The Room in the Dragon Volant') in which the undead 'Richard Beckett' – 'Monsieur Beckett', as he is known in France – is 'taken into the realm of the dead, if only a little way' (xviii). But even in revivifying a once dead Belacqua in three new contexts, 'Echo's Bones' shows Beckett treating his material in a way reminiscent of Walter Draffin's 'book' in 'What A Misfortune': 'he refused to regard it anything more than a dump for whatever he could not get off his chest in the ordinary way' (125). There are probably more 'borrowings' in 'Echo's Bones' than in any of the other stories, so many indeed that they effectively throttle the story's ability to move towards some determined end. The imaginary title of an imaginary book by the imaginary author Mr C[lavius] F[rederick] Earbrass in Edward Gorey's *The Unstrung Harp* (1953) – *More Chains Than Clank* – rather neatly reflects the creative constraints operating in Beckett's 'Echo Bones', even though Gorey could not possibly have known of the story's existence. For far from Beckett rejoicing in a kind of freewheeling fantasia, the evidence suggests he was deliberately hampering any real chance of the impulse to tell a story coming to fruition, and he cannot have been wholly surprised when Charles Prentice felt moved to turn it down.

'Echo's Bones', unlike most of the *More Pricks* stories, has a very simple tripartite structure comprising three 'encounters and contretemps' (127), which have only the figure of Belacqua in common, and which do not permit any interactivity between its three bit-part players, Zaborovna Privet, Lord Haemo Gall and the gravedigger Mick Doyle. The sexual issues arising in the case of the first of these encounters recur in the case of the second, but are largely deferred in this middle 'panel' of the triptych (with Belacqua and Lord Gall obviously the people who matter), and then dropped altogether in the third section, which is largely dependent on re-contextualizing Hamlet's encounter with the logic-chopping functionary in the graveyard towards the end of Shakespeare's play. Given the choice between '*l'Amour*' and '*la Mort*' – which 'Love and Lethe' wants to suggest are much the same thing anyway (90) – Belacqua favours the latter, although he would obviously prefer what Mr Rooney in *All That Fall* calls 'fully certified death' to this semi-purgatorial dreaming back through experiences apparently brought to an end in 'Draff', now having to be gone through again with even less pleasure than the first time. Belacqua has to be a body for the purposes to which Zaborovna Privet and Lord Gall wish to put him, so no doubt it is as well that 'Draff' has seen him buried rather than cremated. Like Peter Schlemiel in Chamisso's classic fairy tale, however, Belacqua cannot cast a shadow, and for all his physical woes (as he sees them) he is really little more than a spirit, 'wandering to find home' (as chapter 1 of *Murphy* will later put it). The extravagantly high spirits of the story cannot in fact conceal that its message is a profoundly gloomy one. A character who has been 'killed off' with relief is now left – like Hamlet in the 'nunnery' speech to Ophelia (Act III, scene 1) – 'crawling between earth and heaven', a resident of neither; he is, as we learn in the third panel of this triptych, no longer even to be found in '[t]he loveliest little lap of earth you ever saw' (173), since the story requires him to be up and about again.

There is a great deal of 'knockabout' on display here (as the story at one point [26] admits; Beckett later uses the same term in the O'Casey review in *Disjecta* [82]), but the deeper levels of grief and anger are never really masked. Beckett's devastation at having lost his father is hilariously transposed by making Belacqua father a child (a girl, when Lord Gall wanted a boy to ensure the succession on the Wormwood estate) with the hapless Moll Gall, and by suggesting that someone (presumably Hairy Quin, though he is not specified) has impregnated the Smeraldina. Lord Gall, who has no *hair*, also has no *heir*. This is one of the best jokes here precisely because, unlike many others, it is left unspoken. But the jokes of which so much is made are a mask for the sadness which cannot be contained. Beckett's real grief, in remaining unexpressed (and still only to be glimpsed in passing in 'Lightning Calculation' a year later), is left unrelieved, making it impossible to know how or whether it might have been eased if expressed more directly. The *More Pricks* 'game' is kept going, but the will to see it through to a resolution has obviously atrophied to almost nothing. 'Echo's Bones' suffers from what Beckett was later to describe, in a review of the poetry of Denis Devlin, as 'the need that in its haste to be abolished cannot pause to be stated' (*Disjecta*, 91), and there was no corresponding 'need that is the absolute predicament of particular human identity' that could be found to displace it.

The long preamble to 'Echo's Bones' perhaps reflects Beckett's uncertainty as to how best to proceed with the story. None of the *More Pricks* stories (not even 'Ding-Dong') begins quite so independently of what is to follow, such that 'Echo's Bones' has to begin again at the beginning (as the narrator emphasizes) on the second page of the typescript. There is a certain amount of hysterical 'fun' in this preamble, but Beckett had presumably decided to have most fun in the dialogue exchanges to follow. Zaborovna Privet materializes (as her name effectively admits) out of nothing, and as something of a 'hedge' against a background in which a dying Galloway cow features briefly. The dialogue between Belacqua and Zaborovna retards any action of the kind in which Zaborovna is most interested; this is not so much the deferment of ultimate pleasure that prolongs its attraction as a reflection of Belacqua's reluctance to act on his own behalf and volition. Zaborovna behaves like the bad fairy or wicked stepmother in a fairy tale, and writhes like the Gorgon of classical mythology (6). But in dialogue she plays a fairly reactive role, unlike Lord Gall, who needs to be proactive if his plot is to 'bear fruit' and who even manages to impress Belacqua from time to time with instances of quick-wittedness that belie his general demeanour as a monstrous oaf, literally and figuratively.

Weighing in at 25 stone (9), Lord Gall is a giant out of the stock-in-trade of fairy tales, and partly intended to be a kind of threat, however harmless he turns out to be. 'Echo's Bones' is at its best in this middle section, because the kind of battle that is taking place between the two men gives each of the combatants some weapons with which to work.

With the gravedigger Mick Doyle, said to be a Dubliner though his speech does relatively little to make this stick, Belacqua is back on safe (home) ground, rather than up in the air on the back of an ostrich, here mysteriously (for a flightless bird) able to convey its passengers over a considerable distance, if at some cost to its strength. The ostrich eventually becomes fatigued, but the real fatigue (which perhaps reflects Beckett's own efforts in the middle section) kicks in during this third section, with Doyle searching for something Belacqua knows he cannot find, and Beckett having to confront something he would prefer to avoid. Maintaining 'Echo's Bones' as it was at its best would have entailed even more effort than Beckett had already expended, and it is hard not to feel that, while Beckett left the surface of the story bristling with as much difficulty as he could muster, it was being undermined from within by difficulties which could not really be brought to the surface.

By the time the story reaches its inconsequential end, the very title has come to seem all too apt; there are so many echoes here that they seem to multiply to infinity, and yet they are little more than the bare bones of material without any overarching purpose to animate. Beckett knew from reading Ovid's *Metamorphoses* that 'Echo's bones were turned to stone' (*DN*, 1101), and the better parts of the story can be seen as 'stony ground but not entirely' as later explored in the 1965 text *Assez* (*Enough*). But Beckett must have felt that he had done enough ('Ample', as Mrs Nixon drily remarks after enduring four stanzas of the doggerel poem 'To Nelly' in the opening scene of *Watt*) in making *More Pricks* a publishable entity in the first place, without having to supply a 'fagpiece' (2) which could only weaken the effect of the whole, however much it might bulk out its substance. He was sufficiently aggravated by Prentice's rejection of the story to write a poem with the title 'Echo's Bones', the 'muffled revels' in the poem becoming something of a retroactive critique of the story's overheated high spirits, deliberately excessive in a failed attempt to 'whisper the turmoil down' (as in the 1929 story 'Assumption', in its own way no less extravagant a product, but without any basis in really profound personal feeling). Beckett included the poem in a letter to MacGreevy (*LSB*, 171); but he felt ruefully obliged (almost) to concede: 'No doubt [Prentice] was right. I tell him so'. It was the things of which the story could not tell that left the bitterest aftertaste to an enterprise unwillingly begun, doggedly continued and then pointlessly revived just when it seemed to be all over. Almost the only benefit to be derived from it was some material added to the last-minute revision of 'Draff' (cf. 'the new little bit at the end' of the letter of 11 December 1933 from Prentice to Beckett; UoR) which gave the final tableau there just the right amount of resignation and resonance to seem an apt 'send-off' to *More Pricks* as a whole, the material which 'Draff' and 'Echo's Bones' have in common being much better modelled in the former than in the latter. It remains a moot point, however, whether 'Echo's Bones' is too much in the spirit of *Dream* to force its way into an 'ideal' *More Pricks Than Kicks*, since there would have been no place for it even in the wide latitudes of the former (with both Belacqua and Beckett's father still alive), just as there was to be no home for it in the more constricted confines of the latter (with them both dead). It may be preferable to situate it within – if always to be detached from – the *More Pricks* ambience, rather than see it as a retrograde step. But there is little doubt that, at the time of its rejection by Prentice, Beckett must have felt that he had been saved – without really deserving such a blessing in disguise – from having in a way dishonoured the memory of his father, more so even than in the story 'Draff', where the humour is less wild, and where the grief is made quietly eloquent, even for a reader without access to the personal tragedy which lies behind it. The story 'Lightning Calculation', which I deal briefly with below, was in part an attempt to make amends where, given the irreversible facts of the matter, no amount of retraction and retrenchment could ever remedy the condition of spirit in which Beckett still found himself. It was only in that story, written some 12 months after 'Echo's Bones', that Beckett could cast a retrospective glance over what had proved to be rather more than just a damp squib in a firework display which had never quite lived up to expectations, and which had in fact only added to a pain that could not be removed. He may not have felt that, in the circumstances, 'Draff' was a wholly appropriate response to 'the entire process of [his father's death], from the falling ill to the interment'; but no doubt 'Echo's Bones' had contributed even more to what had become 'a talkie in his brain of almost continuous performance, featuring himself in postures that impressed him as ignoble' ('Lightning Calculation').

Kicks against the Pricks

Beckett's brief and none too profitable career as a short story writer was extended for a few more months and for a little more money (ten shillings and sixpence; letter to MacGreevy of 18 August 1934) by the acceptance of 'A Case In A Thousand' in the Christmas number of *The Bookman*, the last issue of the magazine. (An odd kind of circle was thereby created, 'Dante and the Lobster' having appeared in the last number of the *émigré* journal *This Quarter* in 1932.) After this Beckett sent an even shorter story, 'Lightning Calculation', to magazine editors (*Lovat Dickson's Weekly* and *Life and Letters*; *LSB*, 243, 247), but it was not accepted.

'A Case In A Thousand'

> *Ah', [Arsene] said, 'the unconscious mind! What a subject for a short story!'*
> (Watt *typescript, HRHRC, 149*)

Although the bibliographers Raymond Federman and John Fletcher first made the existence of 'A Case In A Thousand' a matter of record in 1970 – presumably prompted to do so by Beckett himself – Beckett seems never to have considered the story part of the strict 'canon' of his work. There may in fact be no better example of exactly what Beckett meant when, having recently read Ernst Cassirer's study of Kant in the first few months of 1938, he entered the phrase 'short stories antinomial' in his *'Whoroscope' Notebook* (see my discussion of this Kantian term at the very beginning of Chapter 1). Indeed, the antinomial or ancillary status of 'A Case In A Thousand' seems to have been little altered either by its inclusion in *The Complete Short Prose 1929–1989* (1995, 18–24), by Ruby Cohn's own *Canon* (2001, 67–8) or by the imaginative but limited critical attention which the story has received. This unsurprisingly piecemeal response has, perhaps equally predictably (given the nature of the story, combined with its unstable status), demonstrated the inability of commentators to agree how best to assess it. For any interested party – and there have not been very many – there are still at least three questions which remain unanswered: Is it helpful to bring Joyce into the equation? Is it helpful to apply psychoanalytic concepts? Is it most helpful to apply those concepts, and then show them to be inadequate? Perhaps no treatment of the story can hope finally to resolve these issues, given the way or ways in which 'A Case In A Thousand' makes its own case, or refuses to do so. There are, however, as I shall subsequently show, some alternative approaches which shed some light from outside the fragile, or simply too indeterminate, confines of the story as it manifests or fails to manifest itself. 'A Case In A Thousand' actually sheds a good deal of retrospective light on what Beckett had been trying to achieve with *More Pricks* and how he needed to move beyond it, and still further beyond Joyce, to continue creatively. In his *Dubliners* stories, Joyce had famously and fastidiously practised an art of 'scrupulous meanness', but 'A Case In A Thousand' is much meaner and much less scrupulous. Gone are the elaborate strategies and verbal exuberance of *More Pricks*, and in their place an oddly quiet voice seems to prevail. So quiet, indeed, that one of the key 'points' in the story – a revelation which might with Joyce have led to an 'epiphany' – is simply omitted, or rather mentioned without this supplying any 'elucidation' of its content (24). This is a gesture which seems very much in accord with 'No, I *won't* say everything, I *won't* tell you everything' (*Dream*, 72), but here it occurs in a context from which any 'I' presence seems to have been entirely removed.

It was never, of course, part of Joyce's purpose in *Dubliners* to 'say' or to 'tell' everything; if it had been, he would hardly have needed to adopt a mode of 'scrupulous meanness'. But with Joyce this did not mean that he deliberately flaunted his refusal to supply the necessary information, or flouted the convention that an author must at least attempt to do this. 'A Case In A Thousand', in complete contrast to Joyce, has no intention of satisfying this 'requirement'. John P. Harrington has treated 'A Case In A Thousand' as 'Beckett's *Dubliners* story', but Beckett is here in many ways further from Joyce than he had ever been before, even if the unnamed location of the 'action' of the story is Dublin (cf. O'Brien, 200–1), and even if the story is not obviously very daring from any other point of view. The parallels which Harrington adduces with Joyce's 'A Painful Case' (37–40) in his interesting but ultimately unconvincing essay surely 'take longer to meet than most' (*Disjecta*, 78), and so far as I can see cannot usefully be said even to meet at infinity.

Nor do the numerous pages of psychology notes taken by Beckett at or around this time seem to have had very much bearing on 'A Case In A Thousand' either. Beckett is resolutely objective in his presentation of the facts of this 'case', as if he were demonstrating, and not just simply asserting (as he had done in 'Echo's Bones', 14), that he had no interest in analysing motives for behaviour, simply in offering the outcomes of behaviour. Almost the only memorable shaft of light in 'A Case In A Thousand' is Dr Nye's recognition 'Myself I cannot save', a kind of back-formation from the crucified Christ of Matthew 27.42 (cf. Rabinovitz, 70, n. 16). This is memorable because it is surrounded on all sides by almost toneless gestures of a 'He said/She said' or 'He did/She did' type. We may choose to think that it is a doctor's responsibility (and also his or her job) to try to 'save' the life of someone other than himself or herself, but we swiftly discover this is not going to happen in this case in a thousand, an outcome which seems in some way anticipated by – almost generated by – Dr Nye's sudden shaft of self-awareness (cf. Rabinovitz, 65, and Phil Baker, 2: 'As Nye's self-knowledge deepens, the boy's condition worsens'). In this instance, then, over against 'a suppression of information' (Hunter, 236), we seem to have been given something analogous to what Harrington (40) calls 'ironic manipulation'. O'Hara even goes so far as to propose that this self-involved half-thought is a necessary stage in what may ultimately be a 'possible source of therapeutic recovery' for both Dr Nye and Mrs Bray (1997, 42). It seems much more probable that it was mere perversity that led Beckett, in allowing Dr Nye's thoughts to (as it were) speak for themselves, to feel under no compulsion to speak further on their behalf, which does indeed amount to another kind of 'suppression'. But this is also arguably a way for Beckett to deliberately (if silently) critique the 'talking cure' of psychoanalysis (cf. Rabinovitz, 67), even if Mrs Bray and Dr Nye can with sufficient ingenuity be shown to replicate the different timeframes and intensities of 'mourning' and 'melancholy' as analysed by Freud in a famous section of his *Beyond The Pleasure Principle* in 1920 (Robins, 423), an essay with which Beckett must nevertheless by this point in time have been familiar (cf. *LSB*, 185).

Suppression is also the name of the game in the way 'A Case In A Thousand' tells us almost nothing about Dr Nye, his 'old schoolfellow' friend (20, 24), Surgeon Bor (cf. O'Brien 358, n. 16) or Mrs Bray. There is not very much room in 'A Case In A Thousand' for what we are actually going to be told, and certainly not nearly enough for us to gauge in what light the few events in the story are to be judged. Adrian Hunter speaks of 'the occlusion of perspective' (236) here, which seems very apt, although this is perhaps part of a larger 'occlusion' which seems also to have affected tone, motive, corroborating detail or even significance – in fact, any of the elements which we might, surely legitimately, look for or expect to find in a short story. As Philip Robins says (421), this leaves us with 'an oddly hollow feeling'. Neither the death of Dr Nye (as projected by him), nor the death of his patient, Mrs Bray's boy, prompts the author to a flurry of exclamation marks comparable with those which Beckett applies to Marcel's realization at the Duchesse de Guermantes' gathering late in the *Recherche* (*Proust*; in *PTD*, 77–8), or even to the studied casualness employed in 'writing out' most of the key female figures in *More Pricks* at the beginning of the last story 'Draff':

Thelma née bboggs perished of sunset and honeymoon that time in Connemara. Then shortly after that they seemed all to be dead, Lucy of course long since, Ruby duly, Winnie to decency, Alba Perdue [obviously a *Recherche* too far!] in the natural course of being seen home [by Walter Draffin, of all people, towards the end of 'What A Misfortune']. (167)

This is summary execution if you like. But it takes time and it leaves a mark, whereas the death of Mrs Bray's boy scarcely seems to ruffle the surface of 'A Case In A Thousand', a surface which is almost certainly a mask for other feelings too deep to be expressed. What does leave a mark here is the way the story emphasizes several eminently 'real' details, none of which seems to possess any ambiguity, yet none of which actually *says* anything, much like Mrs Bray's hat, which (we are told) she wears at all times, yet is only mentioned once (22). Equally enigmatic is the fact that Mrs Bray is 'paying no heed' to the complicated 'manoeuvre' which will enable a barge to 'pass through the lock', in due course to be seen 'working clear of the dock', an event which engages the attention of 'three groups . . . one on the bridge and one on either bank' (19) although it seems to have little to do with the primary action of the story. 'A Case In A Thousand' is all the time playing fast and loose with what it discloses and conceals. We are told at every opportunity how someone 'stood', how they 'sat down' or how they 'stretched' out – this in a story with Mrs Bray presumably standing still for hours on end every day – but nothing about the boy in bed. There is no indication whatsoever of what Mrs Bray's boy – Dr Nye and Surgeon Bor's patient – is doing, thinking or feeling, even though we read early on of children 'waiting angrily' for the rain to stop (18) and of 'the distant furious crying of a child' (18).

These supposedly 'real' details, like the umbrella with a handle 'carved in bog-oak to represent a bird' (20), Mrs Bray's nose with a 'strawberry mottle' (20), her breath 'smelling heavily of clove and peppermint' (20) or her eating of an orange (23), seem to possess no real mystery, and yet are left looking mysterious. But these enigmas are completely upstaged – which is perhaps an apt word in such a staged environment – by other elements repeated so often that Beckett can hardly have been unaware of them. In just over six pages of 'A Case In A Thousand' (as reprinted in *The Complete Short Prose*, 18–23) there are more than 50 instances of words denoting looking, seeing, watching, eyes, or other optical or facial indicators, more than 7 per page on average. The word 'face' itself occurs at least seven times, and examples of 'seen', 'saw' or 'sight' six times. Most numerous are 'look' and 'looking' (eight times) and 'watch' and 'watching' (ten times). The reader is being invited to visualize these various, though in fact strictly limited, *scenes*, but is given no help in interpreting what is being insisted upon. We are left a little like the sister who surveys the 'tableau' of Mrs Bray and Dr Nye together behind the screen, and who, having 'peeped' round the corner, leaves them there, 'having *seen* what she had *seen*' (22, my italics).

What the sister had seen is never disclosed, just as Mrs Bray 'did not disclose the trauma at the root' of Dr Nye's feelings for her when he was a boy, when – she alleges – ' "You were always in a great hurry to grow up so's you could marry me"' (20). S. E. Gontarski, in his introductory essay to *The Complete Short Prose* (xxi), treats this 'trauma' as indicative of Dr Nye being as much a 'patient' as the boy, lying stretched out in a 'kind of therapeutic trance' (21), he apparently hopes to help. Cohn (2001, 68) sees the situation as 'a metaphor for ejaculation', perhaps influenced by O'Hara's judgement that Dr Nye's therapy is 'directed at himself' (39). Gontarski himself follows O'Hara in suggesting that the 'trivial and intimate' matter which 'need not be enlarged on here' (24) – as indeed it is not – may very well be 'the young Nye's curiosity about female anatomy, in particular whether or not women have penises' (xxi; cf. O'Hara, 41, with reference to a 1905 paper by Freud, 'Analysis of a Phobia in a Five-Year-Old Boy', echoes of which O'Hara also hears in *'From An Abandoned Work'*). But this is surely to turn a fictional enigma into a real 'case' and to ignore the fact that (as Phil Baker stresses) this is 'a wilfully enigmatic text' (4). It is only on this basis, however, that Gontarski can extend O'Hara's argument by suggesting that the case in a thousand of which the title seems to make so much is 'not (or not only) the young boy's empyema but Nye's disorder, impotence perhaps, as well' (xxi). This may be why 'Dr Nye belonged to the sad men' (18) or – in the absence of clear-cut evidence – it equally well may not. Presumably Dr Nye's interest in 'buttocks, male and female' (19), an interest apparently confined to horses at the beginning of *Dream* (1), could just as easily have made him 'that sad man' (24), without actual impotence having entered into the equation. As *Dream* (199) later puts it, in a passage which obviously had to be omitted from 'A Wet Night' (47), 'the plot looks as if it might begin to thicken'; however, the 'sad man' behind 'A Case In A Thousand' is kept out of sight.

Gontarski's analysis supplies exactly what the story is determined to leave undisclosed, and it takes no account of a very curious letter to MacGreevy of 4 August 1932, written almost exactly 2 years before 'A Case In A Thousand' was published in *The Bookman*. The scene described (*LSB*, 112–13) is not in Dublin, but in London, in St James's Park, and concerns a little boy at play, calling out to his 'Nanny'. Beckett calls the game that the boy is playing 'empty buses', which prompts him, in the letter to MacGreevy, to add both a Proustian colouring (an allusion to the celebrated opening pages of *Du côté de chez Swann*, with the infant Marcel longing for a kiss from his mother before going to sleep; cf. O'Hara, 39) and a wry Beckettian twist, substituting the nanny figure for the mother figure who, in any Oedipal scenario, cannot openly be acknowledged as an erotic focus. The Proustian and quasi-Freudian aspects of the situation were obviously intended to catch MacGreevy's eye. However, as is so often the case with Beckett's analogical plays with pre-existent cultural and/or intellectual materials, what was really uppermost in Beckett's mind in 'having seen what he had seen' was something that could not be seen but could nevertheless be felt: nothing less than an inner drama of loss and gain specific to his own life, with or without the famous '*fort/da*' (gone away/there) game of Freud's grandson to buttress it. It was on Beckett's return from answering a call of nature at Piccadilly Circus Underground Station that he found the little boy and his nanny had left the park. In their absence, and after the fact in writing to MacGreevy, Beckett plays his own game of 'empty buses', spinning an elaborate fantasy of falling in love (principally, it would seem, so as to be in a position to write lots of poems!), having a child and engaging a nanny. Beckett imagines this fantasy nanny in terms of details derived from his own childhood nanny Bridget Bray (the 'Bibby' of *Dream* [8], 'now mother of thousands by a gardener'), who sucked the very same peppermint creams that surface in 'A Case In A Thousand' and who had the very same 'strawberry mottle' on her nose (Knowlson 1996, chapter 1, section 5).

The little boy who had been playing 'empty buses' was obviously of some help in imagining – presenting or re-presenting, as the doctors and psychiatrists might say – the children who are waiting for the rain to stop ('so that they might go out to play', 18). But all the 'play' in 'A Case In A Thousand' – both all the game-playing, and all the theatricality – belongs to Beckett, or to his studiously impersonal storytelling alter ego. It may or may not be profitable to relate this to Joyce's 'classical temper' and the artist-god paring his fingernails, but the balance of probability suggests the latter. Literary creation, in this configuration, comes to seem less a matter of compensatory fantasy and more a matter of forced moves. Far from emulating the Mlle Glain of 'Dante and the Lobster' and 'honing after a penny's worth of scandal' (12), Beckett seems intent on burying still further the scenes, primal or otherwise, which were for him in some kind of causal relationship with the notion of 'trauma'. Beckett knew perfectly well that this was what any more or less accomplished psychotherapist would have expected him to do, and indeed would have required him to have already done for any interpretative analysis to be undertaken on his behalf for his potential benefit. But here Beckett is complying with this 'requirement' consciously, not unconsciously, and in such a way as to ensure that the trauma remains impossible to retrieve.

Mrs Bray and Dr Nye are, we are told, 'making great efforts to speak their minds' (23), but the text seems to be doing exactly the opposite. The net effect is to make actions (which are what we mostly have) speak louder than words, but without the words thereby assuming very much importance. The words actually spoken in 'A Case In A Thousand' remain mundane, functional and without any inflection. All this is happening in a story whose title promises something exceptional. But this case in a thousand turns out to be one of no particular significance. Indeed, the final gesture of the story is towards a quite different case in (no doubt many more than) a thousand, certainly the second such case in the story and perhaps – if Gontarski's analysis is to the point – even the third, with Dr Nye going off to try Wasserman's test on an old schoolfellow friend (24), a friend he has visited 'professionally' at about the midpoint of the story (20). Presumably the results, when they come through, will be no more ambiguous than the diagnosis of the empyema(s) from which Mrs Bray's boy suffers; the test, though the story does not tell us this, is for syphilis (cf. a letter to MacGreevy of 6 February 1936; *LSB*, 314; and the '*spirochaeta pallida*' of 'Echo's Bones', 11). But, as if determined to emulate the nursing sister who has 'seen what she has seen', the story brings the curtain down upon this quite separate issue before anything resembling an 'elucidation' (24) can occur, in yet another refusal to supply what any reader might need to determine the significance of a given detail. Early in the *Proust* essay Beckett claims that Proust is 'not altogether at liberty to detach effect from cause' (*PTD*, 11) – a 'liberty' which the syntax of the phrasing seems almost contrived to confer on Beckett the critic – and presents Proust as having to 'accept regretfully the sacred ruler and compass of literary geometry' (*PTD*, 12). As we have seen with the stories of *More Pricks Than Kicks*, this 'ruler' and this 'compass' had been accepted equally regretfully by Beckett, although where possible, and to the best of his ability, he had tried to undermine them. But 'A Case In A Thousand' is perhaps the first story Beckett had written in which he turns the 'literary geometry' back upon itself by situating (in more than one sense of the word) everything at the level of 'effect' and leaving 'cause' exclusively in the hands of, or in the mind of, the reader.

It is difficult if not impossible to estimate what effect, if any, some 7 or 8 months of psychotherapy had exerted on 'A Case In A Thousand'. But one way or another Beckett had by August 1934 come to realize that there could be nothing more mysterious than a fact clearly described, always provided that the fact in question could be left questionable by the absence of any 'background pushed up as a guarantee' (*Dream*, 13). In his first published essay 'Dante . . . Bruno.Vico..Joyce' (1929) Beckett had praised what he saw as 'the savage economy of hieroglyphics' (*Disjecta*, 28) in Joyce's *Work In Progress* and, although 'A Case In A Thousand' in its plainness is at quite the opposite end of the spectrum from *Work In Progress*, there is perhaps something in its own way as 'savage' at work here. Of Proust, in equally strong terms, Beckett had written, 'His eye functions with the cruel precision of a camera' (*PTD*, 27). While 'A Case In A Thousand' contains nothing which explicitly requires its reader to think in terms of the cinema – as, by contrast, there certainly is in 'Lightning Calculation' ('a talkie in his brain of almost continuous performance'; UoR typescript, page 1) and, to much more dramatic effect, in chapter 11 of *Murphy* – the story is so optically obsessive, and possesses so little literary surface, that it could almost have served as a shooting script. The sheer popular appeal of films in the early days of the 'talkie[s]' must have seemed a very mixed blessing to a writer so suspicious of 'vulgarity' as Beckett claimed to be (*PTD*, 81), but his high-mindedness had got him nowhere. 'I seem to be sailing dangerously near Gide's BANAL', Beckett told MacGreevy (7 August 1934; *LSB*, 217) in the very month that 'A Case In A Thousand', together with his pseudonymous 'Recent Irish Poetry' (supposedly written by 'Andrew Belis'), was appearing in *The Bookman*.

Beckett's letter shows that he was familiar with a passage in a lecture given by Gide in 1900 and collected in the first of three volumes of *Prétextes* (1903, 1911, 1924):

> A great man has but one concern: to become as human as possible – or, to put it better, to become *commonplace* [*banal*]. . . . The wonderful thing is that he thus becomes more personal. But he who flees humanity for himself alone, succeeds only in becoming special, bizarre, incomplete. (31)

Beckett had taught Gide (see Le Juez, 33–48) at TCD, had assessed his shortcomings in *Proust* and 'Le Concentrisme' (*PTD*, 20; *Disjecta*, 39–40), had offered a book-length essay on him to Chatto (letter to Prentice of 8 February 1932) and had experienced difficulties in so doing (letters to MacGreevy of ?27 August and 13 September 1932; *LSB*, 121). Gide remained a reference point in later letters: to Nuala Costello (27 February 1934; *LSB*, 186), to MacGreevy (7 August 1934; *LSB*, 217) and to George Reavey (9 January 1935). But it is only Gide's notion of the 'banal', and not his typical subject matter or style of writing, that has very much to do with 'A Case

In A Thousand'. Indeed, it seems probable that with this story, as with the stories of *More Pricks* as a whole, Beckett had no real or useful models to follow. He could, for example, as O'Hara seems to want to suppose (39), have fallen under the spell of Franz Kafka's 'A Country Doctor', a story which generates a sequence of enigmatic and dreamlike events and in large part depends upon the doctor's difficulties in saving anyone, himself included (cf. Dr Nye's 'Myself I Cannot Save', 18). But Kafka's 'A Country Doctor' is, after all, narrated by the doctor himself, and neither Kafka nor Gide can really help to explain what makes Beckett's 'A Case In A Thousand' such a curious and beguiling, if ultimately unsatisfactory, experiment. There seems to be nothing we can derive from the story itself which will explain why such a studiously impersonal manner has been applied to material that focuses on personal distress, only for it to be left uninflected and effectively primed to frustrate any reader's 'natural' desire to detect some significance in what occurs. This is an exceptionally odd outcome, given the way in which the extratextual evidence suggests that Beckett, feeling 'incomplete' in himself, was worried that he might be becoming more 'personal', even after having done his level best to ensure that *More Pricks* would not openly betray its origins in his own life – the very material that *Dream* had been wholly dependent on.

Beckett was indeed 'sailing dangerously' – as per the MacGreevy letter, and as half-suggested by the canal barge – in more than one sense of the phrase. This, we may well feel, was the real 'case' beyond the 'Case' at issue, which the story of its very nature (its own 'call of nature', as it were) obscures rather than clarifies. The late Rubin Rabinovitz's judgement, 'Those who hunt too eagerly for Oedipus may find themselves being lured into the abode of the sphinx' (69), warmly endorsed by Ruby Cohn (2001, 68), looks the shrewdest assessment of the evidence available in the story as published. But even that cannot confidently be said to be a judgement which the story itself is in any position to endorse. The interpretation of 'A Case In A Thousand' remains, more than 70 years from its publication and with no critical consensus having emerged in the interim, dependent not on what little the story chooses to foreground but very much on what it leaves 'incomplete' at the narrative level.

It may ultimately be preferable to consider the issues in 'A Case In A Thousand' in a larger context, against the background of the *More Pricks* 'fiasco'. There was undoubtedly a need on Beckett's part to dump Belacqua, the 'principal boy' of two disasters, one unpublished (*Dream*) and one published (*More Pricks*), or to find some way of getting free of him. There was a similar need to get beyond Peggy Sinclair, Ethna MacCarthy, and friends and family generally. But the great disaster for Beckett was the death of his father on 26 June 1933, some 18 months before 'A Case In A Thousand' was published in *The Bookman*. This was an event from which Beckett could not free himself, even though he only admits as much by way of the 'talkie . . . of almost continuous performance' in 'Lightning Calculation' (UoR, typescript, page 1). Indeed, to say, as O'Hara does, that 'Beckett deals directly with a subject previously evaded' (42) is to forget that there was one major subject that he was finding it no more possible to deal with here than he had in the earlier 'Echo's Bones' story, which had led to both stories generating what 'Lightning Calculation' calls 'postures that impressed [Quigley] as ignoble' (typescript, 1). In the light of the loss of his father, even with what pages and pages of his psychology notes could tell him about familial relationships dysfunctional or otherwise, any idea that this 'may be Beckett's only psychological story with a happy ending' (O'Hara, 42) looks a lot less helpful than the fact that 'the piece ends less on a catharsis than on a sly anti-climax', as Phil Baker concludes (4).

Since January 1934, Beckett had been having three sessions a week with Dr Wilfred Bion, 'one of those new mind doctors' (Maddy Rooney in *All That Fall*). 'A Case In A Thousand' seemed to imply, some 7 or 8 months into these analytic sessions, that there was really nothing to be done, although there were still more than 10 months of meetings with Bion to follow. (Phil Baker very aptly suggests that Dr Nye is 'both patient and analyst, Beckett and Bion', 5.) Even in February 1935, with 'Lightning Calculation' sent out to editors, Beckett could tell MacGreevy that he was 'terribly tired of all the psychic evidence' (*LSB*, 245), and it was not until it was all over, and until *Murphy* had been finished, that he could begin to see how his analysis with Bion had helped him to better understand himself, even with a definitive 'cure' still far to seek. If there is indeed 'a distaste for doctors' in 'A Case In A Thousand', as Ruby Cohn proposes (2001, 68), the distaste almost certainly extends to psychotherapists, even if Beckett is understandably reluctant to broadcast it. Cohn's view is in accord with Phil Baker's emphasis on 'the wretchedness of believing in psychoanalysis', given that the story is 'providing no biographical data for the vulgar Freudian' (2, 4) and as such may well be 'an Oedipal parody' (2), as indeed even O'Hara seems finally prepared to concede: 'The hypothesis of an Oedipal complex . . . cannot hold up' (39).

If Beckett himself found anything positive in 'A Case In A Thousand', perhaps it was the fact, independent of any prevailing therapeutic orthodoxy or actual analysis, that he had conducted his own exercise in self-therapy. Far too light, and far too unstable a vessel, to bear any of the weight that he had left visible in the *More Pricks* stories, 'A Case In A Thousand' nevertheless drew a line in the sand, beyond which Beckett was never much disposed to venture again. He had effectively written *finis* to the whole *More Pricks* experience by closing off access to his various traumas. By abandoning any pretension to depth he had also created the kind of space which could only be filled by a quite different modelling of materials.

For 5 years, from June 1929 (with 'Assumption' in *transition*) to August 1934 (with 'A Case In A Thousand' in *The Bookman*) – publications representing the cutting edge of the avant-garde to the more placid pastures of the middlebrow monthly magazines – Beckett had struggled to make the short story an appropriate medium for his complex vision. In one last move he wrote 'Lightning Calculation', which he thought 'very short' and 'very tenuous', and very probably ideal fodder for the *Evening Standard* (*LSB*, 243). 'Lightning Calculation' is so short (two typewritten pages, UoR) that there is hardly sufficient space for a story to materialize and so tenuous that nothing very like one threatens to emerge. Almost the only telling detail in what emerges from this study of the 'low spirits' of a figure called 'Quigley' – a name later to be given to Murphy's Dutch uncle, 'a well-to-do ne'er-do well' (13) – is, as pointed out in my concluding remarks on the story 'Echo's Bones' above, the inability to 'forget his father's death', which revolves in Quigley's brain like the 'almost continuous performance' on an endless loop in a very private cinema. (This is the origin of the 'spool' image in the description of Murphy's last moments [157], and there is a much later variation on the same theme in the sixth of the *Texts for Nothing*: 'The news, do you remember the news, the latest news, in slow letters of light, above Piccadilly Circus, in the fog?' [25].) In the event 'Lightning Calculation' was not to be lit up in neon, or to become news of any kind, but to be put away in a drawer. But Beckett must soon have realized that – as far as his troubled transactions with the form of the short story were concerned – it was time to emulate the tinker of 'Walking Out' (95) and Doyle in 'Echo's Bones' (25), and call 'Game ball' on a game that had to be considered lost (cf. *SBT/A*, 16, 208). With the 'ancient punctured themes' of *More Pricks* (174) receding, Beckett was, much like Belacqua at the end of 'A Wet Night', 'only too happy' (75) to move on, at least until *Murphy* proved in its own way to be something less than plain sailing.

Murphy was also to become a matter of 'encounters and contretemps' (127) although, largely by virtue of a much improved adaptation of means to ends (cf. Pilling 2010), it left Beckett sufficiently comfortable to write about three-quarters of the novel (almost all of the first nine chapters) within 3 months of its inception, a rate of strike which would have left *More*

Pricks finished in less than half the time it actually took. *Murphy*, Beckett must quickly have realized, could only be accomplished within a through-composed form and format in which control might be exercised with fewer, or less debilitating, compromises. The struggle with an alien medium had not produced the desired outcome, any more than psychoanalysis had done. It was to be back to 'ars longa' (*Dream*, 168), after what must have seemed like far too long a foundering in a strait of two wills.

Chapter 3

How It Went in the World

1. The Early Reviews

Federman and Fletcher's bibliography lists seven reviews of *More Pricks* on its publication in 1934, with some well-known names, either of the time or later – Arthur Calder-Marshall, Gerald Gould, Peter Quennell – sitting in immediate judgement on an author virtually unknown in literary London, and only known to people in the Joyce circle in literary Paris. Two of these reviews are reprinted in the Graver and Federman *Critical Heritage* collection (42–4), one by the poet and critic Edwin Muir (originally printed in the *Listener*, 4 July 1934), the other by the anonymous reviewer of the *Times Literary Supplement* (26 July 1934), identified as Alex Glendinning by Derwent May (201). Both of these reviews show that the book need not have been the publishing disaster it turned out to be. Muir acknowledges that it is 'very difficult to describe', but credits Beckett with 'a subtle and entertaining mind' and thinks that *More Pricks* is an 'exploration' which is 'very much worth following'. Between these statements Muir writes: 'The author has been influenced by Mr James Joyce, but the spirit in which he writes is rather that of Sterne', showing 'the particularity of both', even if 'he does not nearly come up to them'. Muir's soft-pedalling of Joyce here could have been more profitably followed up by later commentators than has sometimes been the case (see Addenda 1).

In the *TLS*, Glendinning thought it an 'odd book', but also felt that there was a 'definite, fresh talent at work in it'. He makes no mention of Sterne, but he discusses Joyce sensibly, and he has certainly done his homework:

> Part of 'Draff' is transcribed from an earlier prose piece of Mr Beckett's which appeared in *Transition* ['Sedendo et Quiescendo', March 1932] and showed strongly the influence of Mr Joyce's latest work [*Work in Progress*] – a dangerous model. There is still more than the setting of

Dubliners to remind us of this writer, but a comparison between the piece in *Transition* and the present book shows how much Mr Beckett's work has gained from discipline of his verbal gusto.

Glendinning could hardly have been expected to see, amidst so much that remains unclear in 'Sedendo et Quiescendo', that it was in essence an attempt on Beckett's part to expel Joyce from his system, a necessary voiding if any real creative progress of his own was ever to be made. But the praise of 'the chapter or episode which describes Belacqua in hospital ['Yellow']' as 'perfect in its way' makes Glendinning's judgement of *More Pricks* as 'an uneven book . . . unlikely to appeal to a large audience' look less damaging, even if the book was only to find a pitifully small audience. Glendinning effectively anticipates this by saying: 'His book sometimes invites us to compare Mr Beckett with one of his characters [Walter Draffin, in 'What A Misfortune'], an author, who thought out a very pretty joke but could find no one subtle enough to appreciate it'.

The other weeklies and the daily newspapers did not help matters. Three early reviews not listed by Federman and Fletcher (see instead the Knowlson biography, 1996, 184 and 738, n. 71–80) emphasize the book's shortcomings, with only a few plaudits to compensate. On 22 May 1934, readers of *The Morning Post* were told, 'The meaning of *More Pricks Than Kicks* completely eludes me'. On 26 May 1934, Richard Sunne in *Time and Tide* wrote: '[Beckett's] allusiveness is often merely smart . . . it is too clever a book to be first-rate'. On 9 June 1934, the reviewer in *John O'London's Weekly* pointed out that 'every sentence is tortured out of its natural shape in the hope of impressing the reader with the author's cleverness'. In the *Dublin Magazine* (IX, July–September, 1934, 84–5) one 'H.N.' spoke of it as 'a book that glitters and will make holiday for highbrows', attempted to cover himself by adding 'Those who are not highbrows must also admire that glitter', and then rather spoilt the broth by quoting a typically sour quatrain from a poem by Roy Campbell ('On Some South African Novelists') questioning the whole point of applying 'the snaffle and the curb' where there might really be no horse on which they could be used. In none of these reviews is there anything as penetrating as the judgements of Edwin Muir and Glendinning. Nor, perhaps understandably, do any of these reviews suggest, as the anonymous 'puff' in the *Observer* (6 May 1934) dares to do, that one day *More Pricks* might benefit from the provision of explanatory notes, although Muir's analysis of the 'style of presentation' ('witty, extravagant and excessive') and the *TLS*'s 'wealth of observation and . . . erudition' effectively point in that direction. It has taken until now for anyone actually to provide them (see Chapter 5).

2. The Belated Afterlife

After his success with *Godot, Endgame* and the so-called trilogy, Beckett came under pressure from his publishers to reprint *More Pricks Than Kicks*. He had briefly and half-heartedly toyed with the idea of writing 'a new series of yarns' in the mid-1930s; the letter to MacGreevy of 6 February 1936 has him jokingly proposing as possible titles *Less Kicks Than Pricks* and *More More Pricks* (*LSB*, 313). But as time passed nothing of the kind emerged. By 1952, with *L'Innommable* seen as 'about the end of the jaunt' and likely to be going into production soon – it was in fact published a year later – Beckett told the young Irish writer Aidan Higgins that the only stories from *More Pricks* which he could remember were 'Yellow' and 'Dante and the Lobster' (letter of 8 February 1952; HRHRC). In a letter to Kay Boyle (4 March 1957; HRHRC) Beckett wrote: 'I find these stories very unsatisfactory and do not propose to have them re-published'. In writing to her again a few months later, during which time Kay Boyle must have written some kind of essay on one of the stories (presumably 'Dante and the Lobster'), Beckett told her: 'It's one of the most sensitive, imaginative, inseeing, painstaking comments I've read. I came out of it almost beginning to like the story myself'. This marginally more positive mood did not last for long. Beckett told Barbara Bray in a letter of January 1959 that he was re-reading the stories, but in a letter to her in the November of that year (TCD) wrote: 'Wouldn't open More Pricks for a king's ransom. I remember Yellow vaguely, and Dante and the Lobster, the others not at all, not a clue. Glad you got something from them, don't know how you do it'. On 31 June 1961 he told John Calder (UoR MS 2073) that *More Pricks* was 'unobtainable' and that there was 'no question of republishing it'. In a letter to Barbara Bray of 22 August 1962 (TCD) he spared her blushes, as it were, by substituting an arrow device for the 'prick' element in the title, almost as if to wish it away!

But it could not be wished away so easily. In late April 1964 Beckett told Bray in a letter (TCD) that he had reluctantly agreed to a John Calder reprint of *More Pricks* and would obviously have to let Barney Rosset of Grove Press do likewise. But by early October, reading the proofs (cf. my discussion of 'The Smeraldina's Billet Doux' in Chapter 2), Beckett was finding this hard going, as he confided to Bray; in due course Beckett told first Barney Rosset and then John Calder that he simply could not allow them to proceed. (The proofs of this jettisoned Grove Press edition were offered for sale at Sotheby's a few years ago, showing very few corrections, suggesting that Beckett had very little stomach for it well before he had got as far as 'The Smeraldina's Billet Doux', which in the event became something of a last straw. He very probably did not even re-read 'Yellow' and 'Draff', or could not bring himself to do so, given the fact that, either in part or in whole, they were dependent on the sudden death and subsequent burial of his father.) Once again pressed on the matter, Beckett was prepared to allow a limited mimeographed edition of 100 copies (Nelson, xvi) 'for scholars only' from John Calder in 1966 (followed by a second hundred in 1967), but he told Marion Boyars (11 May 1967; UoR) of Calder & Boyars that *More Pricks* was 'a work which I have banned!', obviously still thinking back to, and still aggrieved by, the Irish 'Register of Prohibited Publications' in 1935 (cf. *Disjecta*, 86 ff.). In agreeing to a Marie Kean radio reading of selections from his work, Beckett stipulated to Calder (13 September 1969; UoR) that she could not read 'Dante and the Lobster', 'nor any other part of *More Pricks Than Kicks*'.

Beckett's personal 'ban', which ensured that *More Pricks* remained virtually unobtainable, obviously left it in the limbo to which he had consigned it in the 1930s. The book had gone more than 30 years without being re-read, and no doubt Beckett sincerely wished it would remain buried for another 30. Whatever blame Beckett might still have wished to attach to the medium of the short story, never really a comfortable medium for him, must soon after publication have come to seem irrelevant in the face of a blame better exercised on his own early 'itch to make' (Harvey 1970, 273). It was in this spirit, but with the inestimable benefit of hindsight, that Beckett warned Aidan Higgins not to make 'the silly mistake we all make of publishing too soon' (letter of 22 April 1958). (Higgins was trying to interest publishers in his own collection of short stories, *Felo de se*, published by John Calder in 1960.) All that mattered, Beckett told Higgins, was to 'work, work, writing for nothing and for yourself'. What mattered to the world of publishing, however, was Beckett as a bankable asset, especially after he was awarded the 1969 Nobel Prize in literature. Far from there being, as is claimed by the narrator of *Murphy* (chapter 5), 'no return game between a man and his stars' – perhaps a wry reflection on the failure of 'Belacqua redivivus' in 'Echo's Bones' to pass muster – a return game was preparing behind the scenes.

After the Nobel, it was no longer 'too soon' for *More Pricks*, but much too late, or at least too late to be other than 'a game that must be lost' (a phrase Beckett had taken from Beaumont and Fletcher's play *Philaster* (in the subsection 'For Interpolation') into *Murphy* and had jotted down in his *'Whoroscope' Notebook*; cf. *SBT/A*, 16, 208). By 31 January 1970 (Nelson, xvii), however – much like Murphy playing chess against Mr Endon – Beckett had 'capitulated' (letter to Kay Boyle 20 March 1970; cf. a similar letter of 5 February 1970 to John Kobler; HRHRC). In a letter to Ruby Cohn of 2 July 1970 (UoR), Beckett told her that the Calder reissue had just been published, and in due course there was also an edition from Grove Press (who first published *More Pricks* in 1972, the first time the book had ever appeared in the USA). In the circumstances, Beckett obviously could not prevent the book from dissemination by the usual routes. He wrote 'OK' in his best terse manner in a letter to Marion Boyars after she asked for his agreement to a Spanish translation (22 June 1971; UoR), and from that point on he could not avoid the fact that a book which he loathed and had personally 'banned' was, once again (by this time nearly 40 years on), available to almost anyone wishing to read it. (Whether Beckett himself ever re-read it in proof after 1970 is seen as unlikely by Cassandra Nelson [xvii]; he had ground to a halt in 1964, as indicated above.) Beckett had, one way or another, been 'damned to fame' too successfully for him to be allowed the luxury of *More Pricks* sleeping sound in its long oblivion. Shortly before his death an audio tape of the actor Barry McGovern reading 'Dante and the Lobster', sponsored by the Allied Irish Bank with the financial assistance of the Irish Arts Council, appeared from 'Paycock Publications' under the title *The Abbey Reads/A Tribute to Samuel Beckett* (a recording issued as ABB 013; 1986), without any let or hindrance to inhibit a thoroughly worthwhile enterprise.

3. The Longer Perspectives

As the academic study of Beckett got under way, *More Pricks Than Kicks* could still only be read in its first edition of 1934, and *Dream of Fair to Middling Women* only in typescript. Ruby Cohn, in one of the first major monographs on Beckett (*The Comic Gamut*, 1962), does not refer to the latter, of which she seems then to have been unaware, but her chapter 'Early Elegance' (10–44), which deals with *More Pricks* and other early work by Beckett, still looks bright and helpful today, by no means a last word, but for a first word 'elegant' in its own right.

In his groundbreaking 1964 study *The Novels of Samuel Beckett*, John Fletcher interweaves *Dream* and *More Pricks* in a chapter called 'Belacqua', without really separating the Belacqua of one from the Belacqua of the other. The problem John Fletcher faced was that *Dream* was not then available for public scrutiny (it only became so in 1992), and *More Pricks* was long out of print. Fletcher's account is engaging, but almost 50 years on inevitably looks rather colourless. And Fletcher was self-evidently concerned with the *novels* of Beckett. There is no chapter on 'The Art of the Storyteller' in Fletcher's later (1967) *Samuel Beckett's Art*, although in all truth the 'art' of the 'storyteller' can be – as hopefully I have demonstrated – just as readily illustrated in the case of *More Pricks* as it can in the case of *Dubliners*, and in some ways much better than it could be in the case of Beckett's later *Nouvelles*.

The late Raymond Federman's *Journey to Chaos* (1965) places *Dream* in an appendix (209–11), but the second chapter ('Belacqua and the Inferno of Society') deals with *More Pricks* in the terms proposed in the subsection's title: 'Social Reality: Lethargy, Doubt and Insanity'. There are some heavy-handed judgements ('Belacqua is detestable', 35), but the chapter had its uses at the time, with *More Pricks* still not back in the public or 'social' domain. When the book was finally reprinted in 1970 (the limited edition of 1966 changed nothing), the academic community was still struggling to come to terms with the issues raised by Beckett's 'trilogy' (a word he himself loathed) and the turbulence created in the wake of *Waiting for Godot* and *Endgame*. With the best, or what looked like the best, the enemy of the good, *More Pricks* was effectively buried by the work that had come after it. There was the general feeling that, in writing about Beckett's prose fiction, the book had to be 'visited', but one did not need to stay for long.

The late Rubin Rabinovitz (in his 1984 study *The Development of Samuel Beckett's Fiction*) stayed long enough to write 35 pages on the short fiction, 15 of them on the unpublished 'Echo's Bones' and the published 'odd man out', 'A Case In A Thousand'. Rabinovitz usefully begins by separating *More Pricks* from *Dream* (36), but having proposed that it is 'more like an episodic novel' (36) he persists thereafter in calling it a novel, and then shifts around within the collection (as it might be more appropriate to do with something that really was a novel) without ever really characterizing any individual story, or recognizing how different they are one from another. As Rabinovitz could not possibly have known, when Beckett felt it incumbent upon him to own up to his book but prudent not to give its actual title, as in his application for a lectureship at the University of Cape Town, he called it *Short Stories* (*LSB*, 524). Beckett's application was also unavailable to Leslie Hill ('the collection of stories, or episodic novel', 7), and to S. E. Gontarski who, in leaving *More Pricks* out of his compilation of texts for *The Complete Short Prose 1929–1989*, claimed that it was 'as much a novel as a collection of stories' (xiii), having earlier emphasized that 'short fiction was a major creative outlet' (xi) for Beckett. Rabinovitz helped move matters forward, and it is still refreshing to find him treating *More Pricks* as worthy of attention in its own right. But he clearly does not find the book as compelling as Beckett's later fiction.

Robert Cochran (1991) confines himself to Beckett's 'short fiction' and in dealing with *More Pricks* makes a number of very useful points about details easily missed. His claim that the 'later' stories (by which he means as per the order in which they appear) are 'better' (17) is not based on any attempt to deal with the matter of when each story was written. Cochran is extremely sensitive to the dynamic structures operating across *More Pricks* (e.g. the way in which a planned death leads to 'nuptial' in 'Love and Lethe' [91], and a 'bridegroom' of a kind suffers an unplanned death in 'Yellow'; 164), and within its self-imposed limits his account remains one of the best of its kind.

There is a much larger volume of coverage in Anthony Farrow's *Early Beckett*, also published in 1991, which has much to recommend it, especially the close reading of 'What A Misfortune', an outstanding piece of analysis. But his book as a whole suffers from problems of structure and organization and, because of its terms of reference, cannot help leaving *More Pricks* looking a rather poor relation of the much richer *Murphy*, which is also part of Farrow's brief.

There are a number, although not a large number, of single essays on *More Pricks* in symposia and in the periodical literature, and each of these has the advantage over most book-length studies of not having to be concerned with issues of development, or judgements of value, in which *Murphy*, say, will inevitably emerge the victor. The most interesting of these are given in the bibliography to this study.

In doctoral theses, isolated references to *More Pricks Than Kicks* have become increasingly frequent, but only two (of those known to me) offer sustained coverage. Harry Vandervlist's 1991 thesis is very useful, but only a handful of essays have emerged from it, and *More Pricks* only occupies a portion of the thesis. Vandervlist makes useful comparisons and contrasts with Joyce (49–50, 55), rightly points out that the collection as a whole 'resists suggesting larger coherences in which its overall unity might be located' (56) and emphasizes that this is a fiction which, like its protagonist, tries to be nowhere for as long as possible.

Outstanding in every way, but unfortunately still lying recessed in the library of Columbia University in New York City, is Jeri L. Kroll's 1974 doctoral thesis. Some material from it appeared in consecutive issues of the *Journal of Beckett Studies* in the later 1970s, but these essays give only a limited idea of Kroll's expertise over some 150 pages on *More Pricks* in a thesis of about 365 pages. Kroll's achievement in this thesis is the more remarkable, given how very little material of a personal or archival kind was then available to her. Kroll is by far the most sensitive and resourceful apologist Beckett's stories have ever had, and it seems somehow symptomatic of the 'adverse fate' ('Walking Out', 98) of Beckett's stories that so very few readers can readily access the one account which might have put *More Pricks* more securely on the critical map and helped to generate the cut-and-thrust, or the oxygen, of genuine critical debate.

For the general reader, the most serviceable brief account of *More Pricks* now available is probably the one provided by the critic who began 'it all': Ruby Cohn, in her *A Beckett Canon* (2001). This is a model of astute and sensitive compression, and in its necessarily short space shows how far matters have been taken since 1934. Cohn would be the first to agree *mutatis mutandis* with Ferrers Howell, writing on Dante in his 1920 study (9), that 'it must not be forgotten that it is more profitable as well as more interesting to read [Beckett] than to read about him'. This may not yet be quite 'how it is' for *More Pricks Than Kicks* in the world to which it has, after many difficulties (some of its own making), been restored. But without scholars believing this could be the case it will only continue to be misprized, neglected, underestimated or simply misunderstood. At least the Faber 2010 reprint gives both the general reader and the specialist scholar the opportunity to discover otherwise.

Chapter 4

The Statement of a Compromise

The only thing disturbed by the revolutionaries Matisse and Tal Coat is a certain order on the plane of the feasible.

('Bram Van Velde'; *Three Dialogues*)

More Pricks Than Kicks has been aptly described as a book that is 'openly exasperated with its own procedures' (Vandervlist 1991, 71), and I have tried throughout this study to show why it could hardly have been otherwise, given the almost irreconcilable tensions out of which it grew. The total failure of the overly ambitious *Dream* left Beckett with 'ars longa' (168) so radically 'désuni' (138) that any move forward was likely to be – and, worse still, to feel – a 'forced move' (*Dream*, 43). *Dream* had in its own way been obliged to confront the fact that 'going up the rigging' (139) could only be temporary, and that there had to be a return to 'steerage-class' (139) sooner or later. The section of *Dream* in which this realization occurs ('UND') was almost certainly written close in time to Beckett's translation of Rimbaud's 'Le Bateau ivre' in April or May of 1932; Prentice acknowledged how helpful he had found 'UND' in a letter to Beckett of 5 July 1932 (UoR). The extraordinary career of Rimbaud, who had waved a magic wand over the domain of poetry only to abandon literature and head for Abyssinia, created a myth to which Beckett was very ready to subscribe, which is one reason why Belacqua in 'UND' heaves a 'foaming spit' overboard into the 'ocean greyhound' (*Dream*, 136, 137). But within the myth of Rimbaud was the poet's own stern sense that a 'visionary' solution (cf. *LSB*, 73) could only lead to disappointment. In a painfully honest self-examination beginning 'Qu'est-ce pour nous, mon coeur . . . ', Rimbaud had stoked up a fiery fury (a 'feu furieux') only to be forced finally to recognize: *'Ce n'est rien: j'y suis; j'y suis toujours'* [It's nothing: I'm here, still here] (203). Back in Dublin after 2 years in Paris, Beckett was 'still here', with a novel that nobody wanted and a handful of short stories that were also not going anywhere. What, he must have asked himself – much as Belacqua does in 'Yellow' – were to be 'his tactics in this crisis?' (154).

Beckett's first move was to try to focus less on flying high and more on the kinds of experiences anyone might have. 'Ordinary' things – going out in the country with one's girl ('Fingal'), wandering aimlessly about the streets ('Ding-Dong'), attending a Christmas party ('A Wet Night'), undergoing a *minor* operation after an overnight stay in the hospital ('Yellow') – would occupy a space previously (in *Dream*) treated fantastically, and too often the mere pretext for aesthetic speculations. It had to be by way of the ordinary that the extraordinary could still be conjured, rather than the other way around as in *Dream*. *More Pricks* accordingly became a study, or series of studies, in the art of disaster averted and conclusions left inconclusive, resistant to completion. Mark Nixon has shown how in later works Beckett inscribes a 'tension between demise and survival in the compositional process itself' (2009, 23). But there is nothing quite so sophisticated as that going on here, simply a determination to keep the process of composition alive long enough to generate a sufficient number of stories and make them echo back and forth between one another. The only 'moral' to be deduced from this was that the 'public' (*Dream*, 161) was not ready for anything more bracing, but Beckett had already praised Proust for being 'completely detached from all moral considerations' with 'no black cats and faithful hounds' (*PTD*, 66, 89) to keep the public happy. The 'happy ever after' of comedy was out of the question, but so was the gloom of tragedy. Decades later Beckett was to adapt a prose text by Chamfort to say: 'The trouble with tragedy is the fuss it makes / Over life and death and other tuppenny aches' (*Collected Poems*, 125). There was only one way out: tragicomedy.

Tragicomedy (as, for example, found in the so-called problem plays of Shakespeare) typically requires a broad canvas to make its complex effects work in a way that will keep both elements of the blend alive, which is one reason why it is not often an obvious asset in the more confined space of a short story, despite several notable examples of stories that leave one uncertain whether to laugh or to cry. It seems to be a natural consequence of writing tragicomedy that the reader is left with an uncomfortable, and sometimes dissatisfying, uncertainty whether to have a long face prepared to soften into a smile or to maintain a mild countenance ready to take on a grimmer aspect. The mixed mode is effectively embodied in 'A Wet Night', where the 'home of tragedy' (the Queen's Theatre in Pearse Street, 44) is left to figure against events in 'real life' which are neither truly tragic nor merely funny. As Leslie Hill's emphasis on 'purgatory' (10) implies,

Beckett's preference for what is 'middling' (as advertised in the very title of *Dream*) is in many ways in accord with his love for the middle section of Dante's *Divine Comedy*, the *Purgatorio*, over the *Inferno* ('the static lifelessness of unrelieved viciousness') and the *Paradiso* ('the static lifelessness of unrelieved immaculation'), because Purgatory is 'a flood of movement and vitality released by the conjunction of these two elements' (Dante . . . Bruno.Vico..Joyce; *Disjecta*, 33). If the 'visionary' had to be brought down to earth, and if the earth had to be seen as purgatorial ('On this earth that is Purgatory'; *Disjecta*, 33), Beckett's 'spirits of rebelliousness' had to be scaled down accordingly, and given a tragicomic colouring. Beckett's response was to make light of the tragic sense of life but keep his comedy serious, to make a 'fuss' over showing that it was difficult simply to laugh at, or difficult to come to terms with, or just plain difficult. The mixed mode of tragicomedy creates an unstable environment which can never be quite resolved, like the musical ('plagal') phrase in the January 1932 poem 'Dortmunder'. The laugh and the tear, as Belacqua discovers in 'Yellow', are impossible to separate.

This is one reason why 'Yellow', the story of a death, is alive throughout (with both literal and metaphorical exclamation marks), and one reason why Beckett gives the name 'Miranda' (derived from the heroine of the tragicomedy *The Tempest*) to the day-nurse, the 'divine creature' to whom Belacqua entrusts his glasses as they go 'down in the lift' to the operating theatre. Tragicomedy ensures that, in *More Pricks*, it is always a matter of both/and rather than either/or. The death of Belacqua gives a new lease of life to his sometime best man Hairy Quin in 'Draff', and the focus in 'Draff' falls not on the burial, but rather on what leads up to it, and what leads away from it. In almost all the stories (with the possible exceptions of 'Dante and the Lobster' and 'Yellow') the focus falls precisely *not* where we would expect to find it, as if Beckett felt that would be too artless a resolution of any story, short or long. Focus is one of the primary casualties of *More Pricks Than Kicks*. In each and every story it is difficult to establish or maintain a perspective, and the continuity, or rather discontinuity, of story succeeding story runs counter to the impulse anyway. *Murphy* is in many ways an unconventional novel, but it is always dependent on some of the 'unbreakable' rules of novel writing, even when it only pays lip service to them. However much Beckett may have learned from the longer and more complex *More Pricks* stories (notably 'What A Misfortune') in his handling of a larger cast list brought in and out of focus around the 'fundamental[ly] unheroic' hero (as Beckett describes Murphy in the entry for 18 January 1937 German Diaries, which also claims, 'It is impossible to controvert

Murphy as construction'), the novel is through-composed in a way that simply cannot operate in *More Pricks Than Kicks*. In *More Pricks* we have to learn new ways of thinking and looking in each case, and then remain flexible enough to do away with them, finding others to set in their stead, until they too manifestly fail to work. This strategy would have crippled any possible novel based on these materials, as Beckett had already demonstrated to his own satisfaction (if no one else's) in *Dream of Fair to Middling Women*, which is always exploding away from any nucleus in an exhilarating but alarming centrifugal fashion, and can only ever produce 'tattered starlings in the devil's blizzard' (36).

Within the tragicomic spirit of the enterprise, Beckett wanted to keep the darker tones hidden and emphasize the lighter ones. This is clear in what is almost the only exception to Beckett's virtual silence on the subject of *More Pricks*, a letter to Nuala Costello of 10 May 1934 identifying 'major influences'. If Nuala Costello took Beckett's list of these influences at all seriously – he had identified them as Grock, Dante, Chaucer, Mandeville and Uccello – she had only to reach for her *More Pricks* to confirm that two of them (Dante and Uccello) were indeed to be found (in the first and last stories of the collection), and two more (Grock and Chaucer) were part of the mix in one other story ('A Wet Night'), the former by way of his catchphrase, the latter by way of 'The Man of Law' and by a quasi-Chaucerian dependency on type figures among the gallery of bit-part players and guests at the Frica's party. Presumably Nuala, a cultured and intelligent woman, was rather thrown by Beckett's mention of Mandeville, first because of who he was, and then because of the way in which he had been kept recessed in *More Pricks*. (Bernard de Mandeville, the satirical eighteenth-century author primarily known, if no longer often remembered, for *The Fable of the Bees*, is never mentioned by name in *More Pricks* and survives, if he survives at all, in a few phrases in 'What A Misfortune' contrasting 'private vices' and 'public virtues', the key concepts of Mandeville's *Fable*.) But no doubt long before Nuala Costello went looking for Mandeville, it had occurred to her that Beckett's list of major influences was more a matter of smoke and mirrors than an acknowledgement of genuine indebtedness. Beckett's first three names gesture back some years before *More Pricks*, to *Dream* and even earlier. The last two are from the stories then freshest in his memory ('What A Misfortune' and 'Draff', both of which were supplanted by 'Dante and the Lobster' and 'Yellow' in later life). But none of the five had had the kind of impact on *More Pricks* which would have justified the elevation of any one of them to the status of a major influence. Like the Belacqua who is *of* Dublin but not really *in* Dublin, each of these five 'influences' is part of the fabric or the furniture of *More Pricks*, but not an overarching factor in the composition of the stories. There were, in fact, other figures with a stronger claim: Keats for one, Robert Burton for another, Thomas à Kempis for yet another, and a host of lesser lights ('William Cooper', Pierre Garnier, Victor Bérard, Max Nordau, W. R. Inge, etc.) all chipping in from start to finish (see Chapter 5 for documentation in this connection). Beckett's purpose, if we can call it that, in identifying five major influences was obviously to burlesque the very idea that in an enterprise like *More Pricks* he could have been under any influence at all. In its casual and off-the-cuff way, the letter to Nuala Costello speaks volumes: *More Pricks*, it suggests, is one of a kind, without portfolio, the product of not wanting to be like anyone else. Even the role played in it by Schubert, a composer who was no more a writer than Uccello, leaves Beckett able to disavow any influence by way of the policy of 'flagrant concealment' analysed in Chapter 2.

It would be difficult to claim that 1933, the year in which *More Pricks* came to seem viable, was a turning point for Beckett, especially if, in the early years (as the late play *That Time* reconfigures them), he was, like Voice C, 'always having turning-points' (*Krapp's Last Tape*, etc., 101), a pattern which was not in fact to change very much over the decades. But it was in 1933 that circumstances conspired to impose change on a creative mind 'confused' as to how best 'handle heterogeneous entities' (*Dream*, 34), immensely adept at generating a 'concert of effects' (*Dream*, 12), but so 'enmeshed' in them (*Dream*, 3) that no one move seemed any better than any other. A sometime lover and a beloved father were dead. A book of poems (*Echo's Bones and Other Precipitates*) was beginning to take shape, with George Reavey likely to be (as indeed he was to prove) a kindly light at the end of that tunnel. In an exploratory spirit Beckett was beginning to add a more detailed knowledge of English literature (cf. Pilling 2006b) to the continental influences which had figured so largely in his studies and not just as a consequence of his 'short stay abroad' ('Fingal', 18). He had also begun to investigate the history of philosophy, develop an existing interest in art and art history and broaden his sense of history generally. Even with the old world ('the old pact' of *Proust*; *PTD*, 22) gone – or going – it was still in essence 'the old story of the salad days, torment in the terms and in the intervals a measure of ease', as in 'Ding-Dong' (31). But rather than just exercising his erratic 'fidgets' (*Disjecta*, 81), Beckett was putting out feelers for relief. He had realized that the aesthetic of *Dream* was much too hit-and-miss to take him very far, and that a compromise would have to be found, even if it was a compromise with which he was far from comfortable. And it must have gradually become clear that, for anything like 'new life' to come into being, the very idea of Belacqua (whether as in *Dream* or as in *More Pricks*) simply had to be abandoned; his death was a kind of 'necessary' death (Kroll 1978, 11, 33, 36).

How great a part Beckett's developing interest in philosophy played in all this we cannot be certain, and he was not to be offered the opportunity to express any aesthetic views (in public, at least) until given column space beyond *More Pricks Than Kicks* and beyond Dublin, in the more promising literary climate of London in the summer of 1934. But for 'an inkling of the terms in which our condition is to be thought again' ('The Capital of the Ruins', *As The Story Was Told*, 28), the history of philosophy offered Beckett ideas and structures that helped him think in ways that would have been beyond him in *Dream*. In a review of Giovanni Papini's *Dante Vivo* (in its 1934 English translation) Beckett found '[r]elief' (*Disjecta*, 81) from a suffocating emphasis on literature as morality by proxy (the '*morale negotium*' of Dante's letter to Can Grande) by way of 'Nietzsche's hyena' (*Disjecta*, 80–1), an image from the first part of the subsection 'Skirmishes of an Untimely Man' of *The Twilight of the Idols* (1889). Nietzsche uses this image to describe Dante as 'the hyena who *writes poetry* [Nietzsche's italics] in tombs', (513), a phrase which no doubt caught Beckett's eye in large part because he himself had mentioned Dante's tomb in Ravenna (in the Piazza Byron!) in 'A Wet Night', and was in any case alert to mentions of Dante wherever they were to be found. But Beckett must almost have reflected ruefully that the skirmishes he had himself conducted in *More Pricks Than Kicks* had proved just as 'untimely' as any of Nietzsche's, that his own poetry was still unappreciated and that he had been reduced to the bread-and-butter business of reviewing. Long before Nietzsche, a philosopher who could be read as a creative writer, Beckett had responded warmly to Schopenhauer (a major influence on *Proust* in the summer of 1930), but in moving forward from Schopenhauer to Nietzsche he had also moved from metaphysics and pessimism to a more '*fröhliche Wissenschaft*', or joyful wisdom, or had at least supplied himself with a potential antidote to the pessimism that was always threatening to cloud even the brightest horizon. Ultimately, Beckett's enthusiasm for Nietzsche, which seems to have been in part based on seeing Nietzsche as just as hostile to 'ars longa' as he himself had become (letter to George Reavey of 23 June 1934, telling him 'j'ai Zarathustra [*Thus Spake Zarathustra*] sous la main'; *LSB*, 212), was not to survive the more deep-seated commitment to Schopenhauer, and subsequently to Dr Johnson. But there are obvious traces of the 'hyena' in *More Pricks Than Kicks*, and perhaps it is no accident that one of the grotesques in the story 'What A Misfortune' is given the name Hermione Näutzsche, since her first name enables Beckett also to underwrite the tragicomic vision of Shakespeare in *The Winter's Tale*, as if his own tales were to be taken as neither one thing nor another.

Beckett had read Schopenhauer in Dublin, and Nietzsche in London, but it seems to have been in London, in the summer of 1932, that he had first given serious attention to the study of philosophy, a subject which he had never been formally taught. His first source for this new enthusiasm, pursued with his usual obsessive attention to detail, was Archibald Alexander's *A Short History of Philosophy*, from which Beckett took typewritten and handwritten notes, now at TCD, on early Greek philosophy, with a special emphasis on the Pre-Socratics. There are details in these notes which must date from before Beckett put the finishing touches to *More Pricks Than Kicks*. It was from Alexander, for example, that Beckett took the 'Delian diver' reference in 'Yellow' (149); Alexander mentions this early in the *Short History* as Socrates' view on the difficulty of understanding Heraclitus of Ephesus (28). Alexander also (29) discusses Heraclitus' view that it is 'not possible to step down twice into the same stream', which Beckett uses in 'Echo's Bones' and elsewhere. (The reference to Thales and the line in the 1932 poem 'Serena I' summarizing his idea that all things are full of gods are also from Alexander). Beckett's typewritten notes also include three quotations from Heraclitus as presented by Alexander: 'Moistened soul of the drunken is unwise'; 'The driest soul is the wisest and best'; and 'When fire is quenched by damp, reason is lost' (32). These quotations seem perfectly adapted to Belacqua's situation in 'A Wet Night', and the gardener's loss of reason in 'Draff'. In Beckett's longhand notes on Heraclitus there is also the quotation 'It is the same thing in us that is quick and dead, awake and asleep, young and old', together with the comment 'That is the game of draughts that Time plays everlastingly', both derived from John Burnet's *Greek Philosophy* (62), which were presumably entered too late for 'Dante and the Lobster' and *More Pricks* as a whole, but which in the case of the latter at least seems to have given Beckett an image worth developing in the game of chess in *Murphy*. Beckett seems to have first read Wilhelm Windelband's great *History of Philosophy* – of significant importance in relation to *Murphy* (cf. C. J. Ackerley, 'Demented Particulars' and Matthew Feldman, *Beckett's Books* [especially chapter 3]) – after the completion of *More Pricks Than Kicks*. But much of Windelband on the Pre-Socratics strikes a chord with Beckett's stories, notably his presentation of the views of the Milesians (Anaximander and Heraclitus) on the ways in which 'things change their form', and in particular his discussion of 'rarefaction' and 'condensation' (Windelband, 48; these distinctively Milesian practices are also used later by Windelband to dissociate Pythagoras from them). Windelband shows that for the Milesian school of philosophers these activities lead to an important conclusion as regards 'the development of the present state of the world out of the prime matter' (48): 'it is necessary to assume a ceaseless process of world-formation and world-destruction' (49). The idea of 'ceaseless process' seems better adapted to the wild and whirling words of *Dream* than to the controlled climate of *More Pricks*, but Windelband's two terms describe, even if Beckett only discovered them after the fact, what he had been obliged to do in moving on from the one to the other. *More Pricks*, Beckett's first really serious attempt to school his wilder tendencies, *condenses* by having to live within the restrictions of shorter forms and *rarefies* by having to accept some diminution of density. In practical rather than philosophical terms, 'condensation' affects the structure of the stories, and 'rarefaction' permeates their content. Both these activities make for a more manageable body of material, without necessarily forcing an idiosyncratic vision to give up some of its distinctiveness. It 'make[s] things easier' ('Yellow', 153) by leaving the difficulties to be perceived by the reader rather than persistently harped upon, or theorized about, by the writer who, even in remaining hidden behind his handiwork – in many ways more so than Joyce ever was – is still more or less openly masquerading as the narrator.

It is entirely characteristic of Beckett's method in *More Pricks Than Kicks* to make things easier for himself by making them more difficult for the reader. Obliged, as we seem to be, to read the stories more closely than their sometimes casual, and occasionally rather colourless, surface may actively encourage us to do, we are also being asked to do the opposite: to look away from what is 'given' in the direction of something that is not, strictly speaking, there. What results is a kind of narrative astigmatism. This, for Beckett, is a counterbalance to '[t]he influences of nature' and a legitimate exploitation of 'the disruptive intelligence' which helps to put, and to keep, the 'jizz' (*Disjecta*, 83) in a form or format which, for him, was otherwise inimical to it and overly dependent on formulae. Whatever 'unity' the stories may appear to possess, Beckett wants to subvert and disturb it, occasionally for merely local effects, by being as 'disruptive' as the form will allow, even if this clearly cannot be done in anything like so determined and formidable a manner as in the jettisoned *Dream of Fair to Middling Women*. As Leslie Hill says, 'The stories highlight not the dialectical unification of contraries, but the evanescence of unity, the movements of constant displacement at the core of apparent stability' (8). As *Proust* puts it, in addressing 'the dual significance of every condition and circumstance of life', 'the most ideal tautology . . . involves only an approximate identification, and by asserting unity denies unity' (*PTD*, 69–70).

By far the most famous, or most often quoted, moment of displacement and denial in the *More Pricks* stories occurs at the end of the first story ('Dante and the Lobster'), when, as Belacqua consoles himself with the thought that it will be a 'quick death' for the lobster (but also for 'us all'; 14), a voice from nowhere intervenes to object 'It is not'. This is not so much a case of 'exacting the tumult from unity' (*Disjecta*, 83), but rather a brutal assault on a 'natural' desire, a consolation piously maintained, which is being exposed to a withering critique. The 'disruptive intelligence' is, for Beckett, a disintegrating demon, but nevertheless an agent of integrity, 'the integrity of the eyelids coming down before the brain stroms of grit in the wind', as Beckett describes it in a letter of 18 October 1932 to Thomas MacGreevy which has his early poems for its focus (*LSB*, 136; with 'stroms', as found in *Dream* [4, etc.], substituted for 'knows' as published). This is one reason why, in 'Yellow', Belacqua decides to 'close his eyes, he would bilk the dawn in that way' and thinks to himself: 'What were the eyes anyway? The posterns [the back door, or alternative entrance] of the mind. They were safer closed' (153). There is of course, as we soon discover, no guaranteed safety in closing one's eyes, since there is no looking at what never can be seen, and no looking away from it that will guarantee a benign outcome. One has to try to do both, if not at one and the same time, then with as much flexibility as can be mustered in a given instance. But only the narrator has the ability to empower the reader with 'dualism in multiplicity' in a composition 'under two signatures' (*PTD*, 11). Daniela Caselli aptly cites an entry in the *'Whoroscope' Notebook* which she describes as 'a text that simultaneously incites us to see and not to see Dante' (2009, 23), and the *More Pricks* stories are continually playing blindness off against vision and vice versa, as if any disclosure could at some point be retracted and exposed as bogus or simply inappropriate. At one level at least, Beckett obviously relishes the fact that narratives under pressure to deliver a 'suitably' complex series of twists and turns over a more or less determinate number of pages must, to a greater or lesser degree, depend upon differential perspectives of engagement and disengagement, juxtaposing looking *at* with looking *away*, as if looking at anything necessarily entailed looking away from something else.

Looking away is what the narrator does in 'Walking Out' after Lucy has been 'dreadfully marred' from being hit by a Daimler; 'Now it is Belacqua's turn to carry on', he observes imperturbably, as if nothing had happened (103). It is also what the crowd does in 'Ding-Dong'. A shocking accident (what Molloy would call an 'absurd mishap'; 29) occurs, and no one is moved, or only physically, one up the queue for the cinema. The 'wisdom' of *More Pricks* seems to be that accidents will happen; as Vladimir tells us in *Waiting for Godot* there is '[n]othing to be done'. You might, like Belacqua with the lobster, want to prevent them, but you cannot. And, anyway, one 'good' accident deserves another. Belacqua cannot save the lobster, and later, at what we might naturally suppose to be a rather more important (because human) moment in 'Yellow', he cannot save himself (compare Dr Nye in 'A Case In A Thousand'). The stories are repeatedly gravitating towards disaster (*not* tragedy) and then veering away from it. They play the short-story 'game' of containing at least one incident of note (typically a potentially disastrous one), but they subvert the convention from within by passing it off as something too familiar, too mundane, for comment or undue grief. Even in 'Draff', a story which could hardly have been written without Beckett's grief at the loss of his beloved father, the darker tones are kept at bay, even when the darkness falls over the cemetery. 'Draff' begins, appropriately enough, with the cold print of a newspaper announcement, and briefly imitates a telegram, as if to drain away emotion, before proceeding to examine the way in which every survivor pays lip service to the victim, while still having to get on with their own lives.

The very writing of short stories was, for Beckett, a matter of 'having to get on', and in more than one sense of the phrase. Given that he was later to enjoy (or endure) world fame, the aspect of this which seems most to affect the fabric of *More Pricks* in the larger view is the way each of the stories *seems* to conform to conventional narrative expectations, only to show that this convention is *really of no value*. This is the Beckettian equivalent of what the great Argentinian writer Jorge Luis Borges identifies in his 1950 essay 'The Wall and the Books' as 'perhaps' the defining feature of 'aesthetic reality': 'the imminence of a revelation that is not yet produced' (5). Borges, quite unlike Beckett in this as in most other things, felt no compulsion to add to the stock of novels in the world, though he was happy enough to read and even review them (as *The Total Library* shows). Beckett wanted in *More Pricks* to satisfy his two wills, the one gravitating towards a kind of totalized entity (resembling a novel, if not actually attempting to be one), and the other gravitating towards an exploded entity in which 'the units of continuity have abdicated their unity' (*Dream*, 138). One reason why *More Pricks* has never been accorded a wider critical welcome is that Beckett has left the collection looking both disparate and all of a piece, with a number of critics (as discussed in Chapter 3) privileging the latter aspect over the former, even though Beckett never fooled himself into thinking that he had written a novel, or even a novel *manqué*, *Dream* having served him (im)perfectly well as an example of the latter.

If we review the *More Pricks* stories in their published order as separate entities, but treat them as having kindred characteristics, one feature which they all have in common is an end, or ends, towards which they point i.e. a *raison d'être* designed to put some flesh on the idea that time is short, as of course (if only as regards the space available) it is bound to be in a short story, and that one had better busy oneself in getting on with finishing things off. 'Dante and the Lobster' foregrounds this by way of the lunch/lobster/lesson emphasis. In 'Fingal' it takes longer to emerge, but is finally revealed as the asylum: ' "Do you know what that is?" he said, "Because my heart's right there" ' (19). In 'Ding-Dong' the comparable refuge is the public house. In 'A Wet Night' the focus is on the Frica's party to come. In 'Love and Lethe' everything points forward to a suicide pact. In 'Walking Out' the movement forward is towards the wood. In 'What A Misfortune' a similar role is played by the marriage ceremony to come. Even 'The Smeraldina's Billet Doux', which of its very nature is unlike all the other stories, is orientated towards Belacqua arriving on the '23th' of December, the day before Christmas Eve. In 'Yellow' everything is a prelude to Belacqua's operation. And in 'Draff', the 'decent' sequence of events has to be, first, the burial of Belacqua, and only then the wooing of his widow by Hairy Quin. (Almost as much attention is given to the latter as to the former; the Smeraldina, whom we have never seen with a live husband in *More Pricks*, has given birth by the time she reappears in the story 'Echo's Bones', although we are not told who the father might have been.) Without these 'triggers' there would be no way 'to go on' and 'to carry on' (cf. *Dream*, 195, 'Now we really must be getting on'). But in none of these cases is there a resolution of the expectation which has been the enabling element in the story, even when the event envisaged as the *raison d'être* does actually take place (the party in 'A Wet Night', the wedding in 'What A Misfortune', the committal of Belacqua's coffin to the grave in 'Draff'). Events of this kind are displaced from where we might ordinarily expect to find them – supposing they were ever intended to be the focal point of the story – and placed in a context in which they cannot function in this capacity. Even when such decentering is not possible – 'Dante and the Lobster', 'Love and Lethe' and 'Yellow' are the most obvious examples – the expectations which a given story has built up are brought crashing down.

The idea of 'having to get on', if only to the next moment, destroys the perspective that has enabled suspense to occur. As an idea it cannot be articulated fully because its effect would be thereby dissipated. But Beckett increasingly hints at it, in privileging, if only for a moment, a kind of 'flash forward' which falls 'outside the enceinte of our romaunt' (*Dream*, 185). He gives one of these to Belacqua in 'Love and Lethe' (his 'boast' on 91), another one to Belacqua 'like a stock at gaze' in 'What A Misfortune' (139), and hints at another in 'Yellow' ('Years later . . . ', 160). In 'What A Misfortune' the technique is extended even to Hairy Quin ('One of these fine days . . . ', 126) and to Otto Olaf ('The days that came after . . . ', 116; 'He died in the end . . . ', 130). It is as if time, 'that double-headed monster of damnation and salvation' (*Proust*; *PTD*, 11) can be imagined as having an ideal fluidity and flexibility which is quite unlike its manifestation in the 'real' world, but which is perfectly adapted to 'aesthetic reality'. Time, indeed, has to be imagined in this way, because otherwise it would be impossible either 'to go on' or 'to carry on'. The thrust forward is, of course, only really available to the narrator, and it is only the narrator who can see the collection as a whole, as in the footnotes (81, 101, 109, 177, 180) and in the four reminders (of 'A Wet Night' in 'What A Misfortune', of 'What A Misfortune' and 'Yellow' in 'Draff', and two more references back in 'Echo's Bones'). But for all practical purposes each story can begin as if the time which must have elapsed between one appearance of Belacqua and the next has simply not existed. Belacqua's apparent inability to remember the past (other than when haunted by the 'spectre' of Lucy in 'What A Misfortune', which is perhaps precisely one of the most important misfortunes of that story) means not only that he can never 'develop', but also that he can never 'cod' himself by indulging in 'nostalgia' (*Dream*, 240). And it subserves both of Beckett's 'two wills', since it is not only Belacqua who has 'a strong weakness for oxymoron' (32). It enables the production of stories about Belacqua, while never suggesting that there might be some kind of continuity in these events, a continuity from which the lead character might begin to construct a more settled sense of identity. Beckett's desire is to do away with motivation as ordinarily understood, and to adopt '[t]he simplest course' and 'have done' (82–3) with narrative supports of (as he sees it) dubious validity. But in *More Pricks* he recognizes (as he had not attempted to do in *Dream*) that he must *seem* to comply with at least some of the narrative supports which simply cannot be removed. The tactic of 'whispering the turmoil down' (as asserted rather than demonstrated in the case of the unnamed protagonist of 'Assumption' in 1929) replaces the notion that it can be shouted down. And the cream of the jest is that it can be performed with a figure *of the same name*, who is *not the same*. The Belacqua of *Dream*, whose 'young thought' is 'stocked . . . and confused in a way that was opposed to its real interests' (35), had proved there to be counterproductive, or productive only of confusion. But *More Pricks* sees its Belacqua more coolly, and even as an organizing agent he is less important in his own right than for what he contributes to the 'having to get on' which will enable the enterprise to continue.

This 'having to get on' is allied with the tactic of 'looking away' in 'Yellow'. Belacqua has come to the point where he decides he will 'draw the blind, draw both blinds' to block out 'all the morning sun' which is streaming in, and so contributing to 'this dribble of time' (7 hours of waiting; 159). The whole story depends upon this 'dribble of time', with all the time indicators (and there are many) pointing forward to Belacqua's operation, an operation which occupies no time at all since it never actually occurs, Belacqua dying too soon. Most of Belacqua's efforts in 'Yellow' are devoted to dealing with the unusual situation in which he finds himself and to devising a protective refuge, from the world, from time passing. As part of this strategy he comes up with a 'plan', 'tactics' which might ameliorate this 'crisis'. The plan is elaborately developed over several paragraphs, but comes to grief (as the planner himself later will) in two one-liners: 'How did he proceed to put this plan into execution? / He has forgotten, he has no use for it any more' (156); 'By Christ! he did die! / They had clean forgotten to auscultate him!' (164). (These are the only two occasions in 'Yellow' when this 'double indemnity' device is applied as a structural principle.) The 'has' in the first of these two quotations is very carefully judged; the reader is almost bound at that point in the story to ask 'Why?' It obviously prepares the way for, without openly signposting, Belacqua's demise, much as the many references to his 'late family' also do. But the reader is allowed, and indeed encouraged, to forget it, as the narrative gets on with its business, and as the night-nurse '[breaks] in upon him' (156) for the second time. Only in the last words of the story, however, can it be 'seen' that the same tactic has been employed for the second time, both to terminate the life of Belacqua and to end the story in a 'suitably' dramatic manner.

More Pricks Than Kicks works in the spirit of Thomas Hardy's 'if way to the better there be' by at least sneaking a glance at the worst, and turning away from it. The collection as a whole leaves its reader with the largely useless 'wisdom' that everything depends on your angle of vision. In 'Fingal', Belacqua wants to avoid an entanglement, while a part of him is also quite keen to promote it. In 'Walking Out', the story is not really concerned with what kind of marriage Belacqua and Lucy may have (what story ever is anyway, literature being much more interested, like Mirabell and Millamant in Congreve's *The Way of the World*, in how best to prepare for it), but with something *out*side normal bounds, something not very likely to promote marital harmony. Yet harmony of a kind is restored, and the verbal 'shrug' with which 'Walking Out' ends is, on the face of it, cordial and in its way kindly. In 'real' terms, of course, cordiality and kindness are, at the end of the story, beside the point and (in every sense) beyond it. We are effectively being asked, without the question being foregrounded, to decide what is 'important' by way of the 'little things' which the stories contain. Yet *More Pricks Than Kicks* shows that complete indifference cannot be sustained, and that there is always 'some sentimental factor in play (or at work) complicating the position' (175). The very title 'What A Misfortune' contains the idea that all terms, and all terminations, especially the 'termination' of marriage as it typically ends a comedy, may need to be looked at a little more closely. *What* exactly, it asks, is a misfortune? And what would it be like to experience good fortune? Who has good luck and who has bad luck? And what is luck, when you look at it closely? A subset of fate, destiny or determinism? Or just something that happens? (Compare Kroll 1978, 34–5, on how the very idea of 'misfortune' is developed and changed after 'What A Misfortune', in 'Yellow' and 'Draff'.)

Looking *at*, then, is always in some sense a matter of looking *away*, or looking more closely than we normally look. The gaze of the author is a privileged one, but it is not something which he insists upon. You can take it or leave it, he seems to say, as he had in fact said in *Dream* (13). If you take it, you can enjoy the subtle shift from the 'great [C] major symphony' of the public bar to the idea of heavenly infinity in the shtick of the ticket-seller. If you leave it, well, there are other things going on. They're just not as interesting to the author, that's all. But he can hardly expect to control what you find interesting. If you started out by surrendering your authority to him, as to some extent you had to do, you soon enough discover that ultimately neither you nor he has any left to give away.

* * *

It was not only an 'adverse fate' (101) that affected the ability of the public to see what Beckett was up to in *More Pricks Than Kicks*. He knew, as the public obviously could not, just how much he himself had been 'hoisted' with the material he was dredging up from a 'deep source' (*PTD*, 32), even if he had kept 'on the move' ('Serena III') and had pretty effectively covered his tracks. He must quickly have discovered that *More Pricks* would not be quite the 'bone-shaker' which he had imagined he might subsequently ride away on once *Dream* was done (139). But having salvaged a book of short stories from a wrecked enterprise, Beckett could easily see that he had shaken up more than a few dormant bones in the short story genre, which were not to be found in Joyce, Maupassant, Chekhov or even Ronald Firbank. It was a cage that Beckett wanted to rattle, but not with such ferocity as to actually destroy the bars which kept it together. He was 'in a strait' because he had narrowed his perspectives, and his 'two wills' could not help but clash with one another, generating forces that could only with difficulty be kept on speaking terms. It was time to find out what happened if it really was the case that 'The whisky bears a grudge against the decanter' (*PTD*, 21–2). The form, the cage, the decanter was bound to win, irrespective of the public's ability to understand what the author was up to. But not before Beckett had given it a serious run for its money, even if *More Pricks* was, like Belacqua, 'doomed' (79), not only making him very little money, but also leaving his publishers out of pocket.

Chapter 5

Notesnatchings: Allusions, Borrowings and Self-Plagiarisms in *More Pricks Than Kicks*

Let them perish, those who have uttered our words before us: *'pereant qui ante nos nostra dixerunt'*. Beckett had found this phrase in one of Birkbeck Hill's footnotes to his great edition of Boswell's *Life of Johnson* (vol. 2, 358, n. 4), and was obviously much taken with its long history, stretching back from St Jerome to the fourth-century grammarian Aelius Donatus, and beyond him to the dramatist Terence, a provenance rather strikingly confirmative of the very wisdom which the tag conveys. It became a personal favourite of Beckett's, occurring twice in the *'Whoroscope' Notebook*, in a letter to MacGreevy of 21 January 1938 (*LSB*, 590), in the 'Addenda' to *Watt* and in a revised formulation of the phrase in two letters of October 1971 to Barbara Bray (TCD). The burden of the Latin tag is not far removed from the implications of the Christian doctrine of 'let the dead bury their dead' in St Luke's Gospel (9.60), an idea which Beckett adapted after the war by way of Mercier exclaiming 'Blessed be the dead that die!' in *Mercier and Camier* (95). (This heartfelt cry derives from Revelation 14.13, but Mercier effectively reverses the biblical meaning by leaving out the concluding words of the phrase – 'in the Lord' – as if Beckett really could not free himself of the dead who had died. The original text, as published by Minuit in 1970, reads 'Heureux les morts qui meurent!' [Paris: Minuit, 201], quoting from the French *Sainte Bible*.) But in the early 1930s it seems reasonable to suppose that what primarily concerned Beckett, before the death of his father changed everything, was finding a justification for the morally questionable aesthetic practice of 'notesnatching' by which he was in part enslaved, and in part liberated. (An undated letter to MacGreevy of early August 1931 shows Beckett thinking of this activity as a combination of demonic possession, perhaps with the *Discours de la Méthode* of Descartes as a kind of analogy [cf. 'Discours de la Sortie', *Disjecta*, 42], and 'self-pollution', as frowned upon by orthodox religious doctrine [cf. *DN*, 447].) In the early years, irrespective of the format in which he was writing – poem or prose fiction, since plays only came later – it was Beckett's practice to quote, usually in tandem and more or less creatively adapted, materials derived from his reading, applying them in contexts quite other than those for which they had originally been intended, as well as to recycle phrases and situations that he had himself devised out of his own personal experience. Many of these triggers were jotted down in his *'Dream' Notebook,* for the most part with chapter and verse omitted, presumably in order to allow Beckett the illusion that there was nothing new under the sun (as in the first sentence of the novel *Murphy*), that everything was a woven tapestry or 'text' – like the 'Text' poem first published in 1931 in *The European Caravan*, and like the prose-poem 'Text' published in 1932 in *The New Review* – and that what he was seeing as a common stock of material could be legitimately used. It was as if nothing could be open to censure, given the way in which previous literary practice had sanctioned the practice, in what amounted to a general free-for-all. *More Pricks* gives this activity as much dignity as it will bear by gesturing in the direction of a 'palimpsest' (88). It seems likely that the Birkbeck Hill quotation, no doubt soon seen as no longer Birkbeck Hill's insofar as it ever had been, served Beckett subsequently as a kind of *ex post facto* confirmation – itself of 'suitably' obscure provenance, and hidden away in a footnote – that he had been on the right track in this regard all along.

In an age like ours which prizes originality, sincerity and authenticity (itself a 'jargon', in the view of the philosopher Adorno), Beckett's early reliance on 'those who have spoken our words before us' is bound to seem something of a desperate remedy, as if an 'itch to make' (Harvey, 273) were being scratched too often for the wound or abrasion underneath to have much of an opportunity to heal. But in *Dream* and *More Pricks*, this radical commitment to an almost homeopathic regime paid dividends; it gave Beckett the opportunity to demonstrate that 'those who have said our words before us' could be co-opted to speak *for* us and to stand in our stead. The construction of new combinations ('the art of combining', as the 1965 prose text *Assez/Enough* calls it; *Texts for Nothing, 94*) was to prove of long-term utility to Beckett, even when quotations from others diminished almost to nothing, and self-plagiarism had become his preferred mode of 'excavation' (*PTD*, 29). (As early as his *Proust* essay, written in 1930, Beckett had identified 'that most necessary, wholesome and monotonous plagiarism – the plagiarism of oneself' [*PTD*, 33]; and the very writing of *More Pricks Than Kicks* was predicated on 'plagiarism of oneself', from *Dream*, or –increasingly – from the stories as they came to be written.) Reading the Beckett in Beckett is often, if not always, a relatively straightforward matter. But to register the presence of 'those who have said our words before us' is much more demanding, especially when they have been so effectively kept 'out of sight' (cf. Caselli 2005, 82, quoting the *'Whoroscope' Notebook*).

To get the most out of the 'palimpsests' in *More Pricks*, which are so much less visible than their counterparts in *Dream*, they need to be seen and confronted, in what can be regarded as an ancillary addition to the ways in which the stories can be 'ordinarily' read, but also as complementary to them. *More Pricks Than Kicks* has never been considered (except perhaps briefly and jocularly, in the 'puff' for the book in the *Observer* on 6 May 1934) of sufficient difficulty and density to merit an annotational approach of the kind that has been applied to *Dream of Fair to Middling Women*, *Murphy*, *Watt*, and a number of the many other post-war works which constitute the received idea of Beckett in the minds of most readers and scholars. But it should really come as no surprise to find that *More Pricks*, a survivor in the aftermath of *Dream*, is much more complex than it appears at first sight, and in places quite as challenging as much better known works by Beckett. His unusual, if not unique, habit of 'snatching' notes from here, there and everywhere is one of the most striking features of all Beckett's early work in English, and what follows is intended to increase a reader's enjoyment and understanding of a book which was never perhaps destined to become anything like a popular favourite, but which shows how hard Beckett laboured to bring *More Pricks* to a level with which he might begin to feel comfortable.

Here, unlike in the main body of the book, I follow the published order of the stories for the sake of clarity. The page numbers refer to the 2010 Faber paperback edition and, in the case of 'Echo's Bones', to the Dartmouth College typescript, with the Faber edition of the latter currently still in *limae labor*.

Biblical references are selectively cited from Ackerley (1999), which contains many more items than are noted here.

Even the details given here are themselves only a selection from what could be an indigestibly large list. For fuller discussion of some entries, and of related issues, see my *Beckett's 'Dream Notebook'* and *A Companion to 'Dream of Fair to Middling Women'*. *DN* numbers refer not to the pages of my edition, but to the numbers of the items there given in square brackets.

To save space, the following abbreviations are used: 'DL' = 'Dante and the Lobster'; 'DD' = 'Ding-Dong'; 'AWN' = 'A Wet Night'; 'LL' = 'Love and Lethe'; 'WO' = 'Walking Out'; 'WAM' = 'What A Misfortune'; 'EB' = 'Echo's Bones'.

'Dante and the Lobster'

3

Belacqua was stuck in Slote (2010, 16) reminds us that Dante the pilgrim is '*within* the moon' (my italics) and that 'for the pilgrim, being stuck in the moon is a sign of his spiritual progress towards God, whereas for Belacqua it is still just an aporia'.

He was so bogged in *Dream*, 'bogged' (177) is applied to the Belacqua experiencing difficulties in his entanglements with the Alba.

the canti in the moon a famously demanding and often obscure section of Dante (*Paradiso*, Canto XI ff). Piccarda (who is mentioned in *Purgatorio*) is in Canto III. Beatrice first appears in the *Divine Comedy* in Canto I of *Inferno*, but is present throughout *Paradiso*. In a 1958 letter to Barbara Bray (TCD), Beckett told her that he had recently tried to re-read *Paradiso* with as little success as when he was young, and he said the same in letters to Mary Hutchinson (9 April 1958, HRHRC) and Kay Boyle (12 April 1958, HRHRC), in the latter dating his previous reading back '30 (odd) years ago'.

neither backward nor forward in Dante's *Purgatorio*, Belacqua refuses to move merely from indolence (cf. Beckett's Belacqua in 'DD' [31]), but here Belacqua is unable to do so given his fruitless endeavour to understand an 'impenetrable passage'. Kay Gilliland Stevenson has suggested that he has chosen the wrong time ('morning') for Dante's Moon Cantos, which begins at noon, but (see the next note) the primary point is that because of his temperament he is actually the wrong person to absorb whatever wisdom they may contain.

a rapid shorthand of the real facts Belacqua's inability to understand is not because he, like Dante, is a 'misinformed poet', but because he instinctively disavows the very premise on which the information is given. Slote (17) comments: 'Beatrice's explanation of the spots on the moon is part of the pilgrim's instruction in how to properly read the signs of divinity'. And he adds: 'She is not merely explaining an astronomical phenomenon, rather she is imparting divine wisdom'.

impatient to get on to Piccarda cf. *Dream*, 130.

quodlibet that is, a subtle, sophistical or merely debatable point, derived from Burton's *The Anatomy of Melancholy* (hereafter Burton), '*Dream*' *Notebook* (hereafter *DN*) item 990, with all subsequent references to the item number of the entry, and not to the page number. The word is also used in 'AWN' (72), and both instances anticipate, although they are quite independent from, Beckett's interest in 1935–6 in Geulincx's *Quaestiones quodlibeticae* (*SBT/A*, 16, 141).

4

a very nice affair   'nice' in the sense of requiring, and rewarding, care and discrimination, which Belacqua demonstrates here; in *Dream* (120) the author suggests that his use of dots is 'nice' (in both of the senses of the word, the common and the more sophisticated).

an old Herald   probably at least 4 years old at the time of writing this story; this, like the paper purchased in 'AWN' (47), is the *Evening* ('Twilight', *Dream*, 182) *Herald*, Belacqua typically (cf. 'WAM', 127) preferring to spend the morning in bed; here, as Stevenson points out (37), he has perhaps, in Dantean terms, been active too early to hope to succeed.

McCabe the assassin   see Kroll 1977, *passim*. The Beckett/Péron translation of *Anna Livia Plurabelle* (1930) has McCabe in it (*L'Herne* 1985, 420), but the equivalent passage in Joyce's *Finnegans Wake* does not.

a bathos   not in the 1932 version; 'bathos' is noted in the *'Whoroscope' Notebook*, among materials from Kant and Mauthner; 'Bathos', in a phrase from Kant's German, is in one of the 'Addenda' to *Watt*.

the stump of the loaf went back into prison   a pervasive metaphor in *More Pricks*: cf. 'dungeon' ('Fingal', 18; 'AWN', 70); 'his patron's spirit had left its prison' ('WAM', 118); 'look nervously round for prisons and palaces' ('WAM', 125); 'his heart gave a great leap in its box' ('Yellow', 161).

no such thing as a sparrow in the wide world   probably thinking of Shakespeare's *Hamlet* (a recurrent point of reference, cf. 6, etc.) and the 'special providence in the fall of a sparrow' (Act V, scene 2), but also of Augustine (*DN*, 37).

5

done to a dead end ... waiting   the bread takes longer to 'die' (into toast) than McCabe will, Belacqua hoping he may experience a 'quick death'.

Cain   cf. *Dream*, 129–30 and Dante, *Paradiso* II, 51 (and also found at *Inferno* XX, 126 and *Purgatorio* XIV, 133); a figure also invoked in the unpublished 1932 poem 'Spring Song'. Beckett is here also adapting details from Genesis 4.2–15.

a true saying   from 1 Timothy 1.15 and 3.1; repeated on 10, and used again in 'Yellow' (155) and 'EB' (1).

6

Butter was a blunder   derived from a phrase in J. G. Lockhart's life of Napoleon (*DN*, 37), and recycled in 'EB' (24).

like smiting the sledded Polacks on the ice   derived from *Hamlet*, Act I, scene 1.

bringing tears   cf. Belacqua and tears elsewhere (70, 87, 105, 155, 162).

burnt, not fully dressed   from Leviticus 7.

horse behind the tumbrel   adapting the proverbial phrase 'the cart before the horse', with the 'horse' – if only by virtue of the syntax – in front here.

Most days, about this hour   cf. Belacqua's regular habits in *Dream*, 126–7.

He knew a man . . . Gorgonzola   added to the 1932 version. Angelo, one of the waiters at the Cochon de Lait restaurant, is mentioned at least twice in letters to MacGreevy (*LSB*, 27, 32).

7

washing his hands like Pilate   Matthew 27.24; cf. the surgeon in 'Yellow' (164).

8

his feet were in ruins   this is one reason why Belacqua 'waddle[s]' (47). *Dream*, after noting that Belacqua 'waddled' (126), tries to explain this 'demolition' (128), but leaves out of account the fact that, in imitation of Joyce, Beckett would sometimes wear shoes that were too small for him. *Dream* (117) has 'the ruined melody'; the Ottolenghi in 'DL' has a 'ruined voice' (11); Otto Olaf in 'WAM' speaks in 'a ruined whisper' (133); the voice of one of the nursing assistants in 'Yellow' is 'in ruins' (163); the groundsman in 'Draff' is 'a fine man in ruins' (173). Later, in 'WAM', another Beckettian alter ego, Walter Draffin, who is only 'five foot five' (114), a 'little creature' with a 'little face' (125), wears 'shoes a size and a half too large' (114), which are part of his 'fantastic upholstery' (136) and help to explain why he 'shuffled and shifted his feet like one surprised in a dishonourable course of action' (136).

9

old bitch of an aunt   anticipating 'old maids . . . old hens' (9) and 'base prying bitch' (12) and the Kerry Blue terrier of 'WO'; the poet Carducci (9) is 'an intolerable old bitch' in the 1932 version (230).

her blackguard boy   not in the 1932 version.

Il Cinque Maggio   a poem in homage to Napoleon, on his death, by the novelist of *I Promessi Sposi*, Alessandro Manzoni (cf. ' [. . .] "Is that *promessi?*" ' in 'AWN' [71]). Whether the fifth of May also had any personal significance for Beckett, in terms of the date of composition of 'DL' or its submission to *This Quarter* in 1932, seems unlikely ever to be known, though it may have done. In 1932 he certainly had good reason to regret a death on 7 May, the assassination of Paul Doumer, which – given that he had no current *carte de séjour* to enable him to stay in Paris – obliged him to leave a few weeks later.

Napoleone di mezza, etc.   from J. G. Lockhart's *Life of Napoleon* (ed. cit. London: William Tegg, ?1867, 3; *DN*, item 15).

Pellico   Silvio Pellico, Italian author (1789–1854), principally remembered for *Le miei Prigoni* (*My Prisons*) [1832], here remembered because of McCabe in Mountjoy.

Carducci   in the 1932 version (230) Carducci is described as an 'intolerable old bitch' (cf. 9, 12). See Beckett's TCD notes (*SBT/A*, 16) and a letter of 'c. 18 to 25 July 1930' to MacGreevy (*LSB*, 33).

10

make it up . . . against the next time   that is, investigate it in readiness for the next lesson (cf. 16), but with the implication that any explanation will necessarily be fabricated.

Bating   Dublinese, used again in 'WAM' (130) and 'EB' (24). In the 1932 version: 'Except . . . '

Oliver the improver   in the 1932 version: 'Oliver the barman'. Earlier on the same page of the *This Quarter* printing there is the phrase 'He did not see how [Belacqua's lunch] could have been improved on'; 'improved on' is, as it were, improved upon by 'superseded' in 1934.

Lepping   cf. *First Love*; *The Expelled*, 79; and *The unnamable*, 126 .

11

Signorina Adriana Ottolenghi   a character based on Beckett's Italian teacher, Bianca Esposito; cf. 'Ottolenghi' (*Disjecta*, 32).

went prestly in   that is, quickly; cf. 'Presto' (Swift) in 'Fingal' (26).

obiter   that is, casually, or in passing; later (in 'Yellow') again applied to 'conversation' (157), as it had been by Robert Burton (*DN*, 844), and by Beckett in *Dream* (162; cf. 24, 195).

a lady of a certain age   cf. 'Yellow' (163).

She would look it up in her big Dante   a perfectly naturalistic detail, but Slote (18) very shrewdly points out that 'just as Beatrice receives her wisdom straight from God, so too must Ottolenghi defer to a higher power'.

compassion in Hell   cf. 'EB' (11).

qui vive, etc.   used by MacGreevy as an epigraph to his poem 'Fragments'; probably 'the phrase you want' (Beckett to MacGreevy 'before 5 August 1930' (*LSB* 35, and n. 1, 37); Beckett asked MacGreevy if he had retained the '*qui vive* . . . ' phrase in a letter of 6 January 1931. The phrase is from Dante's *Inferno* 20:28, and is 'one of his rare wan smiles' (*The Lost Ones*, *Texts for Nothing* etc., 103).

12

clutching her cat   the situation here is an extrapolation of the phrase 'something the cat brought in', a phrase used by the Polar Bear, with 'dog' for 'cat' in 'AWN' (70); cf. the cat mentioned on 161.

The grey hairs of her maidenhead   adapted, adding a sexual ambiguity, from 'maidenhair' in the 'rare' *Oxford English Dictionary* sense 5 of 'a maiden's hair'; cf. *DN*, 1066.

honing after   that is, longing for, or (in certain circumstances) lusting after, as in 'EB' (4); Burton, *DN*, 818 (where it is 'home' which is longed for); cf. a 'honing after' or longing for the dark in *Dream* (51).

13

Let us call it Winter   in 'real' terms this would not be necessary: Henry McCabe was hanged on 9 December 1926. A possible indicator that 'DL' was written over the spring or early summer of 1930.

and a moon rise   like an equally obliging moon at the end of Act 1 of *Waiting for Godot*; cf. 'the moon on the job' in 'Draff' (180) and the 'toy moon' of 'EB' (18).

A lamplighter flew by   cf. the lamplighters of *Dream* (156).

Jonah and the gourd   from the Old Testament book of Jonah 4.10.

a jealous God   Exodus 20.5.

whatever flowers die   perhaps with half an ear to a line in the song 'Danny Boy': 'And if you come, when all the flowers are dying . . . ', that is, in winter ('Let us call it Winter'), not 'when summer's in the meadow'.

14

Take into the air my quiet breath   from Keats's 'Ode to a Nightingale' (cf. *LSB*, 21); the phrase is used in a semi-erotic situation in *Dream* (107).

and then lash into it   cf. 'Yellow': 'She lashed into the part with picric and ether' (160).

It is not   Cohn (2001, 391, n. 11) records Beckett once jokingly telling her that he had considered changing this to 'Like Hell it is'. Slote (19) sees the phrase as a 'synchronic disjunction' set against the way allegory is typically 'sustained diachronically (i.e. through narrative)', having previously pointed out (18) that 'Belacqua winds up in hell, after having started in heaven'.

'Fingal'

17

a memorable fit of laughing   this becomes a 'frame' for the story on being reprised in its last paragraph; cf. 'Yellow' (162).

not much more than a burrow   cf. the 'two holes to a burrow' in 'DD' (36).

sad animal   cf. the 'animal spirits' in 'EB' (1): the notion here (the phrase is repeated on 21) is derived from one popularly attributed to Aristotle, to the effect that all humans are naturally sad after sexual intercourse, which does not seem to have occurred here; alluded to by Winnie [!] in the play *Happy Days*.

don't they look lovely, so dreamy   'lovely' is here very much Winnie's word (cf. 21), but later it becomes Belacqua's ('WO', 97, 99; 'Yellow', 158, 159), and he is buried in 'the loveliest little lap of earth you ever saw' ('Draff', 173; see note to Uccello below).

east wind   perhaps with some thought of Mr Jarndyce in Dickens's *Bleak House*, but Belacqua is presumably looking east, or at least watching the effect of a wind blowing from the east.

She began to admire this and that   later 'admiring the theories of swans and the coots' (25); cf. Beckett's father 'admiring the view' on a walk they had taken together (letter to MacGreevy of 23 April 1933, *LSB*, 154).

the Cena   the Leonardo da Vinci 'Last Supper' at the Brera in Milan; the 'rime' with 'villain' is Shakesperean pronunciation, as in Act I, scene 2 of *The Tempest*.

Madame de Warens   the 'Mamma' to Jean-Jacques (cf. 28) Rousseau's 'little one', who is introduced in Book II of his *Confessions*, whom Rousseau later abandons (cf. Winnie here).

tesserae   mosaic tiles; the second use of recondite Latin (cf. 'passim' in the first paragraph), and as such preparing for 'Roman' to come (19).

18

a magic land   cf. *Dream*, 161.

Lamartine (the '**Alphonse**' of a few lines below) French poet and (later) government officer, author of the lyric 'L'Isolement', which contains the line: 'Un seul être vous manque, et tout est dépeuplé', which is to be found in the notebooks towards *Murphy*, and was adapted by Beckett for the title *Le Dépeupleur* (*The Lost Ones*).

champaign cf. *Dream* (9, 43), 'WO' (96) and 'EB' (24), 'across a travesty of champaign . . . ' in the late 1931 poem 'Enueg I', and *Mercier and Camier* (81).

Impetigo a skin ailment from which Beckett periodically suffered, recorded in letters to MacGreevy of ?17 September 1930 and 8 October 1932, and described in the latter as a 'toga mollis' or soft covering. cf. the Smeraldina thinking of 'your poor sore face', which seems to be part of 'what is on you that makes me love you so greatly' (145).

water to drink in a dungeon from *Dream*, 108. Later adapted to the fairy tales of Charles Perrault (in 'AWN': 'a pint of Perrier'; 70).

a land of sanctuary cf. 'sanctuary' (*Dream*, 40), and Walter Draffin in 'WAM' (139), but here designed to set up Belacqua 'safe' at the end of the story (27).

smoking a cigar identified as a sign of 'buccal' homosexual tendencies by Garnier (*DN*, 481); Belacqua smokes cigarettes in 'Yellow' and cigars in 'EB'; Beethoven 'smokes a long pipe' in a *DN* entry (1105) from Romain Rolland; Jeri L. Kroll (1974, 360, n. 3) considers the likelihood that Lord Gall may be homosexual.

women' [. . . /19] **dream'** thinking of Beckett's first novel, soon to be jettisoned.

Cincinnatus legendary Roman exponent of agriculture, perhaps via Brewer's *Dictionary of Phrase and Fable* [hereafter Brewer]; imported from *Dream* (191).

all anyway on the grass the mention of the grass links Winnie to the 'rank grass' where the bicycle is 'lying' (20). But Winnie is to die 'to decency' ('Draff', 167).

Roman . . . across the estuary as if they were, like Caesar, 'crossing the Rubicon'; cf. the 'Napoleonic' Poet ('as though he had just brought an army across the Beresina') in 'AWN' (47), used in *Dream* (203), so written before 'Fingal', though the one motif may perhaps have generated the other.

as wax in her hands cf. the footnote to 'WO' (101).

a quiet puella that is, a girl, in most cases (as here?) a virgin; from Burton (*DN*, 913, 916, 928); yet more Latin.

who shall silence them cf. *Dream* (234), where it has been first tried out on 188; cf. Beckett's translations of a prose poem by André Breton and Paul Eluard for the Surrealist issue of the magazine *This Quarter* (V:I, April 1932, 76). The question is repeated (and extended) in 'AWN' (71).

If she closed her eyes she might see something a precondition for real vision, as distinct from mere seeing, in Beckett's estimation, which he often thought of in connection with Rimbaud's 'Les Poëtes de Sept Ans' (a point of reference several times in 'EB'), and as conducive to poetry (cf. 'yeux clos', *Dream*, 21). In 'WO', Lucy, with a name derived from the patron saint of eyes and seeing, has a 'sudden vision' (101) which tells her more than all the looking she engages in. In 'Yellow', Belacqua decides that the eyes are 'safer closed' (153), but the late 1932 poem 'Serena II' had already decided: 'it is useless to close the eyes'.

the round tower anticipating '**Martello**' (20), and perhaps inevitably (though the real scene is the issue) thinking of the opening of Joyce's *Ulysses*.

20

red chapel of Donabate for a photograph, see O'Brien, 231.

as full of towers as Dun Laoghaire of steeples cf. 'kindergartens of steeples' in the late 1932 poem 'Serena II'.

21

Dr Petrie world-famous archaeologist Dr Flinders Petrie.

this machine anticipating the theft of the bicycle; but cf. the 'clockwork' Chas of 'AWN' (45). Hamlet uses the phrase 'whilst this machine is to him' in Act II, scene 2 of the play to express his discomfiture with corporeal life.

funeral meats . . . marriage tables from *Hamlet*, Act I, scene 2.

a square bawnless tower a tower without a fortified outwork, enclosure or 'enceinte' (*Dream*, 185).

sursum corda still more Latin: the injunction to 'lift up your hearts' in the Roman Catholic Mass, later (in 'WO') revealed as Belacqua's periphrasis for voyeuristic activities.

22

The crenels on the wall I find as moving . . . cf. the 'vulvate gnarls' found moving by Ruskin in 'EB' (9).

as a little fat overfed boy   cf. the first words of *Dream*: 'Behold Belacqua an overfed child' (1), and the 'little fat boy' of 'WO' (96). Presumably to compensate for being overfed as a child, Belacqua eats nothing but a sandwich and some scallops across the ten stories of *More Pricks*, and nothing but garlic in 'EB' (7).

the idea of a sequitur from his body to his mind   thinking of Descartes and the pineal gland; more Latin added to the mix.

Jean-Jacques sprawling   from Rousseau's *Confessions* (I, vi), from where Mme de Warens has earlier been taken (23). There are two entries from Rousseau's *Rêveries d'un promeneur solitaire* in *DN*, 332, 333 (cf. *LSB*, 145, 228), and one from *La Nouvelle Héloïse* (*DN*, 331; via Praz). Rousseau is (with Lavater) one of the two 'best Swiss' (*LSB*, 282), and Beckett read him again in 1934 (16 September 1934; *LSB*, 228), but with some reservations.

caul   cf. the circumstances surrounding the birth of the title character of Dickens, *David Copperfield* (cf. Mrs Gummidge in 'AWN', 73).

punctilio   cf. *Dream*, 240, in phrases altered for 'AWN'.

hugger-mugger   that is, privately, clandestinely, as in Shakespeare, *Hamlet*, Act IV, scene 5; taken over from *Dream* (109).

23

over the wall, through the chord of yellow   anticipating the 'grand old yaller wall' of 'Yellow' (159), but also (like many of the *More Pricks* stories) with music, and musical terms, in mind .

his panting   cf. 98, 118, 180, etc.

Dr Sholto   a surname probably derived from the murdered Major Bartholomew Sholto in Arthur Conan Doyle's *The Sign of Four* ('almost certainly a character modelled on Oscar Wilde'; Michael Coren, *Conan Doyle*, London: Bloomsbury, 1995, 58; cf. Mary Power's essay on 'Fingal'). Sholto is presented here 'with a brow' (like the Student of 'AWN', 59) because he thinks of himself as an intellectual, although in these circumstances he does not think to much effect apparently.

Malahide!   thinking of McCabe, the 'Malahide murderer' (10); Kroll (1977), 48, n. 5.

25

Winnie still sees   the first of relatively few 'flash forward' moments (a device first tried out in at least two 'years later' excursions in *Dream* [129, 185]) in the collection, which serve further to disrupt narrative continuity.

Compare: 'One of these fine days Hairy will observe' and Otto Olaf who 'died in the end of a clot' ('WAM', 126, 130), and the Matron 'Years later' in 'Yellow' (160). But by then Beckett must have known how he would get to the 'end' of *More Pricks*, or how it might benefit from some revision.

the last ditch   thinking of the Malebolge (cf. *Dream*, 168) in Dante's *Inferno*.

I was born on Lambay   Lambay Island; see photographs in O'Brien (71, 228).

Swift and his 'motte'   The enigmatic relationship between satirist Jonathan Swift and his friend 'Stella' (Esther Johnson) figures in any number of biographies of Swift. The most recent biography of Swift known to Beckett was a collaborative effort (published by the Dublin company Maunsel in 1934) on the part of his friend Joseph Hone and Hone's Italian friend Mario Rossi (letter to MacGreevy of 5 January 1933; *LSB*, 150), whom Beckett had helped in some capacity, though he had doubts about the book. Madame de la Motte, an oppressed and imprisoned figure under the cruelties of Marie Antoinette, is referred to in the 1932 poem 'Sanies II', and in *DN*, 396. In 'DD', the pedlar, a 'woman of the people' as the old man in 'Fingal' must presumably be a 'man of the people', also uses the word 'motte' (39) for the girlfriend that Belacqua (for once) lacks.

he had read it in an old Telegraph and he would adhere to it   probably a reflection of Beckett's preference for the *Evening Herald*; cf. 'the old *Herald*' of 'DL' (4).

26

Little fat Presto ... camomile   'Presto' (cf. 'presto' in line 23 of the 1932 poem 'Spring Song') is Swift's nickname for himself in the *Journal to Stella*, from which Beckett has combined two completely unrelated phrases many pages apart (as noted by Frederik N. Smith, 31).

27

Taylor's public-house in Swords   for a photograph, see O'Brien, 239.

drinking and laughing   Ackerley (2008, 63), pointing out that the American edition reads simply 'drinking', thinks that the English original 'accentuat[es] the notion that [Belacqua] is an escaped lunatic'. If so, the old man who has been 'showing signs of excitement' and spoken 'hopefully' on 28, has anticipated it, and become (unknown to himself) 'off' and 'unsluiced' in much the same way as Belacqua has been and will be. With 'and laughing' omitted, there can be no late *ricorso* to 'the memorable fit' of the opening sentence of the story.

'Ding-Dong'

31

to move constantly from place to place   cf. 'on the move' (33) and 'keep on the move' in the poem 'Serena III'.

the Furies   as in the Greek tragedies of Aeschylus; they recur in the unpublished 1932 poem 'Spring Song'.

salad days   a time of youthful inexperience, from Shakespeare, *Antony and Cleopatra*, Act I, scene 4; cf. *Dream*, 43 (which is one reason why the phrase **the old story** is used here to create a kind of paradox) and *DN*, 248.

bogged in indolence   a translation of *impaludito in pigrizia* (*DN*, 315), apparently 'a Beckettian coinage, allusive to *Inferno* XX and VII' (Caselli 2005, 63); borrowed from *Dream*, 121.

32

Pylades and Orestes   a pair of Greek mythological heroes who became a byword for friendship (cf. the David and Jonathan figures in Gaelic in 'EB'); probably by way of several pairs of friends listed in Burton (*DN*, 813).

abode   a kind of back-formation from 'the author of the Imitation' (see next note), derived from *DN*, 563; used in *Dream*, 5 (twice).

author of the Imitation   *The Imitation of Christ*, traditionally ascribed to the German mystic Thomas à Kempis. Beckett knew it (see *DN*, items 558–65, 573–9, 584–603) in the Ingram translation under the alternative title 'Musica Ecclesiastica'.

glad going out and sad coming in   from the same; *DN* (with the Latin and the English), 576; in accordance with the 'reverse' spoken of here the story has no 'sad coming in' at its end, but rather a contented staying out.

internus homo   from the same (*DN*, 578).

a strong weakness for oxymoron   itself an illustration of the rhetorical term.

33

this 'gress' or 'gression'   formed in part by removing the 're-' prefix from 'regress' and 'regression' as found, as perhaps Beckett already had, in the writings of psychoanalysis. Beckett recycles 'gress, pure and mere gress' in relation to 'hav[ing] been saved the trouble of moving' in his discussion of 'anabasis' in a letter of 27 February 1934 to Nuala Costello (*LSB*, 186). He had first met the notion of anabasis, a journey, on reading the famous poem *Anabase* by Saint-John Perse in 1931, which had been translated by no less a figure than T. S. Eliot. Beckett had been invited to review the latter (*LSB*, 59, 73), but seems to have declined, having been unmoved, or at least not having moved as requested.

vaudeville cf. *Proust* (*PTD*, 92).

all the tulips and aerugo 'aerugo' is rust or verdigris; cf. 'the green tulips' of a September 1931 letter to MacGreevy (*LSB*, 88), also found in the poem 'Enueg II'.

Tommy Moore's plinth the statue to the poet Thomas Moore in College Green, atop an underground toilet (cf. 'AWN').

Buridan's ass a proverb based on the absurd supposition that an ass situated equidistant between two bales of hay would perish from hunger by being unable to choose between them; probably by way of Brewer, but with the opening of *Paradiso* IV no doubt also in mind; the phrasing 'could not . . . move . . . backward or forward' recalls to mind Belacqua at the beginning of 'DL' (3).

ebbing from the shingle Farrow (108) hears an echo of Matthew Arnold's 'Dover Beach', which can be heard a good deal more audibly, though it is still distant, in *The Calmative* (32).

Itself it went nowhere, only round and round anticipating the Heaven of the pedlar (42).

34

a star the horizon adorning omitting the phrase 'of the east' from the popular hymn 'Brightest and Best of the Sons of the Morning'.

Down Pearse Street previously Brunswick Street, as Chas reminds Caleken Frica in 'AWN' (57), a story which begins in much the same locale in central Dublin, only later to move on east and south.

Perpetuis, etc. the TCD charter undertakes to provide for 'the education, institution and instruction of youth, and of a student in arts and faculties to exist in perpetuity, henceforth and for ever'.

35

Here he was known perhaps thinking of the sentences beginning 'By them that knew him . . . ' (*Dream*, 126). In both contexts it is implied that Belacqua cannot really be 'known'.

manoeuvre probably prompted by readings in Garnier (*DN*, 440) and, earlier, a collection of citations relating to the hand (*DN*, 252–5).

the weary proletarians   cf. 'AWN', 43: 'lashing into his dinner like any proletarian' (with the 'lash into it' idea from 'DL' [14]; *Dream* [200] has 'eating his dinner').

36

aliquots   exact divisors or factors of an integer or quantity.

ebriety   from the French word *ébrieté* (drunkenness).

the only place where he could come to anchor   contrast the Alba in *Dream*, whose soul is her only 'poste restante' (177), who has no use for an anchor (192, 193) and who 'puts not her trust in changes of scenery' (176).

at home in his own great armchair   cf. the 'poltrone' of *Dream* (147) and *DN* (417).

the trituration of the child   her reduction to powder.

37

all the way from Tommy Moore   the 'plinth' of whose statue is first mentioned on 37; the statue itself is referred to at the beginning of 'AWN' (43).

spoiling porter   in 'AWN', Belacqua favours hostelries 'where the porter was well up' (44; emphasized for a second time later in the same paragraph). Here either his 'old itch [cf. 'EB', 13] and algos [Greek for 'pain']' have contrived to disimprove it, or the 'spectacle' he has seen as if in a vision (36) has lasted longer than his drink can stay 'up'. In the next paragraph it will be 'dying', and ultimately 'dead' (39) as the 'dribble of time' (159) takes effect, in spite of the extra 'tuppence' (39) which Belacqua has given to the pedlar. In 'AWN', Belacqua's porter is 'despondent' (47; in *Dream*: 'at half-mast' [204]).

38

Master of Tired Eyes   the name given, in default of any known name, to an old master acquired in 1928, a painting of an old woman in Dublin's National Gallery in Merrion Square, mentioned in a letter to MacGreevy of 13 September 1932 (*LSB*, 121). For a reproduction, see O'Brien, 140. It is now (James Knowlson tells me) described as 'Flemish School, c.1540'.

sweet style   a reference to the thirteenth-century *dolce stil nuovo* of Dante and some later contemporaries; cf. Winnie in *Happy Days* on the 'old style'.

the just and the unjust   taken over from *Dream*, 130. Ackerley, 'Bible' (69), invokes the rain of Matthew 5.45, but Beckett is thinking here of the 'light' from the 'Cain' figure first met with in 'DL' (5). Cain, and part of this phrase, are in the 1932 poem 'Spring Song' (the phrase is on line 56).

tuppence a piece   cf. the 'penny heaven' of *Dream* (194) and the 'penny-a-line vulgarity' of *Proust* (*PTD*, 76).

39

'Rowan' . . . 'rowan an' rowan an' rowan'   there seems to be no reason to suppose that this is a kind of backhanded homage (like the 1932 acrostic poem 'Home Olga') to Joyce, whose only play *Exiles* focuses on the marriage of Richard and Bertha Rowan. But Beckett quotes: 'The Vico road goes round to meet where terms begin' (cf. *Finnegans Wake*, 452) in 'Dante . . . Bruno.Vico..Joyce' (*Disjecta*, 23), and was obviously fascinated by the idea of circularity, even if ultimately disposed to reject it, with Belacqua here voluntarily self-exiled from Heaven.

yer motte   as also previously in 'Fingal' (25).

white voice   partly derived from a French idiom meaning 'to say one thing, then the opposite', but possibly simply plain or colourless; cf. 138 ('WAM'); *Dream*, 186 and *DN*, 975.

cantcher   cf. Mick Doyle in 'EB' (25).

Belacqua tarried   perhaps, given 'went away' just above, half-remembering a jingle of the Fool in Shakespeare's *King Lear*, Act II, scene 2, containing the phrases 'But I will tarry, the fool will stay . . . The knave turns fool that runs away' – with Belacqua as fool, and the woman of the people in some ways wiser than he is. But both of them are moving 'away'.

'A Wet Night'

(Adapted from *Dream of Fair to Middling Women*, 199ff, with only some of the numerous differences in phrasing between the two texts noted here.)

43

Hyam's   a well-known Dublin tailor.

Mistinguett   Parisian entertainer; the 'chalets of necessity' (*DN*, 490) are street urinals or pissoirs, perhaps combined here with thoughts of 'the great and good Lord Chesterfield' and his 'necessary house', as in Murphy's 'sheet' attempting (as it turns out, to no purpose) to arrange for the 'disposal' of his 'body, mind and soul' after death in chapter 12 of *Murphy*.

happy body   having used the underground toilet; cf. 'EB' (10) and Sproule's exclamation 'Happy dawg' in 'WAM'(124).

the strom   the bustle and confusion, from the German, but also used by Rimbaud in the prose poem 'Mouvement' (*Les Illuminations*) and by Beckett in his translation of 'Le Bateau ivre' ('turgent stroms'). Taken over from *Dream* (4, 119, 139), and used again in the 1933 poem 'Serena I'.

The lemon of faith jaundiced   cf. 'the lemon of lemons' (*Dream*, 79), derived from Augustine (*DN*, 104).

Gabriel   'prophecy' in the vicinity suggests the Angel Gabriel and the annunciation to Mary; but cf. 'the Abbé Gabriel' in 'WAM' (138), a contemporary figure once known, mainly in occult circles, for his idiosyncratic cyclic theory of history.

Doubt, Despair and Scrounging   from Burton (*DN*, 996); cf. Caselli (2005, 65–6).

the blind paralytic   as already met with in 'DD' (34).

Wanderjahre . . . a sleep and a forgetting   the first part of Goethe's *Wilhelm Meister* combined with Wordsworth's 'Ode: Intimations of Immortality'. cf. the 'years of wandering' in the 1934 Goethe-inspired quatrain 'Gnome'.

44

a sign   from the Bible (all four Gospels, but also throughout the Old Testament), but probably here primarily thinking of T. S. Eliot's 'Gerontion'.

cloud of latter rain   from the Biblical book of Proverbs 16.15, with gratitude emphasized; *DN*, 555; cf. the last line (28) of 'it is high time lover' (HRHRC), a revision of the poem 'Return to the Vestry', and 'EB' (1).

a waste of poets and politicians   'a waste of' replaces 'the sand of' in *Dream* (200), with Beckett no doubt of thinking of Shakespeare's Sonnet 129 ('Th' expense of spirit in a waste of shame'), but also the better to prepare for the 'waste of water' in the poem 'Calvary by Night' later (54).

cantilena   cf. *Dream*, 201 (and also 125); cf. Dante, *Paradiso*, XXXII, 97.

the Fire Station   cf. O'Brien, 167–8, with a photograph of it on 169.

45

Savonarola   notorious Renaissance Florentine hell- and fire-raiser, burnt at the stake for excessive zeal construed as heresy.

Homer hour   derived from Victor Bérard's translation into French of the *Odyssey* (*LSB*, 90); *DN*, 715; compare 'indigo hour' later, in 'WAM' (110) and 'Draff' (174).

Chas . . . of French nationality a character based on Beckett's French friend Georges Pelorson (later Georges Belmont); 'Jean du Chas' (as he is later here, 69) is the (non-existent) French poet of Beckett's 1930 skit 'Le Concentrisme' (*Disjecta*).

Skeat Dr W. W. Skeat, editor of Chaucer and author of a famous *Etymological Dictionary of the English Language,* much beloved by James Joyce, among others.

Paganini legendary 'demonic' violin virtuoso and composer of phenomenally difficult musical pieces for the instrument.

the song in his head derived from the 'simple cantilena in his mind' of the previous paragraph (cf. the 'UND' section of *Dream* [125] and also 201), but there are two songs about to emerge, Harry Lauder's 'Roamin' in the Gloamin' (as 'Ramble . . . in the twilight', from Belacqua) and the first line of the popular parlour piece 'Love's Old Sweet Song' (from Chas; cf. *Dream*, 167). The quickly popular 'With a Song in my Heart' by Richard Rodgers and Lorenz Hart was first heard in Britain in the 1930 C. B. Cochran revue show.

the Hibernian Dairy also mentioned in 'DD' (34): there the little girl went to fetch milk and bread, with her death as it were 'guaranteed' by the Monumental Showroom which we only now discover to have been close at hand; here Chas has 'butter and eggs'.

clockwork cf. 'clockwork cabbages' (of Balzac), *Dream*, 119.

Bartlett John Bartlett, Victorian compiler of concordances (hence '**a mind like a tattered concordance**' above), most famously to Shakespeare, a copy of which Beckett owned, and also of books of quotations.

Fair . . . to meedling thinking of the jettisoned *Dream* (as again later in 'WAM'; 128).

The poem moves, eppure adapted from a famous, but slightly ambiguous, remark of Galileo's (roughly translatable as 'and yet it moves') which lies behind the 'That's not moving, that's *moving*' line in the 1930 poem 'Whoroscope'.

ars longa *not* mentioned here by Chas, but ruefully reflected on by the implied author of *Dream* (68); proverbially always contrasted with *vita brevis*.

Limae labor, etc. cf. 128; also used in 'Serena I'; from Horace 'The Art of Poetry' (one of three direct quotations from Horace in *More Pricks*): 'the painstaking use of the file and delay' (line 290), but of course it was not 'delay' that had held up *Dream*, and fewer pains were taken in writing it than had been required for *More Pricks*. Beckett was 'presented with a lovely polyglot edition of Horace' (letter to MacGreevy of 8 November 1931: '[I] haven't the guts to start into it'; but cf. the 'polyglot splendours' of 'WAM', 121), and it was still in his library at the time of his death.

46

casa Frica   the home of Caleken Frica, about to appear ('Behold the Frica'), a character based on Mary Manning, who had appeared before this in *Dream* (180): 'Caleken' by way of Cooper (*DN*, 375), and 'Frica' by way of old Norse mythology and the Fricka of Wagnerian opera. She reappears (as does the Count of Parabimbi) in 'EB' (5, 15).

Service Flats   municipally assisted dwellings for the poor; similar provisions in London (cf. Ackerley 1998, 76) are described in *Murphy* (chapter 5) as 'malignant proliferations of urban tissue'.

Havelock Ellis   (1859–1939) pioneer editor (the *Mermaid* dramatists), essayist (*From Rousseau to Proust*, etc.) and sexologist (*Studies in the Psychology of Sex*, six volumes, 3rd edition, 1910).

frankly itching to work that which is not seemly   from *DN*, 749 (St Paul's definition of sodomy in his Epistle to the Romans).

Portigliotti   from Mario Praz, *The Romantic Agony* (original Italian edition of 1930); *DN*, 258. Most of what follows is 'added' to 'AWN' from *Dream* (179), long before the Frica's party gets into full swing.

Sade's 120 Days   the notorious pornographic fiction *The 120 Days of Sodom* by the Marquis de Sade, which Beckett had not yet read. Early in 1938 he toyed with translating it for Jack Kahane's Obelisk Press (Knowlson 1996, 293), and later proposed (and undertook) some translations from Sade for Georges Duthuit to use in post-war *Transition*, translations which never appeared.

Brignole-Sale   also from Praz; *DN*, 258.

shagreened   thinking of Balzac's novel *La Peau de Chagrin*; cf. 'the famous fatal skin' (*Molloy*, 51), where the length of the novel seems to have made the character (and no doubt his author) wish it were shorter.

A septic pudding   a phrase jotted down in *DN* (547) and used in *Dream* (179, the source for the whole of this description).

absinthe whinny   cf. Lord Gall on Pernod in 'EB' (17), with a number of equine references (here mostly associated with the Frica, for example, 68; this tactic is begun with the 'fetlock' and 'shod foot' of the Syra-Cusa in *Dream*, 33). It begins to look as if the first name of Winnie Coates in 'Fingal' may have a meaning that the story has decided not to emphasize (given that there is a bicycle to steal away on), but 'WO' renews the equation with Lucy and the jennet.

seldom one without two   cf. *Dream*, 11: 'never one without two' and 'never two without three' in 'LL' (88).

a little saprophile   a medical term for a bacterium inhabiting putrid matter; he reappears on 61 and 63; in *Dream* (203, etc.) he is a 'macaco', a Spanish version of the monkey better known as a macaque, which in the typescript of *Dream* replaces 'acavus' (a type of snail).

golden eastern lay   from line 32 of Tennyson's 'To Edward FitzGerald', the 'translator' of *The Rubaiyat of Omar Khayyam* via *DN*, 1157.

the Grosvenor   a well known hotel on Westland Row; see O'Brien, 174.

The golden eastern lay   from *DN*, 1157, where it is identified as a phrase from Tennyson's 'To Edward FitzGerald', author/translator of the *Rubaiyyat of Omar Khayyam* (cf. 'Omar', *Dream*, 197).

Wally Whitmaneen   an Irishization (cf. 'penny maneen', *Dream*, 100) of the great American poet and democrat Walt Whitman, but the implication is that the poet may be a homosexual. Lord Gall's sexuality in 'EB' may be more ambivalent than he would like to admit (cf. Kroll 1974, 360, n. 3), and of course the Belacqua of *Dream* is more than once thought of as a 'principal boy' (19, 38, 40).

the impression of having lost a harrow, etc.   cf. 'Censorship in the Saorstat': 'the Irish are a characteristic agricultural community in this, that they have something better to do than read' (*Disjecta*, 87).

47

Beresina   or, as more often nowadays, the 'Berezina', a river on the then border between Russia and Poland, crossed by Napoleon in November 1812 on his retreat from Moscow, after appalling losses which, in France, have made the name synonymous with catastrophe. The difficult crossing is described in Lockhart's *Life*, although Beckett does not note it in the Napoleon notes in *DN*. Presumably the 'point' here is that the poet's attempt to dominate Belacqua, and his satisfaction at having apparently boxed him in, are about to fall flat, with Belacqua actually having the drop on him by virtue of the local knowledge which enables him to effect a retreat more readily than Napoleon could.

give it a name   Dublinese; cf. 'EB' (27).

He waddled out of the bar   as in *Dream* (203), but there Belacqua's peculiar way of walking has earlier (175) been seen by the Alba as a consequence of his posteriors being 'on the big side' for his boots. Later, Chas describes Belacqua's way of walking as 'zigzagging' (57).

Stendhal's Comte de Thaler   from *DN*, 903; a very minor figure in part II, chapters 4 and 8, of the French novelist's *Le Rouge et le Noir*. Beckett's copy (UoR) was purchased in September 1926 for examination purposes.

drank despondent porter   cf. the 'spoiling' and 'dying' (37) and ultimately 'dead' porter (39) of 'DD'; not in *Dream* at this point (204), although *Dream* has the phrase 'at half mast', omitted here (to be recycled in 'Draff' [176] and in the poem 'Malacoda', begun at about the same time).

ptosis   not in *Dream* at this point (204); a medical term for the slackening or loosening of an internal organ, here of the intestinal organs or **viscera** in the trunk of the body or, by extension, of the buttocks (cf. the 'Panpygoptosis' of Miss Dew in chapter 5 of *Murphy*).

A woman, etc.   tried out in *DN* (948 ff.), probably as copied straight out of a daily newspaper.

48

the curate   Irish term for the barman or bartender.

Grock   not in *Dream* at this point (204), but this figure is more specifically associated with the Alba in 'AWN' than his more numerous manifestations in *Dream* would permit. 'Grock' was the stage name of the Swiss clown Charles Adrien Wettach (1880–1959), whose tag line was (in the German quoted here) 'Nicht möglich', an almost untranslatable phrase, and here extended (cf. 'Ouayseau bleheu . . . '; 'WAM', 118), either to sound more Swiss or simply to look morestrange and to catch the eye. Its literal meaning is 'not possible', but in the circumstances could perhaps be read as 'it's not on' or 'it's no go'. It is certainly 'no go' in one sense of the phrase when it is voiced in the same emphatic manner later (73), Belacqua having emerged from Casa Alba. But Beckett seems, on the evidence of *DN*, 1026 (where he adds the French phrase 'sans blague' in brackets; cf. *Dream*, 174) to have also understood it to mean something like 'no joke' or 'no kidding' or 'it's no laughing matter', as if to insist on the truthfulness or seriousness of what may seem to have been passed off as a merely flippant anecdote or occasion; hence Beckett's use of 'I assure thee', with or without the German 'doch doch', in the poems 'Enueg II' and 'Spring Song' (with Grock added in line 39 of the latter). Grock crops up repeatedly, always in scenes of sexual arousal and/or bafflement in *Dream*, (e.g. 9, '*Inquit Grock* . . .', 115, 204, 237: '*Voice of Grock* . . .') Beckett adopts his tag again, with a comment in French added, in a letter to MacGreevy of 9 October 1933, but without any obvious sexual dimension intended (*LSB*, 166).

began to worry lest the worst should come to the worst   in *Dream* (204): 'began now to be harassed by dread les[t] the robe should turn out . . . to be backless', probably altered so as to echo 'hope for the best [a]nd expect the worst' in 'DL' (10).

Venerilla   from Burton (*DN*, 871), perhaps with the implication that she suffers from the pressures of venery, which of course may sometimes lead to venereal infection.

eye of the mind   from the opening of W. B. Yeats's play *At The Hawk's Well* (1916), a favourite of Beckett's; cf. 'WAM' (137).

[Beckett at this point omits a paragraph describing how 'fashionable Dublin' is preparing for the party to come (*Dream*, 206–7), one of only two paragraphs cut in transposing this material into 'AWN', although individual phrases often differ. The phrase 'a few pothooks and hangers' in this paragraph in *Dream* is, for example, recycled in 'WO' (98).]

49

her mind is at prayer-stool   as distinct from a body being 'at stool'.

winding up the weights of her mind   cf. the clock(s) given by Thelma to Belacqua as a wedding present in 'WAM' (122). The Alba is, unlike most of the *More Pricks* women, associated with the 'mind', no doubt partly because Ethna MacCarthy, the real-life model for the character, was not available (to Beckett) in any other way.

the belle of the ball . . . the belle . . . the ball   in *Dream* this passage (207) is anticipated on 203 by: 'And she. In her scarletest robe. And her broad bored pale face. The belle of the ball. Aïe!' (omitted from 'AWN', 46), the motif having first been used very strikingly, emphasizing the near-homophony, in a conversation between Belacqua and the Alba on 197, where it effectively becomes an echo of the Smeraldina's 'Bel!'. Beckett is probably half-thinking of the character Belle-Belle (cf. 'WAM') in the fairy tales of the Comtesse d'Aulnoy (*DN*, 1141) and the 1932 poem 'Sanies II'. Beckett told Aidan Higgins, in a letter of 3 December 1951, and in the context of what must have been on the part of the latter a well-meant but in the event fruitless enquiry: 'Bel-Bel [*sic*] somewhere in Perrault [the confusion between Perrault and the Comtesse d'Aulnoy was habitual with

Beckett] and Belacqua somewhere in Purgatory can hardly be the same man' (HRHRC).

she might have mercy, etc.   derived from Burton (*DN*, 994); cf. the newspaper report on the death of Nemo in *Dream* (182).

of a palm . . . assume   an addition; not in *Dream* (208).

50

the exploit   altered from *Dream* (208) perhaps to echo 'DL' (10): there, Belacqua's lunch; here, the Alba again thinking forward to the party, where she intends to make a big impression, and does (61 ff.).

she might have mercy on whom she would   Burton; *DN*, 994.

humiliter, etc.   derived from Kempis; *DN*, 560.

strait   derived from Augustine, 'amid the strife of . . . two wills'; *DN*, 155; cf. 'A village just one long street . . . A strait' (*Mercier and Camier*, 33).

Dan the first   Chaucer, so designated by Tennyson in 'A Dream of Fair Women'; but the quatrain which follows is from an anonymous, popular, obscene, anti-clerical Spanish squib.

The Polar Bear   a character based on Beckett's TCD Professor, T. B. Rudmose-Brown. Beckett later registered, in a letter of 13 September 1932 to MacGreevy, some regret at having included this travesty of someone who had more than once been kind to him (*LSB*, 121), but of course he could do little, and in the event did nothing, to make amends, any more than he did with the other real-life models for other characters, notably 'the Smeraldina'. Only Winnie Coates (in 'Fingal') and Thelma (in 'WAM') have no obvious real-life equivalents, and even the latter can (just about) be seen to point towards one (see note below).

a big old brilliant lecher   added to *Dream* (209) by way of the Alba's description of Ronsard as 'a comic old lecher' (175).

The Lebensbahn . . . of the Galilean   Christ's 'way of life'; the fact that the Polar Bear 'never used the English word when the foreign pleased him better' is not in *Dream*, but the number of languages used in 'AWN' (German, Latin, French, Italian, Spanish, etc.) suggests this is more true of the narrator than the character.

sirreverence   human faeces, not in the equivalent passage in *Dream*; given as from Tobias Smollett (cf. Smith, 48) in the 'For Interpolation' section of the *'Whoroscope' Notebook* (*SBTA*, 16, 232, item 157); cf. the 'human turd' in 'LL' (87).

51

the woman taken red-handed   that is, in adultery, as in John 8.3–12, a context which lies behind a phrase in the 1931 poem 'Alba', and perhaps also the 'girls taken strippin' in the 1933 poem 'Serena III'.

Lazarus   from the Gospels of Luke and John; later, in the 'Denis Devlin' review of 1937–8, used to call the good judgement of Jesus into question (*Disjecta*, 92).

Empedoclean   Beckett had read about Empedocles of Agrigentum (who committed suicide in attempting to prove his divinity by jumping into a volcano) in Archibald Alexander's *Short History of Philosophy* and, probably later, in Wilhelm Windelband's *History of Philosophy*.

Nemo   a major character in Jules Verne's *Twenty Thousand Leagues Under the Sea*; a minor one, but nevertheless (with Grock) one of the crucial demiurges or *éminences grises* of *Dream*, with Beckett also prompted to adopt this name by way of three Latin phrases in Burton (*DN*, 757).

coratés   that is, kindred vagabond spirits (hyphenated in the equivalent passage in *Dream*).

his hairless voice   'hairless' is added to the text of *Dream* here, with Beckett presumably thinking of bald but 'Hairy ['indeed hairy', that is, clever, cunning in 'Draff', 179] Quin'; the motif of hair links this section to the next ('The hair of the homespun Poet', 53) and the section after ('The Frica combed her hair', 55); the motif of baldness is derived from Nordau (*DN*, 635) and from Stephen Dedalus on Aristotle in *Ulysses* ('Bald he was and a millionaire').

Hexenmeister   a magician or sorcerer; a Beckettian reflex where (as here) Mozart (and no doubt Sarastro in *The Magic Flute*) is concerned (cf. the Mörike review in *Disjecta*, 62, and 'Yellow', 163), but in *Dream* it is simply 'infant prodigy' (210).

urtication   from Cooper (*DN*, 403); flagellation with nettles.

52

mathematician   adapted from Augustine; *DN*, 93.

the burden of his fare   cf. 'EB' (16).

Chas's girl was a Shetland Shawly   we meet her early in 'TWO' in *Dream* (143), and also later there (149, 178); a figure apparently based on Georges Pelorson's girlfriend and, subsequently, wife.

cinched   Dublin slang for clothes proving something of a tight fit; cf. in the HRHRC revision of the poem 'Casket of Pralinen . . .': 'I want you to cinch up your song'.

divulgation   a word also found in 'LL', 87; from Jules de Gaultier thinking of Kant on 'the moribund'; *DN*, 1145; used again in a letter to Nuala Costello of 27 February 1934 (*LSB*, 185).

53

a rat's back   a severe cut, unlike the long hair fashionable in 'the nineties'. cf. ' "Am I all right behind?" ' (128).

d'occasion perhaps in both senses   in that it conforms to Goethe's definition of 'occasional poetry' as spontaneously lyrical, but also in that it is 'second-hand' (too much influenced by Joyce, with perhaps Rimbaud's 'Clearance Sale' from *Les Illuminations* also partly in mind). It is also of course intended for an actual occasion, the party to come.

54

Calvary by Night   recycling a number of motifs associated with Joyce; cf. 'the Calvary of pity and remorse' in *Proust* (*PTD*, 44) and 'Calvary through the shock-absorbers' (*Dream*, 82). cf. also 'the waste of waters' (*Dream*, 134).

Ruby . . . Mrs Tough   anticipating 'LL', so naturally enough not in the corresponding passage in *Dream* (which has 'the Smeraldina-Rima' and 'Mammy', 214) and presumably added after the composition of 'LL'. In 'LL' we are told that 'the hair of our heroine is black' (81; see the note on this, below), which points back to the 'sabine coiffure' here, and prefigures the Smeraldina in 'Draff', whose hair is also black (168).

mammae   cf. 'Draff' (171) and the poem 'Serena III'.

cutwaters   the bows of a boat; cf. 'EB' (15).

Sistine!   as in the Sistine Chapel in the Vatican; anticipating 'limey' and 'frescosa'(cf. *Dream*, 215) subsequently (56).

56

how many pebbles in Tom Thumb's pocket   from a Charles Perrault fairy tale (not, as seems to be being suggested, the Brothers Grimm); *DN*, 1130.

sweaty Big Tom   Tommaso Masaccio; Beckett is probably thinking of the 'Madonna and Child' painting in the London National Gallery with its striking use of cobalt blue (cf. *Dream*: 'cobalt devil' [5]). Masaccio, Vasari tells us, was physically clumsy and was nicknamed 'hulking' (as In Browning's 'Fra Lippo Lippi'); Beckett had studied Browning's poem and had read Vasari in his uncle William Sinclair's copy (*Dream*, 156); 'bloodfaced Tom' is also in the early poem 'Casket of Pralinen . . . '

all things . . . were as they were taken derived from Burton (*DN*, 822).

premature . . . too soon derived from a *faux-naïf* narrative strategy in chapter 3 of Dickens's *David Copperfield* (either referred to or adapted on 57 ['shabby man and often moody'; *DN*, 1126 and 71).

whose name we shall never know a phrase adapted from the *Journal* of Jules Renard; *DN*, 231.

looking della Robbia babies cf. 'like a starved della Robbia' (*Dream*, 162), but adding a phrase from Burton (*DN*, 907), used again (of Zaborovna) in 'EB' (4).

57

Duke Street's thought changed from 'Camden Street's' in *Dream*; cf. 'the usual Duke Street complications' (126). The 'thought' in question is probably idle pub talk (cf. O'Brien, 75).

Owen later (by way of 'the sweet mouth') 'identified' as Owen Glendower, as in Shakespeare's *Henry IV*, Part 1, Act III, scene 1.

shabby . . . moody from chapter 10 of Dickens's *David Copperfield* (cf. 59, 71, etc.), as cited in *DN*, 1126; cf. 70 (of Belacqua as 'shabby hero') and *Dream*, 85 ('a taste of the moody').

hushabied not used in *Dream* (which has 'as fondly as she durst', 217); derived from the name of a character in Shaw's play *Heartbreak House* (1914).

Man of Law cf. Chaucer's *Canterbury Tales* (as also for the Wife on Bath on the following page).

his face a blaze of acne cf. *DN*, 1024, amid a collection of entries on the theme of excessive alcohol consumption.

son of Han from H. A. Giles, *The Civilisation of China* (London: Williams and Norgate, 1911), hereafter Giles; *DN*, 520.

prong . . . keen and bright from *DN*, 939.

58

What . . . not exactly a question and with no question mark (as earlier [55]: 'Would she bite her tongue off, that was the interesting question' [58]; for 'bite', cf. 'EB', 27), though 'AWN' is full of questions (e.g. 45 [three], 47, 48 [four], 49, 50, 56, 57 [six], 58 [four], 59, 60, 61, 62 [three], 71 [five], etc.), as indeed all the stories are.

The Beldam from Burton; *DN*, 831; also on 119.

Poor little Dandelion!   the dandelion is diuretic and popularly known as 'pissabed' (Fr. *pissenlit*); Caleken's sister is said to be 'in bed, unwell'. *Dream* (218) reads 'Poor little Pissabed!'

tall Tib, slender Sib   names from Burton; *DN*, 895; this incomplete 'list' is effectively trumped by Caleken's list of the drinks available when next she speaks.

Cup! . . . Ching-Ching!   the 'point' of this list, one item longer even than the names above, is to establish that the party is an alcohol-free zone: they are all soft drinks, which is no doubt one reason why Belacqua, earlier 'well adrift' on Chas mentioning the party, says 'Alas' (46). cf. Belacqua to the Alba at an earlier point in *Dream* (197): ' "They have announced cup. So far", he said bitterly, "as I am concerned, they have announced cup and you" '. Belacqua is of course by now (as will later emerge) getting well oiled in his 'lowly public' (47) and, partly as a consequence and not just because it is raining, is 'soaked through and through' (67) by the time of his arrival at the Frica's.

Great cry, etc.   probably by way of Brewer.

59

a violist d'amore with his instrument in a bag   the viola d'amore is in the tenor register of the family of viols, and famous for its sympathetic strings, enabling the instrument to produce a deep and full sound. In the event this figure only speaks twice (64), obviously with *amore* uppermost in his mind, or perhaps his 'instrument' of *amore* down below.

the saprophile   first mentioned on 46 as 'an anonymous politico-ploughboy'; he reappears on 61.

a disaffected cicisbeo   later (63) said to be 'declining'; cf. 'WO' (96).

Jemmy Higgins   later (61) identified as the hooker in the rugby union team Bective Rangers; earlier, as 'Jem Higgins' in *Dream* (152–4) he writes an absurd love letter to the Alba.

arrived now in a body   cf. the disappearance of the pub customers 'in a body' in *Mercier and Camier* (38).

60

Smoerrbroed   in *DN*, 532.

I did his epitaph in the eye   cf. *DN* (1072), with 'in the eye' added to lines from Tennyson, and *Dream* (137), where 'in the eye' is applied to Beckett's 1932 translation of Rimbaud's 'Le Bateau ivre' (twice borrowed from in 'EB'). The phrase meant something like 'flagrantly fraudulent' to Beckett.

For other uses of writing as a point of reference, with suggestions of finality and a kind of crystalline permanence, see 'WAM' (116) where the wedding invitation looks 'like an epitaph' to Walter Draffin, and 'Draff' (180), where Hairy Quin cannot remember the 'inscription' Belacqua would have wanted for his headstone.

Belisarius   a Byzantine cavalry commander (c. 505–65) under Justinian.

old Norn   as in old Norse mythology (an equivalent to the Greek Furies, a spinner of the Fates), but probably thinking of the uses to which it had been put by Richard Wagner (cf. *Dream*, 37–8) in his opera tetralogy *Der Ring des Nibelungen*, notably in *Götterdämmerung*.

Uranus . . . Neptune   from Sir James Jeans; *DN*, 1048.

an apple of gold and a picture of silver   from the biblical book of Proverbs; *DN*, 566.

The Parabimbi waxed stiff   a 'natural'(?) response to the Polar Bear's dreadful joke, itself playing on the stiffening properties of wax; used in a different context in *Dream*, 181. But the phrase is borrowed from Kempis (*DN*, 577).

61

dauntless daughter of desires   derived, with some thoughts of Lockhart (*DN*, 66) from Dean Inge (*DN*, 695), his description of St Teresa (quoted from in 'EB').

she mounted the estrade   a French word for a daïs or platform, here sounding as pretentious as (no doubt) the Frica could wish, probably first encountered by Beckett in reading Proust's 'Un amour de Swann' in the *Recherche*.

gravitational nets   probably derived from reading Sir James Jeans (*DN*, 1059); cf. the 'fish . . . gaffed' by the Alba in 'EB' (19a).

62

They all do   thinking of Mozart's opera *Così fan tutte*, the title of which points obliquely towards feminine infidelity in its general presentation of how all human beings behave; cf. 'EB' (26). But 'Some do abstain' below adapts the title of a novel by Ford Madox Ford, *Some Do Not*, published in 1924.

ricordandosi del tempo felice   'recalling the happy time'; (mis)quoted (Caselli 2005, 67–8) from *Inferno* V, 122.

Woe and Pain   from a poem ('Dark Rosaleen') by James Clarence Mangan; taken over from *Dream*, 172.

like sunbeams through cracks in cucumbers derived from Giles (*DN*, 534), combined with an image from *Gulliver's Travels*, Swift being much more in evidence (though not always explicitly, or by name) in *More Pricks* than he was in *Dream* (which has this slightly differently on 223).

63

unintelligible world from Wordsworth's 'Lines Written a few Miles above Tintern Abbey'.

whirligig derived from Burton (*DN*, 829), where it is 'Cupid's whirligig', and used again by Belacqua in his wedding speech ('WAM', 132).

daggers of rain derived from Burton (*DN*, 874; repeated, 1179); added to *Dream*, which simply has 'and the rain', etc. (224), although Beckett omits from 'AWN' what Belacqua does next there, an 'eye-suicide' *à la* Rimbaud ('Les Poëtes de Sept Ans').

baby anthrax that he always wore just above his collar anticipating 74, 'Yellow' ('the tumour the size of a brick that he had on the back of his neck', 156) and an exclamation by Hairy Quin in 'Draff' (177); cf. *Dream* (where the anthrax is first mentioned on 29), 225, and the 1931 poem 'Enueg II', line 25: 'shining round the corner like an anthrax'.

he catted in *Dream* (225): 'he was sick'; cf. in 'EB': 'Belacqua spewed' (17).

64

Wipe them boots adapted from a quite different situation in Lockhart's life of Napoleon (470; *DN*, 56), and later used again in 'EB' (3).

gentle peace from Shakespeare's *Henry VIII*, Act II, scene 2.

Justice and mercy reprising issues first raised in the mind of Belacqua after leaving the Ottolenghi to take the lobster to the house of his aunt (13). This initiates a paragraph considerably revised from the corresponding passage in *Dream* (226), which at this point (for once!) is less concerned with narrative embellishments and much more so with simple and straightforward physical activities.

Dogberry a constable (and clown) in Shakespeare's *Much Ado About Nothing*.

his incorruptible heart cf. 'Malacoda', 'Echo's Bones' and *Murphy* (Lawlor 2009, 55–6).

65

Belacqua halted, etc. in *Dream* (226) this paragraph is simply a short (and thereby halted) sentence: 'Belacqua halted and waited'.

lion ... fox   from the title of Wyndham Lewis's 1927 study of the role of the hero in the plays of Shakespeare.

his Leix and Offaly head   the implication is that the Civic Guard is little better than a country bumpkin (like Dogberry). Beckett's interest in distinctively Irish heads surfaces in the 'Trueborn Jackeen' notes, where the 'first inhabitants' of Ireland are described as 'short, dark, dolicocephalous [i.e. with wedge-shaped heads]'; cf. 'wedgehead' later, earlier used in *Dream* (69, 159).

haeres caeli   'an heir of heaven' from Kempis (*DN*, 587; *Dream*, 226); and cf. Donne, Sermon XXXIV (618).

his fall from the vague grace of the drink   thinking of Joyce's *Dubliners* story 'Grace' (cf. Farrow, 111).

loop like an eight   cf. the sign for infinity towards the end of the 'Denis Devlin' review (*Disjecta*, 93); the next phrase seems to point to Stephen Dedalus in the library scene in *Ulysses* ('Scylla and Charybdis').

66

the dirty low-church Protestant!   derived from *Dream* (100), later repeated in an expanded form in 'Yellow' (163); cf. letter to MacGreevy of 18 October 1932 (*LSB*, 134). There is more (implicitly) Protestant material on 125 and 164.

beating his bosom thus bared   derived from Ovid (*DN*, 1116); not in *Dream* (227), but found again in 'EB'; most of the rest of this paragraph is also altered, and the sudden appearance of the Smeraldina as a ghost, with a musical quotation (*Dream*, 228–9), is omitted, the musical phrase and the spectral presence being reassigned (twice) to Lucy in 'WAM'.

a breast of Bisquit   Bisquit is a brandy (which is the Alba's favourite tipple); the brand is not specified in *Dream* (228).

67

she whinnied   in *Dream* 'bugled' (229); 'whinnied' reprises 46, and is part of the persistent equating of the Frica with a horse, deriving from a phrase in Burton ('a generous mare': *DN*, 912).

Here ... I float   an exchange tried out in *DN* (527), where it is 'boxed'.

He dried himself as best as he might   with Beckett thinking back to Burton (*DN*, 771), and perhaps also of Leopold Bloom on the seashore with Gerty MacDowell in the 'Nausicaa' episode of *Ulysses*; 'his cambric pochette' replaces 'his Paris pochette' (*Dream*, 228).

dilated   from Garnier's *Onanisme* (*DN*, 475), with Burton (*DN*, 823) half in mind also; adapted to Beckett's poor job prospects in a letter to MacGreevy of after 15 August 1931 (*LSB*, 84); used in a different context in *Dream* (1).

68

the mice were beginning to enjoy themselves   reinterpreting the line 'Nothing was stirring, not even a mouse' from the popular song 'The Night Before Christmas'.

goose . . . flying barefoot   derived, via *Dream* (108), from Burton, who has 'going' and is discussing women weeping; *DN*, 864 (and also 1179);

from McCabe   is, unsurprisingly, not present in the equivalent passage of *Dream* (230), but has obviously been added to echo 'DL'.

in a dream   as has indeed happened, 'in' the jettisoned novel *Dream of Fair to Middling Women*; cf. 'all this would happen to him again, in a dream or subsequent existence' ('WAM', 139).

toga virilis   a badge of honour, but here (it is not in *Dream*, 230) with an implied critique of 'the Shawly'; associated by Beckett with Garnier's discussion of syphilis (*DN*, 486); cf. 'toga' in the 1937 poem 'Ooftish' ('toga virilis' in unpublished versions). In a letter to MacGreevy of 8 October 1932 Beckett applies the word to his own outbreak of impetigo, one of several he suffered at this time.

Toutes êtes, etc.   from *Dream*, 52 (where it is 'given' to 'Jean du Chas'); *DN*, 397; from Cooper's citation of the quatrain, which is from Jean de Meun's portion of the *Roman de la Rose*.

69

that shabby hero   cf. 57 ('a shabby man'); not in *Dream*; taken over from *DN*, 1126; one of several borrowings in 'AWN' from *David Copperfield*.

vernier   a scientific category of measurement, derived from reading Sir James Jeans (*DN*, 1055).

him with the bile-tinged conjunctivae   from *DN* (1024), like the acne of the Man of Law (57).

She addressed herself to the Jew   preceded in *Dream* (232) by the sentence 'Then she supposed Jem [Higgins] could drive her home', Jem Higgins being (slightly) more of a presence there than he is here. The Alba's need to be seen home is omitted at this point of 'AWN', but brought back for 'WAM' (134) and 'Draff' (167).

nonesuch   as if translating 'nonpareil', although no doubt the figure in question is something of a 'sensitive plant'. Presumably, given the context,

Beckett is thinking of his readings in the 1929 *Complete Poetry and Selected Prose* of John Donne, published in London by The Nonesuch Press; the 'nonsuch' in 'The Calmative' (21), however, is the plant.

70

sottish mot   cf. the so-called 'profound mot' of 'WAM' (125) and the 'sottish jest' in 'Yellow' (163).

pint of Perrier   adapted from the fairy tales of Charles Per*r*ault; in *Dream* (233) simply 'a drink of water', as earlier, in 'Fingal' (18).

Move up in the bed   first used in *Dream* on 98 by 'Mammy'; cf. *Disjecta*, 79.

Rose Marie   a 1924 Broadway musical, later a film; not in *Dream*.

the six ways in which they could arrange themselves   anticipating Quigley's biscuits in 'Lightning Calculation' and after them Murphy's; and, much later, the looks of the academic committee, and dozens of other calculations, in *Watt*.

71

promessi   with reference to the great Italian novel *I Promessi Sposi* (*The Betrothed*) of Alessandro Manzoni (cf. 9: '*Il Cinque Maggio*'). In 'WO', Belacqua and Lucy are 'merely betrothed' (96), but in real life Beckett and Peggy Sinclair were never formally engaged.

Sheffield more hilly than Rome   a 'fact' recorded in *DN*, 1045.

bicuspid   from Jules de Gaultier (*DN*, 1149).

Who shall circumcise their lips . . .   Farrow (117) gives four biblical citations for this, two from Deuteronomy, and two from Jeremiah. The previous question is echoed in 'Fingal' (19), written later.

Maestro Gormely   is obviously, musically speaking, gormless ('executed'); Beckett and his brother Frank played relatively simple Scarlatti pieces as teenagers.

Plato . . . Boehme   derived from Dean Inge (*DN*, 705).

estrade   as indicated above, Proust uses this word for a daïs or platform at a salon in 'Un amour de Swann' in the first part of the *Recherche*.

presented her teeth   that is, smiled; 'from the teeth outwards' is in *DN*, 1015.

Vinegar . . . on nitre   from the book of Proverbs 25.20 (*DN*, 567, with 'songs to a heavy heart' added), a phrase used again in a letter to MacGreevy of ?19 August 1936 (not in *LSB*).

Mrs Gummidge . . . coverture   in *Dream* (235): 'coucherie'; Mrs Gummidge is a character in Dickens's *David Copperfield*.

72

before his soul heaved anchor   i.e before he lost hope; derived from Burton (*DN*, 992); cf. *Dream*, 190, 192, 193, 205.

a wolf . . . by the ears   from Burton (*DN*, 914).

Motus!   in *Dream* (?incorrectly) as 'Lotus!' (235); probably derived from Jules Laforgue's poem 'Pétitions'.

turned a little yellow, as well he might   from Burton (*DN*, 946); anticipating the Eiffel Tower on 73.

Brobdingnag   from Swift, *Gulliver's Travels*, Book II; **dumb crambo** is a parlour game similar to charades; neither of these are in *Dream* (235).

When with indifference etc.   'borrowed' (but altered) from Augustine; *DN*, 182; cf. 'quodlibet' in 'DL' (3).

73

Eiffel Tower   the famous Parisian tower is repainted every 7 years; the most recent re-painting relevant here was in 1931, as noted in *DN*, 935.

torrents of speed   *recte* 'spleen', as in *Dream*, 236 (1934 edition 236, 1970 edition 111).

Can you pay this man   in *Dream* Belacqua first uses this phrase to his friend Lucien on arrival in Paris (33).

Je t'adore, etc.   taken over from the taxi ride in *Dream* ('Sedendo et Quiescendo'), 66. The phrase is from a poem in Baudelaire's *Les Fleurs du Mal*.

Tire la chevillette, etc.   from the 'Red Riding Hood' fairy tale ('Le petit chaperon rouge') of Charles Perrault; *DN*, 1070.

his baby anthrax   first mentioned on 63.

Nisscht mööööööglich   the Swiss clown Grock's trademark tag (here sounding very Swiss), comprising a number of meanings (as indicated above). In *Dream* (239), which simply has '*Voice of Grock* . . . ', this marks the end of section 'THREE'.

A divine creature, native of Leipzig   in *Dream*, less guardedly, a prostitute (239), probably one that Beckett had actually encountered in Germany (perhaps in Kassel) in January 1932 (the phrase 'round about the following Epiphany' has here been added to *Dream*, 239), who figures in the poem 'Dortmunder'. The Joycean portmanteau word that follows on 74 is tried out in *DN*, 1178.

74

the rain fell   cf. the 'softly falling' snow at the end of Joyce's 'The Dead' (and the 'soft rain' falling in *Dream*, 145), the rain here deriving in part from Portia's 'quality of mercy' in Shakespeare's *The Merchant of Venice*, as again later in *Murphy* (chapter 4) and *Mercier and Camier* (25, 96).

darkness visible   from Milton's *Paradise Lost*, Book I, line 63; but probably taken from Book 3, chapter 2 of Fielding's novel *Joseph Andrews*, which Beckett read in October 1932 (*LSB*, 129), too late for *Dream* (240). Beckett uses the phrase again in *Company* (24).

he took off his perfectly good boots and threw them away   Farrow's suggestion that this motif was prompted by the galoshes in Joyce's 'The Dead' seems over-ingenious, but this may have been Beckett's way of suggesting, to himself if to no one else, that he needed to rid himself of Joyce's influence.

belly-ache   later a 'pain' relieved, with Beckett probably thinking of how Augustine 'turned to God' (as Belacqua does not) on suffering a 'pain' in the chest; *DN*, 161.

the bridge over the canal, not Baggot Street, nor Leeson Street, but another nearer the sea   identified by O'Brien as the Huband Bridge (195), with a photograph on 196. This curiously specific nonspecificity is added to *Dream* (compare 240–1), and O'Brien's map (194) shows that Belacqua must be moving slightly north and east (a little closer to the poor suburb of Irishtown, where the Toughs in the next story, 'LL', live), rather than proceeding directly towards Ballsbridge (a destination of sorts, but supplied only in *Dream* [241]), which is further south, and in the direction of Foxrock. His move in *Dream* precedes 'an enormous pain in his stomach' (240), but here he is given 'such a belly-ache as he had never known' presumably because this 'revoke[s]' the 'small gain in the matter of ease' occasioned by throwing his boots away (a detail not given in *Dream*).

the knee-and-elbow position   cf. *Dream*, 81; resembling the position adopted by the figure Belacqua whom Dante meets in *Purgatorio*.

75

a spectacle   in part a reminder that Belacqua has shaken off his glasses.

more in sorrow than in anger   from *Hamlet*, Act I, scene 2; contrast the 'sorrow and anger' of the parson in 'Draff' (170).

'Love and Lethe'

79

Ruby   a 'ruby', *Dream* (96) tells us, is Dublin slang for the last drink left in the bottle (cf. 91), and is an apt name for a character intending to be involved in a last hurrah, and imbibing one brandy (80) and three double whiskeys (88–9) during the course of a (quite *short*) short story. Her father suffers from alcohol-induced cyanosis (*DN*, 1020; cf. 1021–4 also).

admirably preserved though well past the change   cf. 'she whose life had changed' in 'Yellow' (163).

What time is he coming?   the first of an unusually large number of questions in 'LL'; we soon learn that Ruby is 'inclined to resent all these questions'.

the dicky   a small area to be used at a pinch for a passenger in a sports car with only two seats; cf. 85, and Lucy at the end of 'WAM' (140).

80

She could not bear to be idle   as we are told again on 84, as if the narrator shared her need to keep busy.

It was half-past two, that zero hour, in Irishtown   the time when the pubs close for an hour in the afternoon; cf. 'DL' (9) and Neary and Wylie early in *Murphy*.

However.   a narrative intervention, with no follow-up, also found in 'WO' (99) and 'WAM' (129).

81

thirty-third or -fourth year of her age   this is oddly precise in a collection which typically gives no information of this kind. Thirty-three is taken to be the age of Christ at his death; Molly Bloom in *Ulysses* is thirty-three.

the Magdalene . . . Perugino   reproduced in O' Brien (140–41); Ruby is later 'more bawdy Magdalene than ever' (87–8).

the hair of our heroine is black   because (as anticipated in an addition to 'AWN', 55) 'inherited' from the Smeraldina of *Dream* (cf. 'pitch black hairs' [144] and 'The hair was as black as the pots' in 'Draff' [168]); *Dream* gives the Alba 'the blackest hair' (155). The detail 'not ginger' suggests that Beckett is trying to distance the figure from the real-life Peggy Sinclair, although Beckett obviously relished fiction's ability to transpose and interchange features that are fixed in real life. In *Dream*, despite 'Mr Beckett' telling us that 'the two girls [the Smeraldina-Rima and the Syra-Cusa] simply had to be compared' (35), the distinctions between them, and later between them and the Alba, are for the most part maintained, with the different sections of narrative helping to keep them apart. But these largely clear-cut distinctions tend to become slightly blurred in *More Pricks* (with the Lucy of 'WO' and 'WAM' a later version of the Syra-Cusa, and Ruby indeterminately situated just outside that magic circle). This strategy obviously could not possibly have been registered by a reader in 1934, but Beckett re-doubles it by suggesting some equivalences, for all the physical differences between them, in his presentation of the Belacqua/Hairy Quin/Walter Draffin material (cf. Kroll 1974, 344, showing how in 'Draff' 'his best friend Hairy adopts some of Belacqua's mannerisms').

atomic despair cf. 'atomic tempo of species' in the revised (A. J. Leventhal) version of the poem 'Whoroscope' (HRHRC), in the last line of material inserted previous to the published version's line 65; the Georges Belmont version of the poem has 'atomic frequencies' linked to 'species', and both versions must presumably postdate Beckett's August 1932 reading of Darwin, although at this point in this story, which was probably written in the summer of 1933, he seems to have Sir James Jeans more in mind.

sun of a binary . . . syzygy from Sir James Jeans (*DN*, 1061); cf. 'binary' (*Dream*, 28) and 'syzygetic stars' in Beckett's sonnet 'At last I find . . . ', a poem 'given' to Belacqua in *Dream*; the **meteorite** and the **metal of stars** below were no doubt inspired by the same source.

in the days of hot blood perhaps (in a collection with numerous allusions to Shakespeare's *Hamlet*) remembering, 'Now could I drink hot blood' (Act III, scene 2).

82

a series of staircase jests curiously close to the phrase 'mémoire de l'escalier' in a letter to MacGreevy of 2 July 1933 (*LSB*, 165), a week after the death of Beckett's father.

hem of her garment in the Bible 'his' (Jesus's) garment in Matthew 9.20; cf. line 32 of the early poem 'Casket of Pralinen . . . ' and *Dream* (143).

ebriety repeated from 36; drunkenness by way of Fr. 'ébrieté'.

A mental home was the place for him cf. the Portrane Lunatic Asylum in 'Fingal', where Belacqua has his 'heart' (19), and the Magdalen Mental Mercyseat in *Murphy*.

felo de se literal or metaphorical suicide; cf. *Dream* (183, of the demise of Nemo).

83

Empedocles cf. the note to 54.

John of the Cross from Dean W. R. Inge (*DN*, 607); cf. Belacqua as 'dud mystic', 'borderman' and 'John . . . of the Crossroads' in conversation with 'Mr Beckett' (*Dream*, 186).

bang from T. S. Eliot, *The Hollow Men* (1925), on how the world ends, which is also how this story ends.

Philosopher Square . . . Molly Seagrim Beckett first read, and much admired, Fielding's great novel in late 1932 (cf. Belacqua as 'a kind of cretinous Tom Jones' in 'WO', 96). This prefigures the 'inevitable nuptial' later (91), and pays Ruby a backhanded compliment of a kind, although her mind is on the 'bang' and (in the event) on the whiskey.

chartered at untold gold by the hour this 'swagger sports roadster' anticipates the 'fast but noisy' three-wheeled Morgan of 'WAM' (126, 140). In 'Draff' the 'greatly improved' Hairy Quin arrives 'in a car of his very own' (171), but one which 'conk[s] out' (179).

a growler a four-wheeled taxicab struck by a three-wheeled sports car, and reduced accordingly; cf. a Kassel character in *Dream* called 'the Grauler', who 'drove them [Belacqua and the Smeraldina] up to [the Wirtschaft] in his superb machine' (106).

84

Peter Malchus's ear the name of a servant of the High Priest whose ear is cut off by Simon Peter. The story is told in all four gospels, but the name is given only in the gospel of John 18.10–11.

Victoria Bridge as also mentioned in imagining a similar journey down to Irishtown (and beyond) in the 1933 poem 'Serena III' (line 17); for a photograph, see O'Brien, 76.

like a cuckoo making good, as it were, the perceived deficiency in the scene in 'WO' (103).

bee . . . sting thinking of Lucas Cranach's canvas 'Venus and Cupid' of 1524.

a heavy lunch at the Bailey. The truth was not in him apart from toast and cheese in 'DL', and some scallions in 'WAM', the Belacqua of *More Pricks* eats nothing, and has presumably only consumed alcohol in this instance. On 'the Bailey' (in Duke Street; cf. 57, 126), see O'Brien, 75.

85

cyanosis a condition, often caused by excessive intake of alcohol, turning the face blue; *Dream*, 62; *DN*, 1020 [from Sir William Osler's 1892 textbook

The Principles and Practice of Medicine; personal communication from Mark Nixon]; the condition is inherited by the alcoholic Mick Doyle in 'EB' (22), and the idea is applied to youth in chapter 9 of *Murphy*. In the AJL revised texts (HRHRC, ?1933) of the poems 'Casket...' and 'For Future Reference', Beckett substitutes 'cyanosed' for 'blood-faced' in the first and for 'red-faced' in the second. Ruby drinks heavily, like Lord Gall (three black velvets, followed by Fernet-Branca) and Mick Doyle in 'EB' (11, 17, 22 ff.).

Lot Mrs Tough as Lot's wife, but Beckett is thinking of the cities of the plain, as in 'Fingal' and in Proust's *Recherche*, as well as of course Sodom and Gomorrah in the Bible. Lot is the implied speaker of the 'To My Daughter' poem (a revision of 'Hell Crane To Starling') in the Leventhal 'POEMS' material at the HRHRC, Austin, Texas.

I can't relish a Dublin phrase, tried out (with several others) in *DN*, 642; cf. *Dream*, 192.

Blue Birds alluding to the fairy tale 'L'Oiseau Bleu' by the Comtesse d'Aulnoy, which is (mis)quoted from in 'WAM' (118); cf. the 'blue bird' of *Dream*, 120, and *DN*, 1132–3.

safely stowed thinking of Hamlet after the killing of Polonius (Act IV, scene 2); also used in 'Draff' (171).

Socrates... and the hemlocks cf. the 'Philosophy Notes' on Plato and the circumstances of Socrates' death (TCD).

86

The revolver Beckett probably has in mind, even in this very different situation, Stendhal's famous observation that politics, in a novel, is like a pistol shot at a concert (in *Le Rouge et le Noir*). The 'rule' (as found, for example, in Chekhov's *Literary and Theatrical Reminiscences*, ed. Koteliansky, 1923, 23) that, a writer having introduced a gun into the proceedings, it must go off, is of course one that Beckett will be perfectly happy to comply with (91), but with his own purposes of flagrant concealment in mind.

foul old skirt... off with it cf. the 1933 poem 'Serena III': 'girls taken strippin that's the idea' (line 22).

87

Ruby, greatly eased cf. 'EB' (5, 22, 23).

told Ruby he had got it compare Belacqua to the Alba at the end of 'AWN': 'Have you got it' (72). Here, as immediately explained, the 'it' that Belacqua has 'got' is the reason for 'the astounding thing' of the previous page (86), but this example also echoes the use of 'IT' twice in close succession earlier (82).

as in a quicksand   repeated, for Hermione, in 'WAM' (133); cf. the 1933 poem 'Serena III': 'the sands quicken in your hot heart'.

larches   as at the Becketts' house in Foxrock; cf. 87, 'WO' (96), 'Draff' (173), and the 'posses of larches' of the late 1932 poem 'Serena II'.

Synge   from his *In Wicklow and West Kerry*, purchased by Beckett in 1926.

The city and the plains   thinking of Proust's *Sodome et Gomorrhe* section of the *Recherche* (in the first English translation: 'Cities of the Plain').

breasts with pimples   cf. the poem 'Serena II'.

A human turd   cf. 'sirreverence' in 'AWN' (54), the last item 'For Interpolation' in the *'Whoroscope' Notebook*, which Beckett had found in Smollett's *Humphry Clinker*; and the 'étron' of *LSB*, 185.

fantoccini   (It.) puppets of the Commedia dell'Arte.

Punch and Judy   cf. *The Unnamable*: 'this gnawing of termites in my Punch and Judy box' (53).

88

Harlot's Progress   the most famous of the many series of engravings done by Hogarth (cf. the 'pothook' in the first line of the 1933 poem 'Serena III' and the 'pothooks' of 'WO', 98); this is linked to the sometime prostitute Mary Magdalene in the Perugino painting (first mentioned on 81) in the immediately antecedent phrase.

Pavane   alluding to Maurice Ravel's composition 'Pavane pour une Infante défunte' which exists in both a piano version and a version for orchestra. Ravel variously claimed either to have liked the sound the title made, or to have had no particular dead Infanta (cf 'Infanta defunctus' in *Dream* [83] and 'The Infanta' in 'The Possessed', *Disjecta* [100]) in mind, or to have been thinking in terms of a kind of 'ideal' Infanta such as might have been painted by Velasquez. Beckett soon himself, aptly enough, has a Velasquez Infanta in his sights. Beckett refers to playing a piano duet version of 'The Infanta' in a letter to MacGreevy of 8 February 1935 (*LSB*, 245; see also 241). In an earlier letter (27 August 1934) Beckett writes about what he considers a doubtful attribution to Velasquez. A different Velasquez canvas is referred to in 'Draff' (171).

pale cast   of thought, which 'sicklie[s] o'er' the 'native hue of resolution' in Act III, scene 1 of *Hamlet*.

Velasquez   an 'Infanta' (probably familiar to Beckett only from a reproduction) here partly prompted by Ra*vel*; cf. the Velasquez painting mentioned in 'Draff' (165), and Velasquez references in letters to Morris Sinclair (*LSB*, 214) and to MacGreevy (July 1934).

pensums   a word (an imposition, duty or task) first used in *Proust* (*PTD*, 93), and again later in *The Unnamable* (21); borrowed from Schopenhauer.

apple cart   alluding to a Bernard Shaw play (1929) which Beckett did not much care for, and which he later described, having obviously been somewhat upset by it, as 'unpsettable' (Knowlson [ed.], *Exhibition*, 1971, 23; quoting from a 1956 letter to the actor and producer Cyril Cusack).

If he did not pull it off now   this picks up from 'told Ruby he had got it' and Ruby 'not bothering to ask what' on 87. The story has many an 'it' with no clear antecedent given; cf. 'Have you got it' in 'AWN' (72), which turns out to be enough money for a taxi home. Beckett may have been thinking here (as in 'AWN') of Lenehan's 'it', and perhaps also of the gold coin (a guinea), in Joyce's 'Two Gallants', a story featuring two figures who might just possibly become – although in the event, unlike Ruby and Belacqua here, they do not become – sexually active, as one meaning of 'gallants' would justify. Corley and Lenehan in Joyce's story have money rather than sex as their principal concern, as Belacqua in 'What A Misfortune' also will (110–11).

the screw turned up as it always does   perhaps thinking of Hardy, early in *Jude the Obscure*: 'But nobody did come, because nobody does' (I:4).

89

a palimpsest   as implied, one inscription placed over another; cf. 'WAM', the number-plate removed by Hairy Quin *en route* to Belacqua (127).

Never two without three   adapting, and extending, the 'seldom one without two' of 'AWN' (46).

O Death in Life . . . no more   days that 'shall not return'; from the 'Tears, idle tears, I know not what they mean' stanzas of Tennyson's 'The Princess', as invoked in *Dream* (149) and – unwittingly no doubt – also by the Smeraldina in her billet doux ('tears! tears! tears!', 143).

Kreuger   from *DN*, 605; the Swedish 'Match King' Ivar Kreuger who, embroiled in financial difficulties, committed suicide in March 1932, and who is also remembered, or almost remembered, in *Malone Dies* (104). In *Dream*, Nemo, not a 'chevalier d'industrie', commits suicide (or 'Felo-de-se from Natural Causes', 183) very differently. Murphy experiences a kind of mental suicide in chapter 11 of that novel, but before the gas takes effect, as Beckett emphasized in a letter of 29 April 1951 to Mania Péron.

90

The problem of precedence from Bourrienne's *Memoirs of Napoleon* (London: Richard Bentley, 1836), vol II, 264; *DN*, 53.

'The Pope the puke' 'quoted', as if any reasonably informed reader might know it, from Beckett's privately revised (?1933) version of the 1930 poem 'Whoroscope' (Leventhal papers, HRHRC).

We . . . are gone astray thinking of the lyrics of the 'Whiffenpoof Song' as originated at Yale University in 1910, but also of the babes in the wood and the Hansels and Gretels of fairy tale.

slaves of the sand-glass cf. 'The shuttle of a ripening egg combs the warp of his days' in the headnote to the 1930 poem 'Whoroscope', and 'sands' in the 1933 poem 'Serena III'.

As though there were only the one in the world Ruby may perhaps be thinking of Jesus's 'In my father's house are many mansions' (John 14.2).

91

coenaesthesis cf. *Dream*, 32, 123; later used again in 'Draff' (167); derived from Nordau on 'general sensibility'; *DN*, 664, and also 666.

starry cf. Belacqua on the boat home in *Dream* (136), looking up at the 'starfield' (137), and a number of other references to the stars in Beckett's early work, culminating in the star-chart of *Murphy*. Beckett may well have been thinking of Kant's famous description of the 'starry' sky (together with the continuation which qualifies the statement and renders it doubtful), as expressed in a jotting found in the Psychology Notes at TCD (MS 10971/7/6), and remembered for the third of the *Three Dialogues with Georges Duthuit*. Some of the Psychology Notes appear to date from 1933, which would be consistent with a late date of composition for 'LL'.

the revolver went off as earlier Ruby's skirt did (86); cf. the note on the revolver, also on 86.

in terram from Garnier's *Onanisme* (*DN*, 426), in a discussion of Onan's sin in the Bible, spilling his seed on the earth; cf. 'frigged up, in terram' in a letter to MacGreevy of 18 October 1932 (*LSB*, 134).

The finger of God later 'Digitus Dei' cf. Exodus 8:19; cf. 'Serena III', written in late 1933 (probably close in time to 'LL'): 'Jesus Christ Son of God Saviour His Finger'.

white feather adapted from Lockhart's life of Napoleon (537); *DN*, 62.

one competent to sing of the matter the great French Renaissance poet Pierre de Ronsard, 'the Ronsard' of *Dream* (68, 175) and a presence in the

1929 poem 'Return to the Vestry', Beckett having visited his grave on a summer holiday in 1926. Cf. the 'competent poet' Dante in a footnote to 'Draff' based on the *Convivio*, II, 1 (Caselli, 2005, 74, 92), and Racine and Gide described as 'competent psychologists' in the Rachel Burrows lecture notes. The linguistic aspect of the 'joke' here is specifically French (even if the idea is universal), and a much later French writer, Paul Valéry and his poem 'La fausse morte', also seem to be in the mix, given Beckett's intention to translate 'LL' into French with the title 'Mort plus précieuse' (*LSB*, 212), a phrase from Valéry found in *Dream* (72) with the words 'que la vie' added.

full of music   in the early work of Beckett, up to and including *Murphy*, 'music' (as a word, the source of an image, or a simple 'fact') is rarely without some connotation of sexual, or at least amatory, activity; and at least two of the 'Poèmes 38–39' continue the association. The connection is less clear after the war, but can still be seen or heard in works as diverse as *Happy Days* and . . . *but the clouds* . . . , among others.

'Walking Out'

95

One fateful, fine Spring evening   'fateful', because of the 'adverse fate' preparing, or being prepared (96); 'fine', because all's well that ends well and (almost) all will end well, if only for Belacqua.

Croker's Gallops   cf. 'Croker's Acres' in *Not I*, and again in *Company*, a place close to Beckett's childhood home, near the Leopardstown racecourse. The faint suggestion that someone might 'croak' is misleading: only the jennet dies, and in doing so makes no sound. The mention of 'Pretty Polly that great-hearted mare . . . buried in the vicinity' is, in the event, more ominous; this horse is presumably the 'old racemare' of *Dream*, 127.

no horses were to be seen   later in the paragraph there is no cuckoo (cf. 103) and, in the next paragraph, 'there were no cats'.

the race-course of Chantilly   Beckett visited, and was impressed by, the Musée Condé at Chantilly in June 1934, but must obviously have been to Chantilly during his 1928–30 years in Paris.

Leaning now on his stick   here, and *now*, a support; later used by the Tanzherr to administer a 'brutal verberation' (105). Camier's stick (*Mercier and Camier*, 97) 'was my father's', but other sticks have appeared there earlier (8, 30, 39, 63).

the sky was Mary's cloak   that is, blue.

Only the cuckoo was wanting   a detail recurring on 103.

a matter of some difficulty to keep God out of one's meditations   cf. *Mercier and Camier* (59): 'Contrary to a prevalent opinion, there are places in nature from which God would appear to be absent'.

preferring this time of year to the late Autumn   in a letter to MacGreevy, during the first month of writing *Murphy*, Beckett told his friend that he would like to live in a perpetual September (*LSB*, 273).

past my best   almost immediately revised to 'past the worst of his best', but of course worse (and better?) is to come.

unable to move on   unlike the 'bogged' figure in 'DL' (3; cf. 'DD', 33), this Belacqua can move forward, but it proves a mixed blessing.

96

dereliction   derived from Dean Inge; *DN*, 696.

Tom Wood   anticipating Belacqua as 'Peeping Tom' (cf. *Dream*, 72, and 'Tom's in his hedge/creeping and peeping', 'The Possessed', *Disjecta*, 99); cf. 'Serena II': 'it is useless to close the eyes'.

Larches, however, he knew   cf. *Molloy* ('It was a larch tree. It is the only tree I can identify, with certainty'; 35), and *Malone Dies* ('trees he could not name'; 31).

little fat boy   compare section 'ONE' of *Dream*, 'Fingal' (22), and the similarly little (and fat) daughter of someone (a girl whom Beckett was teaching) in a letter to MacGreevy of 25 July 1933.

reseda   a shade of green; from *Dream*, 4; cf. 'Draff' (168).

cicisbeo   cf. the 'disaffected' and subsequently 'declining' cicisbeo of 'AWN' (59, 63); probably directly derived from Nordau (*DN*, 612), but Beckett no doubt first encountered the word in the second paragraph of Stendhal's *La Chartreuse de Parme*.

Tom Jones   cf. the reference to the Philosopher Square and Molly Seagrim in 'LL' above (83), but Beckett did not read Fielding's novel until late 1932, so this analogy presumably could not have been present in the version of 'WO' sent back to Beckett by the agent J. B. Pinker in August 1931.

the next list of fields   cf. the 'tesserae of small fields' in 'Fingal' (17).

champaign   from *Dream*, 9; also used earlier in 'Fingal' (18), and later in 'EB' (15), in the late 1931 poem 'Enueg I', and in *Mercier and Camier* (81).

The wall was too high hence the 'vigorous heave' applied to the 'grey hunkers' of the bitch; but Beckett is no doubt reapplying elements from the situation in *Dream* (194), with the Alba thinking Belacqua would 'get over' his difficult problems with 'Personality', and the narrator stepping in to mention 'another story, a far far better one', without of course specifying which one, 'Walking Out' having been already rejected by J. B. Pinker. Earlier in *Dream* (49) this last phrase is used to explain why 'the Syra-Cusa', a portrait of Lucia Joyce, has been considered 'hors d'oeuvre' (as indeed she largely is in *Dream*). Shloss (194, 282) chooses to interpret the phrase 'a far far better story' as referring to Joyce's use of aspects derived from his daughter in the depiction of Issy in *Work In Progress/Finnegans Wake*, but it seems safer to see the double emphasis on a 'story' in *Dream*, a kind of novel, as pointing (in)directly to 'Walking Out', a rejected story about a 'Lucy' who is on the point of being rejected, and an abortive love affair involving more than one rejection among its real-life participants. The middle sound in Lu*ci*a Joyce's first name is of course itself doubled in the '*cici*sbeo' (94) and '*cici*sbei' (102) here, and the use of Italian (cf. Lucia's brother's name Giorgio) was second nature in the Joyce family. In a letter of 9 August 1934 to Stuart Gilbert (who knew Beckett), telling him that *More Pricks* had been published, Joyce said of Beckett: 'He has talent, I think' (*Letters*, vol. 3, ed. Ellmann, London: Faber and Faber, 1966, 316), having noted – or not noted, depending on how one looks at it – 'One of the characters is named Lucia [*sic*] but it is quite different. She is a cripple or something'. In a kind of explanation for being so vague on the subject, Joyce added: 'Haven't time to read it. But looked at it here and there before quitting Paris'. Joyce was of course famously 'blind' in regard to Lucia, and would no doubt have resisted the implications of 'Walking Out' if he had been in any position to see them. But as the note on 'in a sudden chaos of mind' on 101 below shows, Beckett certainly knew what he had intended, and was probably relieved that neither Joyce nor anyone else had been able to work out what he was up to. There was to be no comparable outcome in the matter of 'the Smeraldina', her 'billet doux', and the still grieving Sinclairs, where the equation with Peggy Sinclair obviously could not be finessed so successfully, since Beckett had happily enough connived at it, and indeed effectively insisted on it.

97

a strange equipage cf. 'This grotesque equipage' ('WAM', 139). The word 'equipage' is typically used of accoutrements, adornments or apparatus; in 'WAM' it is applied to a 'tomb-deep armchair on casters'.

a complete down-and-out . . . very busy with something cf. line 21 of the November 1931 poem 'Enueg I': ' . . . a gang of down-and-outs would seem to be mending a beam'.

The sun beamed down cf. Dublin 'flooded with sunshine' in 'WAM' (127), and 'all the morning sun' in 'Yellow' (158, 159). The weather is 'more than merely clement' for the burial ceremony in 'Draff' (175). Belacqua, like Watt after him, is generally 'lucky with his weather' in *More Pricks*, in spite of the pouring rain in 'AWN'.

the bitch made herself at home cf. 'the blue bitch's affront' ('EB', 20). In *Mercier and Camier* (48) , 'wetting his trousers' refers to Camier's immoderate laughter.

'Game ball' he said/98 After that further comment was impossible cf. 'EB' (25), and the present-day catchphrase 'Game over'.

pot-hooks probably with half an eye on the painter and engraver Hogarth's serpentine line of beauty, as in the 1933 poem 'Serena III'.

flourish with his stick like Corporal Trim in Volume IX, chapter 4 of Sterne's *Tristram Shandy*.

her magnificent jennet cf. the 'ginnet' of 'EB' (8).

panting cf. the 'footsore Achates', a different kind of 'faithful dog', who 'pants his pleasure' in the 1933 poem 'Sanies I', Hairy Quin in 'WAM' (118) and the sea 'panting' on 180.

I got up on the roof cf. Camier's question: 'Would you have me go up on the roof?' (*Mercier and Camier*, 61).

Sister Ann from Charles Perrault's Bluebeard story 'La Barbe-Bleue'. In a personal communication, Seán Lawlor has reminded me that, while Belacqua does not actually (like Bluebeard) kill his wives, they have a distinct tendency to die after consorting with him.

99

Fünklein derived (misspelt, probably deliberately) from Dean Inge; cf. *Dream*, 17 ('Fünkelein'); *DN*, 690.

I have the chinks Dublin slang for diarrhoea, which is what 'Sedendo et Quiescendo' ends with (*Dream*, 74); the word 'chinks' is used in *Dream* (85) and in a letter of c. 7 September 1931 to MacGreevy.

Lovely Lucerne, lovely Lucy omitted (by accident?) from the 1970 Calder & Boyars reprint, and all other reprints, but present in 1934. Only restored in the 2010 Faber paperback. Apart from the obvious wordplay of this one liner, 'Lucerne' may be a 'coded' substitute for Zürich, about thirty miles away, where Lucia Joyce was taken for psychiatric treatment in 1933.

with its suggestion of the Nobel Yeats W. B. Yeats was awarded the 1923 Nobel Prize for literature, the first Irish writer to be thus honoured, and Beckett may have had in mind here the lines 'everything that's lovely/Is a brief, dreamy, kind delight' from the poem 'Never give all the heart'.

the hard bust cf. the 'Bilitis breasts' of the Syra-Cusa (*Dream*, 33, 84).

100

to walk it off there are numerous instances in *More Pricks* of Beckett using an unexplained and unassigned 'it' for the purposes of *double entendre*, or simply to set up situations in which an addressee is 'not bothering to ask what' ('LL', 87).

the devil's bath translating from Burton's Latin ('*balneum diaboli*'); *DN*, 765.

devil's finger the middle finger, the longest; cf. 'digitus diaboli' in *DN*, 748, 'Digitus Dei . . . for once' in 'LL' (91), Celia in chapter 3 of *Murphy*, and the tracing of Anna/Lulu's name in a cowpat in *Premier Amour* (*First Love*).

sursum corda cf. 'Fingal' (21); the phrase also occurs in the Beckett/Péron translation of Joyce's *Anna Livia Plurabelle*.

pastoral clamour cf. 'pastoral' and 'fairy tale' early in 'WAM' (110), and the quasi-pastoral scene in *Molloy* (165ff.).

101

as wax in her hands the footnote redirects us back to 'Fingal' (21), and must obviously have been added to the 1931 version of 'WO'.

forbad them at this point to fund their ways that is, forced them to go in different directions; cf. the poem 'Sanies I', and a letter to MacGreevy of 13 May 1933: 'He [A. J. Leventhal] thought funds ways home had something to do with paying her tram fare!' (*LSB*, 159). The idea of 'home', and indeed the word 'home' (missing here), is the point at which the 1932 poem 'Spring Song' comes to a kind of repose (line 89), and in *More Pricks* is on three separate occasions associated with the Alba (74, 128, 161).

in a spasm a phrase echoed in the November 1931 poem 'Enueg I', but borrowed from a phrase in a MacGreevy poem ('Crón Tráth Na nDéithe' [Twilight of the Gods]) which Beckett told him was 'a great phrase' in a letter of sometime after 15 August 1931 (*LSB*, 84).

living with him like a music that is, in harmony.

102

pinetum   a plantation of different varieties of pine, for either scientific or ornamental purposes.

wie heimlich!   Ger., 'heimlich' meaning 'secret', but in the 1934 edition (cf. n. 43 to Cassandra Nelson, 'Preface', xxiii) this reads '*wie heimatlich!*' (153), as if 'the pretty little German girl' is thinking back to scenery nearer home. In combination with the **pinetum** these two instances anticipate, 23 years later, 'Could have been happy with her ['Effie', the heroine of Theodor Fontane's novel *Effi Briest*], up there on the Baltic, and the pines and the dunes' in *Krapp's Last Tape*. Fontane's novel was apparently one of Peggy Sinclair's favourite books, but Beckett seems not to have read it until 1937, after her death, and much too late for *More Pricks*.

Tanzherr   an accomplished dancer, as Belacqua in *Dream* claims that he wishes he could be, but is not (93). cf. 102, where he 'jazzed neatly out of the line'.

wood . . . mischief   thinking of Dante in *Inferno* astray in the wood of error, but probably also of woods and forests in any number of fairy tales; Molloy will later get into difficulties in a forest in part one of *Molloy*.

secret things   from Dante *segrete cose* (*Inferno* III, 21; Caselli, 2005, 79, n. 39, citing Harvey); cf. 'Enueg I'; cf. also 'secret occasions' in 'Draff' (177), with a footnote alluding obliquely to Dante. 'Secret things' seems apt enough in this voyeuristic context, but the full phrase 'not so closely as to screen the secret things beyond them' is probably also Beckett's way of acknowledging (if only to his own satisfaction) that he is engaged here in recycling real-life material deriving from his involvements with Peggy Sinclair and Lucia Joyce which, with both them still alive (in 1931), he has felt constrained to 'screen'.

smoke . . . pines   adapted from a *Journal* entry by Jules Renard (*DN*, 238), and from *Dream*, 52. cf. the 'flower of smoke' in the 1931 poem 'Alba'. The phrase **fume of signs** is such an odd phrase in this context that one might be forgiven for supposing it a compositor's error for 'sighs'; but it is a kind of signpost, pointing towards the end of the story, and no doubt the idea that 'there is no smoke without fire' was not very far from Beckett's mind. Only with access to *Dream*, with its 'pine of *ashes*' (52; my emphasis), is the real subtlety of this very complex moment fully available.

Lucy, groping in a sudden chaos of mind, saw nothing   one of the few 'clues' that Lucy might be modelled on Joyce's daughter Lucia, who had mental problems and who suffered from a squint (hence, presumably,

'Lucie/opticienne' as seen with 'Jude', the sensual/spiritual hero of Hardy's last novel, in the poem in Lucien's letter in *Dream*, 21, and again on 73). For **saw nothing**, cf. 'Fingal', 19.

Poor little Lucy! a 'movement of compassion' (11) on the face of it; but cf. '(poor little Thelma!)' and 'poor Otto Olaf' in 'WAM' (129, 133).

103

jennet a cross-breed, unable to propagate itself; cf. the ginnet in 'EB' (8). An event similar to this occurs in the Somerville and Ross novel *The Real Charlotte* and causes the death of the character Francie. In a letter of August 1963 to Barbara Bray (TCD), Beckett mentions how he gave up riding after sustaining a painful injury on falling off a horse (presumably during early Dublin days) in the Phoenix Park, a memory also stirred by writing to Bray's two daughters 3 years earlier.

darkling thinking of 'Darkling I listen' in Keats's 'Ode to a Nightingale', and also perhaps of a remark by the Fool in Shakespeare's *King Lear*.

housetop from Kempis (*DN*, 603); cf. *Dream*, 83 and 'WAM', 112.

the first corncrake of the season cf. *Molloy* (13, 159). In the second of these two instances Moran says 'I listened to a nightingale', almost as if he has just been re-reading either this very story or Keats's famous Ode!

The velvet third of the cuckoo's note; cf. 'LL', 84.

pineal eye alluding to the pineal gland believed by Descartes to be the place where mind and body interact; but cf. the pines and the **pinetum** earlier (102).

a flutter the nearest the story will come to glimpsing, underclothes obviously being out of the question,the nightingale (a bird more often heard than seen) of Keats's ode, from which some of the details of this scene are taken.

staring vacantly into the shadows the apparently dispassionate response here is anticipated in *Dream* (72): 'up he rose and apprehended without passion round and about the Sabbath brushwood foothill couples'.

his feet that were so raw with one thing and another cf. 'DL': 'his feet were in ruins' (8).

105

verberation a beating or battering on the rump; from Cooper (*DN*, 355); cf. *Dream*, 97.

valour probably via Carlyle (*DN*, 293); cf. *Dream*, 117.

tempus edax the idea of time as 'the devourer of all things' occurs in Horace, whom Beckett read after being given a 'polyglot' edition late in 1931 (letter of 8 November 1931); but the phrase *tempus edax rerum* is in Ovid, *Metamorphoses*, 15, 234. cf. the Swift/ Sheridan quatrain 'All devouring . . . ', quoted by Anne Atik, 85.

the gramophone. *An die Musik* in a letter to MacGreevy of 31 December 1935 Beckett told him that it was a pity that there was no gramophone recording of Elena Gerhardt singing Schubert's song (in italics in 1934), given that there was an inferior version of it (as he thought) by Elisabeth Schumann.

place in the sun from Pascal, *Pensées* no. 295 (cf. 'Draff', 176).

'What A Misfortune'

109

so happy married picking up from the end of 'WO' (105), anticipating the Rooneys and 'How to be happy though married' in *All That Fall*.

He could produce no tears . . . over-indulgence discreetly alluding to too many 'teary ejaculations' (*Dream*, 4) of a different kind, beginning with the opening pages of section 'TWO' of *Dream*, but also thinking of 'AWN' (70) and preparing for 'bu[r]st into tears' (118). Cf. 'weeping' in 'Yellow' (155–6), and Hairy and the Smeraldina unable to produce tears in the 'death-chamber' (172) in 'Draff'.

small stock of pity . . . the current quick cf. '*qui vive*', etc. in 'DL' (11) and 'pity is quick with death' in the (?1929) poem 'Text'; from *Inferno* XX (Caselli 2005, 67–8).

public . . . private thinking of Mandeville.

110

sprayed with . . . human civet that is, human smells, with Beckett probably thinking of Shakespeare's *King Lear*, with Lear asking for his 'imagination' (his mental condition) to be sweetened; 'civet' also occurs in *As You Like It*. Ackerley (2008, 61) links 'civet' in *Murphy* with Swift's *A Tale of a Tub*.

odours he snuffed up derived from Augustine; *DN*, 204.

dearworthy from Dean Inge; *DN*, 694, on St Teresa.

the dust and the clay of the ground from Proverbs 8.26. cf. 'the dust of the world' ('EB', 1; *Dream*, 31, 78, 111; *DN*, 553).

throttle them gently cf. 'DL', the dying flowers of 13; and Mr Rooney of *All That Fall* wanting to 'nip some young doom in the bud'.

pastoral motiv . . . fairy tale need cf. for the pastoral aspect, 'EB', 25.

indigo hour the two other comparable instances (45, 174) have 'Homer' instead of 'indigo'; from Bérard; *DN*, 715.

ipsissimosity from Nordau, discussing Nietzsche; *DN*, 670; taken over from *Dream*, 113.

Saint George thinking of the Red Cross Knight of Book 1 of Edmund Spenser's *The Faerie Queene* (hence the elder bboggses' daughter's name: Una). The bboggses live in North Great *George* Street in Dublin (cf. O'Brien, 68).

Mildendo the metropolis (i.e. London) of Lilliput in Book I of Swift's *Gulliver's Travels*.

better worlds cf. Lucy's eyes at the end of 'WO' (105).

divine frenzy possibly with the 'heroic frenzies' of Giordano Bruno in mind, but there may also be the Orlando of Ariosto's *Orlando furioso* in the mix.

111

Her name it was Thelma Beckett's way of emphasizing that her name was *Thel*ma may be a 'coded' reference to Adrienne B*ethell*, whose wedding in May 1933 was a major event in Dublin. In late 1937, but perhaps earlier also, Beckett had some kind of sexual relationship with Adrienne Bethell. Cf. Kroll (1978, 20) on other aspects of the name 'Thelma'.

younger daughter presumably Otto Olaf, like the Professors of *Dream* and also like the Mandarin in that novel, lacks the 'gust' to sire sons (116), as indeed Belacqua does (so frustrating Lord Gall's plan) in 'EB' (10, 19a).

old men . . . young men from Diderot's 'Ceci n'est pas un conte'; *DN*, 583.

Venus Callipyge from Cooper; *DN*, 351.

toilet requisites and necessaries cf. the same phrase used by Mercier to describe what he first thinks of as having been in the sack that has disappeared (*Mercier and Camier*, chapter 2, 20).

112

kick . . . kiss an elaborate imitation of Fielding's manner, but probably not without some thought of 'KMRIA' in the 'Aeolus' section of Joyce's *Ulysses*.

woman's second passion   no. 471 of the *Maximes* of La Rochefoucauld in the 1976 Gallimard edition reads: 'Dans les premières passions les femmes aiment l'amant, et dans les autres ells aiment l'amour'. Beckett's continued interest in this subject is evident in a passage in the original German jotted down from Goethe's *Dichtung und Wahrheit* in a notebook a few years later (TCD MS 10971/1). In *More Pricks* generally, it is of course Belacqua to whom most readers would want to apply the dictum, rather than the many 'loves' of one kind or another to whom, or to which, the character seems to be temperamentally attracted.

a chartered accountant   cf. 'the chartered recountants' of *Disjecta* (89).

a long losing jenny   a difficult shot in billiards (cf. *Watt*; Ackerley 2006, 31).

She had at least the anagram of a good face   adapted from line 16 of Donne's second Elegy ('The Anagram'), the previous line reading: 'Though all her parts be not in th'usual place'.

swallow . . . eave   adapted from Kempis; *DN*, 603.

keycold   from part 3 of Shakespeare's *Rape of Lucrece*; as in *Dream*, 71.

Coleridge   a view proposed in the first volume (1817) of the *Biographia Literaria*.

ape . . . hell   derived from *Inferno* XXXIII (Caselli, 2005, 70), but a similar phrase meaning 'to die an old maid' is in Brewer. cf. Madden in *Mercier and Camier*: 'Tell the missus to go chase apes in hell' (31).

Beltschmerz   derived from Ger., 'Weltschmerz', of the pain occasioned in and by the world, to describe a stomach-ache (cf. Belacqua's 'bellyache' on 75).

113

He wore a belt, etc.   from the songs of popular parlour repertoire; Beckett remembered it, and quoted a fuller version of the second verse, in a letter to Barbara Bray postmarked 22 June 1987 (TCD).

A real three dimensional organ   Belacqua's 'word and honour' on this looks misplaced, given Walter Draffin as 'presumptive cuckoo' (cf. the cuckoo lacking in 'WO'). But it sets up the 'organist' (cf. 'Assumption') of the wedding ceremony (130, and on 132 regaining 'control of his instrument').

114

a vast white brow   for Beckett the brow, typically and indeed stereotypically, is an index of creativity (*Dream*, 141, of 'Mr Beckett') or of intelligence

('The Student' in 'AWN', 56). But the 'white brow' which intrigued him most was the '*bianca fronte*' (Dante, *Paradiso*, III, 14) in a passage translated in *DN* (1097) and adapted for use in *Dream* itself (174), also used in line 4 of the 1930 poem 'From the Only Poet . . . ', and again in the spoof lecture of 1930 'Le Concentrisme' ('un caillou à peine visible contre un front exsangue'; *Disjecta*, 37). Beckett's letter to Mary Hutchinson of 9 April 1958 (HRHRC) shows him still puzzled as to why the Spirits of the Moon appear to the Dante of *Paradiso* to be as shadowy as a pearl on a white forehead, and still trying to understand Beatrice's explanation of the phenomenon.

a cap for every joke   cf. one of Hairy Quin's three nicknames, 'Capper'.

His name was Walter Draffin   Draffin because of Beckett's working title for the collection, *Draff*. But why Walter? As a kind of homage to the Middle High German poet Walther von der Vogelweide? Or a nod in the direction of the author of the (pornographic) *My Secret Life*?

115

Juliana of Norwich   from Dean Inge; *DN*, 673 and 709; her 'all shall be well and all manner of thing shall be well' occurs in *Dream* (9, 125).

Oppoponax, etc.   perfumes, from Burton; *DN*, 891 (cf. *Dream*, 149).

any Mozart sonata whatsoever   cf. a letter to MacGreevy of 1 February 1933 mentioning the A minor sonata ('I think there is only one').

Augener's edition   long-established music publishers.

Saint Tamar   there is no Saint Tamar. Tamar, a daughter of King David, is raped by her half-brother Amnon in 2 Samuel 13. The setting, said to be Glasnevin [but cf. the note on 129], is a tacit reminder of the largest Dublin cemetery close by, but Beckett is also thinking of the largest medieval church in Ireland, St Nicholas's in Galway, which he had visited with his brother Frank (letter of 8 October 1932; *LSB*, 127–8).

Saturday, 1ˢᵗ August   as in 1931, almost certainly some 2 years too early for the composition of this story.

116

a little enjambment   he explicitly voices his objection to Hairy on 125; Hairy, who is said to be 'one of the coming writers' (117), seems not to know what an 'enjambment' is, thereby 'confirming' the point made at the end of this paragraph.

He slaked it a second time   continuing the 'theme', extrapolated out of the implications of the name *Draff*in, begun on 114, where he is reported as having 'made up' in private for drinking 'a little in public', and where his 'abuse' of Otto Olaf's decanter is noted. The association (begun with 'quenching' on 116) is further established later with 'his glass of Golden Guinea' at lunch (135) and again when, in toasting the happy couple after the ceremony, Walter 'dealt himself a slow uppercut with the glass' and 'unleashed what was left of the glorious bumper' (137). Drinking is, of course, also prominent in 'LL', 'DD', 'A Wet Night' and, to a lesser extent, 'DL' and 'Fingal'.

117

quick honeymoon, which fiasco   Beckett associated the word 'fiasco' with the impotent Octave figure in Stendhal's novel *Armance* (letter to MacGreevy of 26 April 1935); cf. *Dream*: 'when the thing fiascoes' (64). The word 'quick' is typically associated by Beckett with death.

Belacqua came back into the picture   cf. 'Capper the faithful companion simply faded away' (122).

Hypothalamion   a witty back-formation from Spenser's two marriage hymns, 'Epithalamion' (on the brink of marriage) and 'Prothalamion' (after it), here with an ominous 'hypo-'prefix, indicating a lowering, a reduction.

Capper Quin, for so we must call him   this Quin, in his size and in his significance, is a substantial figure; here he is Belacqua's best man, and later (in 'Draff'), when he is still presumably 'one of the coming writers' – though unable to come up with an inscription – he is seen propositioning Belacqua's third wife, the widowed Smeraldina, to let him become a kind of substitute Belacqua in her affections. In 'EB' (15), the Smeraldina is '[f]estooned with babies', presumably (though Hairy is not explicitly implicated) after being made pregnant by Quin, who later in the story (21) is remembered as 'Mr Quin' by Belacqua in conversation with Mick Doyle. Here 'Capper' (but also 'Tiny' and 'Hairy'), he is later 'doomed' (79), like his friend Belacqua, to prove expendable for all practical narrative purposes in the notebooks towards *Watt* – in the opening scene of the novel proper his name is attached to a hotel – irrespective of what he can 'cap' in *More Pricks*. Thus himself substituted, Camier's 'That must be someone who does not exist' at the end of *Mercier and Camier* (97), becomes something of a joke at his expense, as does his appearance in the dream of 'the Saxon' at the end of *Malone Dies*. We are twice told in quick succession here that Hairy 'broke down' (as does the 'car of his very own' [171] in 'Draff' [179]), almost as if Beckett were already planning his later and more spectral appearances, when he is very far from being the 'best man' for the job.

glabrous   bald (cf. Lord Gall in 'EB', 11); Garnier (*DN*, 454, 485) links baldness and impotence, so perhaps Hairy is not the father of the Smeraldina's child in 'EB'!

panting his pleasure   cf. the 'footsore Achates' of the Easter 1933 poem 'Sanies I', Lucy panting in 'WO' (98) and the sea panting in 'Draff' (180).

Ouayseau, etc.   a travesty of the refrain in the best-known of the Comtesse d'Aulnoy's fairy tales, 'L'oiseau bleu' ('The Blue Bird'; cf. Mr Tough in 'Love and Lethe', 85); *DN*, 1132, 1133. One fairy tale effectively generates another in **a snow-white bride** a few lines below.

and bu[r]st into tears   as he has earlier done ('AWN', 70), and as later Hairy and the Smeraldina are unable to do ('Draff', 172), although the latter is full of tears in her billet doux (143). Cf. Belacqua keeping back his tears in 'Yellow' (155). In 'EB' (3, 4), tears are seen as signifying babies, with Beckett no doubt thinking of St Augustine's 'The son of these tears shall not perish' (*DN*, 89).

the usual wings   either alluding to 'the viewless wings of poesy' in Keats's 'Ode to a Nightingale' or a glance at a song by Mendelssohn (cf. the 'Eggs Without Words' of *Dream*, 86), 'Auf Flügeln des Gesanges', better known as 'On Wings of Song'.

119

Oh well is thee   Psalms 128.2.

Otto Olaf sang a little song   cf. the groundsman in 'Draff' (181).

big blank beldam   Burton; *DN*, 831.

Purefoy triplets   perhaps thinking of the Purefoy baby in *Ulysses*, but the name also occurs in Book IV, chapter 1 of Swift's *Gulliver's Travels*, a work very much in Beckett's mind during this story.

Columbus   traditionally associated (as mentioned in a letter to MacGreevy of 8 October 1932; *LSB*, 128) with having left on his journey (to the West Indies, as it turned out, although *LSB*, 132, fn 2, suggests it was on a journey to Iceland) from the west of Ireland, where Thelma and Belacqua are to honeymoon. Cf. Kroll (1978, 25).

nine   the result of adding 'seven' and 'two pins'; but almost certainly with some thought of Dantean numerology in the *Divine Comedy* and the *Vita Nuova*, as discussed in that connection (and in connection with other writers) in 'Dante . . . Bruno.Vico.Joyce' (*Disjecta*, 32).

Pope Celestine the fifth   as in Dante's *Inferno* III; noted in TCD MS 10966, fol. 3 (Caselli, 2005, 80 fn 47).

120

mouth ajar   like the seamstresses imagined masturbating by Garnier; *DN*, 475; the 'dilated nostrils' of Mrs bboggs earlier belonged to the Frica in 'AWN' (67), where the horse analogy was more developed.

Alba Perdue   as later, in 'Draff' (167) [see the note there on the 'lost' real-life original of Alba]; later in 'WAM' she becomes 'Miss Perdue', lost and missed.

121

loud rending noise   via Giles; *DN*, 509; cf. 'a frightful sound as of rent silk' ('EB', 6).

The bodice had laid down its life to save hers   cf. *Dream*, 152; adapting John 15.13; cf. the parson in 'Draff' (178).

Struldbrug   from Swift, Book III, chapter 10 of *Gulliver's Travels*.

an infant prodigy   cf. Mozart in 'AWN' (51).

polyglot splendours   thinking of the not so very recent (November 1931) gift – cf. a quite different 'present' in the next sentence – to Beckett of a polyglot Horace, a handsome book of which Beckett was particularly fond, still in his library at his death. But *More Pricks Than Kicks* is an unusually 'polyglot' kind of book, with words and phrases from French, Italian, German, Spanish and Latin, and with many English words of Greek origin (perhaps especially here in 'WAM'), as well as coined words (e.g. 'ipsissimosity', 110; 'cherharming', 111, etc.) 'EB' adds a name (Zaborovna) derived from Russian, and some attempts at Gaelic (cf. 'Slainte' in 'WAM', 137; and Hairy on 177).

122

tossed and turned   like Augustine (*DN*, 122), and as he will again later (127); compare Hairy in 'Draff' (174, 'for various reasons' [!]).

canticle of the ring-doves   thinking either of the 'Spiritual Canticle' of St John of the Cross, which begins with an allegorical figure, the Bridegroom (cf. the end of 'Yellow'), talking to the Soul about a 'small white dove', or (Ackerley 1999, 123) of the Song of Solomon. There may also be some thought of Paul Valéry's poem 'Cantique des Colonnes' from the 1922 collection *Charmes ou Poèmes* (which contains 'Le Cimetière Marin', cf. 'Draff', 180).

beyond rubies   from the book of Job 28.18; cf. *Dream*, 50, 146.

Superfoetation   from line 6 of T. S. Eliot's quatrain poem 'Mr Eliot's Sunday Morning Service' (*Poems*, 1920). A biological term meaning multiple impregnation of an ovary, resulting in twins or larger multiple births (cf. 'multiparas', *Disjecta*, 87, and the fecund 'Mammy' of *Dream*, 75, etc.).

123

Two large orchids   an oblique innuendo, by way of the etymology of the Greek *orkhis*, conjuring up the testicles (cf. *che sciagura d'essere senza coglioni*, in Voltaire's *Candide*, one point of origin for the title of this story), an analogy no doubt lost on a florist in *Mary* Street.

do I wake or sleep?   from Keats's 'Ode to a Nightingale'.

dilated   partly from Garnier (*DN*, 475) as earlier, but with Burton uppermost this time (*DN*, 823); cf. *Dream*, 113.

124

Shekinah   via Carlyle; *DN*, 298.

125

eyes to the sky   adapting Psalm 121: 'I will lift up mine eyes unto the hills, from whence cometh my help', also alluded to in the *Nouvelles* ('The Expelled', 6; and obliquely in 'The End' also: 'Most of the time I looked up at the sky', ibid., 50) , but here all that Sproule sees is 'the day in the form of a beautiful Girl Guide galante'.

Whom should Hairy meet . . . but Walter Draffin   the exchange between them is brief and consists largely of borrowed (stolen) quotations, with Hairy in particular earning another of his nicknames ('Capper', as he is again introduced in 'Draff', 171), and the two men are indeed described as only 'on speaking terms'. But the exchange is kept brief probably because, by this point in time, both characters are being remodelled as possible substitutes for Belacqua in a story often dependent on substitutions.

spruce and keen   from Burton, speaking of a 'new ground hatchet'; cf. *Dream*, 32 and *DN*, 877.

This is where I stand   probably thinking of the Protestant Luther's 'Here I stand' stance at the church door in Wittenberg.

the Liffey swim   an annual race (since July 1920) of a mile and a half at high tide, which now usually takes place in late August or early September; the subject of a well known painting by Jack B. Yeats.

blue-eyed cats   from chapter 19 of Darwin's *On the Origin of Species*, which Beckett had bought and read in the summer of 1932. The phrase is quoted in an August 1932 letter to MacGreevy (*LSB*, 111). cf. the 'varieties' and 'species' distinction, probably also from Darwin, in 'Draff' (171).

The mole is never sober   this supposedly 'profound mot' (cf. 'sottish mot', 'AWN', 70; 'sottish jest', 'Yellow', 163) depends on the fact that moles, being blind, can be re-interpreted (via 'blind drunk') as 'never sober'.

rose   setting up Walter's gloss, overpage (126), on Alexander Pope, *Essay on Man*, I, 200: 'Die of a rose in aromatic pain'.

126

a funeral passed   thinking in part perhaps of section six of Joyce's *Ulysses* ('Hades'); presumably not a good omen, with a wedding to follow. Cf. 'Let women come thrice abroad: baptism marriage & burial' (*DN*, 971; from Burton).

the defunct   a sneak-preview, suitably depersonalized, of the dead Belacqua in 'Draff' (172, 173), perhaps explicable in part because 'WAM' and 'Draff' were composed close in time to one another; cf. the next note.

One of these fine days Hairy will observe   anticipating 'Draff', and presumably added to the story after 'Draff' had been conceived, although what is envisaged here is not in fact quite what occurs there. This 'flash-forward' ploy had been tried out in *Dream* (185, 'years later . . . '), and is partly reanimated in 'Yellow' (154, 'there is a good time coming for [Belacqua] later on'), 'Yellow' being very probably finished, if not necessarily begun, quite close in time to the writing of 'WAM' and 'Draff'.

the Morgan   Beckett owned the three-wheeler model of this famous sports car with its unusual ignition procedure; his erratic driving brought him before the magistrate Mr Reddin (later just about visible as 'Mr Nidder, strange how one fails to forget [!] certain names' in the *nouvelle* 'The Expelled'; 10) after an accident on Christmas Eve in 1931 (Knowlson 1996, 143). cf. the 'wake of objurgation' provoked by Belacqua in 'LL' (83). Hairy Quin is (like Walter Draffin earlier) a kind of *alter ego* for Beckett, who will later 'reward' him, and metaphorically himself, with the Smeraldina in 'Draff'. Later 'the Alba-Morgen' (136, possibly with an Arthurian resonance added, but also 'Germanised') adds something to this exceptionally complex configfuration, but in real life, Beckett's friend A. J. Leventhal did not reward him with the favours of Ethna MacCarthy. Beckett's sensitivity to the dangers of driving is reflected in an odd instance of life almost imitating art, as recorded in a letter to MacGreevy of 7 September

1933, Beckett having been knocked off his bicycle in Dublin by a careless motorist.

127

hymeneal insignia   from *DN*, 434.

a backfire that broke the obliging fellow's arm   a hand-cranked engine by way of a starter handle and a 'slot' in the radiator could sometimes occasion such an injury, even when carried out by an experienced driver.

Uebermensch   by way of Nietzsche's *Thus Spake Zarathustra* (cf. a letter in French to George Reavey of 23 June 1934; *LSB*, 212); Hermione Näutzsche is introduced to the fray on 129.

the back number-plate   cf. 'LL' (89).

the winged attendant   thinking of Mercury, the messenger of the gods in Greek mythology, but the insignia of the Morgan marque featured wings.

the cruel stroke of midday   adapted from 'the prick of noon' (and the hand upon it) in Shakespeare's *Romeo and Juliet*, Act II, scene 4; cf. 'DL' (3) and 'Yellow' (151).

like the Florence of Sordello   as in Dante's *Purgatorio*, VI, and remembering a paragraph in *Dream* (23–4), Sordello there being a 'troubadour of great renown'.

all postures painful   derived from Augustine; *DN*, 122 (from which 'tossed and turned' [as here and, earlier, on 122] also comes, to return in 'Draff' [174]); anticipating Otto Olaf on 132: 'that most painful of all possible positions'. The Alba is suffering her 'old pain' (130), inherited from *Dream* (151,154).

128

voice, after so long silence   it 'grate[s]' because Beckett is thinking of a phrase in Dante (*chi per lungo silenzio parea fioco*, Virgil to Dante the pilgrim in *Inferno*), as recorded in notes to Canto I (Caselli 2005, 243); Beckett 'translates' the phrase as 'hoarse after long silence' in the *'Whoroscope' Notebook* entry; 'fioco' is usually translated 'faint' (Caselli 2009, 28–33, esp. 29 and n. 9). The protagonist of *From An Abandoned Work* claims he suffers continually from a sore throat (*Texts for Nothing*, etc., 59).

you perish in your own plenty   after this remark Belacqua is 'feeling his eyes moist', tears being sometimes associated by Beckett with the conception of children (e.g. 'EB', 4); adaptations of a phrase from Augustine (*DN*, 89).

If what I love, etc.   adapted from Ovid's *Metamorphoses* (*DN*, 1115), with perhaps Burton (*DN*, 824) also in mind.

Dum vivit, etc.   'while he was living he was either drinking or pissing', in italics in 1934 (194); from Burton (*DN*, 768).

The Quaker's get   'get' is Dublin slang for 'lowest of the low' or worse; Beckett speaks of 'a whore's get version' of 'WO' that he had sent to J. B. Pinker in a letter to Charles Prentice of 15 August 1931 (*LSB*, 82).

129

stout and scallions   scallions are small pungent onions; cf. 131. This is only the second 'meal' (after the lunch in 'DL'), and the last, that Belacqua eats in the whole collection, although he claims to have had 'a heavy lunch' in 'LL' (84), presumably heavy in liquid.

At the Church of Saint Tamar   O'Brien suggests that this fictional church is modelled on St Peter's in Phibsborough (192–3), though Beckett may also be thinking back to St Nicholas's church in Galway as in a letter to MacGreevy of 8 October 1932 (*LSB*, 128), which also mentions Christopher Columbus.

in her bosom   a place to 'moor' in *Dream*, 3 (where it is Abraham's bosom), as subsequently here, Bridie being overcome by the bridegroom's bad breath.

omphalodes   probably thinking of the Martello Tower as an 'omphalos' or belly button in Joyce's *Ulysses*; but here for good reason in the plural.

Morgante and Morgutte   characters from the comic epic and burlesque poem by Luigi Pulci (1432–84), *Il Morgante* (1483), in which M*a*rgutte, a giant, dies laughing at a jest (cf. 'Yellow') of Morgante's. Beckett probably read about Pulci in John Addington Symonds's *Italian Literature* (two volumes in his *The Renaissance in Italy*).

crowded into a shade   of the trees 'wheree'er you [the loved one] walk'; adapted from Pope, *Pastorals*, from which there are entries in the *'Whoroscope' Notebook*, but here probably mediated principally via a much-loved song of Handel's.

Hermione Näutzsche   an unlikely name, but only one among many; a hybrid joining the famous philosopher and the redemptive agent in Shakespeare's *The Winter's Tale*, neither of them known to be 'nymphomaniac', although of course the real-life original (assuming there was one) may have been.

the precise remove of enchantment   adapting the familiar wisdom to the effect that 'distance lends enchantment to the view'.

Ecce, etc.   'Behold' (Lat.), most famously used in 'Ecce homo' (Pilate bringing out Christ to face the people); O'Brien discusses (140–3) a Titian canvas with this title, and Beckett also knew Joyce's 1932 poem 'Ecce puer' very well. He may also have known the 1923 book of George Grosz grotesques *Ecce Homo*. 'Behold' is the first word of *Dream*.

130

organist ... loft   cf. 132 and also 'the buffoon in the loft' at the beginning of Beckett's 1929 short story 'Assumption'.

Drink a little, etc.   adapted from Swift, letter XXI of his *Journal to Stella*.

He died of a clot   as Beckett's father did; cf. Lawlor 2009, 53, and later in 'WAM': 'the fatal result as aforesaid' (137).

dehiscence   glossed as 'the opening of a pod at maturity' in *DN*, 453, where it has been taken from Garnier; the word had been borrowed by Beckett for *Dream*, where it becomes a kind of 'principle' of aesthetic composition (116, 138). Beckett later detected 'dramatic dehiscence' in Sean O'Casey's *Juno and the Paycock* (*Disjecta*, 82).

Joseph Smith   a founder of the Mormon movement, and a believer in polygamous marriage.

131

Mens mea, etc.   'Lucia irradiates my mind with her mind', from Burton; *DN*, 868; any passion Beckett may have felt for Lucia Joyce had considerably diminished both before and during the writing of *Dream* in 1931–2, but *More Pricks* gave him the opportunity of convincing himself that it was no longer a matter of importance, if by no means wholly forgotten (hence the numerous mentions of Lucy in 'WAM'), and some of his letters show that he was not wholly immune to Lucia Joyce's charms even in 1934 and 1935.

marasmus   from Garnier (meaning a wasting away of the muscles); *DN*, 464.

the Unbuttoned Symphony   referring (with the help of Romain Rolland's biography [*DN*, 1107], but also by way of Schubert's Eighth [the so-called Unfinished] Symphony) to Beckett's favourite Beethoven symphony, the Seventh, and quoting from the accompaniment in the lower instruments of the orchestra (as again later on 140, though only one of these two musical quotations is notationally correct). These musical quotations also occur (again twice) in *Dream*, each of them as if they were a kind of doorbell chime (cf. *Dream*, 106, the studio of Herr Sauerwein), as to a salon (the Frica's) or to a 'house of ill fame' (*Dream*, 229). Neither of the examples here is explicitly linked to the Smeraldina (as in *Dream*); both are here linked to the memory of the dead Lucy. For further discussion of Beethoven, Schubert and Beckett's 'covert resurrectionism', see Lawlor (2009, 66, n. 23).

the famous viticultural passage . . . Olives?   thinking of Psalms 128.3: 'thy wife shall be as a fruitful vine . . . thy children like olive plants'.

muscae volitantes   flying mosquitoes.

Dürer cartoon   of two hands clasped in prayer; Beckett possessed a reproduction of this image.

Maupassant   the phrase is from the story 'Divorce' (see my discussion of this in the body of the text).

132

Be present, etc.   from the fourth verse of the marriage hymn 'The voice that breathed o'er Eden' with words by John Keble.

Sidneian heart   alluding to 'Look in thy heart and write' from Sir Philip Sidney's *Astrophel and Stella*; cf. a letter to MacGreevy of 22 June 1933, and the same idea in 'Yellow' (153), in 'EB' (2) and as travestied in a late squib, not quite a *mirlitonnade*, in English.

suilline   swine-like; probably via Darwin.

crystallisation   a concept famously explored by Stendhal in *De l'Amour*.

most painful of all positions   derived from Augustine, *DN*, 122; cf. 127 above.

so whorled in its disposition   a description 'justified' by the fresco analogy to follow; but cf. also the 'vulvate gnarls' of 'EB' (9), which are associated with Ruskin.

a Benozzo fresco   thinking of the Gozzoli frescoes in the chapel at the Palazzo Medici-Riccardi in Florence, and specifically those depicting 'The Journey of the Magi' in procession, which are across the east, west and south walls of the chapel (Knowlson 2006, 119–20, with colour reproduction).

Ass and all   this comment by the Alba, of 'indescribable bitterness', depends (as James Knowlson has shown) on special knowledge of one of the two fresco scenes of 'The Vigil of the Shepherds', a large painting of an ass with huge ears prominently displayed on the wall over the entrance to the right-hand sacristy of the Medici-Riccardi chapel, staring directly at the viewer (Knowlson 2006, 121, with colour reproduction).

133

Raise me up Mr Quin   probably thinking of Augustine's 'My love weighs me up . . . ' from *DN* (198), used in *Dream* (105).

Hermione . . . as in a quicksand   cf. 'LL' (87), probably written close in time to 'WAM', and 'Serena III' (written by 9 October 1933): 'the sands quicken in your hot heart'.

to make a mess of it   cf. Winnie in 'Fingal' (26).

great perturbation   from Burton, writing of 'tenses' (*DN*, 733), but put to a different use here, as also in the 1931 poem 'Enueg I', twice in *Dream* (1, 133) and again in chapter 10 of *Murphy*.

in a ruined whisper   cf. Belacqua in 'DL' (8) and 'Draff' (173).

right lung . . . left lung a distinction also made much later, in *Waiting for Godot*.

134

Italianate Irishman   derived from notes Beckett took on the Elizabethan dramatist, an 'Italianate Englishman', John Lyly (TCD MS 10971/3, notes on the 'University Wits'; *SBT/A*, 16, 130).

limae labor   cf. 'AWN' (45), and also used in the late 1932 poem 'Serena I'. Alluding to Horace (one of three direct references in *More Pricks*, with another to come in 'EB'): 'the painstaking use of the file [and delay]' (*Ars Poetica*, line 290).

is he not insured?   cf. the Smeraldina in 'Draff' (179).

135

husks off the ice with '**The sweets**'   in the near vicinity this glances towards *Hamlet*, 'the funeral bakemeats' (cf. 'Fingal', 21) and 'the sledded Polacks' ('DL', 6).

saw, clearer than ever before   here, a 'beer-engine'; later, with the same phrase suggesting an even 'clearer' vision (140), the mule and the beaver; a motif linking Hairy and Belacqua (cf. the note on the Morgan). For the beaver, cf. *Dream*, 63.

She was a very strange girl   cf. Ruby in 'LL', in the estimation of her mother Mrs Tough (85); varied later in the paragraph to 'She was a most strange girl'.

oniromaniacs   people mad for, or maddened by, dreams or fantastical illusions; derived by a kind of back-formation from the various manias listed by Nordau (*DN*, 662).

Swift, rebuking the women of this country   the rebuke described (perhaps prompted by thoughts of Swift/Presto using his feet [cf. '**those feet**' here] to 'walk like camomile' in 'Fingal' [26]) is from letter XVII of his

Journal to Stella. Beckett's interest in feet begins with 'DL' (6), and extends here (114) to Walter Draffin's heels, and also his shoes.

fit for nothing better than to be laid aside Smith (30) notes the 'bawdy pun'. In 'Fingal', Winnie, as if to punish her for her 'decency' ('Draff', 167), has been – from Belacqua's point of view – very effectively 'laid aside', like the bicycle on which he makes his getaway.

136

contesting an election there had been a general election in Ireland in January 1933.

like a pelican a bird in legend famous for its care of its children; derived from Musset; cf. Lucien's *Dream* poem (21), which Beckett 'adopted' as his own in the HRHRC *Poems* list (Leventhal collection).

penetrate . . . façade echoing *Dream*, 46; a phrase Beckett had found in the *Journal du 'Faux-Monnayeurs'* by André Gide (on whom he hoped towards the end of 1932 to write a short book for Chatto's 'Dolphin' series, soon to be wound up).

Shekinah for the second time (cf. 124), in a story making much of doubles; *DN*, 298.

Semper ibi juvenis, a Late Latin version of the Isle of Avalon into which Arthur passed after his death, intended to function in conjunction with the reference to Avalon in Walter's speech some 20 lines below. The text quoted apparently derives from a late 6th century chronicler, and is displayed at Glastonbury (information kindly conveyed by Dr Mark Nixon). This is perhaps Beckett at his most recondite, ensuring that the work which the quotation is designed to do, the whole *point* (as it were) of these being supposedly 'the first words that he came across in his head', has been totally obscured for the best part of 80 years!

137

buckler cf. *DN*, 133, from Augustine; the word recurs in 'EB' (10).

I close these eyes, etc. Beckett typically associates closed eyes with the Rimbaud 'eye-suicide' of 'Les Poëtes de Sept Ans' (cf. 'EB'), but the vision induced here seems to be tilting at the early work of WB Yeats (whose play of 1916 *At The Hawk's Well* was revived at the Abbey Theatre in Dublin in July 1927); cf. the late 1932 poem 'Serena II': 'it is useless to close the eyes', and the 'yeux clos' that prompt Lucien's poem in *Dream* (21).

Ui Breasail the Irish equivalent of the lost world, or other world, of Atlantis.

the Siamese haecceity from Lat. *haecceitas*, often rendered 'this-ness'; probably one of the few borrowings from Windelband (Tufts translation of *A History of Philosophy*, 2nd ed., New York: Macmillan, 1907, 341), which Beckett may not have begun to read until mid-1933; Windelband uses the word in his discussion of 'the definite individual Form' as found in Duns Scotus and Scotism. The form imagined here is both duplex and narcissistic.

no two stars . . . Saint Paul   1 Corinthians 15.41.

white voice   derived from Burton (*DN*, 975; *Dream*, 186); cf. 39 (the voice of the pedlar in 'DD'), and a letter to MacGreevy of 4 [*recte* 3] November 1932 (*LSB*, 139).

138

I have to thank, etc.   'The wedding speech in "What A Misfortune" is the protagonist's most clever statement in the volume' (Kroll 1974, 339).

torrents of meiosis   that is, of understatement (cf. 'hyperbole', 120). But in coming close to being a contradiction, the phrase is perhaps designed to remind us that Belacqua 'had a strong weakness for oxymoron' ('DD', 32).

Belle-Belle   a character in a fairy tale by the Comtesse d'Aulnoy ('Belle-Belle, ou le Chevalier Fortuné'); *DN*, 1149.

vis a tergo   a back view, as with the 'massive flitches' on 133; used again in 'EB', and in the essay 'Recent Irish Poetry' (*Disjecta*, 71); Freud's 'Wolf-Man' claimed he had seen his father make love to his mother from the rear (hence 'run her behind', of the car, on 132). Anticipated by 'all right behind' and the 'posterior aspects' of 128, and (almost) by 'Ass and all' (132).

rising to the occasion   continuing the 'crystallisation' process begun on 132. One of the best 'jokes' in the story is that weddings promote sexual relations between the guests (here 'the Skyrm and Näutzsche', earlier Walter and the Alba) rather than the sexual future of the principals (with Thelma seemingly condemned to remaining 'Miss bboggs . . . henceforward'; she is still 'Thelma née bboggs' on 167).

Tiny Hairy Capper Quin   *three* nicknames for once, as if he really were 'enormous' (117).

spiritual body   cf. the 'spiritual equivalent' in 'Draff' (178, 180).

Abbé Gabriel   cf. *Dream*, 134 (and perhaps also 'Abbot' on 161): an eccentric cleric and professor of mathematics at the University of Caen who proposed a complicated theory of history, based on cycles of 744 years, on which he based predictions, including (in 1925) cold winters to come. Astronomical prediction and divination, and notions of celestial influence, obviously interested Beckett more than his irony about them permitted him to disclose (cf. 'Whoroscope', and the 'star-chart' in *Murphy*, and some jottings in the 'Whoroscope' Notebook from the *Encyclopaedia Britannica* putting matters on a more 'respectable' basis). But the Abbé Gabriel was presumably not an ideal person to thank in a bridegroom's wedding speech, unless you happened to be looking forward with some qualms, as Belacqua, given his temperament, obviously is.

the whirligig that is, the world turning, creating time as it can be seen on a clock (cf. 117). As in 'AWN' (65), revised from *Dream* (224). Derived from 'Cupid's whirligig' in Burton (*DN*, 829).

Plutarch Beckett told MacGreevy he had bought a Plutarch in a letter of 5 January 1933, and in another letter to him (23 April 1933; *LSB*, 154) said that he had not yet made much progress with it.

This bivalve world cf. 'succulent bivalve' (*DN*, 639).

Selah a Hebrew word of obscure origin found in the Psalms, traditionally taken to mean a blessing of 'forever'.

139

we leave it to the reader to determine an abdication of responsibility comparable with the 'we beg leave' moment in 'LL' (83).

Walter took sanctuary cf. the 'land of sanctuary' in 'Fingal' (18).

like a stock at gaze that is, like a senseless or stupid or stupefied person; derived from the 'gazing-stock' in two biblical contexts (Nehemiah 3.6; Hebrews 10.33), but perhaps remembering Hardy's Jude Fawley 'filled with an ardour at which he mentally stood at gaze' (*Jude the Obscure*, I:6).

He opened the wicket into the lane probably thinking of the Beckett home Cooldrinagh in Foxrock, as again with Moran leaving home in part two of *Molloy* ('So we came to the little wicket-gate'; 133, but first mentioned on 51). But in this earlier instance Beckett may also have had in mind Christian in Part I of Bunyan's *The Pilgrim's Progress* meeting Mr Worldly Wiseman: 'I tell you, sir, I am going to yonder wicket-gate before me; for there, as I am informed, I shall be put into a way to be rid of my heavy burden'. So heavy is Christian's 'burden' that, although he has a wife and children, 'I am as if I had none', which Bunyan quotes from Corinthians 7.29. Belacqua of course now has the 'burden' of a wife, if not for long, or for much 'further' (140; cf. 'Draff', 167).

grape . . . grasp probably thinking of the Tantalus of Greek myth (cf. *PTD*, 13 and an entry from the 11th edition of the *Encyclopaedia Britannica* in the *'Whoroscope' Notebook*).

140

Belacqua threw them a tub   Beckett is here effectively throwing a tub (cf. a retrospective view of the 'little story' told early on in *Dream*; 178, looking back to 10 ff.) of his own making by way of an obvious reference to Swift's *A Tale of a Tub*, a tub which is designed to catch the eye without disclosing any real substance or significance, but which is well adapted to assisting Belacqua in making an exit from the situation, with the story now almost over. But the mule and the beaver to come (134) are another kind of 'tub', and actually part of a much more serious and thoroughgoing purpose in this story, the delicate nature of which means it can never be openly or directly acknowledged: an actual or metaphorical impotence at least in part occasioned by the dead hand of the past (Lucy) and Belacqua's thoughts of a cold and grim 'Abbé Gabriel'-like future.

atra cura   from Horace (*Odes*, 3, 1, 40): 'dark care', Lucy as a ghostly presence at the back of the car and at the back of Belacqua's (and perhaps also Thelma's) mind. Lucy dead appears more often (eight times) in 'WAM' than she does in the story that features her ('WO'). This is the third direct quotation from Horace in *More Pricks*, and the last (with one more to come in 'EB'), and it is used again in the (?1934) revision ('Weg du Einzige!') of the 1933 poem 'Sanies I'. It may perhaps have been prompted by a recent reading of Hardy's *Tess of the d'Urbervilles*, where 'Black Care' occurs in chapter XLI, but the phrase was almost proverbial.

babylan   from *Dream* (50, 89, etc.), but derived from Stendhal's letter of 13 December 1826 to his friend Prosper Mérimée, with Beckett thinking of Stendhal's novel *Armance* (as in letters to his friend MacGreevy of 18 August 1932, a section omitted from *LSB*, 119, and again, Beckett having re-read *Armance*, on 26 April 1935). A deliberate way of advertising, albeit by way of a word difficult to 'read' (a 'strange word' on 140), Belacqua's fears that he either will be, or for his peace of mind may need to be, sexually impotent.

Something to eat?   a persistent concern of the Smeraldina in *Dream* (25, 75), here inherited by Thelma, whose 'What is it?' is also designed to remind us of the title of this story, the real reference point of which cannot be acknowledged without offending public decency; 'Draff' has the Smeraldina dreaming of letting herself go 'in the arms of a man of her own weight at last', Quin being a massive man (hence his nickname 'Tiny').

baba   as in the ice cream confection known as a 'rhum-baba', but the implication here may be that Thelma is thinking of babies, or that Belacqua sees them in her eyes (as he will again in the eyes of Zaborovna Privet in 'EB', 3–4); a notion derived from St Augustine (*DN*, 89) and from Burton (*DN*, 907).

the mule . . . a beaver, flogging it   an exceptionally complex metaphor, its 'strange'-ness simply assumed and highlighted rather than explained, re-animating a kind of St George and the Dragon motif (cf. North Great *George*'s Street and Una via Spenser's Red Cross Knight earlier) as if it were heraldic (cf. 'rampant' (103); 'appaumée' on 171). The mule as a hybrid is unable to propagate itself as a species, and the beaver is 'known' to castrate itself at the sign of danger (cf. *DN*, 819). This is also a reworking of the Apollo-Marsyas situation used as a reference point in *Proust* (*PTD*, 79).

Gone west   in the late summer of 1932, Beckett had visited Galway with his brother Frank, and very much enjoyed the trip (*LSB*, 128); but the journey west (as in Joyce's 'The Dead', where the journey only takes place in the mind of the mental traveller, the sleepy Gabriel Conroy) is traditionally associated with death, because of where the sun sets. The phrase 'went further' is no doubt Beckett obliquely remembering, and registering, a real journey, but also thinking in terms of going one better than Joyce. We learn later (in 'Draff') that Thelma died of 'sunset and honeymoon that time in Connemara' (167), which distinguishes her from the Michael Furey figure in 'The Dead', who either metaphorically or literally dies from the cold.

They went further   at once an oddly flat, and an oddly ominous end, which is *not* an end, the 'point' of which is expanded in 'EB' when Lord Gall recalls that 'the Lord laid a curse on the mule and the ginnet, whose gist was that they should [being hybrids unable to propagate their species] go no farther' (9).

'The Smeraldina's Billet Doux'

143

tears! tears! tears!   thinking of a famous Tennyson lyric from 'The Princess', which continues . . . 'I know not what they mean' [!].

Nägelnackt   Ger., 'stark naked'; in *Dream* (55–6): 'naked! naked!'

at last be the Geliebte   by analogy with the 'ferne Geliebte' of Beethoven (*Dream*, 56, 138; *DN*, 1106, 1109).

Sturm über Asien, etc.   the films have Vsevolod Pudovkin in common; in the first he was the director, in the second the lead actor.

if it comes to Dublin in *Dream* (56): 'if it comes to Paris' – a rather more likely eventuality.

144

the man she loves thinking of the Gershwin song 'The Man I Love' (the phrase appearing below).

wahnsinnig! the literal meaning is 'insane', the colloquial meaning is 'terrific'; another threesome (cf. 'tears' [143] and 'Bel!' [145]).

the man is a bit of a fool but dances quite well cf. the Tanzherr of 'WO' (102).

a blue letter issued to a student whose work has been in one way or another unsatisfactory.

145

everything that is on you the prepositional mistake sets up the impetigo in the next note.

your poor sore face cf. the impetigo from which Belacqua is suffering in 'Fingal' (18), to which the less than accommodating Winnie Coates takes exception. The Smeraldina has 'inkspots' on her face (143), but is apparently unaware of the famous *black* American close harmony group, despite having a friend in 'Amerika'.

How long? How long? adapted from Psalms 4.2, as in *Dream* (82), and as parodied ('How square, O Lord, how square!' in 'The Possessed', *Disjecta*, 99).

Die Grosse Liebe a (1926) book by Paul Wiegler, made into a film, but too late for this Smeraldina to see it, by Otto Preminger in 1932.

how could you ever doubt me? in *Dream* (59): 'doupt', with the spelling focused on a consonantal cluster much more frequent in German than in English. cf. Beckett's emphasis on how 'sophisticated' English is by comparison with other languages, as instanced by the different words for 'doubt' (*Disjecta*, 28).

146

Goethes Faust quoting from Gretchen's song at the spinning wheel in Part 1, famously set by Schubert.

Do you remember last summer probably referring to the summer of 1929, during which Beckett spent time with Peggy and the Sinclair family in Kragenhof, near Kassel (*LSB*, 11; cf. *Disjecta*, 37). The misspelling 'dose' (for 'does') looks ominous.

147

Der Tag wird kommen, etc.   from the tragic conclusion of Grillparzer's play *Des Meeres und der Liebe Wellen*, with Beckett perhaps also thinking of 'Oft in the stilly night' (one of Thomas Moore's *Irish Melodies*, resurfacing in *Nacht und Träume* many years later). Beckett quotes 'old leaves that have known the long joys of summer' from Grillparzer's play in *Malone Dies* (58), without revealing that he is doing so.

Arschlochweh ... gone to the Schweiz   the Smeraldina's piano teacher in *Dream* (14, 18, etc.), of Swiss origin.

the 'thing' you wrot about my 'beauty' (as you call it)   presumably the (?1929) poem 'Casket of Pralinen ... ', in which the issue of beauty is raised, although the word 'beauty' is found in several of Beckett's very early, for the most part jettisoned, poems. It may or may not explain the reference that Beckett uses the word 'thing' to refer to 'Sedendo et Quiescendo' as sent back by Charles Prentice in a letter to MacGreevy of August 1931 (*LSB*, 83).

that marvellous pain again that we did in the mountains   cf. 'the old pain' of the Alba ('WAM', 130), and Molly Bloom as a 'Flower of the mountain' at the end of Joyce's *Ulysses*.

P.S. One day nearer to the silent Night!!!   in this context the phrase brings us nearer to the 'silent night' which will fall on Belacqua in the next story (as anticipated, unwittingly, in 'die stille NACHT!!!' from Grillparzer), although the reader of 1934, having got this far and having registered that Christmas is coming, would be much more likely to think of the German carol 'Silent Night'.

'Yellow'

151

The night-nurse ... turned on the light   a motif first used in 'Assumption': 'She ['the Woman'] turned on the light' (*transition*, 16–17, 1929, 270); cf. Liebert in *Dream* (48), who 'insisted on turning out the light'. According to *Murphy*, in the view of Miss Counihan, 'It is only in the dark that one can meet' (chapter 10). Belacqua immediately switches the light off, switches it on again (152) to postpone daybreak, and then off again (153), only to find 'it threw shadows'.

Hardy's Tess   in a letter to MacGreevy of 12 December 1932, Beckett tells him that he has been given (by his father) Hardy's novel to read while he is in hospital: 'Will I ever read it?' He obviously read at least as far as chapter

XXV (from the section titled 'The Woman Pays', Hardy's Tess effectively becoming one of the many women in this story), and probably to the end. Hardy has 'sorrow' whereas Beckett has 'grief', so the phrase has indeed been a little 'manipulated'. For 'opportunity', cf. 'EB' (3).

down for twelve   thinking of Dante (as in 'DL'), but more particularly of Mercutio (to the *Nurse*) in Act II, scene 3 of Shakespeare's *Romeo and Juliet* and 'the bawdy hand of the dial' (in *Murphy*, chapter 10, this becomes 'the bawdy innuendo of eternity'). We are told that here, at least, Belacqua is more than usually 'saucy' (precisely, and perversely, in circumstances hardly propitious for *sexual* intimacy), and at the end he is absurdly ready to become a 'bridegroom', with disastrous results (as previously for his wives, so now at last for him too).

a bistoury   a scalpel; the French equivalent ('bistouri') is in Stendhal's *Armance*.

152

bastardo   as again on 153; this Belacqua who is 'tired' of himself resembles the one in 'WAM' who suffers a 'loss of interest in himself' (139).

Huguenot guts   Beckett liked to believe that the family were descendants of Huguenot émigrés to Ireland, but 'guts' here is probably in the light of Hamlet's words after the killing of Polonius (see the note on 'family guts' below) in Act III, scene 4 of Shakespeare's play (cf. 'safely stowed' from Act IV, scene 2, on 85, soon to be encountered again in 'Draff'; 171).

Daybreak . . . nasty birth   a distaste borrowed and adapted from *Dream* (174), found again in 'EB' (24), and *Molloy* (146); cf. the 'placenta' of the 1932 poem 'Spring Song' (line 79), and the 'placenta de l'aurorore' in Lucien's letter in *Dream* (21).

I am what I am   probably thinking of Swift in his 'madness' repeating the Old Testament self-definition of God; cf. 'Le monde et le pantalon': 'je suis ce que je suis' (*Disjecta*, 136). The motif is reprised on the first page of the typescript of 'Lightning Calculation' (UoR).

the tortures of the damned   thinking of Dante's *Inferno*, but probably also of the 'Hell Sermon' in Joyce's *A Portrait of the Artist as a Young Man*.

153

the local doc   the anaesthetist who appears at the end to 'put him off' in no uncertain fashion (164). 'EB' (24) speaks of Belacqua being 'bumped off'.

the handy man at hand   cf. the note to 'handy Andy' (158) below.

family guts thinking of 'I'll lug the guts into the neighbour room' (*Hamlet*, Act III, scene 4), after the killing of Polonius; hence the 'neighbour room' of the asthmatic (who is not yet dead!) overhead.

An asthmatic later (by way of the 'yaller wall' [159]) equated with Bergotte in Proust's *Recherche*, Proust having been an asthmatic.

the livelong day cf. the Easter 1933 poem 'Sanies I': 'all the livelong way'. A Beckettian favourite, found again in *Malone Dies*, and twice in *The Unnamable*. Less obviously, perhaps, in 'LL', Ruby Tough is not expected to live long, and in 'Yellow', Belacqua (and perhaps the asthmatic also) is not fated to do so.

as Crusoe laboured in chapter 4 of Defoe's *Robinson Crusoe*. Beckett's correspondence with Barbara Bray shows him re-reading *Robinson Crusoe*, with mixed (but for the most part positive) feelings over a summer holiday. Cf: '[I] curse the day . . . / . . . I was not born Defoe' ('Sanies II').

The posterns of the mind the back door or alternative entrance, Beckett having probably first encountered the word in a quite different context in reading J. R. Green (cf. *LSB*, 150), but the word is used earlier in 'What A Misfortune' (139) in another context, just after Belacqua and Thelma have 'opened the wicket' *behind* the house.

finding a comfortable position cf. the 'tossed and turned' motif from Augustine in 'WAM' earlier, and later in 'Draff'.

bourgeois poltroon Beckett associates 'poltroon' with *poltrone* (It., armchairs) in *Dream*, 145 (cf. *DN*, 417).

the last ditch cf. Winnie in 'Fingal' (30), with the ditches of the Malebolge in Dante's *Inferno* (XVIII ff.) in mind, as in *Dream*, 168.

154

could no more go back into his heart cf. *Dream*, 44, 122; adapted from Augustine; *DN*, 101. But cf. also the 'Sidneian heart of Skyrm' in 'What A Misfortune' (132), thinking of the last line of the first poem (travestied in a late English squib/*mirlitonnade*) in Sir Philip Sidney's *Astrophel and Stella*.

to lie on his back in the dark anticipating a wish of Murphy and the position of the 'you' in *Company*.

the grocer's sense of honour probably remembering the 'warm-hearted' grocer of 'DL' (8).

there is a good time coming for him later on cf. *Molloy*: 'I have a good time coming' (45).

What were his tactics in this crisis? adopting an oddly objective narrative stance, partly perhaps to set up 'How did he proceed to put this plan into execution?' later (156), but almost certainly a nod, in this last but one of the *More Pricks* stories, to the last but one section of Joyce's *Ulysses* ('Ithaca') with its thoroughgoing question-and-answer technique. But there are actually fewer questions asked in 'Yellow' than in, say, 'A Wet Night', which in some thirty pages asks nearly fifty, or 'Love and Lethe', which contains on average almost three a page.

hope for the best also Belacqua's hope in 'DL' (10).

Flitter the – cf. 'The [piano] strings are in flitters' (*Watt* 59). All subsequent reprints (but not Faber 2010) fill in the dots with 'fucker'.

Donne the quotation (in italics in 1934, 235) is from the tenth of the *Paradoxes and Problemes* ('That a wise man is known by much laughing'), probably as read in the Nonesuch Press *Complete Poetry and Selected Prose* volume edited by John Hayward, first published in January 1929. Cf. similar material on the inside of the back cover of the Schiller Theater *Krapp's Last Tape* notebook, in the TCD Philosophy Notes, and Heraclitus and Democritus appearing once again in a kind of tandem in the *mirlitonnades* 'flux cause' and 'samedi répit'. Farrow emphasizes that Donne is 'pro-witty' and 'anti-lachrymose' (171), but the popular wisdom to the effect that 'laughter is the best medicine' is presumably Beckett's more general target.

155

between contraries no alternation because of the 'coincidence of opposites' or 'identified contraries' in the philosophy of Giordano Bruno (*Disjecta*, 20).

ultra-red and ultra-violet cf. 'ultra-violet' in 'Draff' (167); from Sir James Jeans on the Doppler effect; *DN*, 1061.

a more dreary morning Bill Beckett's last words were, apparently, 'What a morning' (9 October 1933; *LSB*, 165). A letter from Beckett (on the first of his two admissions to the Merrion St Nursing Home) to MacGreevy of 5 December 1932 (*LSB*, 145) mentions the 'morning sun' emphasized later on this page, and once again mentioned on 152.

a true saying from 1 Timothy 3.1, as previously (twice) in 'DL' (11, 15), and in *Dream* (40).

flaws of dawn derived from chapter 9 of Dickens's novel *Little Dorrit*; first used with wind (*Dream*, 139), later with saliva (187), and later still (in 'EB', 27) with 'tramontane' (from It., *tramontana*, a cold wind from the north or the east).

the dilemma probably thinking of an entry in *DN* (914) in which Beckett reminds himself what Burton meant by the phrase 'holding a wolf by the ears' (already adapted for use in 'AWN' [72]').

an impression almost of gallantry cf. Belacqua being 'incapacitated ... from gallantry' in 'Fingal' (17).

Bim and Bom popular Russian clowns, who were twins; names given as nicknames to the Clinch twins in *Murphy*.

he was obscure at the same time 'obscene' in the 1970 Calder & Boyars reprint (176), presumably a compositor's error, followed in the Picador paperback edition. Heraclitus has long been known as 'Heraclitus the Obscure'. Cf. a letter to MacGreevy of 23 April 1933; *LSB*, 154–5), which registers Beckett's regret at not being able to get to the library in TCD to study Heraclitus and the other Pre-Socratics. Beckett's notes on the early Greek philosophers are mainly taken from Windelband and from John Burnet's *Greek Philosophy: Thales to Plato* (but see the next note).

Heraclitus of Ephesus ... that Delian diver among Beckett's typewritten notes on philosophy (taken from Archibald Alexander, *A Short History of Philosophy*, 1907, etc.) is a quotation from Socrates on the subject of the 'Delian diver' who would be needed to unlock the obscurities of Heraclitus. It appears under the heading 'Heraclitus of Ephesus' (1908 [2nd] edition, 28).

the tumour the size of a brick in *Dream* it was only a 'baby anthrax' (29), as again in 'AWN' (63, 73).

156

not quite the word cf. 'no other word for it' (159) and the 'surgical' quality of Murphy which is said to be 'not quite the right word' (*Murphy*, chapter 4).

ohne Hast aber ohne Rast adopted by Goethe as his motto: 'without haste but without respite'. Goethe uses the phrase, linked to 'Wie das Gestern' ('like a star') in the second of the *Zahme Xenien*, an influence on the 1934 poem 'Gnome', and a point of reference in Beckett's later life also. In this 'not quite the word' context, self-evidently not the right language (compare '*Au plaisir*' [157]), and the Beckett/Belacqua aesthetic is utterly different from Goethe's, being much more a matter of feeling 'ardour and fervour absent or faked' (*LSB*, 121; cf.'fervent/ ardent', ibid., 130).

157

That made her third appearance cf. 'Now she appeared for the fourth or fifth time' (164).

What a Life! Beckett may have known, and if so been amused by, a comic book with this title (a book now often considered proto-surreal) by 'E. V. L.' [E. V. Lucas] and 'G. M.' [George Morrow], subtitled 'An autobiography', first published by Methuen in 1911.

There was no controverting this repeated on 159. All the 'controverting' in 'Yellow' occurs at the very end, given the 'manipulated' structure of the story. cf. 'There is no controverting *Murphy* as structure' (German Diaries entry for 18 January 1937).

Au plaisir this French phrase replaces 'farewell' (in line 55 of the published 'Whoroscope') in the revised (A. J. Leventhal) version of that poem (HRHRC).

a mighty rushing sound of starched apron cf. the 'sound as of a rushing mighty wind' in Acts 2.2 heard by the Apostles at Pentecost, with the Holy Ghost inspiring them to speak in tongues, just as the day-nurse Miranda will later prove 'bilingual' (154).

conversation obiter from *Dream*, 24; cf. 'DL' (11); from Burton; *DN*, 844.

Like that, all in a rush etc. cf. 'Like that, all in one word' ('AWN', 74).

But he stupidly elected to linger on in the bed with his uneasy load Smith (30, 180, n. 14) points out that 'uneasy load' is from Book I of Swift's *Gulliver's Travels*. This is one of more than a dozen sentences in 'Yellow' beginning with the word 'but', a tactic which helps to create a sense of conflict understandable in the circumstances as they appear (and as they turn out), generating an undercurrent preparing the way for an unexpected (but 'predicted') outcome.

158

the sun, that creature of habit anticipating the sun in the first sentence of *Murphy* (from Ecclesiastes 1.9), but 'rainfall' (73) is relatively rare in *More Pricks*, and certainly rarer than it would typically be in Dublin. This is one (small) way of not rewriting Joyce's *Dubliners*.

Aschenputtel the German version of the fairy tale 'Cinderella' as collected by the Brothers Grimm, who are mentioned in a letter (in French) to Maurice Sinclair of 27 January 1934 (*LSB*, 177), and much later, in an undated letter of January 1955 to Pamela Mitchell (UoR), which supplies a source for the last words of 'Draff' (181). 'Foreignness' (a recurrent feature of 'Yellow') is another way of indicating that this is not *Dubliners*, however many Dubliners may be in it.

Putting out me good fire   cf. the fire and the 'antiphlogistic' of 'Draff' (178), although Belacqua is buried, not cremated, which is just as well given that in the event he was obliged to return in 'EB'. The fire here makes the ward, and later the operating theatre, the 'charnel-house' Belacqua thinks it is (156). Vladimir, in Act II of *Waiting for Godot* (Faber and Faber, 1981, etc., 64) uses the term 'charnel-house' (twice) on seeing 'corpses' everywhere, as the tramps disagree about whether or not you have to 'look'.

She screwed round on her knees   cf. 'WO': 'The way screwed uphill' (102).

That's right   cf. ' "Are you right?" ' at the end (164).

handy Andy   possibly thinking of the title of a once famous comic novel by the Irish writer Samuel Lover [!], first published in 1842, subtitled 'A Tale of Irish Life'. If so, in ironic counterpoint to a tale of Irish death.

159

the old yaller wall   for the Proustian analogies, see my discussion, and (among several) also Zurbrugg's discussion (221–3). Cf. the wall in 'Fingal' (23), 'The lemon of the walls whined like Vermeer's' (*Murphy*, chapter 10), and Arsene's wall in part 1 of *Watt*.

sanies into a bucket   a discharge of blood and pus (*DN*, 1035), the phrase having been borrowed from *Dream* (108). Later in *Dream*, in a paragraph omitted from 'AWN' (228), the association of 'sanies' with sound is maintained in the phrase 'sanies of music'.

Wincarnis   a tonic wine (cf. 164 and 'The Wincarnis cousin' of a letter of 27 December 1934 to MacGreevy).

She took a quick look at his neck   cf. 'theatre nurse in *Yellow* from the neck down' in 'Draff' (178).

Top . . . and bottom   cf. 'she had the weapon into his bottom and discharged' (162).

160

That voluptuous undershot cast of mouth, the clenched lips   borrowed from 'her lips . . . resulting in a faintly undershot local sensuality' in the 1929 story 'Assumption' (*transition* 16–17, 270), and from 'the fine full firm undershot priapism of underlip and chin' (*Dream*, 69).

Miranda whom we met first on 157. Cf. *Proust* (*PTD*, 45): 'unlike Miranda [in Shakespeare's *The Tempest*], he [Proust's Marcel] suffers with her whom he has not seen suffer', a phrase adapted in *Dream* (11).

bump of amativeness as again on 160, and in 'EB' (7); cf. 'his baby anthrax' (73) and *Dream* (29).

fag-end Belacqua having been smoking all morning; cf. 'fagpiece' in 'EB' (2).

as a bride's adorned from the book of Isaiah (61.10), but here to set up the 'bridegroom' at the end (157).

limits . . . to Democritus cf. Neary's gift of his tractate 'The Doctrine of the Limit' to Miss Counihan in *Murphy* (see Feldman, 2006, 69, and Beckett's 'Philosophy Notes' at TCD). Belacqua oversteps these 'limits' by immoderate laughter at a joke which, in a sense, becomes the death of him, having earlier survived the 'memorable fit of laughing' in 'Fingal' (17).

161

long nose derived primarily, with the sexual undertones of the story being maintained, from reading Ernest ('Erogenous') Jones on zones of the body (TCD MS 10971/8/12), but perhaps also thinking of the most famous accoutrement of Cyrano de Bergerac. A long nose, or something like it, would not be of much use to Belacqua, given where he is.

cooling her porridge cf. 'the partner of my porridge days', what a good and chivalrous wife should be, from Giles; *DN*, 542; cf. 'EB' (15).

cor anglais cf. the 'far bugle' of *Dream* (84).

the cat perhaps thinking back to Mlle Glain's cat in 'DL' (12); cf. 'there were no cats' in 'WO' (95).

those two that night in a bed from Burton; *DN*, 993; but there is of course only one in bed here.

Lister the discoverer of antiseptics.

162

Army Service Corps the capital letters replicate the first three letters of 'A*sch*enputtel' earlier; the 'evacuation' is anticipated by 'Merde!'(161), and by the 'salts' on 156.

all would yet be well adapting the famous tag of Juliana of Norwich, from Dean Inge (cf. *DN*, 613, 709 and *Dream*, 125), with perhaps just the faintest suggestion, given the outcome later, that death is a consummation devoutly to be wished.

163

dirty . . . high-brow   expanding a phrase used earlier ('AWN', 66); adapted from *Dream* (100).

Hexenmeister   a magician or sorcerer; cf. the Mozart of 'AWN' and the Mörike review (*Disjecta*, 62).

the ends of his pyjamas tucked like a cyclist's into the sinister socks   cf. the Easter 1933 poem 'Sanies I': 'clipped like a pederast as to one trouser-end'.

a cow's toe   cf. Belacqua's toe, the 'lang tootsy' of 160, and Beckett's 'Cow' notes at TCD.

she whose life had changed   as, we shortly discover, Belacqua's will, and as Proust's Bergotte's life has done. This nurse has seen Belacqua's 'yellow' face, just as Belacqua has tried and failed to close the blinds on the 'yaller wall' (159), and will suffer 'yellow yerks' (164). In 'EB', the colour yellow is associated with death by way of the 'yellow beam' (26) and 'yellow eye' (27) of Mick Doyle's lantern. Murphy's favourite colour is yellow.

164

It was like a dream   cf. Caleken Frica feeling that 'all this' has happened before 'by hearsay or in a dream', with the novel *Dream* (where nearly all of the 'all this' of 'A Wet Night' [68] has indeed already 'happened') also probably in mind.

His hour was at hand   from Matthew 26.45.

There was no blinking at the fact   cf. 'At this all-important juncture . . . Belacqua found himself blinking' (155). 'There was no controverting this' (157, 159), and 'there could be no question about that' below.

his glasses   last '[shaken] off' at the end of 'A Wet Night' (74).

No smoking . . . in the operating-theatre   cf. 'No smoking in the torture chamber' (*Dream*, 71), with Beckett remembering a disturbing complex of feelings, and also a sexual encounter, in Nuremberg in April 1931 (repeated in 'EB', 1), preparing for **antechamber** a few lines below. cf. the 'death-chamber' of 'Draff' (171), a story in which Belacqua will (like Beckett's father) be buried rather than cremated. In *Dream*, 236 (though not in 'AWN') Belacqua follows the Alba out 'through the door of the torture-chamber' (the party at Casa Frica). Nuremberg and 'No smoking' are remembered by Beckett as late as 2 November 1971 in a letter to Barbara Bray (TCD).

washing his invaluable hands   like Pontius Pilate; cf. the grocer in 'DL' (7) and Una bboggs in 'WAM' (120).

antechamber   probably with half an eye on the French phrase 'faire antichambre', to dance attendance upon; *DN*, 1090. But some thought of Ante-Purgatory in Dante's *Purgatorio* is no doubt also present here.

bridegroom   probably derived directly from the description of the martyrdom of the Protestant Dr Rowland Taylor during the Reformation, as described by J. R. Green in *A Short History of the English People*: 'All the way Dr Taylor was merry and cheerful as one that accounted himself going to a banquet or a bridal' (1926 ed., chapter VII, section 2, 365). The entry 'like the Vicar of Hadleigh hastening to the tar-barrel (Green, 365)' is in the 'Whoroscope' Notebook, and must date from late 1932 or early 1933, when Beckett was 'reading nothing but a little history (Greene) [*sic*]' (letter to MacGreevy of 5 January 1933; *LSB*, 150). But Beckett may also have been thinking of 'fresh as a bridegroom' in Shakespeare's *Henry IV*, Part 1, Act I, scene 3, and also of Christ as in the terms discussed by Dean Inge (*DN*, 688). Belacqua has been 'fresh' in a rather different sense in at least his mental dealings with some of the nurses, but as Cochran points out (16) Beckett's principal concern here is with reversing the 'proposed death becomes actual nuptial' structure of 'LL'.

under his vestments   thinking of him as a 'vestryman' (*Dream*, 79), that is, a potential or actual sexual partner (cf. 'EB', 17, and the 1929 poem 'Return to the Vestry'), who would presumably need, as 'best man' (in one sense or another) to be (in one sense or another) 'all togged up'.

yellow yerks   seen by Farrow as nitrous oxide, or laughing gas (172).

One of the best   heard by Farrow as 'warmed-over words from the wedding toast' (178).

By Christ! he did die!   presumably, in the terms proposed (but then disavowed) in 'DL', this would qualify as 'a quick death' (14). But Belacqua has a 'timeless mock' in 'Draff' (173), and 'Echo's Bones' requires him to be 'up and about' again (1), which leaves the issue a little less clear-cut.

to auscultate him   that is, to listen to the beat of his heart with a stethoscope. Belacqua dies, as Beckett's father did, of a heart attack. cf. the asthmatic 'coughing his heart up' (153), 'His heart gave a great leap in its box' (161), and Dr Nye in 'A Case In A Thousand': 'his heart that knocked and misfired for no reason known to the medical profession' (*Complete Short Prose*, 18–19). The 1931 poem 'Enueg II' has 'the old heart' and the 1936 poem 'Cascando' has 'the old plunger'. Beckett mentions his heart palpitations in letters to MacGreevy of 24 February 1931 (*LSB*, 69) and 18 October 1932 (*LSB*, 136), and Knowlson (53, 717) states that they began before

Beckett's twentieth birthday. He experienced acute episodes in July 1933 (close to the composition of 'Yellow'), and recurrently thereafter (e.g. July 1937, March 1955, etc.).

'Draff'

167

in a Nursing Home   the Elgin Nursing Home in Lower Mount Street; for a photograph, see O'Brien, 156–7.

coenaesthesis   from Nordau (*DN*, 664, 666); cf. 'LL' (91).

Alba Perdue in the natural course of being seen home   as of course she had been (by Walter Draffin) at the end of 'WAM' (128). Here she is 'equated' with Proust's Albertine (the focus for a section of Beckett's *Proust* essay [*PTD*, 45–63], and the heroine of *Albertine perdue* in the *Recherche*). It is as if Beckett had realized by late 1933 that Ethna MacCarthy, the real-life original of the Alba, was by now definitively lost or 'perdue' from his point of view (she remains 'Miss Perdue' ['WAM'], as well as still being 'the Alba', in 'EB' [19, 22, 27]). If so, the strategy invites comparison with the 'fact' that the death of Lucy takes place 2 years after her accident (first paragraph of 'WAM'), which almost certainly refers to Beckett's difficulties with Lucia Joyce (and more particularly her father) in 1930, which he had certainly not forgotten by late 1933.

only sail in sight   possibly thinking of the Wagner opera *Tristan und Isolde* (also on 162); cf. *Dream*, 48. 'Draff' is unusually dependent on maritime imagery, for example, 'like an old sail in the wind' (168), the 'cruiser' of 175 (cf. *DN*, 714), 'half-mast' on 176, and 'the lee of the windscreen' (178).

ultra-violet   from Sir James Jeans; *DN*, 1061. Part of an exceptionally subtle 'colour-scheme' or spectrum of effects (cf. the note on 'emerald insertions' [169] below) operating in 'Draff'.

Bodies don't matter   derived from a paragraph in *Dream* (15) beginning 'Because her body was all wrong . . . ', with material adapted from a later section of *Dream* (68–9) added to it in due course.

168

birdface   as in *Dream* (15, with variants of the idea on 30, 45, 68, etc.).

Lucrezia   Lucrezia del Fede (cf. *Dream*, 15, 68), the wife of the painter Andrea del Sarto. She is viewed acrimoniously by Vasari. She is presumed to have been the sitter for a famous painting of the Madonna by del Sarto, which Beckett had seen in Florence in 1927. He had studied at TCD under Wilbraham Trench the great Browning poem 'Andrea del Sarto' from the collection *Men and Women*.

costive coryza a cold that gives one a stuffed-up nose or restricted breathing; cf. *Proust* (*PTD*, 20), and 'Le Concentrisme' (*Disjecta*, 41). The typical Spanish word – Ethna MacCarthy was a student of Spanish – for the common cold is 'constipación'.

Szopen, etc. playing with the various spellings of Chopin's name, and with George Sand's nickname for him.

Auber French composer Daniel-François Auber (1782–1871), known mostly (at the time) for his operas.

Field Irish composer John Field (1782–1837), whose 'Nocturnes' are supposed to have influenced Chopin's superior efforts in the genre.

Kleinmeister's Leidenschaftsucherei roughly, 'the passion-seeking of a minor master'; cf. *Dream*, 69.

Mr Beckett as in *Dream* (69, 141, etc.).

the Fulda or the Tolka or the Poddle or the Volga rivers small and large (*Dream*, 69, refers to 'the Seine or the Pegnitz'), a wry nod in the direction of Joyce's interest in rivers (cf. a letter to MacGreevy of 3 February 1931; *LSB*, 65), as used, for example, in the *Anna Livia Plurabelle* section of *Work In Progress/Finnegans Wake*.

sublimation cf. *Dream*, 69, from Freud; cf. 'sublimen of blatherskite' (*Dream*, 74). In a letter of 8 October 1932 to MacGreevy, Beckett described 'Sedendo et Quiescendo' as 'the transition sublimen' (*LSB*, 128).

wedge cf. the 'ancient Irish wedgehead' from *Dream* (69, 159); cf. also the 'Trueborn Jackeen' notes towards an unrealized, ultimately abandoned, Beckett project in the early to mid-1930s (TCD; *SBTA*, 16).

reseda a shade of green; cf. 'WO' (96).

169

emerald insertions no doubt in part because she is the 'little emerald' from the 'Emerald Isle', the Smeraldina, a name derived from that of the gypsy girl who befriends Quasimodo in Victor Hugo's novel *Notre-Dame de Paris*. Peggy Sinclair had green eyes, but the 'black claws' (170) of death are dominant here. The diminutive form of the character's name probably owes something to the words 'li smeraldi' in Dante, *Inferno*, XXXI, but actual or implicit diminution in naming characters is pervasive in *More Pricks*.

the penannular bow-window a striking feature (a window with five panes) in the Beckett family home at Cooldrinagh in Foxrock, referred to by Beckett in a letter to MacGreevy of 31 December 1935, which describes him looking at the ridge of the Three Rock and Two Rock mountains, which to his father's pleasure the young Beckett had compared to a knife edge. Beckett remembered the unusual window in a letter to Barbara Bray postmarked 19 March 1968 (TCD).

Not a flower, etc. from Shakespeare's *Twelfth Night*, Act II, scene 4, the Clown's song, continuing 'On my *black coffin* let there be strewn' [my italics]. Beckett had studied the play during Michaelmas (Autumn) Term at TCD in 1924 (Smith, 168).

a fat drab demon anticipating 'ungulata' (174) and 'devils' (175).

Malacoda a character (with **Scarmiglione** [175]) from Dante (*Inferno* XXI and XXIII; Scarmiglione is only in *Inferno* XXI); both are present in the poem 'Malacoda' begun in 1933 and later revised.

hear his uproarious endeavours not to intrude on the gravel the 'uproarious' noise that Beckett has in mind is Malacoda's *fatto trombetta* (trumpeting backside) in *Inferno* XXI (Caselli 2005, 73).

Mary Ann's leprous features Kroll (1977, 56; cf. 1974, 349) points out that in actual fact one of the victims of Henry Cabe, the 'Malahide murderer', was a servant girl called Mary McGowan, and that it was not she who raised the alarm in the Malahide murder case (as Mary Ann does here) but the gardener.

170

the gardener also a McCabe-like figure (cf. Kroll 1977, 55–6), McCabe having worked as a gardener for the McDonnell family (ibid., 49); in *Dream* (8), 'Nanny' is said to be 'now mother of thousands by a gardener', and this gardener tries to ravish Mary Ann later.

Someone had stolen his rose as on a watering can or (as in *Mercier and Camier*, 25) 'a watering pot'.

mowed down the flowers with hard jets of water derived from the gardener and the 'vanquished flowers' of *Dream* (174); Kroll (1974, 346–7) hears a faint echo of Belacqua as 'a fairly strong young rose' in 'DL' (in the *This Quarter* printing, 226, less equivocally, 'a strong young rose'), and it may strengthen the point to add that 'DL' is a story at the end of which Belacqua's aunt is seen 'tending whatever flowers die at that time of year' (13).

into the heart of the mountains preparing for the car conking out there later (179).

rustless all-steel   a bicycle (probably a Swift); cf. 'Fingal' and the poem 'Sanies I'.

in sorrow and anger   cf. 'AWN' (76).

there where there is no time   derived from Revelation 10.6. Was Beckett perhaps familiar with the use to which Dostoevsky (whose novel *The Possessed* he had read in a French translation in 1931) had put this biblical text through the mouth of Ippolit in part three of *The Idiot?* Ippolit also refers to the 'star Wormwood' (the name of Lord Gall's estate in 'EB') from Revelation 8.11. cf. the parson's quotation from Revelation 21.4 on 178, and the revision of Revelation 21.1 on 180.

171

weaver's shuttle   from the biblical book of Job, 7.6; but the phrase is adapted by Swift in Book III, chapter 3 of *Gulliver's Travels*.

covenanted   derived from Burton, who has Job in mind (*DN*, 884); cf. 'covenants of all kinds' (*Dream*, 122), and 'covenant' in line 46 of the 1932 poem 'Spring Song', in a more obviously (though far from crystal-clear) sexual context.

a man of her own weight   in *Dream* the Smeraldina eats too much (cf. Thelma in 'WAM' on 140); cf. 'The coffin was not going to eat him' (170) and the 'lightly boiled egg' of 170 and 174. Hairy is later (177) said to be 'less obese'. The 'weight' of the Smeraldina is one reason why Beckett has imported, from *Dream* (15), the passage describing her on 167–8, with the emphasis on 'the real button-bursting Weib'.

carrot . . . grease   derived from the *Journal* of Jules Renard, where it describes the termination of sexual intercourse (not apparently an issue here, or not yet) between a dog and a bitch; *DN*, 219.

commerce with the things of time   derived from Augustine; *DN*, 107; for 'improved' cf. 'EB' (16).

a superb shrub of verbena   anticipating 175, which refers back to 'WAM'; remembered again by Moran in part two of *Molloy*, and in *How it is* (10).

safely stowed   cf. Hamlet, after killing Polonius, in Act IV, scene 2 of Shakespeare's play, Beckett (with the help of Hairy Quin in the matter of burial, and in the subtle structuring of the stories) having killed off Belacqua.

swollen paws appaumée   of a hand opened to show the palm, a term often used in heraldry; cf. the 'wide open' hands of Belacqua at the end of 'AWN' (74).

mammae cf. *Dream* (81), 'AWN' (55) and the 1933 poem 'Serena III'.

varieties, which have been ranked as species cf. the travesty of Darwin in 'WAM' (119). The distinctions here are derived from Darwin's *On the Origin of Species* (as in a letter to MacGreevy of 4 August 1932; *LSB*, 111). There are quotations taken from Darwin's famous book (which Beckett thought was 'badly written') in the *'Whoroscope' Notebook*, but the words 'Even Ireland . . . ' perhaps point also in the direction of the ultimately abandoned 'Trueborn Jackeen' project and the surviving notes from it at TCD (*SBT/A*, 16).

Velasquez cf. 'LL' (88); this second Velasquez is a canvas Beckett could never have seen in the flesh, since he never visited Spain; it is in the Prado in Madrid.

hyphen of reality cf. *Dream*, 27: 'hyphen of passion'.

172

at the foot of the bed, like parallels thinking of Donne, 'A Nocturnall upon *St Lucies* Day, being the shortest day', its 'bed's feet' (line 7) as a metaphor of burial being later literalized here, with perhaps the 'two so/As stiff twin compasses are two' in Donne's 'A Valediction: Forbidding Mourning' also in mind.

the dying and the dead cf. the last words of Joyce's 'The Dead': 'all the living and the dead'.

That was where Queen Anne had the gout as claimed by Swift in his *Journal to Stella*, who does not emphasize this in 'The History of the Four Last Years of the Queen' (first published, posthumously, in 1758). Gout is apparently not a common ailment in women.

defunct crusader cf. 'the defunct' (173); '*defunctus*', quoted from Schopenhauer, is the last word of Beckett's *Proust* essay (*PTD*, 93; cf. *LSB*, 36).

Two nouns and two adjectives cf. *Dream*, 157: 'Three nouns, three adjectives'.

Not a stir out of them cf. 'not a stir out of him' in the scene with Mr Conaire in *Mercier et Camier* (42), and 'not a kick in me' of Mr Graves in *Watt* (145).

the girls, Lucy especially Lucy, the first of the *More Pricks* heroines to die (as reported in 'WAM'), lives the longest in Belacqua's memory.

173

toes turned up adapting the popular periphrasis for death and dying, with perhaps some thought of the 'lang tootsy' in 'Yellow'.

Uccello   cf. 'EB' (11; but there a bird rather than the painter, hence 'a genuine Uccello') and O'Brien (142–3) for a discussion and a reproduction of the canvas by Uccello which Beckett most probably had in mind. Beckett's interest in Uccello (and later in paintings rightly or wrongly attributed to Paolo Uccello) seems to have deepened on seeing the painter's frescoes of *Lives of the Church Fathers* during his time in Florence in 1927 6 years earlier, even if these were not the images which he had most in mind here in relation to the *death* of *his* father. The mountains (later 'the purple mountains', 179) are the Dublin Mountains in the near distance: 'The mountains are looking lovely' (letter to MacGreevy of ?3 August 1934).

to make a long story short   a phrase from *Dream* (73), where the man and woman concerned are 'Lucy and Jude', but 'Draff' is not 'a long story' (as 'WAM' is), and the phrase perhaps indicates Beckett's understandably mixed feelings at having to deal with this very painful memory in this 'ignoble' context (cf. 'Lightning Calculation', typescript, 1), with Hairy and the Smeraldina beginning to furnish, as it were, some kind of life together after the demise of Belacqua.

upholstered the grave   cf. the 'garniture' of gorse and heather to go with the headstone on Beckett's father's grave in a letter to MacGreevy of 25 July 1933, and the 'fantastic upholstery' in 'WAM'.

below the surface of the earth   probably with some thought of the Jules Verne popular classic *Journey to the Centre of the Earth*, Beckett having 'borrowed' Nemo in *Dream* in part from his *Twenty Thousand Leagues Under The Sea*. The round-the-world trip imagined in *The Unnamable* is in partial homage to Jules Verne's *Around The World In Eighty Days*, which (as letters to Georges Duthuit indicate) Beckett was reading at the time.

as well she might   originally derived from Burton (*DN*, 946); here echoing the Polar Bear on 72.

timeless mock   cf. 'grinning up at the lid' (175; from *DN*, 643, among several items of Dublin demotic) and Moran in *Molloy*: 'Sometimes I smiled, as if I were dead already' (141).

whom he had known well   like the gravedigger in Shakespeare's *Hamlet*, unwittingly meeting Hamlet alive, believing him to be dead, and Hamlet to Horatio re Yorick: 'I knew him'.

shinning up the larch trees   cf. *Dream*, section 'ONE' and 'LL' (88); derived from 'shinning up the udder rope' (*Dream*, 81; adapting Jules Renard, *DN*, 223).

friend of the family (what family?)   presumably an echo, however faint, of Dostoevsky's comic novel *The Friend of the Family* (*The Village of Stepanchikova* as translated by Constance Garnett) is not intended; the primary echo to which Beckett seems to be trying to alert the reader is in relation to 'late family' in 'Yellow' (146, 147 [three times], 150), and to exploit for his own purposes, in a story arising out of his own father's death and burial, the irony that (unlike Ruby, Thelma and the Smeraldina) Belacqua has no visible father, mother or siblings. The otherwise similar 'up (why up?)' previously (170) has a different effect, although it obviously contrasts with 'down' here (173), and earlier in 'Yellow' (151, etc.).

174

four lovely deaf ears   derived from the 1886 music hall song 'Two lovely black eyes' (cf. the description of Lucy's eyes, after she has died, in 'WAM' [106]), with some thought of Burton (*DN*, 842) also; cf. 'Two nouns and two adjectives' (172).

I don't see the moon   but, as in 'DL', the moon obliges, or is 'obliged', to shine; 'moonstone' on 173 (with thoughts of Wilkie Collins) prepares for this. Another 'up' to set against the 'down, down, down' of Hairy in the grave (173), but imagined here as a ladder 'let down'.

cut to the quick   cf. 'pity is quick with death' (in the poem 'Text'), God's judgement on 'the quick and the dead', and the 'quick death' of 'DL' (14).

made his water   cf. Beckett's notes from Karin Stephens's *The Wish to Fall Ill* (TCD 10971/ 1 [2]): 'Parting with urine and faeces is thought of as making gifts to loved persons'.

Let the essence of his being stay where it was, in liquor and liquor's harmonics   remembering the 'great major symphony' of the bar in 'DD' (40), with Belacqua there lacking the means to 'consecrate his life to stasis', and only able to indulge his whim from time to time.

tossed and turned   cf. Augustine; *DN*, 122. cf. Belacqua in 'WAM' (122) and Hairy Quin in the same story after too much 'liquor' (127), and of course his mental discomfiture in bed throughout most of 'Yellow'.

ungulata   demons.

like a pantomime baby   cf. the 'principal boy' of *Dream* (e.g. 19).

Homer dusk   from Bérard (DN, 715) and originally in *Dream* (28, 31); also used in the January 1932 poem 'Dortmunder', 2nd mention (cf. 'AWN', 45 and the 'indigo hour' in 'WAM', 110).

175

wire bandage of Jalade-Lafont   a character from Garnier; *DN*, 465.

Belacqua had come unstuck   cf. 'EB' (11) and *Mercier and Camier* (88). The 'favour of veronica' is mentioned twice in 'WAM' (135, 140), and the shrub was first mentioned on 171.

That night the weather so mended   as, apparently, it did for the burial of Beckett's father.

black as Ulysses's cruiser   as described in Bérard's *Odyssey* translation (*DN*, 714), with no obvious reference to the title of Joyce's famous novel of 1922 intended. Beckett later (in *Molloy*, and more obliquely in *How It Is*) analogized this with a passage from the philosopher Geulincx.

demon   cf. 'ungulata' above; as in Descartes's *Discourse on Method*.

pale flag   of death; from Shakespeare's *Romeo and Juliet*, Act V, scene 3.

That was what he was there for, that was what he was paid for   reprising an idea found in connection with Cain (cf. 'DL', 11) in the 1932 poem 'Spring Song' (line 55).

grinning up at the lid   cf. *Dream*, 146, and *DN*, 646.

in the nick of time   because 'time pressed' (166), because time is a prison (the parson has imagined Belacqua 'there where there is no time', 170), and because Mr Malacoda's first name is Nick (178). The firm of Nichols organized Bill Beckett's interment (see below).

176

Scarmiglione   cf. the poem 'Malacoda' ('Scarmilion'); a figure from Dante, *Inferno* XXI.

washer   cf. the 'dribble of time' in 'Yellow' (152).

All souls at half-mast   cf. 'Malacoda'.

commit copious nuisance   cf. *Dream*, 36, and 'copious offence of nuisance' (*Dream*, 139).

her voice raised in furious hallali   Fr., the cry of a hunter on spotting his or her prey or target.

butchering a fowl   cf. the boiling of the crustacean in 'DL'.

a place in the sun   cf. 'WO' (105).

a colossal fly   cf. 'my brother the fly' ('Serena I').

God . . . in his heaven   thinking of the most famous line in Robert Browning's poem 'Pippa Passes'.

sure and certain hope   from the service for the Anglican Burial of the Dead.

177

O Death, etc.   followed by two pastiches of 1 Corinthians 15.55, as used in the service of the Burial of the Dead, and transformed again, by Mick Doyle, in 'EB', 21–2.

G. P. I.   General Paralysis of the Insane, as in the tertiary and final phase of syphilis (cf. 'The Possessed', *Disjecta*, 99).

shining straw   from Augustine; *DN*, 90, 111; used in *Dream* (114).

Gaelic   described as 'a tongue ultramedieval' in a letter to MacGreevy of 7 September 1933 (not in *LSB*), although there are some scraps of Gaelic in 'EB' (9, and 25, on the distinction between a 'Gael' and a 'gull'). Gaelic was one language Beckett, like most Irishmen of his time, did not know. In *Mercier and Camier* it is downgraded to the status of a 'dialect' (8).

less obese cretin and spado   cf. for the latter, meaning a person suffering from impotence, 'EB' (7). The word 'cretin' is etymologically related to 'Christian', although, ironically, Hairy later treats the parson with disrespect.

178

secret occasions   cf. 'secret things' in 'WO' (repeated from 'Enueg I'), but this (together with '*bella menzogna*', a beautiful lie, in the footnote, and also in a letter to Georges Duthuit of 26 May 1949) is from the *Convivio* of Dante, and both are derived from the note '*verità ascosa* [hidden truth] *sotto bella mensogna* [sic]' in TCD MS 10936a, fol. 2 (Caselli, 2005, 80, n. 49). Slote (19) shows that to adopt this perspective is to be on the side of poets rather than theologians.

measured, coffined and covered   cf. the same 'trinity' of visits in 'Malacoda' ('thrice he came').

Nick Malacoda   alluding to 'Old Nick', death's nickname, but obliquely referring to the firm of undertakers, Nichols and Co, who (cf. 'Nichol's box' [sic] in 'EB', 26) took charge of the arrangements for Bill Beckett's funeral.

anagogy   the Greek *g* is hard, and 'The dead die hard' ('EB', 1); Beckett had read Dante's epistle to Can Grande on the fourfold interpretation of allegory, and the footnote here mentions a non-analogy.

cock up   a phrase also used, followed by 'up up up', in the late 1933 poem 'Serena III' (there with the 'moon', which is found here on 167).

coals of fire   cf. '"She has been through the fire"' (177), and anticipating 'the house in flames', 'raging furnace' and several more references to fire on 179.

no more death, etc.   left incomplete because the next word would be 'pain' (cf. 124, 141) in the text being quoted, Revelation 21.4; a Christian version of the 'Golden Age' idea behind the Latin hexameters quoted in, and probably deliberately devised for, 'WAM'; the parson has earlier also quoted from Revelation, without it being 'revealed' that he has done so (170).

to save his life   cf. the gossamer of Una in 'WAM' (121). Biblical tradition emphasizes that whoever seeks to save their life must lose it.

New Gefoozleum   cf. 'Paradize' earlier (164); a travesty of St John's vision in the book of Revelation, but probably thinking also of the 'New Bloomusalem' in the 'Circe' chapter of *Ulysses*.

179

fiddle   presumably an allusion to Nero 'fiddling while Rome *burns*', unless Beckett has in mind one of the insignias of the Civic Guard, such as the shillelagh used as the national symbol of an independent Ireland.

the gardener, who had ravished the servant girl   for the sexual potency of another gardener, compare 'Bibby' in *Dream* (8), 'now mother of thousands by a gardener'.

set the premises on fire   in Beckett's notes taken from Karin Stephens's *The Wish to Fall Ill* (TCD 10971/1/[2]): 'Preoccupation with setting things on fire may be connected with erotic fantasies of powerful urination' (cf. '[The groundsman] made his water agin a cypress' [174], and in 'Yellow' [158] the Aschenputtel saying ' "Putting out me good fire" '). Madden, in *Mercier and Camier* (30), describes how, 'having been awkward enough to fecundate a milkmaid . . . I improved this occasion by setting light to the barns, granaries and stables'.

antiphlogistic   as of an antidote to or remedy for fire, also found in a letter to Nuala Costello of 27 February 1934 (*LSB*, 186); there is a photograph of the Tara Street Cossack firefighters in O'Brien; cf. 'dephlogisticate' in *Dream* (53).

he was indeed hairy   that is, sharp, quick on the uptake, less of a 'cretin' (177). Cf. Corley describing himself as 'too hairy' in Joyce's 'Two Gallants' (*Dubliners*, Penguin, 1992, 45).

the house is insured   cf. 'WAM' (134).

come with me . . . and be my love   the best-known source for this is Christopher Marlowe's poem 'The Passionate Shepherd To His Love', but earlier in 1933 Beckett had been reading Donne, who revises its sentiments in one of the least known of his 'Songs and Sonets', 'The Bait'. Marlowe's poem refers to 'steepie mountains', but there are a number of phrases in the much more complex Donne version which seem, even though left undeveloped, closer to the situation here than the more 'romantic' and pastoral conceptions of Marlowe.

In the heart of the purple mountains cf. the Smeraldina and the gardener on 170: 'She sent him flying up into the heart of the mountains'. There may be some play here, given 'the car conked out', with the folksong 'Will ye go laddie, go?', in the lyrics of which are 'wild mountain thyme' and 'purple heather'.

the car conked out cf. how Hairy 'broke down' twice in close succession in 'WAM' (117–18), preparing for 'At last he too conked out' (180).

180

the picture by Paul Henry Irish (Belfast born) painter (1876–1958) internationally known (from the early 1920s onwards) particularly for his landscapes, often using the mountains of the West of Ireland as a backdrop.

boneyard by the sea thinking of the sublimities of Paul Valéry's famous poem 'Le cimetière marin' (written between 1917 and 1920 and collected in *Charmes ou Poèmes*, 1922), and bringing them down a peg or two. But perhaps also with some thought of Thomas Gray, 'Elegy In A Country Churchyard', the 'Country Boneyard' of a letter to Nuala Costello of 10 May 1934 (*LSB*, 209).

her own spiritual equivalent echoing the same phrase in the context of 'Nick Malacoda' on 178; but one 'spiritual equivalent' of the scene here seems, *mutatis mutandis* and in a most daring 'substitution', to be Gabriel and Gretta Conroy (and Michael Furey) at the end of Joyce's story 'The Dead'; cf. Lawlor (2009, 67, n. 38).

how she would shortly gratify Belacqua (by dying, in part or whole) and Hairy Quin (by complying with his wish for '[t]he little something extra' [174]).

an inscription cf. 'EB' (19a). Ackerley (2010, 48) writes: 'The missing words are, almost certainly, "vox et praeterea nihil", a voice and nothing more, as (saith Brewer) the Lacedemonian said of one who plucked a nightingale, the implied epitaph neatly returning the ending to the story of Echo'. Beckett often borrowed from Brewer, but he seems in any case to have found a quite different version of 'missing words', if only 4 years too late, in writing to Arland Ussher (appropriately enough, from Greystones, where his father had been buried; letter of 28 December 1938; *LSB*, 648). In *First Love* (1972; *Premier amour*, 1947), introduced by the narrator with the comment 'my epitaph still meets with my approval', we find: 'Hereunder lies the above who up below/ So hourly died that he lived on till now'. cf. 'How like an epitaph it [the wedding invitation] read, with the terrible sigh in the end-pause of each line' (116).

the moon on the job as it was not on 174; this moon recalls the moon at the end of 'DL' (13), with Beckett delighted to suggest he might still be 'very strong on architectonics' (*Dream*, 178), in spite of having done much to explode them throughout. cf. the Syra-Cusa in *Dream* as 'one of the many that glare. She was always on the job, the job of being jewelly' (50).

the sea tossing . . . and panting Revelation 21.1 (three verses before the quotation used on 171) has 'and there was no more sea'; cf. 'tossed and turned' earlier (174; and twice in 'WAM' also), and for 'panting' cf. 'WO' (98), 'WAM' (118) and Moran in *Molloy* (117).

classico-romantic poking fun at the categories of Mario Praz (from the original Italian version of *The Romantic Agony*); even at this late stage Beckett finds himself in a 'strait of two wills', unable to decide between alternatives.

No gardener for the gardener as a type of Christ (as in his appearance to Mary Magdalen in the gospels) see the once well known short story by Rudyard Kipling (*Debits and Credits*, 1926); but the gardener in Beckett's story is a rapist and arsonist, a deranged counterpart to the groundsman, a different kind of gardener here.

The words of the rose to the rose from Diderot, *D'Alembert's Dream*, but with Beckett effectively emphasizing (as again in 'EB') that these are only roses talking in a closed-off, solipsistic situation, an 'Ephemeral sophism' (*DN*, 581; *Dream*, 189). In *Dream* (175) there is an implicit critique of Diderot's 'storiette'.

So it goes in the world the last words of the Brothers Grimm story 'How the Cat and the Mouse set up House', as Beckett indicated (without specifying which of the Grimm stories he had in mind) to Pamela Mitchell in an undated letter of January 1955 (UoR). The tag has been 'saved' from the wreck of 'EB', where it occurs twice. Beckett uses the phrase, or part of it, frequently in correspondence; two little-known later occurrences are in letters of August 1967 and May 1977 to Barbara Bray (TCD).

A most foully false analogy the footnote serves as a reminder that Lucy is just as much of an (absent) presence here as she had been earlier, and as she was at the beginning, at the end, and indeed on half a dozen other occasions throughout 'What A Misfortune'. By linking her with the Smeraldina by way of the more than usually awkward syntax, Beckett seems to be trying to bury his memories of Peggy Sinclair and Lucia Joyce with the 'part' (177) of himself to be wished away with the 'remains' of Belacqua in the wake of the death of a beloved father (cf. 'down the mine Daddy'; 178). But the 'secret occasions' (178) here are too secret to be openly acknowledged and fully exorcised, and are now very difficult to reconstruct with any accuracy.

Chapter 6

Addenda

the inevitable something more
('Draff')

1. How (or How *Not*) to 'Get Over' Joyce

Analysis of what a man is not may conduce to an understanding of what he is, but only on condition that the distinction is observed.

(*Disjecta*)

In a letter to Charles Prentice of 15 August 1931, enclosing 'Sedendo et Quiescendo' for his consideration, Beckett wrote: 'Of course it stinks of Joyce in spite of most earnest endeavours to endow it with my own odours' (*LSB*, 81). In a letter to Samuel Putnam of 28 June 1932, Beckett wrote (again *à propos* 'Sedendo et Quiescendo'): 'I vow I will get over J.J. ere I die. Yessir' (*LSB*, 108). Critics of *More Pricks* have taken a lot longer to achieve this, and it seems to have been generally assumed that, because Joyce was the key figure in Beckett's youthful aspirations to become an author fit to be published, it must have been Joyce whom he had most in mind in writing *More Pricks Than Kicks*. For what Beckett calls, in a very different connexion, 'relief from this picture' (*Disjecta*, 81), one tends to have to turn to studies of later Beckett texts, notably to scholars like Dirk Van Hulle who are equally conversant with Joyce and Beckett. There are, however, exceptions even in the *More Pricks* literature. Anthony Farrow makes the excellent point that 'whereas form in Joyce derives concentrically from the subject, the form in [Beckett's short stories] is at odds with the subject' (160). Almost the only other commentator to take a similar line, albeit in a study which sees Joyce in Beckett whenever or wherever it can, is P. J. Murphy, who suggests that the 'ongoing debate with Joyce' is 'largely suspended in *More Pricks Than*

Kicks' (96). Murphy pinpoints a phrase in 'A Wet Night' which reminds him of Stephen Dedalus at the beginning of the *Portrait* (85) and mentions five other stories, although he only gives extended coverage to 'Dante and the Lobster' (85–90). For Murphy, in any case, the *Portrait* is – for the study of Beckett as a whole – a much more important point of reference than *Dubliners* or *Ulysses*. The single most astute statement on one of the uses to which Beckett puts Joyce's 'The Dead' towards the end of 'A Wet Night' is perhaps that of Robert Cochran (11), when he quite rightly states that the pastiche in question is 'not so much a gesture of homage as a comic declaration of independence [from Joyce]'. In their essays, Mary Power and Chris Ackerley actually manage to make either almost no mention of Joyce at all (Belacqua as 'an unheroic antithesis of Joyce's Stephen Dedalus'; Ackerley 2008, 63) or only a useful comparative detail using *Ulysses* (Power, 152).

As part of my discussion of 'Dante and the Lobster' hinted, however, there have been persistent attempts to bring *More Pricks* as close to *Dubliners* as it will go, and arguably closer than can comfortably be achieved. A very different picture from the one outlined above emerges in essays by Phyllis Carey and Adrian Hunter (and by John P. Harrington on 'A Case In A Thousand'; see Chapter 2), and from a much earlier book-length study by Barbara Reich Gluck (*Beckett and Joyce: Friendship and Fiction*). Gluck seems to have been the first critic to think that the Joycean notion of 'epiphany' might help to situate what is happening at the end of 'Dante and the Lobster', which is treated as if it were in a kind of creative tension with Joyce's story 'The Dead' (57ff), a tactic briefly replicated even by Ackerley (2009, 287), who employs the term 'epiphantic' to the 'structure' of 'Dante and the Lobster'. Gluck later compares the 'gone west' at the end of 'What A Misfortune' with the famous conclusion of Joyce's greatest story (67), having earlier suggested that 'Love and Lethe' resembles Joyce's 'An Encounter', and having treated the 'tripartite' structures of 'Dante and the Lobster' and Joyce's 'Grace' as comparable, but does not develop either of these insights in the direction that might have led to quite different conclusions. Phyllis Carey, borrowing the term 'anti-epiphany' from her fellow editor, Ed Jewinski, is more Beckettian in spirit, as is Adrian Hunter, who nevertheless believes that 'all Beckett's early stories . . . can be read as counterpoints [a word that is very nearly a *Dubliners* title!] to Joyce' (241).

In these commentators one sees not so much 'the anxiety of influence' (analysed by Harold Bloom as the reaction of a promising neophyte writer to some 'strong' forbear) as the anxiety of the critic intent on tracing an influence where there may, quite simply, not be one. For the Beckett of the 1929 essay 'Dante . . . Bruno.Vico..Joyce' this would be a classic instance of the 'book-keeping' of the 'analogymongers' (*Disjecta*, 19), and it may be that (as I shall subsequently propose in the case of Swift) all criticism suffers from a tendency to analogymongering. Even if this is in fact the case, perhaps some analogies are preferable to others, and though I have no wish to pick fault with the critics discussed above, I do want to emphasize that there is almost no reason to go looking for connections between *Dubliners* and *More Pricks*, even if by avoiding the comparison with *Dubliners* Beckett kept it in mind as somewhere he did not want to go.

Rather than see Joyce as a 'counterpoint' (Hunter, 241), we could ask: what was there in Joyce that Beckett wanted to 'get over'? His 'classical temper', surely, or whatever classical temper was left after the artist, like an absent God or *deus absconditus*, had finished paring his fingernails. For Beckett, the Stephen Dedalus trinity of *claritas*, *integritas* and *consonantia* as constituents of *quidditas* was too mystical, and too much in debt to St Thomas Aquinas, to be of much use to him. Beckett's own vision was of 'ice-floes' (*Dream*, 30) and of 'flottements' (*Dream*, 138), even if such a vision could never guarantee creative success. Much as Beckett admired, and even loved, Joyce ('heroic work, heroic being', as in Beckett's response to being asked for a 'celebrity' endorsement for a Joyce conference in Beirut), his real affiliations were with writers of a less heroic and impersonal cast of mind. There was more for Beckett to learn from unstructured works like the *Journal* of Jules Renard – one of a large number of 'autobiographical' writings that Beckett read in the 1930s – or from novelists like Fielding, who were always reminding their readers of their own presence and participation in the world of their fiction. (This helps to explain why Beckett writes, in his review of Ezra Pound's *Make It New*: 'The suggestion that Fielding was deficient in comprehension of the novel as a form, because we have no notes (no?) from his hand on the subject, is very nice' [*Disjecta*, 78].)

Adrian Hunter quite rightly sees Joyce as the master of a 'scrupulously unarticulated knowingness' (241). Beckett, by contrast, makes his way, not always 'scrupulously', with what can be made out of inarticulacy. As he told Israel Shenker (*The Critical Heritage*, 148), 'I'm working with impotence, ignorance'. Quite why Beckett critics have felt that Joyce must (in some sense other than his primacy in real time) lie behind *More Pricks* remains a mystery. Even when Joyce leaves avenues of enquiry open, his narrative strategies tell us everything we need to know in order to be able to understand a given situation. With Beckett's stories, even when they end with a final, declarative gesture of closure (as, for example, in 'Dante and the Lobster' and 'Yellow'), there is a pervasive breaking of the 'rule' that a story must contain within itself the reasons why it is so and not otherwise.

(Some of the reasons could never have been known to a reader in 1934, and may still not be widely known, if indeed known at all, in 2010.) We may frequently feel in a Beckett story that things might actually have turned out very differently from the way they did, as is almost never the case with Joyce. Joyce, a modern *maestro di color che sanno* – Beckett adapts this, Dante's assessment of Aristotle as the master of those who know, in his two-edged acrostic 'homage' to Joyce, 'Home Olga' (1932) – was for Beckett in the position of 'the more he knew, the more he could' (Shenker interview). As such, Joyce very much resembles the painter Pierre Tal-Coat in the first of Beckett's *Three Dialogues with Georges Duthuit*: 'Total object, complete with missing parts, instead of partial object' (*PTD*, 101), and also the Leonardo da Vinci who, despite his interest in '*disfazione*' (dis-creation) knows that 'for him not one fragment will be lost' (*PTD*, 112).

Beckett's commitment to the 'partial object' helps to explain why, whatever 'unity' the novel *Dream* might seem to possess – and it does not seem to possess a great deal – it can only be 'involuntary' (132), an inevitable but unplanned outcome, or byproduct, of a transaction with only a 'Mr Beckett' (69) to account for it, however varied and numerous its sources and resources prove to be. Even before *Dream*, in the 1929 essay 'Dante . . . Bruno.Vico.. Joyce', Beckett had refused to distinguish 'form' from 'content', and in his TCD lectures he clearly favours the kind of artist – Stendhal, Gide – who 'states' himself *pari passu* with his material, rather than the 'chloroformed' writing of Balzac and his 'clockwork cabbages' (*Dream*, 119; cf. Le Juez, 30 and the Rachel Burrows lecture notes at TCD). Far from being 'chloroformed', Beckett is trying to work with something that is not *formed* at all, in any conventional sense. The attitude never left him: the 'narrator-narrated' of *How It Is* (begun as *Comment c'est* in late 1958) announces in part 3, resignedly but at the same time almost as a *quod erat demonstrandum*, that 'of our total lives it states only three-quarters'. Presumably, if there could be such a thing as a part 4, which there is not, it could only tell us – as the end of part 3 does – 'how it is *not*'.

Beckett had told his students at TCD that Maupassant and the 'Naturalists' (cf. Burrows, 12) had 'no subjectivism', and there was no obvious 'subjectivism' in the apparently impersonal Joyce who, as Beckett must have known, was (as a writer) almost as autobiographical in his impulses as he himself was, and who of course he knew personally, if for the most part *en famille*, which was perhaps not how he would ideally have preferred to know him, especially with his daughter inevitably a bone of contention and a focus of concern within the family unit, and beyond its effective control. There was much more subjectivism in Fielding and Jonathan Swift, whom Beckett returned to – he had read *Gulliver's Travels* as a child – in early 1933. In doing so, it can hardly have escaped Beckett's notice that, even when writing a fiction with Gulliver as its nominal hero, Swift was not undertaking anything so structured, integrated and organized as a novel.

2. A Note on Swift

> ... *those feet* ... *that Swift, rebuking the women of this country for their disregard for Shank's mare, described as being fit for nothing better than to be laid aside.*
> ('What A Misfortune')

Swift was long ago seen as a useful counterpoint to Beckett, notably by John Fletcher in a 1962 essay in French, although no other early commentator developed the possibilities of comparison in any significant way. In 1991 Robert Cochran found 'more than one nod to Swift' (17) in *More Pricks*, but did not take matters much further, leaving it up to his readers to connect Beckett's interest in Swift with the judgement that 'What A Misfortune' seems 'much more harsh' (14) than some of the other stories. Not until 2002 was there a monograph giving the matter a broader context and a more precise focus: Frederik N. Smith's *Beckett's Eighteenth Century*. Smith makes at least two important judgements of *More Pricks*, which, as in most Beckett monographs, receives only limited coverage in the book as a whole. First, Smith notes that whereas French writers are in the ascendancy in *Dream*, English writers are more in evidence in *More Pricks*. Secondly, whereas references to Swift in *Dream* are few – Smith counts just four – they are significantly increased to fourteen in *More Pricks*. Smith also highlights how very well Beckett must have known Swift's *Journal to Stella* to combine in 'Fingal' two phrases a long way apart (31). But Smith says little on why Beckett took a renewed interest in Swift in early 1933.

It was in a letter of 5 January 1933 that Beckett regaled MacGreevy with the Swift anecdote which he was later to use in 'Fingal' (*LSB*, 150), and in three consecutive undated ('Thursday') letters (probably 12, 19 and 26 January 1933) he told his friend that he was doing translations for Nancy Cunard 'and reading Swift', that he had been reading 'more Swift and Donne, without any great pleasure', and that he 'had hopes of a Swift poem'. (The nearest he came to this was 'Sanies I', written close to Easter 1933, with a Swift bicycle mentioned.) Another letter (1 February 1933) finds him reading *Gulliver's Travels*, a version of which he had read in youth. Swift's *Drapier's Letters* had been prescribed for study while Beckett was at TCD, but by mid-1933 Beckett's knowledge of Swift's massive output (12 volumes in the Temple Scott edition, which does not contain any poems) had obviously increased considerably. As Smith shows, and as a letter as late as 1954 (to Pamela Mitchell, UoR) confirms, Beckett knew the *Journal to Stella* very well, but he also knew some of Swift's poetry (less valued than it would be today; see the Costello letter of 27 February 1934 for an unacknowledged quotation from a Swift poem), *A Tale of a Tub*, and almost certainly some of Swift's Irish writings, for example *The Bickerstaff Papers* and 'A Modest Proposal'. Reading these works, as well as helping Joseph Hone and Mario Rossi with their 1934 book on Swift (*Swift, or The Egoist*; *LSB*, 150), may very well have played a part in Beckett exploring Irish matters around this time, the only surviving evidence of which are the 'Cow' notes and the notes towards the abandoned 'Trueborn Jackeen' project (see *SBT/A*, 16, 125–8), for which he turned to the 13th edition of the *Encyclopaedia Britannica*. It may even have been Swift's interest in the history of his own times that later stimulated Beckett to develop his early interest in Napoleon (*DN*, 2–78) and to read other historians: G. P. Gooch (Knowlson 1996, 746, n. 114), Albert Sorel (*LSB*, 249) and J. R. Green's *A Short History of the English People* (letter of 5 January 1933; *LSB*, 150; cf. my notes to 'Draff' in Chapter 5). Swift's sensitivity to the troubled history of English-Irish relations was obviously of use to Beckett in writing a review of his friend MacGreevy's *Poems* (*Disjecta*, 68: 'now that Balnibarbism has triumphed', Balnibarbi being 'The Continent . . . subject to the Monarch of the Flying Island [Laputa]' in Book III of *Gulliver's Travels*). The same point of reference surfaces in the essay 'Censorship in the Saorstat', written a few weeks later in the summer of 1934, where the four-part Censorship Act of 1929 (already obliquely derided in Beckett's 1929 squib for his college magazine, 'Che Sciagura') is described as 'a measure that the Grand Academy of Balnibarbi could hardly have improved on' (*Disjecta*, 87). Swift was never to matter as much to Beckett as Dr Johnson, although Beckett must almost certainly have been intrigued by the uses to which W. B. Yeats had put Swift in a 1930 poem 'Swift's Epitaph' and, most notably perhaps, in the 1930 play *The Words Upon The Window-Pane*. Swift is a notable absentee from the quotations 'For Interpolation' into *Murphy* as found in the *'Whoroscope' Notebook* (*SBT/A*, 16), having perhaps already served his purpose in the later stories of *More Pricks*. Certainly, by 1936, in reviewing the painter Jack B. Yeats's novel *The Amaranthers*, Beckett emphasized that 'there is no satire' (*Disjecta*, 90), as if satire in any way in debt to the Swift of *Gulliver's Travels* was a mode he personally had also gone beyond.

Swift's usefulness to Beckett as a creative writer seems indeed to have been largely confined to a few months in 1933, at which point in time his primary concern was, naturally enough, with generating sufficient material to make *More Pricks* viable. But here, surely, the very fact that Swift was not a novelist, however consummate a narrative artist he might be, was of considerable assistance. Swift as an essayist, with so many various axes to grind, offered Beckett the opportunity to study a mankind for whom happiness was perpetually deferred, a desire that could even be characterized (as in *A Tale of a Tub*) as 'the perpetual possession of being well deceived' in a seemingly infinite play of mirrors shuttling back and forth between madness and reason. Swift's virtual avoidance (outside *Gulliver's Travels*) of any through-composed narrative project with novelistic potential could never have taught Beckett very much about how to organize his own novel *Murphy* (begun in late August 1935), whereas Henry Fielding and even Jane Austen ('I think she has much to teach me' [*LSB*, 129, 139, 207, 250, 253]) offered examples of how the business might best be managed. But one of the peculiar byproducts of the short story form for Beckett was the way in which it offered, in spite of its restrictions, something of the freedom which Swift had enjoyed in the looser genre of the essay: space for anecdotes, incidental obiter dicta, a certain playfulness and, in short, anything that promoted a largely devil-may-care attitude to mask things too painful to directly deal with, about which a writer might care very deeply in private. Beckett had realized, rather ruefully, that – just like the Frica whom he attacks in *Dream* (216, a passage much reduced in 'A Wet Night', with the Swiftian analogy removed) – he himself did not possess Swift's *saeva indignatio*, or savage indignation, that his rage was more intermittent and could accordingly be adjudged 'fabricated'. But Swift had certainly galvanized Beckett for a while, and he was one of the only Irish or Anglo-Irish writers in the pantheon to leave much more than a mark on *More Pricks*, once Beckett could convince himself – wrongly, if many of the critical estimates are to be believed – that he had written a book which could in no way be seen as Joycean. Swift as moralist Beckett could no doubt as easily take or leave as the moral vision of Proust ('his complete indifference to moral values'; *PTD*, 89), but as a maker of fictions, and someone very much given to donning a mask when it suited him to do so, indeed an all-round spectacular performer, he could be of more use to Beckett in the writing of *More Pricks* than most other writers.

3. An Unknown Letter

Charles Prentice wrote to Beckett from Chatto on 6 September 1933 to acknowledge his firm's receipt of the 'stories', and in a very short time set about trying to interest the literati of the day in a writer whom he thought had a bright future, but with a book that would obviously need marketing. In a hitherto unknown letter of 21 September 1933 (brought to my attention by my colleague Andrew Nash, whom I thank most warmly), Prentice wrote as follows to David ('Bunny') Garnett at the offices of the *New Statesman* magazine:

> Dear Bunny
> Here are the four stories from the Samuel Beckett collection that I think most likely for your purpose. Fortunately, after a cast-off was taken here last week, the figures for the different stories were preserved. The lengths are as follows:
>
> 'Dante and the Lobster', 4300 words
> 'Fingal', 3500
> 'Love and Lethe', 4500
> 'Yellow', 5700
>
> 'Dante and the Lobster' has already appeared in 'Transition' [an error for *This Quarter*]; the others have never yet been printed.
>
> I shall not say anything to Beckett but if you want to use any of them, I'll be simply delighted. His address is: – 6, Clare Street, Dublin. But will you let me know, as I'll have to write him a note of explanation for showing you the stories? I'm sure he won't mind, but some sort of word will be necessary.
>
> In any case, if it is possible, would you let me have the stories back fairly soon, as the collection is still under official consideration here, and we have not yet made Beckett an offer?
> Ever affectionately, etc. (UoR MS 2444/150/95)

On 25 September 1933, Prentice conveyed Chatto's offer and indicated how 'delighted' he was to be able to do so. On 16 October 1933, having obviously heard from Garnett in the interim, Prentice wrote back to 'Bunny' at the offices of the *New Statesman & Nation*:

> Many thanks for the return of the Beckett stories; so sorry they weren't any use. (UoR MS 2444/150/379)

The 'difficult birth' of *More Pricks Than Kicks* had begun.

4. A Note on Editions

The most agreeable way to read *More Pricks Than Kicks* is in the first edition of 1934, published by Chatto and Windus; but, since so very few survive, this is hardly practicable for more than a handful of people. The *hors commerce* John Calder edition of 1966 ('For Scholars Only') was a poor, if acceptable, substitute (now itself rare), but obviously not to be preferred to the Calder and Boyars 1970 reprint or to the first mass-market paperback (Picador 1974, with a garish, but imaginative, cover). In every way extraordinary is the weird large print Masterworks 1989 edition which, presumably because of its print size, omits the last four stories (!), but contains the following priceless 'puff':

> *More Pricks Than Kicks* is a favourite amongst Beckett specialists for the whole world of Murphy, Watt and Maloy [*sic*]. It is a compulsively readable introduction to the outstanding writer of our time. Its reissue has been welcomed as a major literary event.

More of a minor literary event perhaps, this large print edition having reduced Beckett's book substantially and having swiftly proved no substitute for the real thing, since too few readers are able to find the book for it to be 'compulsively readable'. The French translation, *Bande et Sarabande* (by Edith Fournier, for Minuit, 1995) was a heroic, but no doubt 'doomed', undertaking, although the cleverly contrived title, paying a double tribute to delicacy and tumescence, shows how to go down with all guns blazing. Still, it has not stimulated a great deal of interpretative activity on the part of French scholars. But of course much the same could be said, *mutatis mutandis*, for the book's standing in the English-speaking world. Happily, precisely when I was preparing this book for the printer, Faber and Faber reprinted an unannotated paperback edition with a preface (see my introduction for criticism of some details relative to the composition of *Dream*) by Cassandra Nelson. The choice of copy text, thankfully, was the 1934 Chatto *More Pricks*, with the few departures from that edition as were deemed necessary noted in a 'Note on the Text' (xvii–xix). Now everyone can possess at least the text of that exceptionally rare book, if not perhaps an actual copy!

Bibliography

Works by Beckett

Reprinted by Faber and Faber (2009–2010) with editorial introductions:

All That Fall and other plays for radio and television (ed. Everett Frost)
Company/Ill Seen Ill Said/ Worstward Ho/Stirrings Still (ed. Dirk Van Hulle)
Endgame (ed. Rónán McDonald)
The Expelled/The Calmative/The End/First Love (ed. Christopher Ricks)
Happy Days (ed. James Knowlson)
How it is (ed. Edouard Magessa O'Reilly)
Krapp's Last Tape and other shorter plays (ed. S. E. Gontarski)
Malone Dies (ed. Peter Boxall)
Mercier and Camier (ed. Seán Kennedy)
Molloy (ed. Shane Weller)
More Pricks Than Kicks (ed. Cassandra Nelson)
Murphy (ed. J. C. C. Mays)
Selected Poems 1930–1989 (ed. David Wheatley)
Texts for Nothing and other shorter prose 1950–1976 [includes *The Lost Ones*] (ed. Mark Nixon)
The Unnamable (ed. Steven Connor)
Waiting for Godot (ed. Mary Bryden)
Watt (ed. C. J. Ackerley)

John Calder or Calder & Boyars publications yet to be reprinted by Faber and Faber:

As The Story Was Told: uncollected and late prose [includes 'The Capital of the Ruins'] (1990)
Collected Poems in English and French (1978)
Disjecta: miscellaneous writings and a dramatic fragment (ed. Ruby Cohn) (1983)
Proust and *Three Dialogues with Georges Duthuit* (1965)

Black Cat Press (Dublin):

Dream of Fair to Middling Women (ed. Eoin O'Brien and Edith Fournier) (1992)

All Beckett's works in French are published in Paris by Les Editions de Minuit.

Published Beckett letters are quoted with permission from *The Letters of Samuel Beckett 1929–1940*, edited by Martha Dow Fehsenfeld and Lois More Overbeck, Cambridge: Cambridge University Press, 2009. Three further selections of later letters are forthcoming from the same imprint. Unpublished letters by Beckett are quoted with permission from the collections at the University of Reading, at the HRHRC at Austin, Texas, and at Trinity College Dublin. All other ancillary material is sourced either in the body of the text or in the Abbreviations, and is for the most part taken from the special collections at the institutions listed above. The *"Dream Notebook"* and the *"Whoroscope Notebook"* are readily accessible in the very extensive collections in all languages at the Beckett International Foundation (UoR), which also holds the typescript of the story 'Lightning Calculation' and xeroxes of Beckett's German Diaries, which will be edited and published in full in 2015. An edition of the typescript of the story 'Echo's Bones', held at Dartmouth College, New Hampshire, is in press with Faber and Faber; *A Collected Poems* including selected translations, edited with a full scholarly apparatus by the late Seán Lawlor and the present author, was published by Faber in 2012. *Samuel Beckett's Library* by Dirk Van Hulle and Mark Nixon (Cambridge University Press, 2013) is indispensable. The six notebooks containing the original manuscript of *Murphy* were purchased by the University of Reading in July 2013, and await accessioning in the Special Collections department of the Library.

On Beckett either generally, or with specific reference to one or more of the stories in *More Pricks Than Kicks*

Acheson, James. 1997. *Samuel Beckett's Artistic Theory and Practice*. Basingstoke: Macmillan.

Ackerley, C. J. 2010. '"Delite in Swynes Draf": husks and lees, sugarbeet pulp and roses in Samuel Beckett's "Draff"'. *SBT/A*, 22, 39–50.

—2009. '"The past in monochrome": (in)voluntary memory in Samuel Beckett's *Krapp's Last Tape*', in Daniela Guardamagna and Rossana M. Sebellin (eds), *The Tragic Comedy of Samuel Beckett*. Rome: Laterza, 277–91.

—2008. '"The last ditch": shades of Swift in Samuel Beckett's "Fingal"'. *Eighteenth-Century Life*, 32:2, 60–7.

—2006. 'Obscure locks, simple keys: the annotated *Watt*'. *Journal of Beckett Studies* (n.s.), 14 nos 1 and 2.

—1999. 'Samuel Beckett and the Bible: a guide'. *Journal of Beckett Studies* (n.s.), 9 no. 1, 53–126.

—1998. 'Demented particulars: the annotated *Murphy*'. *Journal of Beckett Studies* (n.s.), 7 nos 1 and 2.

Ackerley, C. J., and S. E. Gontarski (eds). 2006. *The Faber Companion to Samuel Beckett*. London: Faber and Faber.

Anspaugh, Kelly. 1996. '"Faith, Hope, and – What was it?": Beckett reading Joyce reading Dante'. *Journal of Beckett Studies* (n.s.), 5 nos 1 and 2, 19–38.

Atik, Anne. 2001. *How it Was: A Memoir of Samuel Beckett*. London: Faber and Faber.

Bair, Deirdre. 1978. *Samuel Beckett: A Biography*. London: Jonathan Cape.

Baker, Phil. 1997. *Beckett and the Mythology of Psychoanalysis*. Basingstoke: Macmillan.
Brienza, Susan. 1990. 'Clods, whores and bitches: misogyny in Beckett's early fiction', in Linda Ben-Zvi (ed.), *Women in Beckett: Performance and Critical Perspectives*. Urbana: University of Illinois Press, 91–105.
Burrows, Rachel. 1989. 'Interview' with the editors. *Journal of Beckett Studies* (o.s.), nos 11 and 12, [5]–15 (and the microfilm 'MIC 60' at TCD).
Campbell, Julie. 2001. '"Echo's Bones" and Beckett's disembodied voices'. *SBT/A*, 9, 454–60.
Carey, Phyllis. 1992. 'Stephen Dedalus, Belacqua Shuah and Dante's *Pietà*', in Carey and Ed Jewinski (eds), *Re: Joyce'n' Beckett*. New York: Fordham University Press, 104–16.
Caselli, Daniela. 2009. 'The politics of reading Dante in Beckett's *Mercier and/et Camier* and *The Calmative/Le calmant*', in Daniela Guardamagna and Rossana M. Sebellin (eds), *The Tragic Comedy of Samuel Beckett*. Rome: Laterza, 20–35.
—2005. *Beckett's Dantes: Intertextuality in the Fiction and Criticism*. Manchester: Manchester University Press.
Cochran, Robert. 1991. *Samuel Beckett: A Study of the Short Fiction*. New York: Twayne.
Cohn, Ruby. 2001. *A Beckett Canon*. Ann Arbor: University of Michigan Press.
—1962. *Samuel Beckett: The Comic Gamut*. New Brunswick: Rutgers University Press, 10–44.
Daiken, Leslie. TCD lecture notes (UoR).
Dettmar, Kevin. 1999. 'The Joyce that Beckett built', in Bruce Stewart (ed.), *Beckett and Beyond*. Gerrards Cross: Colin Smythe, 78–92.
Dimock, Wai Chee. 2006. 'Weird Conjunction: "Dante and the Lobster"', in S. E. Gontarski and Anthony Uhlmann (eds), *Beckett After Beckett*. Gainesville: University of Florida Press.
Engelberts, Matthijs, and Everett Frost (eds). 2006. *Notes [D]iverse[s] [H]olo: catalogues of Beckett's reading notes and other manuscripts at Trinity College, Dublin, with supporting essays*. *SBT/A*, 16.
Farrow, Anthony. 1991. *Early Beckett: Art and Allusion in 'More Pricks Than Kicks' and 'Murphy'*. Troy: Whitston.
Federman, Raymond. 1965. *Journey to Chaos: Samuel Beckett's Early Fiction*. Berkeley and Los Angeles: University of California Press.
Federman, Raymond, and John Fletcher. 1970. *Samuel Beckett: His Works and His Critics*. Berkeley and Los Angeles: University of California Press.
Fehsenfeld, Martha Dow, and Lois More Overbeck (eds). 2009. *The Letters of Samuel Beckett 1929–1940*. Cambridge: Cambridge University Press.
Feldman, Matthew. 2006. *Beckett's Books: A Cultural History of Samuel Beckett's 'Interwar Notes'*. London: Continuum.
Fernández, José Francisco. 2009. '"Echo's Bones": Samuel Beckett's lost story of afterlife'. *Journal of the Short Story in English*. Angers: Presses de l'Université d'Angers, 115–24.
Fletcher, John. 1964. *The Novels of Samuel Beckett*. London: Chatto and Windus.
—1962. 'Samuel Beckett et Jonathan Swift: vers une étude comparée'. *Littératures X: annales publiées par la Faculté des Lettres de Toulouse*, 11:1, 81–117.

Friedman, Alan Warren (ed.). 2000. *Beckett in Black and Red: The Translations for Nancy Cunard's* NEGRO (1934). Lexington: University Press of Kentucky.

Gontarski, S. E. 1995. 'Introduction' ('From Unabandoned Works: Samuel Beckett's Short Prose'), in *Samuel Beckett: The Complete Short Prose 1929–1989*. New York: Grove Press, xi–xxxii.

Gontarski, S. E. (ed.). 2010. *A Companion to Samuel Beckett*. Oxford: Wiley-Blackwell.

Gontarski, S. E, and Anthony Ullmann (eds). 2006. *Beckett after Beckett*. Gainesville: University Press of Florida.

Gluck, Barbara Reich. 1979. *Beckett and Joyce: Friendship and Fiction*. Lewisburg: Bucknell University Press.

Graver, Lawrence, and Raymond Federman (eds). 1979. *Samuel Beckett: The Critical Heritage*. London: Routledge and Kegan Paul.

Harrington, John P. 1992. 'Beckett, Joyce and Irish writing: the example of Beckett's "Dubliners" story', in Carey and Ed Jewinski (eds), *Re: Joyce'n' Beckett*. New York: Fordham University Press, 31–42.

Harvey, Lawrence. 1970. *Samuel Beckett: Poet and Critic*. Princeton: Princeton University Press.

Haynes, John, and James Knowlson. 2003. *Images of Beckett*. Cambridge: Cambridge University Press.

Hill, Leslie. 1990. *Beckett's Fiction: In Different Words*. Cambridge: Cambridge University Press.

Hunkeler, Thomas. 1997. *Echos de l'égo dans l'oeuvre de Samuel Beckett*. Paris: Editions L'Harmattan.

Hunter, Adrian. 2001. 'Beckett and the Joycean short story'. *Essays in Criticism*, 51:2, 230–44.

Katz, Daniel. 1996. ' "Alone in the accusative": Beckett's narcissistic echoes'. *SBT/A*, 5, 57–71.

Knowlson, James. 2009. 'Beckett and seventeenth-century Dutch and Flemish art', in Houppermans et al. (eds), *SBT/A*, 21, 27–44.

—2006a. 'Beckett's first encounters with Modern German (and Irish) Art', in Fionnuala Croke (ed.), *Samuel Beckett: A Passion for Paintings*. Dublin: National Gallery of Ireland.

—2006b. 'A note on Benozzo Gozzoli'. *Journal of Beckett Studies* (n.s.), 15 nos 1 and 2, 118–23.

—2002. 'Beckett in the Musée Condé'. *Journal of Beckett Studies* (n.s.), 11 no. 1, 73–83.

—1996. *Damned to Fame: The Life of Samuel Beckett*. London: Bloomsbury.

Knowlson, James (ed.). 1971. *Samuel Beckett: An Exhibition*. London: Turret Books.

Kosters, Onno. 1999. *Ending in Progress: Final sections in James Joyce's Prose Fictions*. Utrecht: Universiteit Utrecht.

Kroll, Jeri L. 1978. 'Belacqua as artist and lover: "What A Misfortune" '. *Journal of Beckett Studies* (o.s.), 3, 10–39.

—1977. 'The Surd as Inadmissible Evidence: the case of Attorney General vs. Henry McCabe'. *Journal of Beckett Studies* (o.s.), 2, 47–58.

—1974. 'Fair to middling heroes: a study of Samuel Beckett's early fiction'. Ph.D. dissertation, Columbia University.

Lake, Carlton (ed.). 1984. *No Symbols Where None Intended: A Catalogue of Books, Manuscripts and Other Material relating to Samuel Beckett in the Collections of the Humanities Research Center*. Austin: HRHRC.

Lawlor, Seán. 2010. 'The "Dream" poems: poems in personae', in S. E. Gontarski (ed.), *A Companion to Samuel Beckett*. Oxford: Wiley-Blackwell, 228–43.

—2009. '"O Death! Where is thy sting?": finding words for the big ideas', in Steven Barfield, Matthew Feldman and Philip Tew (eds), *Beckett and Death*. London: Continuum, 50–71.

Le Juez, Brigitte. 2008. *Beckett Before Beckett: Samuel Beckett's Lectures on French Literature*. Trans. Ros Schwartz. London: Souvenir Press.

McKinley, Grace [Grace West]. 1931. 'TCD lecture notes on Balzac', in James and Elizabeth Knowlson (eds), *Beckett Remembering/Remembering Beckett*. London: Bloomsbury, 2006.

Melnyk, Davyd. 2005. 'Interruption: a Shuah thing?' *Journal of Beckett Studies* (n.s.), 13 no. 2, 110–24.

—2000. 'Recycling Beckett: from *Dream* to *More Pricks Than Kicks*'. Unpublished M.A. research paper (UoR).

Moorjani, Angela. 2009. 'André Gide among the Parisian ghosts in the "Anglo-Irish" *Murphy*', in Houppermans et al. (eds), *SBT/A*, 21, 209–24.

Morrison, Kristin. 1990. '"Meet in Paradise": Beckett's Shavian Women', in Ben-Zvi (ed.), *Women in Beckett*, Champaign-Urbana, IL: Illini Books, 81–90.

Murphy, P. J. 2009. *Beckett's Dedalus: Dialogical Engagement with Joyce in Beckett's Fiction*. Toronto: University of Toronto Press.

Nash, Andrew, and John Pilling. 2011 [1891]. 'Beckett's dealings with the firm of "Shatton and Windup", wholesale, retail and for exportation', in Mark Nixon (ed.), *Publishing Samuel Beckett*. London: British Library.

Nelson, Cassandra. 2010. 'Preface' and 'Notes' to *More Pricks Than Kicks*. London: Faber and Faber, vii–xxiii.

Nixon, Mark. 2011a. 'Introduction' and 'Notes' to *Echo's Bones*. London: Faber and Faber.

—2011b. *'What A Tourist I Must Have Been': Beckett's German Diaries*. London: Continuum.

—2010. 'Beckett and Germany in the 1930s: the development of a poetics', in S. E. Gontarski (ed.), *A Companion to Samuel Beckett*. Oxford: Wiley-Blackwell, 130–42.

—2009. '"Writing Myself into the Ground": textual existence and death', in Barfield, Federman and Tew (eds), *Beckett and Death*. London: Continuum, 22–30.

—2007. 'Beckett publishing/publishing Beckett in the 1930s'. *Variants*, 6, 209–19.

—2006. '"Scraps of German": Samuel Beckett reading German Literature', in Engelberts and Frost (eds), *Notes [D]iverse[s] [H]olo. SBT/A*, 16, 259–82.

O'Brien, Eoin. 1986. *The Beckett Country*. Dublin: Black Cat Press/London: Faber and Faber.

O'Hara, J. D. 1999. '"Assumption"'s Launching Pad'. *Journal of Beckett Studies* (n.s.), 8 no. 2, 29–43.

—1997. *Samuel Beckett's Hidden Drives*. Gainesville: University of Florida Press.

Pasquier, Marie-Claude. 1984. 'La rose et le homard – vie et mort de Belacqua Shuah', in Jean-Michel Rabaté (ed.), *Beckett avant Beckett: essais sur les premières oeuvres*. Paris: PENS.
Pattie, David. 2010. 'Beckett and obsessional Ireland', in S. E. Gontarski (ed.), *A Companion to Samuel Beckett*. Oxford: Wiley-Blackwell, 182–95.
Pilling, John. 2010. 'A critique of aesthetic judgment: Beckett's "Dissonance of Ends and Means"', in S. E. Gontarski (ed.), *A Companion to Samuel Beckett*. Oxford: Wiley-Blackwell, 63–72.
—2009a. 'The uses of enchantment: Beckett and the fairy tale', in Sjef Houppermans et al. (eds). *SBT/A*, 21, 75–85.
—2009b. 'Beckett and Italian Literature (after Dante)', in Daniela Guardamagna and Rossana M. Sebellin (eds). *The Tragic Comedy of Samuel Beckett*. Rome: Editori Laterza, 5–19.
—2006a. *A Samuel Beckett Chronology*. Basingstoke: Palgrave.
—2006b. '"For Interpolation": Beckett and English Literature', in Matthijs Engelberts and Frost (eds). *Notes [D]iverse[s] [H]olo*. *SBT/A*, 16, 203–35.
—2005. 'Something for nothing: Beckett's *Dream of Fair to Middling Women*', in Colleen Jaurretche (ed.), *Beckett, Joyce and the Art of the Negative* (European Joyce Studies 16). Amsterdam: Rodopi, 171–80.
—2004a. 'From the pointed ones to the bones: Beckett's early poems', in Clare Hutton (ed.), *The Irish Book in the Twentieth Century*. Dublin: Irish Academic Press, 68–83.
—2004b. *A Companion to 'Dream of Fair to Middling Women'*. Tallahassee.: Journal of Beckett Studies Books.
—(ed.). 1999a. *Beckett's 'Dream Notebook'*. Reading: Beckett International Foundation.
—1999b. 'A Mermaid made over: Beckett's "Text" and John Ford', in Stewart (ed.), *Beckett and Beyond*. Gerrards Cross: Colin Smythe.
—1997. *Beckett Before Godot*. Cambridge: Cambridge University Press. (See esp. '*Dream of Fair to Middling Women*: "a solution of continuity"' and 'In the interval: *More Pricks Than Kicks*' 56–113.
—1996. 'Beckett's Stendhal: "Nimrod of Novelists"'. *French Studies*, 50:3, July 1996, 311–17.
—1995. 'Losing one's classics: Beckett's small Latin, and less Greek'. *Journal of Beckett Studies* (n.s.), 4 no. 2, 5–13.
Pothast, Ulrich. 2008. *The Metaphysical Vision: Arthur Schopenhauer's Philosophy of Art and Life and Samuel Beckett's Own Way to Make Use of it*. New York: Peter Lang.
Power, Mary. 1981–1982. 'Samuel Beckett's "Fingal" and the Irish tradition'. *Journal of Modern Literature*, 9:1, 151–56.
Rabinovitz, Rubin. 1984. *The Development of Samuel Beckett's Fiction*. Urbana: University of Illinois Press.
Robins, Philip. 1996. 'Beckett's Family Values'. Ph.D. dissertation, University of London.
Shloss, Carol Loeb. 2004. *Lucia Joyce: To Dance in the Wake*. London: Bloomsbury.
Slote, Sam. 2010. 'Stuck in translation: Beckett and Borges on Dante'. *Journal of Beckett Studies* (n.s.), 19 no. 1, 15–28.
Smith, Frederik N. 2002. *Beckett's Eighteenth Century*. Basingstoke: Palgrave.
Stevenson, Kay Gilliland. 1986. 'Belacqua in the moon: Beckett's revisions of "Dante and the Lobster"', in Patrick A. McCarthy (ed.), *Critical Essays on Samuel Beckett*. Boston: G. K. Hall.

Vandervlist, Harry. 1994a. 'Nothing doing: the repudiation of action in Beckett's *More Pricks Than Kicks*', in Daniel Fischlin (ed.), *Negation, Critical Theory and Postmodern Textuality*. Dordrecht: Kluwer, 145–56.
—1994b. '"Rejecting the feasible": discourse and subjectivity in the perverse project of Beckett's early fiction', in Matthias Buning and Sjef Houppermans (eds). *Beckett versus Beckett. SBT/A*, 7, 149–63.
—1991. 'Samuel Beckett's work in regress: a study of the fiction to 1953'. Ph.D. dissertation, MacMaster University.
Van Hulle, Dirk. 2010. 'Figures of script: the development of Beckett's short prose and the "aesthetic of inaudibilities"', in Gontarski (ed.), *A Companion to Samuel Beckett*. Oxford: Wiley-Blackwell, 244–62, esp. 244–50.
Van Hulle, Dirk, and Mark Nixon (eds). 2007. *'All Sturm and No Drang'. SBT/A*, 18.
Zurbrugg, Nicholas. 1988. *Beckett and Proust*. Gerrards Cross: Colin Smythe.

General

Alexander, Archibald. 1907 [etc.]. *A Short History of Philosophy*. Edinburgh: James Maclehose.
Augustine of Hippo, St. 1961. *The Confessions*. Trans. R. S. Pine-Coffin. Harmondsworth: Penguin.
Boland, Rosita. 2005. *A Secret Map of Ireland*. Dublin: New Island. ('Roscommon' section, with the subtitle 'Crex-Crex', 238–43).
Borges, Jorge Luis. 1973 [1964]. *Other Inquisitions 1937–52*. Trans. Ruth L. C. Simms. London: Souvenir Press.
Boswell, James. 1887 [1791]. *Boswell's Life of Johnson*. Ed. George Birkbeck Hill (6 vols). Oxford: Clarendon Press.
Burnet, John. 1914 [etc]. *Greek Philosophy: Thales to Plato*. London: Macmillan.
Defoe, Daniel. n.d. *The Life and Adventures of Robinson Crusoe*. London: Service & Paton.
Donne, John. 1929. *Complete Poetry and Selected Prose*. Ed. John Hayward. London: The Nonesuch Press.
Eliot, T. S. 1963. *Collected Poems 1909–1962*. London: Faber and Faber.
Flaubert, Gustave. 1989. [1869. *L'Education sentimentale*]. *A Sentimental Education: the story of a young man*. Trans. Douglas Parmée. Oxford: World's Classics.
Gide, André. 1959. *Pretexts*. Trans. Justin O'Brien. London: Secker & Warburg.
Hardy, Thomas. 1985 [1895]. *Jude the Obscure*. Ed. Patricia Ingham. Oxford: World's Classics.
Joyce, James. 1960 [1922].*Ulysses*. London: John Lane/The Bodley Head.
—1991 [1914]. *Dubliners*. Ed. Terence Brown. Harmondsworth: Penguin.
Kafka, Franz. 2006. *The Zürau Aphorisms*. Trans. Michael Hofmann. London: Harvill Secker.
Le Fanu, Sheridan. 1993 [1872]. *In A Glass Darkly*. Ed. Robert Tracy. Oxford: World's Classics.
Maupassant, Guy de. 1979. *Contes et Nouvelles*. ['Divorce'; vol. 2]. Paris: Gallimard/ Pléiade.

May, Derwent. 2001. *Critical Times: the history of the* Times Literary Supplement. London: HarperCollins.

Nietzsche, Friedrich. 1954. *The Portable Nietzsche*. Ed. Walter Kaufmann. New York: The Viking Press. [*Thus Spoke Zarathustra*; *Twilight of the Idols*].

Proust, Marcel. 1960. *Remembrance of Things Past*. Trans. C. K. Scott Moncrieff. London: Chatto and Windus.

Rimbaud, Arthur. 1962. *Collected Poems*. Trans. Oliver Bernard. Harmondsworth: Penguin.

Rousseau, Jean-Jacques. 1953 [1781]. *The Confessions*. Trans. J. M. Cohen. Harmondsworth: Penguin.

—1979 [1782]. *The Reveries of a Solitary Walker*. Trans. Charles E. Butterworth. New York: Harper and Row.

Sade, D. A. F. de (Marquis de Sade). 1966. *The 120 Days of Sodom and Other Writings*. Trans. Austryn Wainhouse and Richard Seaver. New York: Grove Press.

Swift, Jonathan. 1958. *Gulliver's Travels and Other Writings*. Ed. Ricardo Quintana. New York: Random House.

Voltaire. 1966. *Candide, or Optimism*. Trans. John Butt. Harmondsworth: Penguin.

Windelband, Wilhelm. 1907 [1893]. *A History of Philosophy*. Trans. James Tufts. New York: The Macmillan Company. (2nd edn).

INDEX

WORKS BY BECKETT

'Alba' 13, 165, 188
All That Fall 1, 35, 102, 115, 190–1
'André Masson' (*Three Dialogues*) 11
Anna Lyvia Pluratself translation 145, 187
Assez/Enough 104, 142
'Assumption' 6, 48, 57, 116, 137, 147, 201, 210, 216
'At last I find . . . ' 177

'Bram Van Velde' (*Three Dialogues*) 126, 182, 236
. . . *but the clouds* . . . 183

'Calmative, The' 155, 173
'Calvary by Night' 82, 158
'Capital of the Ruins, The' 131
'Cascando' (poem) 95, 219
'Case in a Thousand, A' x, 61, 80, 93, **106–16**, 135
'Casket of Pralinen for a Daughter of a Dissipated Mandarin' (revised version) 165–6, 179
'Censorship in the Saorstat' (*Disjecta*) 161, 238
'Che Sciagura' 80, 238
Comment c'est/How it is 8, 223, 227
Company 183, 212
'Concentrisme, Le' (*Disjecta*) 141, 159, 209, 221
'Cow' notes 218, 238

'Dante and the Lobster' 3, 5–6, 17, 19–20, 22–3, 25, 44, **47–56**, 61, 67–8, 80, 84, 88–90, 111, 120–1, 128–9, 134, 136, 143, **144–9**, 153, 155–7, 163–4, 172, 174, 176, 178, 184, 189–91, 194, 198, 200, 203–4, 211–13, 215, 217–19, 222, 226–7, 240
'Dante and the Lobster' (1932 version) 22, 34, 38, 48, 52–3, 55, 106, 147, 222, 240
'Dante . . . Bruno.Vico..Joyce' 1, 113, 128, 157, 195, 209, 234, 235, 236
'Denis Devlin' review (*Disjecta*) 103, 165, 171
'Ding-Dong' 3, 6, 13, 17–19, 23, 25, 27, 29, 39, 43–4, 51, 53, **56–60**, 62, 67–9, 70, 78, 86, 89–90, 93, 103, 127, 130, 136, 143–4, 149, 153, **154–7**, 159, 162, 184, 194, 205, 226
Disjecta 1, 62, 83, 91, 93, 103, 107, 128, 130–1, 133–4, 147, 157, 161, 165, 171, 173, 209, 218, 228
'Dortmunder' 99, 226
Draff (provisional title) 2, 27, 44, 73
'Draff' x, 6–7, 16, 17, 22–3, 28, 30, 36, 46, 47, 50–2, 54, 60–1, 66, 70–1, 77, 79–80, 82, **85–93**, 99, 102, 105, 121, 128–9, 132, 135–7, 139, 146, 148–9, 158, 162, 165, 170, 172, 175, 179–84, 186, 188, 190, 194–6, 203–5, 211, 213, 216, 218–19, **220–32**, 233, 238
'Dream' Notebook 1, 41, 142–4, 152, 154, 156–8, 171–2, 174, 176, 187, 199, 205
Dream of Fair to Middling Women 1, 2, 6, 8, 9, 11–12, 18, 20, 25–6, 30, 32, 36, 38, 43, 51, 58, 60–1, 66–7, 71–9, 84, 87, 92–4, 98, 100, 110, 111, 113–14, 126, 129–30, 134–7, 139, 142–232, 235–6
see also entries for 'Sedendo

Dream of Fair to Middling Women (Cont'd) et Quiescendo'; 'Smeraldina's Billet Doux, The'; 'Text' (prose poem); 'They go out for the evening'; 'Wet Night, A'

'Echo's Bones' (poem) 104, 170
'Echo's Bones' (short story) x, 2–3, 7, 9, 17, 23, 25, 28, 33, 36, 44, 51, 61, 66, 71, 86–7, 89, 91, 93, **100–5**, 112, 115, 121, 132, 136–7, 146–8, 150–2, 156–8, 160–1, 165–7, 169–70, 179, 186, 190–1, 194–6, 202, 204–05, 208, 211, 213, 216–20, 223, 225, 227–8, 230–1
Echo's Bones and Other Precipitates 67
Endgame 64, 120
'End, The' 197
'Enueg I' 186, 203, 228
'Enueg II' 155, 162, 219
'Expelled, The' 197

'Fingal' 6, 13, 18, 22, 25, 26, 30, **39–44**, 47, 51, 78, 82, 84, 88, 127, 130, 136, 138, 147, **149–54**, 157, 164, 173, 184, 187, 189, 194, 204, 208, 212, 214, 216–17, 237, 240
'First Love' 147, 187, 230–1
'For Future Reference' 179
'From the Only Poet to a Shining Whore' 193
'Fragment de théâtre II' 59
From An Abandoned Work 110, 199

German Diaries 28, 98, 128–9, 215
'Gnome' 158, 214

Happy Days 40, 149, 156, 183
'Hell Crane to Starling' 179
'Home Olga' 157, 236

Jack B. Yeats review (*Disjecta*) 54, 91, 238

Krapp's Last Tape 4, 130, 188, 213

'Lightning Calculation' 61, 103, 105–6, 113, 116–17, 173, 211, 225

L'Innommable/The Unnamable 56, 120, 147, 180, 181, 212
Lost Ones, The 148, 150
'Love and Lethe' 6, 10, 22–3, 25–7, **35–9**, 40–1, 45–8, 56, 60, 62–4, 78, 82, 88, 102, 136–7, 143, 164, 166, 175, **176–83**, 187, 189, 199, 203, 206, 212, 219–20, 224–5, 240

'Malacoda' 162, 170
Malone Dies 8, 33, 80, 99, 181, 184, 194, 210, 212
Mercier and Camier 32, 141, 150, 164, 168, 175, 183–4, 186, 191–2, 194, 224, 227, 229
Mercier et Camier 141
Molloy 4, 8, 30, 44, 72, 135, 187–9, 211–12, 223, 227, 231
More Pricks Than Kicks
  academic retrieval of 122–5, 233–5
  autobiographical elements in 23, 28–9, 43, 46, 49, 65–6, 80, 91, 180, 189, 191, 206, 208, 219–22
    see also entries for 'Beckett, William'; 'Bethell, Adrienne'; 'Joyce, Lucia'; 'McCarthy, Ethna'; and 'Sinclair, Peggy'
  conception and composition of 2, 5–8, 10–11, 27, 36, 48, 56, 66
  Dublin and environs in 16–19, 39, 42–3, 49, 51–3, 57–60, 72, 78, 88, 107, 147, 155, 157, 161, 167, 175–6, 178–9, 183, 186, 189, 191, 193, 198, 200, 204, 206, 209, 215, 220, 222, 225, 230
  editions of 97, 125, 186–7, 213, 24
  fairy-tale elements in 80, 104
  proof stage (1934 Chatto and Windus) 7, 14
  proof stage (1964 Grove Press) xiii, 100, 120, 122
  pastoral elements in 31–2, 88
  publishers and 121–2, 214
    see also entries for journals, newspapers and publishers in the General Index

reception by family and friends 4, 62, 97
reviews of 15, 20, 118–19, 139
sales of 3–4, 67, 140
short story as a genre 2, 8–11, 14, 16–17, 19, 25–40, 45, 56–7, 79, 91, 101, 107–14, 116, 235–6, 239
submissions to magazines 12–13, 56–7, 60, 70, 240
word counts in 7, 44 ('Echo's Bones'), 240 ('Dante and the Lobster', 'Fingal', 'Love and Lethe', 'Yellow')

Mörike review (*Disjecta*) 8, 218
Murphy 4, 8, 31, 34, 38, 44, 49, 51, 64, 86, 116–17, 121, 128–9, 132, 142–3, 150, 157, 160, 162, 170, 176, 179, 182–4, 187, 203, 211, 214–18, 238

Nacht und Träume 147, 210
Not I 183
Nouvelles 58, 197

O'Casey review (*Disjecta*) 62, 103
'Ooftish' 172

Philosophy notes 69, 179, 217
'Poèmes 38–39' 183
'Possessed, The' (*Disjecta*) 44, 228
Psychology notes 107, 182
Proust 11–12, 48, 84, 89, 112, 130, 133–4, 137, 140, 142, 157, 166, 220–1, 224

'Recent Irish Poetry' (*Disjecta*) 113
'Return to the Vestry' 38, 183

'Sanies I' 23, 42, 187, 195, 207 (revised version), 212, 218, 223, 237
'Sanies II' 41, 153, 163, 212
'Sedendo et Quiescendo' (*Dream of Fair to Middling Women*) 9, 72, 118–19, 174, 210, 233
'Serena I' 30, 51, 132, 158, 203
'Serena II' 151, 180

'Serena III' 78, 90, 139, 154, 166, 178–80, 182, 203, 224, 228
'Smeraldina's Billet Doux, The' (originally in *Dream of Fair to Middling Women*) x, 6, 7, 9, 25, 30, 61, 71, **92–100**, 120, 136, **208–10**
'Spring Song' 90, 153, 157, 162, 187, 211, 223, 227
Surrealist translations 151

'Tal Coat' (*Three Dialogues*) 236
TCD notes 79, 147, 183, 203
'Text' [poem] 142, 190, 226
'Text' [prose poem] (*Dream of Fair to Middling Women*) 94, 142
Texts for Nothing 49, 148
'They go out for the evening' (*Dream of Fair to Middling Women*) 71
That Time 130
Thomas MacGreevy *Poems* review (*Disjecta*) 238
Three Dialogues with Georges Duthuit 126, 182 *see also* individual entries
'To My Daughter' 179
Translation of Rimbaud's 'Le Bateau ivre' ('Drunken Boat') 126, 158
'Trueborn Jackeen' 171, 221, 238

Waiting for Godot 3, 4, 5, 135, 216
'Walking Out' 6, 13, 14, 24, **26–36**, 39–40, 42, 45–8, 51, 59, 62, 73, 78, 82, 86–8, 90, 92, 125, 134, 136, 138–9, 143, 146, 149–52, 163, 168, 173, 176–8, 180, **183–9**, 191–2, 200, 209, 216–17, 221, 227–8, 231
Watt 1, 8, 51, 104, 106, 141, 145, 192, 213, 224
'Wet Night, A' (originally in *Dream of Fair to Middling Women*) 6–7, 9, 17–18, 22, 25, 47, **70–9**, 84–5, 87–9, 99–100, 110, 127, 129, 131–2, 136–7, 143, 145, 147–8, 150–2, 155–6, **157–76**, 179–81, 193–8, 206, 214–16, 218, 223–4, 226, 239
'What A Misfortune' x, 6, 8, 10, 18, 20, 22–5, 28, 32, 35–6, 40, 46–7, 51–2,

'What A Misfortune' (Cont'd)
60, 68, 70, 73–4, 76–7, **79–89**, 92, 100, 109, 119, 128–9, 131, 136–7, 139, 143, 145–7, 150, 153, 157–60, 162, 169–73, 176–81, 185–7, 189, **190–208**, 210–12, 218, 220, 223–7, 229–31, 237

'Whoroscope' (revised version) 37, 159, 177, 182, 215

'Whoroscope' Notebook 2, 31, 85, 134, 141, 143, 145, 164, 180, 199–200, 238

'Yellow' 6–7, 23, 42, 44, 46–7, 51, 58, **60–8**, 74, 80, 85, 87, 89, 93, 99, 119–21, 127–9, 132–9, 145–53, 165, 170–1, 173, 176, 186, 196–8, 202, **210–20**, 224, 226–7, 229, 240

GENERAL INDEX

Abbé Gabriel 158, 205–7
Acheson, James 56
Ackerley, C.J. 41–3, 65, 132, 143, 153, 156, 160, 192, 196, 230, 234
Adorno, T.W. 142
Aeschylus 154
Alexander, Archibald 132, 165, 214
Anaximander 132
Aquinas, St. Thomas 204
Ariosto, Lodovico 191
Aristotle 149, 236
Arnold, Matthew 155
Atik, Anne 190
Auber, Daniel-François 221
Augustine, St. 1, 75, 158, 164–5, 174–5, 190, 195–6, 199, 202, 204, 208, 212, 223, 226
Aulnoy, Comtesse Marie d' 163, 195, 205
Austen, Jane 239

Baker, Phil 108, 110, 115
Balzac, Honoré de 159–60
Barnes, Julian 9
Bartlett, John 159
Baudelaire, Charles 174
Beaumont, Francis and John Fletcher 121
Beckett, Frank (Brother) 193, 208
Beckett, William (Bill) (Father) death and burial of 6, 10, 14, 36, 61, 66–7, 80, 88, 103, 105, 115, 141, 201, 213, 218–19, 227–8, 230, 232

Beethoven, Ludwig van 96, 150, 202, 208
Bérard, Victor 129, 158, 191, 226, 227
Bethell, Adrienne 191
Bion, Wilfred 115
Bloom, Harold 234
Boland, Rosita 238
Bookman, The 62, 106, 110, 115–16
Borges, Jorge Luis 135
Boswell, James 141
Bourrienne, Louis Antoine Fauvelet de 182
Bowen, Elizabeth 10
Boyars, Marion 121–2
Boyle, Kay 67, 120, 144
Brantôme, Abbé de 42
Bray, Barbara 9, 42, 59, 67, 111, 120, 141, 144, 189, 192, 218, 222
Bray, Bridget 111
Breton, André 151
Bronowski, Jacob 32
Browning, Robert 166, 221, 227
Bruno, Giordano 191, 213
Bunyan, John 206
Burnet, John 132
Burrows, Rachel 79, 183
Burton, Robert 129, 144, 147–8, 150, 154, 158, 163–5, 167–8, 170–2, 174, 193, 197–201, 205–6, 208, 215, 217, 223, 225, 226
Byron, George Gordon Noel (Lord) 131

Caesar, Julius 150
Calder, John 120–2, 241

Calder & Boyars 121–2
Calder-Marshall, Arthur 118
Campbell, Roy 119
Carducci, Giosuè 146–7
Carey, Phyllis 234
Carlyle, Thomas 68, 189, 197
Caselli, Daniela 54, 134, 143, 154, 183, 188, 199, 222
Cassirer, Ernst 106
Chamfort, Sébastien Roch Nicolas 127
Chamisso, Adalbert von 102
Chatto and Windus 3, 10–11, 13–14, 71, 101, 113
Chaucer, Geoffrey 2, 11, 14–15, 91, 129, 159, 164, 167
Chekhov, Anton 9, 20, 140, 179
Chesterfield, Lord 157
Chopin, Frédéric 221
Cochran, Robert 56–7, 124, 219, 234, 237
Cohn, Ruby 5, 20, 56, 106, 110, 122, 125, 149
Collins, Wilkie 226
Conan Doyle, (Sir) Arthur 152
Congreve, William 138
'Cooper, William' (*pseud* James Glass Bartram) 129, 165, 172, 189
Coren, Michael 152
Costello, Nuala 14–15, 58, 69, 81, 88, 113, 129, 154, 230, 237
Cranach, Lucas 178
Cunard, Nancy 237
Cusack, Cyril 181

Dante Alighieri 14, 15, 23, 47, 49–50, 52–4, 62, 68, 74, 77, 96–7, 125, 128–9, 131, 134, 144–5, 147–8, 153–6, 175, 183, 188, 190, 193, 195, 199, 211, 219, 221–2, 228, 236
Darwin, Charles 197, 224
Da Vinci, Leonardo 149, 236
Defoe, Daniel 62
Delius, Frederick 31
Del Sarto, Andrea 220
Democritus 63, 69

Descartes, René 141, 152, 227
Dickens, Charles 20
 Bleak House 149
 David Copperfield 152, 167, 172–3
 Little Dorrit 213
Diderot, Denis 81, 90, 191, 231
Dimock, Wai Chee 53
Donatus 141
Donne, John 62, 64, 70, 88, 96, 171, 173, 192, 213, 237
 'Bait, The' 229–30
 'Nocturnall upon *S.Lucies* Day, A' 91, 224
 Paradoxes and Problemes 69
 'Valediction: forbidding mourning, A' 224
Dostoevsky, Fyodor 20, 223, 225
Doumer, Paul 147
Dublin Anthology, A 57
Dublin Magazine, The 56, 119
 see also entries for 'Alba'; 'Ding-Dong'; and Thomas MacGreevy *Poems* review *under* 'Works by Beckett'
Duns Scotus 205
Dürer, Albrecht 202
Duthuit, Georges 160, 225, 228

Eliot, T.S. 14–15, 39, 46, 155, 158, 178, 196
 'Gerontion', 64, 158
 Hollow Men, The 38, 178
 'Mr. Eliot's Sunday Morning Service' 196
Ellis, Havelock 160
Eluard, Paul 151
Empson, William 31–2
Encyclopaedia Britannica 206
Esposito, Bianca 49, 147
European Caravan, The 142
Evening Herald [Dublin] 54, 145, 153
Evening Standard [London] 116
Experiment 32

Farrow, Anthony 83–4, 124, 155, 171, 219, 233
Faoláin, Seán O 8
Federman, Raymond 106, 118, 123

Feldman, Matthew 132, 217
Ferrers Howell, A. G. 125
Field, John 221
Fielding, Henry 83, 175, 178, 184, 191, 235–6, 239
Firbank, Ronald 8, 140
FitzGerald, Edward 161
Flaubert, Gustave 47, 79
Fletcher, John (critic) 106, 118, 122–3, 237
Fletcher, John (playwright) 31, 121
Fontane, Theodore 188
Ford, Ford Madox 169
Fournier, Edith 241
Freud, Sigmund 69, 108, 110–11, 205, 221

Galileo 159
Garnett, Constance 9, 226
Garnett, David 240
Garnier, Pierre 37, 129, 155, 172, 195–7, 201, 226
Gascoyne, David 4
Gaultier, Jules de 166
Gerhardt, Elena 190
Gershwin, George 96, 209
Geulincx, Arnold 145, 227
Gilbert, Stuart 185
Gide, André 79, 113–14, 183, 204
Giles, H. A. 167, 170, 217
Glendinning, Alex 118–19
Gluck, Barbara Reich 234
Goethe, Johann Wolfgang von 158, 166, 192, 214
Gontarski, S. E. 19, 110, 112
Gooch, G. P. 238
Gorey, Edward 102
Gould, Gerald 118
Gozzoli, Benozzo 202
Graver, Lawrence 118
Gray, Thomas 88
Green, J. R. 212, 219
Grillparzer, Franz 96–8, 210
Grimm, Jacob and Wilhelm (The Brothers Grimm) 86, 99, 215–16, 231

Grock (*pseud* Charles Adrien Wettach) 74, 129, 162–3
Grosz, George 201
Grove Press 100, 120, 122
Guarini, Giambattista 31

'H., N.' 119
Handel, Georg Friederich 200
Hardy, Edward John 35
Hardy, Thomas 35, 64, 138, 206
    Jude the Obscure 181, 189, 196
Harrington, John P. 107, 234
Hart, Lorenz 159
Harvey, Lawrence E. 101, 121, 142, 188
Hayward, John 213
Hemingway, Ernest 17
Henry, O. 16
Henry, Paul 230
Heraclitus 69, 132, 214
Higgins, Aidan 4, 67, 120–1, 163
Hill, George Birkbeck 141–2
Hill, Leslie 28, 123, 127–8, 133
Hogarth, William 180
Hone, Joseph 62, 153, 238
Horace 159–60, 190, 196
Hudson, W. H. 96–7
Hugo, Victor 96–7, 221
Hunter, Adrian 108, 234–5
Hutchinson, Mary 4, 193

Inge, W. R. (Dean) 129, 169, 178, 186, 190, 193, 217

Jeans, (Sir) James 169, 172, 213, 220
Jerome, St. 141
Jewinski, Ed 234
John of the Cross, St. 196
John O'London's Weekly 119
Johnson, Samuel (Dr.) 45, 131, 238
Jones, Ernest 217
Joyce, James 2, 8–9, 14, 16, 19, 27, 34, 96, 106–7, 111, 118, 133, 146, 166, 174, 185, 220, 233–7, 239

Anna Livia Plurabelle 187, 221
  see also entries for *Anna Lyvia Pluratself* under 'Works by Beckett'
'Dead, The' 27, 75, 101, 175, 224, 230, 234
Dubliners 8, 18–19, 51, 74, 171, 215, 216, 234
'Ecce puer' 201
'Encounter, An' 234
'Epiphanies' 49
Exiles 157
'Grace' 171
'Painful Case, A' 107
Portrait of the Artist as a Young Man, A 49, 51, 211, 234, 235
Stephen Hero 49
'Two Gallants' 34, 42, 72, 74, 181, 229
Ulysses 23, 51, 56, 78, 94, 151, 165, 176, 191, 195, 200, 210, 213, 227, 229, 234
Work In Progress/Finnegans Wake 2, 19, 51, 113, 118, 145, 185, 221
Joyce, Lucia 15, 30–1, 91–2, 185, 187, 201, 220, 232
Juliana of Norwich, St. 217

Kafka, Franz 78, 114
Kahane, Jack 160
Kant, Immanuel 2, 106, 145, 166, 182
Kean, Marie 121
Keats, John 35, 96
  'Ode to a Nightingale' 33–4, 50–1, 87, 148, 195, 197
  'Ode on a Grecian Urn' 39
Keble, John 202
Kempis, Thomas à 2, 43, 90–1, 129, 154, 171, 192
Kipling, Rudyard 231
Knowlson, James 28, 111, 156, 181, 202, 219
Kobler, John 122
Kreuger, Ivar 181
Kroll, Jeri L. 28, 46–7, 62, 70, 87, 90, 124–5, 131, 139, 150, 152, 161, 177, 195, 205, 222

Laforgue, Jules 174
Lamartine, Alphonse de 150
La Rochefoucauld 192
Lauder, Harry 159
Lavater, Johann Kaspar 152
Lawlor, Seán 16, 65–6, 91, 170, 186, 201, 230
LeFanu, Sheridan 101
Le Juez, Brigitte 113, 236
Leventhal, A. J. ('Con') 2, 177, 179, 182, 187, 198, 204
Lewis, Percy Wyndham 171
Life and Letters 106
Lockhart, J. G. 146–7, 161, 169, 170, 182
Lovat Dickson's Weekly 106
Lover, Samuel 216
Lucas, E. V. 215
Luther, Martin 197
Lyly, John 203

MacCarthy, Ethna 26, 76, 114, 163, 220, 221
MacGreevy, Thomas 4, 6–10, 13–14, 23, 28, 32, 44, 56, 87, 98–9, 101, 104–5, 110–14, 141, 146, 150, 153, 155, 160, 163, 171–3, 177, 181, 184, 186–7, 190, 194–5, 197–8, 200, 202, 205–7, 210, 213–14, 216, 219, 221, 224–5, 228, 237
Mandeville, Bernard de 14–15, 81, 85–6, 129, 190
Mangan, James Clarence 169
Manning, Mary 160
Manzoni, Alessandro 146, 173
Marie Antoinette 41, 153
Marlowe, Christopher 229–30
Masaccio, Tommaso 166
'Master of Tired Eyes, The' 156
Maupassant, Guy de 8, 9, 79–81, 202, 236
Mauriac, François 9
Mauthner, Fritz 145
May, Derwent 118
Mayrhofer, Johann 35
McCabe, Henry 48, 54–5, 145, 147–8, 222

McGovern, Barry 122
Melville, Herman 20
Mendelssohn, Felix 195
Mérimée, Prosper 207
Meun, Jean de 172
Milton, John 175
Mitchell, Pamela 85, 215, 238
Montaigne, Michel de 61
Moore, Thomas 155–6, 210
Mörike, Eduard 8
Morning Post 119
Morrow, George 215
Motte, Benjamin 41
Motte, Madame de la 41, 153
Mozart, Wolfgang Amadeus 165, 169, 196, 218
Muir, Edwin 20, 118–19
Murphy, P. J. 233–4
Musil, Robert 20
Musset, Alfred de 204

Napoleon Bonaparte 52, 146, 161, 182
Nash, Andrew 240
Nelson, Cassandra 1, 121–2, 188, 241
New Review, The 142
    see also entries for 'Text' (prose poem) under 'Works by Beckett'
Nietzsche, Friedrich 23, 131, 191, 199
Nixon, Mark 127
Nordau, Max 129, 165, 184, 191, 203

O'Brien, Eoin 42, 151, 153, 156, 158, 175–6, 178, 200–1, 220, 225
Observer, The 15, 63, 119, 143
O'Casey, Sean 62, 201
O'Connor, Frank 8
O'Hara, J.D. 108, 110–11, 114–15
Osler, (Sir) William 178–9
Ovid 23, 104, 171, 199
O'Sullivan, Seumas 56–7, 60
    see also entries for the *Dublin Magazine*

Papini, Giovanni 131
Pascal, Blaise 190
Pattie, David 19

Pellico, Silvio 147
Pelorson, Georges (*aka* Georges Belmont) 159, 165, 177
Péron, Alfred 145, 187
Péron, Mania 96, 181
Perrault, Charles 163, 166, 173–4, 186
Perse, Saint-John 155
Petrie, Flinders (Dr.) 151
Pinker, J.B. 13, 27, 56, 184–5, 200
Plato 179
Plutarch 206
Pope, Alexander 31, 198, 200
Pound, Ezra 235
Power, Mary 234
Praz, Mario 160, 231
Preminger, Otto 209
Prentice, Charles 2–3, 6–7, 9–11, 13, 44–5, 48, 56, 71, 80, 89, 91, 100–1, 104–5, 113, 126, 200, 210, 233, 239
Proust, Marcel 23, 65–6, 77, 79, 108, 111, 113, 127, 173, 179–80, 212, 216–17, 220, 239
Pudovkin, Vsevolod 208
Pulci, Luigi 200
Putnam, Samuel 233

Quennell, Peter 118

Rabinovitz, Rubin 107–8, 114, 123
Racine, Jean 183
Ravel, Maurice 180
Reavey, George 12, 32, 36, 83, 113, 131, 199
Renard, Jules 167, 223, 225, 235
Rimbaud, Arthur
    'Bateau ivre, Le' 126, 158, 168
    'Clearance Sale' ('Solde') 166
    'Mouvement' 158
    'Poëtes de Sept Ans, Les' 151, 170, 204
    'Qu'est-ce pour nous...' 126
Robins, Philip 108
Rodgers, Richard 159
Rolland, Romain 150, 201
Ronsard, Pierre de 38, 182–3
Rosset, Barney 100, 120
Rossi, Mario 62, 153, 238

Rousseau, Jean-Jacques 149, 152
Rudmose-Brown, T.B. 164
Ruskin, John 151, 202

Sade, D.A.F. de (Marquis) 160
Saki (*pseud* H.H. Munro) 8, 17
Scarlatti, Domenico 75, 173
Schopenhauer, Arthur 54, 131, 181, 224
Schubert, Franz 23, 33–5, 39, 59, 99, 130, 190, 201–2, 209
Schumann, Elisabeth 190
Schumann, Robert 59
Seaver, Richard 1
Shakespeare, William 23, 31, 47, 53, 56, 62, 68, 75, 102, 127–8, 132, 154, 157–8, 170, 175, 189–90, 192, 199–200, 219
  Antony and Cleopatra 154
  As You Like It 190
  Hamlet 22, 77, 82, 102, 145–6, 151–2, 175, 177, 179–80, 211–12, 223, 225
  Henry IV, part one 219
  King Lear 157, 189
  Merchant of Venice, The 175
  Midsummer Night's Dream, A 75
  Much Ado About Nothing 170–1
  Romeo and Juliet 62, 199, 211, 227
  Tempest, The 56, 68
  Twelfth Night 222
Shaw, George Bernard 167, 181
Shenker, Israel 235
Sheridan, Thomas 190
Shloss, Carol Loeb 185
Shrewsbury, Duchess of 43
Sidney, (Sir) Philip 202, 212
Sinclair, Morris 11, 97, 181, 215
Sinclair, Peggy 26, 30, 46, 61, 66, 86, 93–4, 173, 185, 188, 209, 221, 232
Sinclair, William ('Boss') 166
Skeat, W.W. 159
Sloman, Harold P. 79
Slote, Sam 53, 144, 147, 149, 228
Smith, Frederik N. 31, 41, 154, 204, 215, 222, 237, 238
Smollett, Tobias 164, 180
Socrates 132, 179, 214

Somerville, Edith and Martin Ross (*pseud* Violet Martin) 189
Sorel, Georges 238
Spenser, Edmund 194, 208
Spinoza, Benedict 44
Stendhal (*pseud* Henri Beyle) 79
  Armance 194, 207, 211
  Chartreuse de Parme, La 184
  De l'Amour 202
  Rouge et le Noir, Le 22, 162, 179
Stephens, James 14, 15
Stephens, Karin 226, 229
Sterne, Laurence 186
Stevenson, Kay Gilliland 23, 53–5, 144
Summerford, Colin 13
Sunne, Richard 119
Swift, Jonathan 41–3, 45, 64, 147, 190, 204, 236
  Bickerstaff Papers, The 238
  Gulliver's Travels 170, 174, 195–6, 215, 223, 237–9
  'History of the Four Last Years of the Queen, The' 224
  Journal to Stella 153, 201, 203, 224, 238
  'Modest Proposal, A' 238
  poems 190, 238
  Tale of a Tub, A 207, 238–9
Symonds, John Addington 200
Synge, John Millington 180

Tasso, Torquato 31
Taylor, Rowland (Dr.) 219
Tennyson, Alfred (Lord) 161, 164, 168, 181, 208
Terence 141
Thales 132
This Quarter 16, 48, 56, 147
  see also entries for 'Dante and the Lobster' (1932 version) and 'Surrealist translations' *under* 'Works by Beckett'
Thompson, Geoffrey 80
Thom's Directory 42
Time and Tide 119
Times Literary Supplement, The 118–19
Titian 201

Titus, Edward W. 16, 56
    see also entries for *This Quarter*
Tolstoy, Leo 20
transition/Transition 116, 118–19, 216
    see also entries for 'Assumption';
    'Censorship in the Saorstat';
    'Dante . . . Bruno.Vico..Joyce';
    'Denis Devlin' review; 'Ooftish' and
    'Sedendo et Quiescendo' *under*
    'Works by Beckett'
Trench, Wilbraham 221
Trevor, William 10

Uccello, Paolo 14–15, 129–30, 225
Ussher, Arland 230

Valéry, Paul
    'Cantique des Colonnes' 183
    'Cimetière marin, Le' 196, 230
    'Fausse Morte, La' 183
Vandervlist, Harry 35, 57, 124

Van Hulle, Dirk 233
Vasari, Giorgio 166, 220
Velasquez, Diego 180–1, 224
Vermeer, Johannes 216
Verne, Jules 225
Vogelweide, Walther von der 193
Voltaire 80, 197

Wagner, Richard 160, 169, 220
'Walter' (*pseud* author of *My Secret Life*) 193
Whitman, Walt 161
Wilde, Oscar 8, 152
Windelband, Wilhelm 132–3, 166, 204
Wordsworth, William 158, 170

Yeats, Jack Butler 197, 238
Yeats, William Butler 163, 187, 204, 238

Zurbrugg, Nicholas 216